You're Only
Young
Twice

You're Only
Young
Twice

10 Do-Overs to Reawaken Your Spirit

RONDA BEAMAN, EdD

VanderWyk & Burnham

Published by VanderWyk & Burnham
P.O. Box 2789, Acton, Massachusetts 01720

www.VandB.com

This book is available for quantity purchases. For information on bulk discounts, call 800-789-7916, write to Special Sales at the above address, or send an e-mail to info@VandB.com.

Library of Congress Cataloging-in-Publication Data
Beaman, Ronda.
  You're only young twice : 10 do-overs to reawaken your spirit / Ronda Beaman.
    p. cm.
  Summary: "The science of growing young (neoteny) provides the underlying hypothesis for activities in this book on reviving ten youthful traits: resilience, optimism, wonder, curiosity, joy, humor, music, work, play, learning. Across all, there is love. Reader selects preferred activities for growing young--from the inside out"--Provided by publisher.
  Includes bibliographical references and index.
  ISBN-13: 978-1-889242-25-5 (pbk.)
  ISBN-10: 1-889242-25-X (pbk.)
  1. Success.   2. Rejuvenation.   3. Youthfulness.   4. Conduct of life.
5. Maturation (Psychology) 6. Aging--Psychological aspects. 7. Neoteny--Psychological aspects. I. Title.
  BJ1611.2.B39 2006
  155.6'6--dc22

                                                              2006020034

Manufactured in the United States of America
10 9 8 7 6 5 4 3 2 1

For my parents, Ron and Patt, who gave me my childhood;
my sons, Chase and Sean, who lovingly let me be part of theirs;
and my husband, Paul, whose optimism, humor, and love
keep me young at heart.

Contents

Foreword

No matter what you have accomplished in life so far, chances are you have much more to offer, and some of your best is yet to be revealed. If you'd like to fully optimize the second half of your life, then *You're Only Young Twice* is your guidebook for a gratifying journey.

You're Only Young Twice is about aging from the inside out: re-awakening your energy, resilience, joy, love, spontaneity, wonder, curiosity, and optimism. In this groundbreaking book, Dr. Ronda Beaman, one of the world's foremost authorities on the science of growing young, provides a practical recipe for recouping, recovering, and re-igniting the things you love most about being yourself and being *alive*.

By living more resiliently, you can become younger. For many, the struggles of the first half of life suffocate our aspirations and joy for the second half. The accumulation of life's adversities can take a tragic toll. Beaten down by inevitable setbacks and suffering, previously vital individuals turn away from life's higher promise and retreat into the debilitating clutches of comfort and compromise. Age becomes an exercise in shrinking rather than growing; limiting rather than expanding; staving off rather than taking on; surviving rather than thriving. According to conventional wisdom, aging is *entropy*—a gradual, comprehensive decline and decay of what was once a fully functioning human being.

Too many people consider the second half of life to be about *less*, rather than an opportunity to become and enjoy so much *more*. With the theories in this book and through personal example, Dr.

Beaman boldly and credibly redefines the second half of life. This landmark achievement is perfectly timed for the largest wave of people entering what can be the *better* half of life. Imagine a world of Jimmy Carters and Georgia O'Keefes, where people *like you* discover and bring forth their greatest gifts and contributions—once they are free from the rigid rules of their earlier years.

You hold in your hands a true classic—one of those rare books you will keep on your shelf for countless years as a keepsake and reminder of what was, and of the day you discovered what could be. One of those books you'll want to *live*, not just read. As you harvest Dr. Beaman's rich advice, elevating insights, and grounded wisdom, you'll feel your life force and anticipation for your remaining years grow with each succeeding chapter.

Finally, *You're Only Young Twice* provides a compelling case for us all: When it comes to the final decades of life, rather than aging, you can "youthen." Rather than losing breath, you can gain your second wind. Rather than becoming old, you can be young twice.

PAUL G. STOLTZ, PhD, author of the bestselling book
Adversity Quotient: Turning Obstacles into Opportunities

You're Only
Young
Twice

Introduction

I wrote this book for the same reason you are reading it. If you weren't "of a certain age" you would never have picked up this book. I'm in the middle of my life, with the finish line coming way too fast.

Once I felt the potential for greatness; now I'm feeling the pull of gravity. The awe that once filled me when I encountered something new is being replaced by the *ahh!* of recognition and occasional resentment. Days, weeks, months, and even years are flying by. It seems like every fifteen minutes, it's time for breakfast again! I want to stop the clock, fight Father Time, find the perfect longevity prescription. I want to live like I'm ageless, or be more my "real age." In other words, I don't want to be *old*.

Like you, I want to make the most of the life I have yet to live. But everywhere we turn, it seems that we all share the premise that old age is an affliction; and we must either deny it, succumb to it, or overcome it. "You're only young once," we hear as soon as we turn thirty, and that, my friend, is the end of that. Because of these attitudes, hackneyed homilies, and false promises, we are dying too soon, and aging lasts far too long.

But what if, in mind, body, and spirit, we are not obliged to live a nasty, solitary, prolonged old age, but are enabled by nature to remain youthful? *You're Only Young Twice* fortifies you with

1

research I have discovered, and want to share, that proves the second half of your life can be as exciting, as invigorating, and even more meaningful than the first half. After all, I don't want to be young twice all alone!

This book introduces you to the concept of *neoteny*, sometimes referred to as the science of growing young. It's a theory researched and validated over the past two centuries by noted anthropologists Ashley Montagu, Stephen Jay Gould, and many others. Neoteny is an evolutionary promise that our culture has violated, resulting in a lifestyle that ages us too much, too soon. As a science, neoteny provides highly developed techniques and behavioral options to counteract this damage and reverse aging as we have come to experience it. I like to call this process "youthening."

You will read the latest information to help you uncover your own biases regarding aging. You'll learn to overcome the adversity of aging, and benefit from an approach that maximizes the youthful qualities inherent, but often hidden, in all of us.

If you are a woman aged thirty-nine or a man aged thirty-six, statistics reveal that you are exactly halfway through your life. If you are older, you may be feeling like film director and comic Woody Allen, who said, "I am not afraid of my mortality. I just don't want to be there when it happens!" I have friends who call themselves middle-aged, and I remind them that this is true only if they live to be 123. Until the year 2012, someone in America will turn 50 every twelve seconds. Until the end of life on this planet, 100% of the world's population will face the looming changes of growing chronologically older. It's a consistent demographic!

Unfortunately, the natural and important contributions that age can bring to your life are being artificially and cosmetically delayed or even denied. The total market for cosmetic enhancement products, according to the U.S. Department of Public Health, is nearly $100 trillion per year. That's more than $4,000 for every man, woman, and child in the United States. If you're thinking of having laser resurfacing, Botox, a facelift, an eyelift, liposuction, a tummy tuck, or breast augmentation, you are not alone. In fact, you're among a growing number of men and women who are focused on improving their aging appearance. A press release from the American Society for Aesthetic Plastic Surgery (ASAPS) reported the results of 14,000 questionnaires mailed nationwide to a random sampling of physicians most likely to perform at least three of these top procedures. This sample included plastic surgeons, dermatologists, and otolaryngologists. The ASAPS reported that nearly seven million cosmetic procedures were performed in the United States in 2003, an increase of almost 24% from the previous year. Even more astonishing is the increase in the overall number of cosmetic procedures by 228% since 1997. Between 2000 and 2001, the number of Botox injections increased by 25%, chemical peels were up 23%, and micro-dermabrasion (a procedure designed to remove skin imperfections by abrading the surface of the skin with fine sandpaper or wire brushes) jumped 47%. You can get anti-baldness tonics, non-surgical lifts, liposuctions, animal matter injections, and acid washes. "Doctor, please puff up my frown lines with cow poison, and swab my little face with some hydrochloric acid while you're at it!" You can get eye tucks, laser peels, and neck and forehead lifts. You can pinch it, pull it, color or camouflage it, but for the love of God, don't look your age.

The most popular plastic surgery for men today is a buttocks lift. Although the picture that just went through your mind made you laugh (admit it), it's really quite sad. Admit it.

All this covering and camouflaging is like someone running around in autumn painting artificial green on the beautiful amber and gold leaves. It's futile and foolish—a doomed endeavor.

This is not an anti-aging book. What does *anti-aging* mean? You're against aging. Translation? No more birthday celebrations for you! Satchel Paige's claim, "Old age isn't fun, but it sure beats the alternative," would fall on your deaf—or should I say dead—ears. Okay, let's say you are *pro-aging*. You would like to live. Good choice. This book is not a panacea, a pill, or a promise that you won't get older, because you will and you are. That's the tough news. Most of us think that if we ignore the issue, forget about the facts, or cover it all up with a little make-up, surgery, or a new red sports car, aging will go away. Sorry! Aging is an unforgiving and permanent process for everyone.

Life is a sexually transmitted disease with a 100% mortality rate. No one gets out of life alive. It's going to take honesty, self-examination, and dedication to move your life forward in a positive and meaningful manner as the years pass. Accepting the truth of your aging leaves you open for growth; denial means part of you has already died. These really are your only choices. My advice? Choose acceptance and growth.

Part One of *You're Only Young Twice* is all about the *why* of neoteny. It's a clarion call, reminding us that we have violated our destiny. It teaches us that there is science beyond the physical body; there is a deeper, concurrent science of the soul that can be recovered and invigorated. Rather than disintegrate as we age, we can elevate, investigate, and appreciate ways to live differently, to "grow young," and to reach the full promise of our longer lives.

- *Chapter One defines neoteny and explains why it's possible to grow young from an evolutionary standpoint.* We'll explore the scientific basis for neoteny, and I'll make the case that in truth, we are violating our birthright. Mid-lifers and those older are the most educated, affluent, and fastest-growing segment of our population in history. Yet the majority of books written to assist us in the inevitable transition of aging address this enormous set of issues largely from the outside in, or at best superficially. Even the newest exercise regimens, attitude adjustments, disciplined diets, and cosmetic tweaks ultimately fall short in guiding us to a complete appreciation of our age and an understanding of the possibilities of furthering our development. The pursuit of neoteny and the practice of neotenous traits far surpass these common approaches to aging.

- *Chapter Two provides a concept inventory: an exploration of the stereotypes or misinformation that most of us carry about aging.* The Inventory of Aging clearly reveals that the way we age is up to us. Aging is inevitable, but how we age is completely negotiable. The questions in the inventory, and your answers, show that our beliefs about aging are self-induced. You'll have the opportunity to reflect on your answers, and then redefine the current mainstream model of aging to create a personal, practical model that will lead to a more resilient and robust life. In the process, you are encouraged to begin a Young Twice Chronicle—written or audio—and references to this first and subsequent uses of the chronicle are called out with the marginal icon shown here.

- *Chapter Three prepares you to reclaim the birthright that neoteny offers by using my AGE™ model. Act* in ways that will construct a daily regimen geared toward creating a foundation for neoteny. *Grow* neotenous in your mental, physical, emotional, and spiritual capacities. Then begin to *Evolve* your true self while moving toward higher levels of wisdom and optimism as you discover the possibilities inherent in growing young.

Part Two explains *how* to be young twice using your innate gifts of neoteny. This part of the book asks you to look at how OLD™ you are based on the *Outlook, Language,* and *Drives* you use daily. Among the natural neotenous traits we'll explore are optimism, humor, learning, wonder, curiosity, and joy—all of which tend to wither and become as brittle as our bones as we age. Common sense tells us that if we can reacquaint ourselves with our neotenous birthright, re-engage these dormant traits, and retain them into our later lives, we'll get more years in our life and more life in our years.

To fulfill this potential, so contrary to the gravitational—and deadly—pull of modern civilization, you need a simple, clear guide.

Ultimately, that's what this book is all about. It will show you how to pinpoint, unearth, revive, and fortify your gifts of neoteny so you can die young…and as late as possible.

- *Chapter Four reminds you to look out for your **outlook**, and introduces four of the ten traits that serve as lenses for the neotenous life.* The four traits are resilience, optimism, wonder, and curiosity.

- *Chapter Five gives voice to neotenous traits that add to the **language** of your life.* The traits of joy, humor, and music are inherent in the life of someone who chooses to be young twice.

- *Chapter Six reveals three neotenous traits that are the essential **drives** in living a youthful life.* The three traits are work, play, and learning.

- *Chapter Seven culminates in the ultimate "youthener" connected with living a life that optimizes all the neotenous traits.* This chapter challenges you to incorporate all the messages and meanings within this book to *love* every stage and age of your life.

Part Two features ten Do-Overs: interesting, experimental, educational, creative, or playful techniques designed to re-engage your neotenous traits. The Do-Over is your opportunity to start youthening. Every Do-Over offers ideas and inspiration to adjust each neotenous trait and its practice to suit your time and temperament.

By the time you've reached the last chapter of *You're Only Young Twice*, you'll have an arsenal of accumulated wisdom on aging from the fields of anthropology, sociology, and psychology. You'll have read the practical examples and insights of positive role models who have faced aging with courage, conviction—and sometimes comedy. And you'll have the benefit of my years as a researcher, educator, life coach, and woman into her third box of birthday candles. This book is dedicated to giving you the tools you'll need to create a gratifying, promising, and youthful long life.

Everyone will age, but this knowledge dictates no specific direction. Aging can be creative, not catastrophic. Aging can be liberating, not limiting. All human beings, whether they are ten, twenty, fifty, or eighty years old, are participating in the same process of aging. It's a personal process, yes—but what's most personal often turns out to be universal. Neoteny is not a luxury for the silly. Neoteny is an essential tool for anyone seeking a long and healthy life. Not accessing your inherent neotenous traits is like spending your life hobbling around on your hands while equipped with two healthy but unused legs!

. . . .

"There is no old age. There is, as there always was, just you."
CAROL MATTHAU, SPOUSE OF ACTOR WALTER MATTHAU

. . . .

There is courage in your decision to take the lead in defining and improving your life from the inside out, to appreciate the deeper colors of those once green leaves, and to be a willing participant in the full experience of your life. You will be a pioneer, seeking new vistas and horizons, and helping us all remember how fortunate we are to have the chance not just to age, but to be young twice, young always.

PART ONE

Why
We Really Can Grow Young

You are not old as long as
you are seeking something.

CHAPTER ONE

Oh, To Be Young…More Than Once!

. . . .

"When the self consciously accepts its role in the process of evolution,
life acquires a transcendent meaning."

MIHALY CSIKSZENTMIHALYI, SOCIOLOGIST AND AUTHOR

. . . .

I've had plenty of friends who believed they could build a better body through science. Under a knife, gasping through nonstop exercise, or faithfully following a spartan diet, all of us have been tempted to use some unnatural remedies to cure or stop the natural process of aging. As a professor, I have uncovered vast research confirming again and again that organisms (including you and me) age. Not exactly breakthrough material, but you'd be surprised how many of us still don't believe it. As a personal trainer, I am reminded daily that the equipment we are issued at birth certainly needs to be fed properly and handled with care; but no matter how many sit-ups you do or miles you run, your body will change with time. And as a counselor who specializes in mid-life issues, I have discovered that personality questionnaires, cognitive therapies, and longevity strategies are only momentary diversions that often distract us from the truth of our mortality.

Consistently, people our age say they know there must be something more to life than running from our years. Something inside us needs expression; we feel a deepening urgency to find what's waiting to be born in the second half of our lives. You feel it, too, don't you?

11

The reason that diets and diatribes, potions and pills, and most of the myriad anti-aging methods have done nothing to stop the unnecessary ravages of aging is simply this: We are seeking the wrong solution and asking the wrong questions.

The real question isn't how to stop the process of aging, but how to maximize the evolution of a human being.

. . . .

"We turn not older with years, but newer every day."
EMILY DICKINSON, NINETEENTH CENTURY POET

. . . .

In 1981, noted anthropologist Ashley Montagu published a book called *Growing Young*. I found a used copy in a bookstore years ago. I was instantly intrigued by the title and fascinated by the concept. I was approaching my fortieth birthday at the time, and thought that growing young was certainly a better deal than the current choice I was being offered.

What I learned from Montagu's book, and have continued to develop and research during the past decade, was a viable theory that could alter not just our aging, but our entire focus of living and surviving on this planet. The scientific theory called *neoteny* describes a physical and emotional evolutionary path based on the evidence of thousands of years of life development. Neoteny has been studied and substantiated by scientists from around the world and down the centuries. Neoteny, plain and simple, states that the human species—in body, spirit, feeling, and conduct—is constructed to grow and develop in ways that emphasize rather than minimize childhood traits. As Montagu said, "We were never intended to 'grow up' into the kind of adults most of us have become."

Neoteny directs us, as individuals and as a species, to amplify our playfulness, creativity, joy, love, work, optimism, laughter and tears, song and dance, wonder, and curiosity; to engage these traits as lifelong habits; and to create a pro-aging life experience.

. . . .

"The trick is growing up without growing old."
CASEY STENGEL, LEGENDARY BASEBALL PLAYER AND MANAGER

. . . .

Simply put, neoteny is the process of growing young. As Montagu and others have pointed out, most people who could benefit from this theory are ignorant of it. Every parent who said, "Grow up"; every teacher who taught us to color within the lines; every college counselor who demanded we pick a major at age eighteen; every friend who asked us when we were going to settle down and have kids; every boss who placed us in a small cubicle with clocks and ten-minute breaks—and everyone who views someone over eighty as an old man or old woman whose life is over is violating the evolutionary principles of neoteny. And most important, every time you look at your life in the past tense, forget what you used to dream about, and surrender or minimize the person you are, you violate neoteny and victimize the potential of the life you have remaining. Until today, until this moment, until *now*. Reading this book can change the way you live your life and help you become, perhaps for the first time, the person nature envisioned: youthful all the days of your life.

THE CHILD IS FATHER TO THE MAN: UNDERSTANDING NEOTENY

World-renowned anthropologist Stephen Jay Gould called neoteny the most important and neglected theme of human life and evolution. So why has it been such a secret? Well, look how long it took to find out that chocolate and red wine are good for us!

The concept of neoteny isn't easy to understand. It seems to contradict everything we believe about the role of the adult and the place of the child in our world. And besides, everyone is in such a hurry to teach us algebra, make us responsible, and help us find gainful employment; the idea that we should enjoy youthful pursuits throughout our lives would really mess things up. Yet quietly and doggedly, the principle of neoteny has affected our physical and behavioral evolution.

It's important to understand some of the basic scientific principles of neoteny. Understanding ourselves—what we're made of, what motivates us, and our goals and dreams—involves an understanding of our evolutionary past.

In the early part of the twentieth century, biologists and anthropologists were fascinated by the slow development of humans compared to other primates. This fascination was more than an exploration of Darwin's theory and beyond asking, "Why don't we look more like fish?" What these scientists wanted to know was why we were so different from all other species on the planet in terms of our abnormally slow physical and emotional growth.

Scientists noted many physical traits exhibited by both adult and fetal humans: flat faces, minimum body hair, and large brain size, for instance, and the adult structure or design of human hands and feet match their structure in the human fetus. This is not true of other adult animals. Scientists believed that the preservation of these characteristics, labeled neoteny, must have played a major role in human evolution. Apes, by contrast, start out with youthful appearing bodies and faces, and they look juvenile. They quickly, however, develop *gerontomorphic* (containing Latin root word for "old") traits: heavy brows, large teeth, and a flatter, more elongated face. The net effect of gerontomorphism is to decrease the ability to evolve further, while the net effect of neoteny is the gift of remaining in a state of development. It is to this slow progress of our development that we owe our exceptional human traits.

YOU'VE GOT THE CUTEST LITTLE BABY FACE

Comedian Dana Carvey claims that he was so underdeveloped in high school that he looked like a fetus wearing track shoes. His prominent, bulbous forehead is shared by infant humans and apes. However, the ape soon develops bony growth over its eyes and nose, while adult humans retain small, rounded foreheads throughout life. This minor physical characteristic plays a major role in the appearance of human faces, and in our interpretation of those faces. Even today, a high forehead is considered a sign of intelligence; and preferring wrestling to Wordsworth is considered "lowbrow."

For centuries, a prominent forehead and short nose in a well-rounded face with large eyes and full lips exemplified the feminine ideal...think *babe*. The small, cuddly, neotenous traits of the young child make us want to protect her. Popular dolls and cartoon characters like Teletubbies, Cabbage Patch Kids, and even Mickey Mouse and Betty Boop are configured with fetal traits: small voice, big eyes, and rounded form. That's why they are universally loved.

In his article "A Biological Homage to Mickey Mouse," anthropologist Gould claimed that Disney cartoonists unknowingly softened and juvenilized Mickey as he grew famous. "Since Mickey's chronological age never altered—like most cartoon characters, he stands impervious to the ravages of time—this change in appearance at a constant age is a true evolutionary transformation...The Disney artists transformed Mickey in clever silence, using often suggestive devices that mimic nature's own changes by different routes. To give him the shorter and pudgier legs of youth, they lowered his pants line and covered his spindly legs with a baggy outfit. His head grew substantially larger and its features more youthful. I suggest that Mickey's odyssey in form, his path to eternal youth repeats, in epitome, our own evolutionary story."

©Disney Enterprises, Inc.

If neoteny is visible in our appearance, it's evident in our mating rituals as well. The smooth face and girlish behavior of women is met by equally boyish behavior in males as they playfully tease and smile when flirting. A woman speaking in a high-pitched voice and using cosmetics to make her cheeks pinker, and a man laughing, playing, and acting vulnerable are examples of physical and behavioral neoteny. Anatomy professor Louis Bolk noted, "Adult humans in their traits are sexually mature fetuses." Anyone who has seen the action at a singles bar on a Friday night knows how true that is.

Anthropologist Konrad Lorenz said, "The unique human trait of always remaining in a state of development is quite certainly a gift we owe to the neotenous nature of mankind." Sadly, one of the by-products of our current view of aging is that development has been replaced by stagnation.

FROM DONUTS TO DOLLARS: GROWING AWAY FROM NEOTENY

I have traveled extensively, speaking to groups of all ages. Here's what always happens: If I bring donuts to a roomful of third graders, the kids jump happily up and down, giddy in anticipation of their treat. It's fun to watch. If I bring donuts to a college classroom, the students say thanks—sometimes. When I walk into a roomful of middle managers or CEOs, they're already looking for the donuts, and then they grab one and sit down, usually without making eye contact. I find myself really missing those third graders! You've probably heard the statistic: Children laugh three hundred times a day, while the average adult laughs three times. If you'd been with me at most of those middle-manager events, you'd say three is a generous estimate.

What happens to us between the third and thirtieth grades?

Most of us don't even notice the view anymore when we're in an airplane. We check our watches, go over our e-mails, and avoid talking to the person next to us. We dread seeing a child walk up the aisle, and think, *Please don't let that kid sit next to me.* Why don't we want children next to us? They get excited, squiggle and squirm, and can't sit still. Children are awestruck looking at clouds, counting mountaintops, stretching to see the sun. You know what? They're right. It's a miracle to be in the air; it's a miracle to fly. And we, who are all grown up, fail to notice. In fact, it seems that the older we get, the more we relinquish not just our youth, but also our sense of delight and amazement.

Now, don't get me wrong. The principles of neoteny aren't about you wiggling in a plane seat or jumping for joy because you got a sugar donut at a meeting. I'm not suggesting that we adopt a more juvenile culture, or that we further erode perceptions of the adult role. Certainly some would argue that "releasing the child within" could result in some of our more selfish and base behaviors, with no benefit for anyone. I'm sure we have all sat in meetings with petulant, noisy, self-involved "adults" and wished we could throttle their inner children. However, what I'm really saying about neoteny lies in the realm of the healthy and continued develop- ment of the *positive* characteristics of childhood.

As Montagu discovered, and wrote in *Growing Young*, "From their mature heights, adults for the most part ignore the clear meaning of the child's neotenous traits and crassly believe them as belonging to the same class of behavior as whining, self-centered- ness, self-pity, obstinacy, impatience, impetuousness, practical joking and the like. Indeed, these are behaviors often observed in chil- dren, but they are usually the products of poor socialization of which the children have been victims. What we call 'childish' behavior constitutes a reflection of the inadequacies of the social- izers, and is in no way to be regarded as the expression of the child's natural drives. Equally certainly such behaviors have no relation whatever to the neotenous traits of children."

In other words, the naughty behavior of children is not innate. Our culture requires children to "grow up" into adults, and since all children are taught that this is their chief goal in life, they learn to

accept it unquestioningly. Success for children becomes emulation
of their elders—their often selfish, lazy, critical, cold elders.

I recall helping my son Sean with a history project for elementary school. He was assigned to teach his class about samurai war-
riors, so I suggested making a samurai outfit from cardboard and
foil, and dressing the part when he gave his presentation. He
looked me right in the eye and said in a serious, fifth-grade tone,
"Mother, teachers don't want you to be creative. They want you to
just read your report."

But in healthy socialization, where parents, teachers, and other
socializers understand a child's requirements for growth and development, childish qualities are cherished, nurtured, and cultivated
as the most valuable possessions of our species. From these qualities, all contributions to art, science, music, and thousands of life's
joys spring. From these valuable possessions, we make a life filled
with love, laughter, imagination, and intensity.

What neoteny suggests is not that we remain arrested at the
developmental level of the child, but that we continue to cultivate
the traits we see in children: love, friendship, learning, curiosity,
playfulness, creativity, a sense of humor, and compassionate intelligence. We need to call upon all of these traits throughout our lives,
instead of becoming restricted by the socialization that constrains
so many of us. We need to be open to the world, and to actively
construct our own environment.

At any age, we all possess the innate ability to be like a ninety-
two-year-old woman I know: a petite, poised, proud lady who is
fully dressed by eight o'clock each morning. Although she is legally
blind, her hair is fashionably coifed and her makeup is perfectly
applied. When her husband of seventy years died, she had to move
to a nursing home. After hours of waiting in the lobby, she smiled
sweetly when her room was ready. As she maneuvered her walker
into the elevator, she was given a verbal description of her tiny room.

"I love it," she declared with the enthusiasm of an eight-year-
old presented with a puppy.

"Mrs. Jones, you haven't even seen the room yet...Just wait."

"That doesn't have anything to do with it," replied Mrs. Jones. "Happiness is something you decide upon ahead of time. Whether I like my room or not doesn't depend on how the furniture is arranged; it's how I arrange it in my mind. I've already decided to love it. It's a decision I make every morning when I wake up. I have a choice: I can spend the day in bed recounting the difficulty I have with the parts of my body that no longer work, or get out of bed and be thankful for the ones that do. Each day is a gift, and as long as my eyes are open I'll focus on the new day and all the happy memories I have stored away. Just for this time and this place in my life."

I'm not advocating that you ignore the losses and lessons involved in aging. But I am suggesting you rearrange the furniture a bit: Put problems in the back of your mind and bring the possibilities to the front. At every age, we need time and space to grow and develop. Because most of us aren't spending that time, and can't find that space, we are denying our most brilliant birthright, the uniquely human trait of remaining in a constant state of development. Youth is a gift, but growing young is an achievement.

IT TAKES TIME TO GROW YOUNG

Children (and despite appearances, we were all children once) demonstrate curiosity, playfulness, a willingness to experiment, honesty, energy, and an eagerness to learn every day. They ask questions endlessly. "Why?" "When?" "How?"

My sons, Chase and Sean, could sit for hours in front of a cupboard filled with pots, pans, and spoons. They named their toys, created plays, wrote songs, danced to any beat, and invented their own games with their own rules. They considered everyone a friend, explored endlessly, and were open to any possibility.

Why do so few of us retain these qualities? Why do we stop asking questions, and fear judgment from others? Why do we worry about tomorrow and fail to enjoy today? Could you go an entire day telling only the truth? When was the last time you tried a new food or new skill? When did you last learn something new? We keep getting smaller, tighter, more critical, and less joyful. Adulthood brings most of us responsibility, burdens, and seriousness—and a gradual erosion of the individuals we once were. This is tantamount to *de-evolution*.

The promise of neoteny, and the fulfillment of our evolutionary possibilities, argues that this continual diminishment is a choice, not an edict. As sociologist Mihaly Csikszentmihalyi reminds us in his book *The Third Evolution*, our responses are not genetically fixed, as in other species. We invent our own responses. This unique ability to invent, choose, improvise, and respond rather than react has made us an evolutionary success. In most cases, we can choose youthfulness and vigor, retain the willingness to explore, and challenge orthodoxies with courage and imagination. Consequently, we can re-train ourselves to youthen.

. . . .

Who's Teaching Who?

When I look at a patch of dandelions, I see a bunch of weeds that are going to take over my yard. My kids see flowers for Mom and blowing white stuff you can wish on.

When I look at an old drunk, and he smiles at me, I see a smelly, dirty person who probably wants my money. My kids see someone smiling at them and they smile back.

When I hear music I love, I know I can't carry a tune and don't have much rhythm so I sit self-consciously and listen. My kids feel the beat and move to it. They sing out the words. If they don't know them, they make up their own.

When I feel wind upon my face, I brace myself against it. I feel it messing up my hair and pulling me back when I walk. My kids close their eyes, spread their arms and fly with it, until they fall to the ground laughing.

When I see a mud puddle, I step around it. I see muddy

shoes and clothes and dirty carpets. My kids sit in it. They see dams
to build, rivers to cross, and worms to play with.

I wonder if we are given kids to teach or to learn from?
ANONYMOUS

. . . .

No matter your age, no matter your past, no matter your physical limitations or emotional setbacks, you can undo the damaging
consequences of a belief in ages and stages erroneously correlated
with chronology. Neoteny teaches us that growth is a continuous
process; that instead of "growing out of," we can "grow into" and
"grow with" our original youth-*full* traits.

. . . .

"Only of one thing am I sure: when I dream, I am ageless."
ELIZABETH COATSWORTH, CHILDREN'S AUTHOR

. . . .

Ultimately, neoteny is the factor responsible for the positive
direction of human growth. This book is ultimately directed at *your*
positive and personal growth: growth of your spirit and growth of
your undeveloped powers. In human growth, points out philosopher John Fiske, "lie all the boundless possibilities of a higher and
grander humanity than has yet been seen upon the earth."

The potential we find in neoteny is greater than all of us max-
imizing our lives, although that's important. The astonishing truth
is this: Nothing less significant than the evolution of our species
rests squarely on retaining our neotenous traits. A loving heart does
not sanction war. Childlike curiosity creates interest rather than
fear. And joy gives intense meaning to each encounter. An adult
world balanced by childlike traits would be a better world.

We can direct our own evolutionary path. In her book *The
Heartbeat of Intelligence*, Elaine Matthews argues that our current
DNA cannot help us survive the world we have created. She
believes that the universal implementation of neotenous traits like

love, compassion, curiosity, and wonder will activate new DNA, building these traits into our genes and providing a clear progression from the DNA of matter to the DNA of spirit. Writes Matthews, "Nature's exquisite design for human beings, her evolutionary intention, is for humans to survive planetary catastrophes through our DNA changing and adapting, and that change was designed to take place through love and wisdom."

FROM THE INSIDE OUT

I know you feel it: You have a deep sense that there is more, that something inside you needs expression; and you want to discover the real adventure and purpose of the second half of your life. Now is the time and this is the path. Morrie Schwartz, the teacher immortalized in Mitch Albom's book *Tuesdays with Morrie*, said, "Most people do not believe they are going to die. If they did, they would live their life very differently."

My promise in *You're Only Young Twice* is to guide you in a journey from the purely external aspects of aging to the knowledge you'll need to live your life very differently—from the *inside out*. Writer Anne Lamott recalls, "I took a long hot shower and then stood studying myself naked in the mirror…I wasn't thinking that I looked awful and wanted to look like someone else…I just remembered that sometimes you start with the outside…It's polishing the healthy young skin of that girl who was just here a moment ago, who still lives inside."

I will help you recognize and reacquaint yourself with the magic of your childhood. You can re-activate the young man or woman who still lives inside. Let's discover our neoteny. As mythologist Joseph Campbell said, "All the life potentialities that we never managed to bring to adult realization, those other portions of oneself are there; for such golden seeds do not die."

CHAPTER TWO

"Grow Old Along with Me." Any Volunteers?

. . . .

"Behavior is based on beliefs.
Action doesn't begin in the muscle, it begins in the brain."
PAGE SMITH, AUTHOR AND PHILOSOPHER

. . . .

ACT YOUR AGE: TAKING A PERSONAL INVENTORY

It's no wonder that the topic of aging is dreaded, denied, and depressing. National surveys consistently find that in spite of calendar age, fewer than 10% of the population identify themselves as old. Geriatrics professional Margaret Gullette proposes that age is "internalized, is a stressor, a depressant...a psycho-cultural illness." The images that our culture conjures up about aging make it seem like a life failure. As Ann Landers said, "Inside every seventy-year-old is a thirty-five-year-old asking, 'What happened?'"

Let's take a look at what you currently know or believe about aging. What stereotypes do you hold? What erroneous information guides you? Just how accurate or inaccurate are your perceptions about the aging process and what awaits you? By determining what you presently believe about becoming older, and then examining why you believe it, we can begin to explore your potential for growing young.

Below is a series of statements. Some statements are true, some are mostly true, some are false, and some are mostly false. Most are commonly held beliefs of many people in the United States. Check to see how well you are able to separate fact from fiction.

INVENTORY OF AGING

1. *True or False? The majority of older adults become senile.*

   False. Contrary to popular stereotypes, dementia is neither a normal part of aging nor is it inevitable. Statistics vary depending on the study, but most research estimates that approximately 2% to 3% of older adults in their seventies experience some form of dementia. Of older adults in their eighties, 5% to 10% will have dementia. Dementia statistics jump with adults in their nineties: between 20% and 30%. However, these data include mild as well as severe forms of dementia. The truth: Nine out of ten older adults are getting on comfortably with life. Florida Scott-Maxwell, the eighty-year-old author of *Let Evening Come*, writes, "Personality, character, and even basic wisdom can last far, far into the mental slowness and even confusion of old age."

2. *True or False? Older adults have no desire or capacity for sexual relations.*

   False. Sexuality continues to be an important aspect of an older adult's life. According to TNS, a Houston-based research firm, people fifty-five years and older are likelier than people aged eighteen to thirty-four to sleep nude. There's nothing like old age to make one aware of the marvels of the human body and mind. A friend of mine dates only men over sixty-five because "They have more time for sex, and they take more time for sex!" For the minority of older adults who experience physical problems that may limit their sexual expression, treatments are available. It's also important to remember that sexuality is not just a biological function. Sexuality includes the expression of feelings and self in a variety of ways in an intimate relationship, and encompasses many aspects of being a man or a woman. As poet Maya Angelou said in an interview, "I am seventy-nine years old and someone still calls me darling…That's very good."

3. *True or False? Chronological age is the most important determinant of age.*
   False. Individuals age in many different ways, and the least important of these is chronological age. Your chronological age is simply the number of years since your birth. More important is your functional age—that is, how well you are able to function in your social environment. The three aspects of *functional* age are psychological age, social age, and physiological/biological age. We have all met individuals who are nearing the end of their biological lifespan—but psychologically they are independent, creative, vibrant, and able to meet life's challenges.

   My husband's grandmother is chronologically ninety-four years old, but during our latest visit, it was she who woke us early to get to water aerobics, who made the cookies for unexpected visitors, and who went out that evening to play bridge. As Ram Dass reminds us in his book *I'm Still Here*, "Before we are parents, executives, or seventy-year-olds, and after we have ceased to be those things; before the Ego can begin its work of attaching meaning to itself, clothing itself in identity, we simply are. Behind the machinations of our brilliant, undependable minds is an essence that is not conditional, a being that age does not alter, to which nothing can be added, from which nothing is taken away."

4. *True or False? Most older adults have difficulty adapting to change.*
   False. Older adults are no more rigid than younger adults.

Rigidity tends to be a relatively stable personality character-istic. Individuals who are rigid and have difficulty adapting to change in young adulthood will probably have the same difficulties when they're older. I take my university-level stu-dents in public speaking to an assisted living center so they can deliver their speeches. Perhaps surprisingly, it's the nineteen- and twenty-year-old students who are afraid to try new things, afraid of being harshly judged by peers, afraid to step up and out. The eighty- and ninety-year-old residents teach my students about opening the mind, relaxing the spirit, and having more fun. These residents are dancing the Macarena, trying new foods, and having the most fun. Author Lillian Hellman—and the residents—could remind my students, "It's a sad day when you find out that it's not an accident of time or fortune but just yourself that kept things from you."

5. *True or False? Physical handicaps are the primary factors that limit the activities of older people.*

False. The primary handicap experienced by older adults is the result of age stereotyping and ageism; both have negative impacts. As Michael Harrington wrote in his book *The Other America*, "America tends to make its people miserable when they become old. They are seen as plagued by ill health, they do not have enough money, and they are socially isolated." So there's a very good reason for any negative perceptions you may have about aging. In *Risking Old Age in America*, Richard Margolis notes that we have given in to "a heavy fatalism that recalls Seneca's dismissal of old age as 'an incurable disease'."

The Gray Panthers is a nationwide advocacy group working on issues that impact older adults. Its Television Monitoring Task Force concluded that older people are typ-ically depicted as "ugly, toothless, sexless, incontinent, senile, confused, and helpless." These stereotypes and culturally constructed norms limit the activities and opportunities available to older individuals. In *Old Age: Constructions and Deconstructions*, author Haim Hazan writes, "There is no process in aging itself; the discourse of aging is born of relations within a given culture at a given time." As we know, in many other cultures seniority is associated with respect, obedience, prestige, and social esteem.

6. *True or False? A decline in all five senses is a normal consequence of old age.*

   Mostly true. For the most part, all five senses decline as we age. But in a recent study, the National Institutes of Health discovered that dementia (see question 1) and physical decline are functions of disease, disability, and social-economic adversity—not the inevitable by-products of growing older. While numerous changes in vision occur that are highly correlated with age, dramatic declines in the auditory system may be due more to the accumulated effects of noise than to age. (You pay for those Led Zeppelin concerts in many ways.) People living in low-noise, nomadic cultures do not exhibit a loss of hearing with age. Diet, regular health care, and the astounding technologies currently available can dramatically reduce changes in all five of our senses.

7. *True or False? Older adults are incapable of learning new information.*

   False. Older adults are capable of learning new information. Research states that older adults may take a little longer to learn new information, as compared to chronologically younger adults, and they may use different learning strategies than in their earlier years, but they can and should continue to learn. Additional research has clearly demonstrated that the memory performance of healthy older adults can improve with memory training. "Memory processes are not lost to us as we age," says psychologist Fergus Craik, who is affiliated with the Toronto-based Rotman Research Institute, an organization that studies memory and the higher functions of the brain. "The mechanism is not broken. It's just inefficient." As time goes by, we tend to blame age for problems that are not necessarily age-related. When my younger son can't find his car keys in the morning, I think it's because he is spacey, distracted, or disorganized. When my mother can't find her keys, I think to myself, *She's losing it.* Older adults can benefit from memory courses and mental exercises like puzzles and bridge. And they can maintain a sheer zest and lively interest in friends, family, and hobbies. "A sense of passion or purpose helps you keep learning," says Dr. Robert N. Butler, President of the International Longevity Center–USA in New York. "Lifelong learning and memory requires us to pay attention to our lives, allowing us to discover in them everything worth remembering."

8. *True or False? Physical strength tends to decline in old age.*
   True. Physical strength does tend to decline with age. Of course, exercise can counteract and limit the amount of loss. Someone who is sixty-five and exercises regularly will probably be in better shape and have greater physical strength than a forty-year-old couch potato. The Aerobics Research Institute in Dallas, Texas, has uncovered "astounding" evidence that as little as ten minutes of walking, repeated often during the day, can make an important difference in fitness and well-being. And Dr. Thomas Perls of Beth Israel Deaconess Medical Center and Harvard Medical School says that in terms of lifespan, exercise "is like putting gold in the bank."

   Stanford University physician Ralph Paffenbarger, a pioneer in the epidemiology of lifestyle diseases, studied more than 17,000 Harvard University students for a quarter of a century after their graduations. His conclusions? Every hour spent in vigorous exercise as an adult is repaid with two hours of additional lifespan. It's fun to look at this another way: if you work out for twelve hours every day, statistics say you will never die!

9. *True or False? Intelligence declines with old age.*

Mostly false. The majority of older adults don't experience a decline in intellectual abilities with age. In fact, some forms of intelligence have been hypothesized to increase with age. Poet Wallace Stevens said, "It can never be satisfied, the mind, never." According to neuroscientist Molly Wagster of the National Institute on Aging, new research confirms that contrary to losing 10,000 neurons a day as we age, as previously estimated, "We are not losing brain cells in significant number. The older brain is capable of generating new cells." Dr. Jeffrey Cummings of the University of California at Los Angeles notes that this discovery of neurogenesis reinforces the emerging notion of "how little brain deterioration there is in the healthy individual."

Many of the calamities—or just plain nuisances—previously blamed on aging actually reflect illness, and nowhere is this truer than in the aging brain. If the rest of the body is aging badly, so will the brain. "In normal aging," says Cummings, "there is surprisingly good brain function. Because the brain is the instrument of survival, it has been spared as much as possible from insults that occur to the rest of the body." Of course, with your brain as sharp as ever, you're more likely to notice those insults.

10. *True or False? The majority of older adults say they are happy most of the time.*

True. According to studies from the Institute of Aging, a majority of older adults report high levels of life satisfaction. The more socially active a person remains, the higher the life satisfaction. Mary Jane Kohn, ninety-three, has been living alone in Chicago since her husband died in 1971. "I love going to parties," she says. "There's no point in staying home twiddling your thumbs." There is great value in remaining involved in informal, intimate activities. The same things that built a fulfilling life before age fifty also apply beyond fifty: connecting with other people, feeling useful, and having fun. In addition, health is correlated with life satisfaction. Individuals of any age who are in poor health are likely to experience lower levels of life satisfaction.

11. *True or False? At some point, the vast majority of older adults will end up in nursing homes.*
False. Contrary to the popular myth, most older adults do not reside in nursing homes (more appropriately called long-term care facilities). In fact, only about 5% of adults over seventy-five in the United States reside in long-term care facilities, compared with 24% who are eighty-five or older. A care facility is no longer a place where one goes simply to die. One of the primary services care facilities provide is short-term respite care; a non-well older adult living with family may stay briefly in the facility to obtain care, giving family a much-needed vacation.

12. *True or False? About 80% of older adults say they are healthy enough to carry out their normal daily activities independently.*
True. The vast majority of older adults have no increased need to depend on others more than they did during their earlier adult years. While they might need help if they decide to move the furniture or read the fine print in a dimly lit restaurant, two-thirds of adults aged sixty-five or older describe their health as very good or excellent, and continue to live in their own residences. Great impairment isn't typically seen except as a function of illness (if you have a stroke, you need care whether you're thirty or eighty), injury, or very old age (nearing the early nineties). Even people older than 100 may need no significant assistance from friends or family. Older adults are not significantly

more dependent than young adults; and they are also highly capable of engaging in professional activities, work, or new careers. This is highlighted by the fact that since the late 1960s, based on surveys from *The Chronicle of Philanthropy*, volunteerism among older adults has practically quadrupled, from 11% to 40%. One out of three individuals over age seventy-five is involved in at least one volunteer activity.

13. *True or False? Most older adults are rejected by their children.*
    False. Older adults are not rejected by their children simply because of age. You'll hear people say something like "Mrs. Jones is seventy-five years old, living in a nursing home, and her children never visit. They have tossed her away because she's old." Chances are, Mrs. Jones and her children have other family issues that preclude close contact. (Perhaps they don't like each other.) In reality, studies have demonstrated that more than 70% of older adults have a child living in close proximity (within thirty minutes). More than half of these individuals visited with one of their children within two days prior to being surveyed. Close families do not fall apart simply because the parent has aged.

14. *True or False? In general, older adults tend to be pretty much alike.*
    False. In fact, current census data reveal that the older population is the most diverse or heterogeneous age group. Development consists of the interaction of an individual with the context in which he or she lives, and includes genetic and biological make-up. The older the individual, the greater the impact of the context. In other words, as you age, your life experience changes you in unique ways: You experience different people and events, you make choices, and you learn. Since events and choices differ for everyone, each life experience serves to increase people's diversity across the lifespan. The only time when older adults will demonstrate

homogeneity is in response to disease. Even so, an individual suffering from Alzheimer's disease at age sixty-seven would share similarities with an individual suffering from Alzheimer's at age thirty-four.

15. *True or False? The majority of older adults say they are lonely.*
False. Loneliness is one of the greatest fears that people associate with old age. Yet based on AARP research, more than two-thirds of older adults report being rarely, if ever, lonely. This may parallel the loneliness experienced by young and middle-aged adults. Fear of loneliness is often based on the thought of losing a spouse and the subsequent isolation. But for most people, this fear isn't based on reality. The majority of men remarry after losing a spouse. Women are more likely to become involved in new social relationships and friendships with other widows. Quality-of-life indices have shown that urban living is associated with higher levels of loneliness. Individuals of all ages living in small towns report lower levels of loneliness.

16. *True or False? Old age can best be characterized as a second childhood.*
False. The lifespan is unidirectional. Older adults are still adults, and should be treated as such even if they are incapacitated by illness. What about the myth of role reversal between parent and child? An adult caring for a non-well parent may say that she has taken the role of a parent, and her parent has become more like a child. However, caring for a non-well parent is not equivalent to role reversal. In fact, true role reversal is viewed as dysfunctional.

17. *True or False? More than 15% of the United States population is over sixty-five years old.*
True. The percentage of older adults in the U.S. has been steadily increasing. In fact, census statistics show that the percent of Americans over age sixty-five has risen from less than 5% in 1900 to approximately 15% in 2000. This figure

is expected to reach 22.9% by 2050. The fastest-growing population in the U.S. is the oldest of the old. In 1990 an estimated 36,000 people were more than 100 years old. These changing demographics, also found in European countries and parts of Asia, will have dramatic—and perhaps positive—effects on all facets of culture and society.

18. *True or False? Most older adults tend to be preoccupied with death.*
    False. Death is an inevitable aspect of life. Attitudes toward death are highly variable, but some trends can be noted in the United States. In general, older adults are less anxious and more matter-of-fact about death than younger people. As people move through the lifespan, they lose friends and family members, and begin to accept their own mortality. This enables older adults to speak more freely about death and dying. By contrast, most young adults in the U.S. avoid thinking about or discussing death. If an older adult brings up the topic of death, he or she may be accused of being preoccupied with death. In reality, it's the younger adult who is preoccupied with *not* discussing death.

19. *True or False? Most older adults have incomes well below the poverty level.*
    False. The majority of older adults live above the poverty level. Survey results from AARP show that we have the wealthiest older adult population in U.S. history.

20. *True or False? Older people tend to become more religious as they age.*
    False. One's level of religiosity tends to remain fairly stable across the lifespan. Older Americans do tend to be more religious than younger Americans. But today's elders have always been more religious, reflecting the time and culture in which they were raised.

21. *True or False? Retirement is detrimental to an individual's health.*
    False. Retirement does not kill people. For the vast majority

of older adults, retirement is a positive experience, with an especially high retirement satisfaction for those who planned for their retirement. People who die following retirement usually retired because they weren't well in the first place. A person has a heart attack and consequently retires. That person has another heart attack shortly after, and dies. Retirement didn't kill this retired person: Heart disease did.

22. *True or False? Pain is a natural part of the aging process.*
False. Pain is not a natural part of the aging process. It's a sign of injury or illness. Pain should not be ignored. Unfortunately, people often attribute pain to aging, and wait too long to seek medical help, with negative consequences.

A man goes to the doctor complaining of pain in his right knee. The doctor says to him, "You just have to expect this. You are getting older." To which the man replies, "My other knee is just as old and it doesn't hurt."

It's true that individuals experience more pain as they age, but this is the result of the accumulation of injury or illness. The pain is due to injury or illness, not to age.

23. *True or False? The majority of older adults say they feel irritated or angry most of the time.*
False. Older adults are no more angry or irritated than younger adults. People who are angry or irritated a good portion of the time while young will probably be angry or irritated a good portion of the time in old age. Of course, remaining upbeat can be tough—especially when you can't hear the TV or remember a joke you wanted to tell. But many people become more comfortable with themselves as they get older. In fact, psychologist Michael Brickney, author of *Defy Aging,* says that older people report being happier than younger people. "For most people, our teens and 20s were pretty insecure times."

24. *True or False? Productivity and quality of work decline after age sixty-five.*

   False. Many historians, botanists, inventors, philosophers, and writers have been most productive in their sixties. And the evidence for great works after age sixty-five is plentiful. Actress Sophia Loren said, "There is a fountain of youth. It is your mind. Your talents, the creativity you bring to your life—when you learn to tap this source, you will have truly defeated age." Cervantes wrote *Don Quixote* at age sixty-eight. Goethe finished *Faust* at age eighty-two. I. F. Stone wrote *The Trial of Socrates* while in his eighties. In his acknowledgments, Stone wrote, "Finally, I pour a libation to my Macintosh word processor. Its large, fat, black 24 point Chicago Bold type enabled me to overcome cataracts and write the book." The limits of what we can continue to dream and achieve as we age are only self-imposed. As Henry David Thoreau reminded us, "We are constantly invited to be what we are."

25. *True or False? With age comes wisdom.*

   Mostly false. Wisdom is an illusive concept. Since wisdom is so difficult to define, few studies have been conducted concerning wisdom and age. But some studies have sought to define the concept of wisdom and test for age differences. Research from the Max Planck Institute in Berlin, Germany, defines wisdom as an "expert judgment system in the fundamental pragmatics of life." Individuals possessing wisdom exercise insight, judgment, self-knowledge, and the ability to manage their lives effectively. Using this definition, the research found that older adults perform no better than younger adults. In other words, both young and old people possess wisdom. Even so, some of the highest scores on these tests did belong to older adults. Mencius, who lived during the third century BC, said it best: "The wise man retains his childhood habit of mind."

"More Light!"

That's what Goethe said on his deathbed, and that's what baby boomers, including me, have brought to the study of aging. When I started my neoteny research more than a decade ago, I began compiling the increasing data and new studies about growing older that were coming out daily. Once we boomers started to add some chronology to our resumes, we insisted on better information, additional research, and more light on the matter.

We had changed every other social convention, and now we decided to take on our own mortality. I was surprised at how many myths, stereotypes, and just plain falsehoods had been perpetrated about growing older. I hope that some of the Inventory of Aging answers surprised you, and that you're now interested in your own development and in creating your personal story of aging.

I'm not suggesting that this is all good news and that we should be delighted to grow old. Quite the contrary. There is sadness in seeing our bodies change. Accepting the new image in the mirror doesn't happen overnight. I've heard it said that if you ever want to feel really old, take a walk on a college campus. I teach at two universities and *yikes!* I can verify that. It's fairly humbling. While my parents were out of town not long ago, my grandmother was rushed to the hospital. I was trying to track down my parents, so I brought my cell phone to the class I was teaching. I explained to my students that should it ring, given the circumstances, I would need to answer it. A young woman in the front row looked aghast and very disturbed. I asked her, "Kellie, what's wrong?" Incredulously and with pure disbelief, she said, "You have a grand-mother?" She was shocked that someone as old as I could still have a living, breathing grandmother.

Those reminders that you have become older can be hard to take. But each day, in the classroom of real life, I have a choice: I can choose to deny my growth by pretending that I am still my stu-dents' contemporary, trying to fit in by wearing the latest styles, nipping and tucking as I go; or I can accept my new stage and continue to grow into the person I can and should be. It's not just a choice for me to make—you, too, can make it.

Along with the biological changes of aging are the subsequent changes in self-regard that have an impact on us all as we age. Who am I, now that my body isn't the same? What inside me has *not* changed? How young is my soul, my spirit, my faith, hope, and love? "Youth is just a moment," says author Susan Branch. "But it is a moment you can carry forever in your heart."

CREATE YOUR YOUNG TWICE CHRONICLE

. . . .

"A graceful and honorable old age is the childhood of immortality."
PINDAR, GREEK PHILOSOPHER

. . . .

Throughout this book, you have a chance to explore opportunities to be young twice by reflecting on your opinions, ideas, hunches, and solutions. I suggest that you begin a chronicle of your responses to the questions asked in this book by creating a written legacy in a small notebook, fancy journal, or three-ring binder. (If you dislike writing, keep an audio version!) You can refer to this Young Twice Chronicle and share thoughts with anyone who asks, "What's *your* secret for staying young?"

Start by answering the following questions that refer to the true-false Inventory of Aging you've just read.

- What most surprised you about the answers? What was your biggest misconception about aging?

- Where do you get most of your ideas about aging—from the media? Personal relationships? Ignorance or guesswork?

- Do you have any inspiring role models of happy, successful, or healthy aging? What specific characteristics of those role models do you admire? What about negative role models of aging? What do you want to avoid?

- How do you feel about your own aging? What do you look forward to, and what do you fear? Consider specifics like career, family life, health, finances, and personal growth and development. Quickly write down your initial reactions.

Now, write down your thoughts based on this statement: *After reading the answers in the Inventory of Aging and considering my own reactions to aging in the questions above, I need to make the following adjustments to my current perception of my goal and ability to become young twice.* Be specific. For example, you could decide that when faced with a new challenge, "I will quit telling myself that I'm too old to do that." Or you might decide this: "It will help me grow young if I try one new thing every day."

Three big obstacles hold people back from changing their lives:

1. Fixed psychological patterns

2. Fixed ideas

3. Social situations or life circumstances

Mark Twain said, "Life would be infinitely happier if we could only be born at the age of eighty and gradually approach eighteen." We can all relate to Twain's idea because it's part of our fixed psychological pattern: our inbred cultural regret about aging. Our life circumstance may be that we are eighty, fifty, or anywhere in between; but no circumstance, and no number of years, can cancel out the ability of humans to change—if we *choose* to change.

The information in this book, as well as your Young Twice Chronicle, gives you the raw material to alter your fixed psychological patterns and ideas about aging. Daily, you'll face the challenge of using this information to create a new life circumstance that establishes neoteny as your foundation for fulfilling the potential inherent in the longer life many of us are living now. In essence, you will create a blueprint to become younger day by day, year by year.

I don't intend to deprive you of your old age. You've earned it. In fact, I think everyone over seventy-five should have an honorary doctorate in life. But I do want you to have the tools to control your aging, care for it, and celebrate it. That's the promise of neoteny. In short, that's the point of being young twice.

THE WHOLE TRUTH...

. . . .

"At eighty I believe I am a far more cheerful person than I was at twenty or thirty. I most definitely would not want to be a teenager again. Youth may be glorious but it is also painful to endure. Moreover, what is called youth is not youth; it is rather something like premature old age."

HENRY MILLER, WRITER AND ARTIST

. . . .

There is a fundamental lie at work in our currently held beliefs about aging. The lie? *To be young is to be whole, and to be old is to be impaired or broken.* We identify too much with the body rather than the consciousness it contains. As Joseph Campbell said, "Am I the bulb that carries the light, or am I the light of which the bulb is the vehicle?"

Until very recently, most people dreaded aging because they saw it as a decline into disease and disability. Yet research shows that by the time you reach sixty, you don't much mind your gray hair or life's other small irritants. In fact, studies by researchers for *The Journal of Experimental Psychology* found that older adults retain fewer negative images, and are more apt to have a balanced outlook, than their twenty-something counterparts. Researchers attribute this difference not to fading brainpower, but to our tendency to worry less as time goes on.

According to these studies, things get better as you get older, or at least they seem to. Researchers showed a series of pictures to 144 healthy participants aged eighteen to eighty. Some of the images were "Hallmark happy" (an old man and a young boy fishing) and others were troubling (an airplane in flames). When questioned later, younger volunteers tended to remember the negative photos more than they did the neutral or pleasant ones. Older people, though, recalled relatively few of the disturbing pictures.

Seniors, the researchers believe, may consciously decide not to spend their remaining years brooding. "I've had so many older adults tell me they wouldn't get out of bed in the morning if they focused on all of the negative things that have happened in their lives," says Susan Turk Charles, PhD, lead author of research on aging and assistant professor of psychology and social behavior at the University of California at Irvine. "Memory is powerful— thoughts can dictate your feelings. If people, young or old, focus on the negative aspects of life, they're more likely to become depressed. As people age they are more likely to focus on the positive, meaningful, and emotional connections."

Our willingness to believe the worst about aging, to dwell on the downside and ignore the upside, is a reflection of human history and human nature. Given today's advances in medicine, technology, and lifestyle options—such as understanding and implementing the tenets of neoteny—we can look beyond biological processes. We now have opportunities for growth and change throughout our lives. The challenge you find in this book is the same as that issued by author Jean Huston: "Think of yourselves not in a second childhood, but on a second level of complete development."

It's been pointed out that the purpose of a baseball game is not to play as many innings as possible. The purpose of a symphony, too, is not to postpone the final note. And what of the purpose of life? It's not about growing old: It's about coming of age.

. . . .

"For age is opportunity
no less
Than youth itself, though
In another dress
And as evening
Twilight fades away
The sky is filled with stars
Invisible by day."

HENRY WADSWORTH LONGFELLOW, POET AND EDUCATOR

. . . .

CHAPTER THREE

Seventy Years Young or Forty Years Old?

The meaning that we attribute to our lives and system of values fully defines and determines the meaning of our old age. If our society, our families—or at least if we who are older—defined aging as an *opportunity* rather than a *problem*, the meaning of our lives and the value of our age could and would be improved, and probably celebrated.

In Okinawa, you're not even considered an adult until you're fifty-five years old. You are old at eighty-eight, and then the village gives you a celebration at ninety-seven for becoming a child again. In fact, these celebrations are so normal and frequent, they have spawned an entire cottage industry of second childhood party planners! Imagine how you would feel living in a culture that believes you become an adult at fifty-five, instead of in our culture—a society that sends you a senior citizen discount card when you turn fifty-five!

The principles of neoteny challenge us to rethink current values, consider new meanings, and create an age-irrelevant life experience. In *Ageless Body, Timeless Mind*, physician Deepak Chopra argues, "The field of human life is open and unbounded. At its deepest level, your body is ageless, your mind timeless." This deepest level of life is deeper than your wrinkles, and more concerned with your gray matter than your gray hair. The deepest level of ageless and timeless self is based almost completely on retaining the characteristics of youth, on practicing the principles of neoteny. Retaining, however, demands re-training.

THINKING MAKES IT SO

As I hope you discovered in the previous chapter, you are carrying some baggage about aging—and that baggage can bring serious consequences. A recent study in the *Journal of Personality and Social Psychology* looked at people over age fifty in the small town of Oxford, Ohio. The study found that people with a rosy view of growing old lived an average of seven and a half years longer than people with gloomy outlooks. In fact, this optimism advantage was greater than factors like low cholesterol, low weight, regular exercise, and not smoking.

Harvard University psychologist Ellen Langer and a research team from Harvard conducted an even more remarkable study. The entire study is recounted in her book *Mindfulness*. Men ranging in age from seventy to eighty-five were sent to an isolated retreat setting, which was outfitted with the same furniture, clothing, music, and even food found in their lives twenty years earlier. This group was compared with a similar age group, which had been placed in a contemporary setting and asked only to *think* about things from their lives twenty years prior.

Langer wanted to answer this question: Since negative stereotyping and negative thinking lead to unhealthy images of aging, can we reverse this line of thinking and thereby improve health? By creating a state of mind that these men had experienced twenty years earlier, Langer wondered if their bodies could also "backtrack" to a more youthful state.

Langer tested her hypothesis by comparing the effects of the two experiences. In the first group, participants made a psychological attempt—surrounded by physical reminders—to be the people they were twenty years earlier. The second, or control, group participants merely focused on the past of twenty years. The study was also designed so that when it came to content, the two groups would be essentially occupied with similar thoughts; in other words, they read the same books, viewed the same programs, listened to the same music, and played the same games.

The major difference between the two groups that could account for any difference in results would be the context in which the experiences took place. For the experimental group, the context was the way things were twenty years ago. For the control group, the context was the present. The challenge was to get the experimental group "into context," and then get them to go about their usual routines.

As Langer recounts, "We placed an advertisement in a newspaper calling for male subjects over seventy years old. Those in reasonably good health were selected as our research participants. We arranged to take them to a country retreat for five days, where they were encouraged through props and instructions to either step back into the past or to view the past from the present."

The research team took several measurements of the participants the day before the experiment began, and again on the fifth day of the experiment. They measured physical strength, perception, cognition; and taste, hearing, and visual thresholds. Measurements included handgrip, bi-deltoid breadth, triceps skin fold, finger length, weight, height, gait, and posture. Vision was measured with and without eyeglasses, and a series of paper and pencil maze tests was administered to measure speed of completion and accuracy.

Previously, all participants had been asked to complete an inventory of likes and dislikes from twenty years earlier, including information about jobs, activities, relationships, joys, worries, and other key criteria. They were then asked to write this inventory in the present tense. The first group lived in rooms filled with magazines, music, movies, and memorabilia from twenty years earlier. While the control group was involved in the same discussions and activities as the first group, this group did not live in re-created past surroundings.

Some startling results emerged from this experiment, and differences between the two groups ranged from striking to suggestive. Compared to the base measurements of performance taken at home, before they participated in the study, at the end of the study both the experimental and control groups showed significant improvement in some measures. For instance, independent and impartial observers evaluated facial photographs at the beginning and end of the study. Observers found that on the whole, after the experiment, all the men looked younger by about three years. Hearing also tended to improve uniformly. Improvement in psychological functioning was seen in both groups, indicated by increasingly efficient performance on the memory tests over the course of the experiment.

The men in both groups gained an average of three pounds during the study, with hand strength increasing steadily during the week. In addition, says Langer, "Our measure of joint flexibility and finger length increased to a significant degree for the experimental group." Langer also noted a greater increase in sitting height for the experimental group, and greater gains in manual dexterity, vision, and memory than in the control group.

Langer's hypothesis was affirmed: The state of a person's *body* can be "turned back" if the person's *mind* can be shifted back. In fact, positive changes of all kinds were found in these men at an age when growth and development are considered arrested or in decline. In other words, by just thinking that they were younger, and by surrounding themselves with things that reminded them of their youth, both their bodies and their minds were measured and found to "youthen." This certainly gives additional credence to the adage "You're only as old as you feel."

This study confirms that the regular and "irreversible" cycles of aging that we witness in the later stages of human life may simply be a product of specific assumptions about the way we're supposed to grow old. The study actually supports—dare I *say* proves?—the entire premise of *You're Only Young Twice*. Imagine a world where we didn't feel compelled to carry out limiting mindsets about aging. Imagine a place that insisted we're not even adults until we're fifty-five years old. Think of yourself getting that second childhood party at age ninety-seven. If we nurtured our neoteny, we might have a greater chance of replacing years of decline with years of growth and purpose.

As a scientific theory, neoteny asserts that there is still a young spirit inside each of us, and that the characteristics of our youth are the same characteristics we must use to recapture our youth. If we can re-harness these characteristics, then, like the men in the study, we too can begin the process of growing young.

In her book *Mindfulness*, Dr. Langer describes three essential mindsets conducive to positive aging:

1. Creation of new categories

2. Openness to new information

3. Awareness of more than one perspective

 In your Young Twice Chronicle, take a moment to rate yourself on each of these mindsets. Do you consider yourself open and aware? If not, it isn't going to get any easier from here. Instead, what do you need to do to create a life situation that frees you to grow young?

You must consciously—or as Langer calls it, *mindfully*—make adjustments, choose changes, and broaden your experiences as you did when you were young. Otherwise, you are choosing to grow old. There is a vast chasm between growing older and *being* old. People who are still growing are not old; and the "old" are people who have stopped growing. I know twenty-somethings who are already old and seventy-somethings who aren't. Don't you?

I LOVE THE EIGHTIES!

I was an aerobics instructor for almost fifteen years. I mean the full-blown, legwarmers, high impact, loud 1980s beat, microphone screaming *Four more!* kind of aerobics instructor. I loved it. I had always wanted to be a dancer, and this was as close as I was going to get. This slightly embarrassing testimony does have a point (and I finally removed my sweatband, by the way). To this day, listening to the music from that era, watching old television shows, and bringing out the vintage clothes still makes me happy and lifts my spirits when I'm down. I crank 1980s music whenever I do chores around the house, much to my husband's chagrin; but the house gets cleaner, doing laundry is fun, and I'm moving so fast that he doesn't have to help.

When I work out now, I still use my music tapes from the classes I taught. I've always thought this music makes me run faster and feel stronger. I'm also happier and peppier using these tunes than using today's music.

Now, because of Langer's study, I know why—and I know it isn't my imagination. I am unconsciously recreating a part of my life from twenty years ago; and like the men in the Langer study, I'm not only stronger, but I'll bet my fingers are longer and I'm sitting taller! To explore ways to further change my mindset, I went to my local athletic club and started teaching an aerobics class, minus the legwarmers. Now I have a cadre of participants who think they are just working out, but I know we are all growing young physically *and* mentally.

Here's more proof that age is an inside-out job: The National Institute of Aging conducted a study under the direction of George Vaillant, MD, that found that ancestral longevity, cholesterol, stress, parental characteristics, childhood temperament, and general ease in social relationships did not affect aging. Instead, said Vaillant, "The keys to successful aging are in self-care and love."

I'm not suggesting that you create your life today to replicate your life of twenty years ago, or that you crawl inside yourself and forget what time, day, or month it really is. But are there things from your past that you loved to do? Books, music, photos, and television shows that were enjoyable? Then why not pull them out, reactivate them, and enjoy the opportunity of being young twice? As physicist Ernst Mach says, "It is utterly beyond our power to measure things in time. Quite the contrary, time is an abstraction, at which we arrive by means of the change of things." Recalling emotions, remembering moments, or dancing to your favorite tunes are all valuable exercises in growing young. By savoring a little dose of nostalgia and immersing yourself in self-care—based on some pretty astonishing science—you may not even need those reading glasses by the time you finish this book!

Take a moment to answer the following questions in your Young Twice Chronicle:

- What was your favorite music or recording twenty years ago?

- What was your favorite book twenty years ago?

- What photos, works of art, or souvenirs of your life twenty years ago can you scatter around?

- What foods did you enjoy twenty years ago that you could eat again?

- Could you reconnect with a friend from twenty years ago?

Pearl of Wisdom

Our culture has created an unnatural dread and denial of aging. By contrast, it's the natural order of our species to continually experiment and enjoy our vital, youthful characteristics from twenty years past, and earlier. Retaining your own childlike characteristics will give you the power to be like a woman I knew named Pearl.

Pearl was seventy-eight years old when she decided to head back to school and get her degree. When younger students asked her how old she was, she would reply, "We're all only as old as the last time we said 'No' to life."

Pearl sat in the front row of my history of education class. I could count on her to be the person who had really read the assignment and could answer the questions, offering colorful commentary and varied perspectives. After all, Pearl was a living example of the history of education. She was fun to be around, she shared cappuccinos with her classmates, and she instantly made friends. To anyone who asked, Pearl said she had returned to school to become a teacher, marry a rich orthodontist, retire, and travel! Pearl eventually joined my fitness class, too, and always took her preferred place at the front of the room. She moved to her own beat, wore the brightest-colored workout clothes, and drank a cold beer when the workout was finished.

Pearl gave a final presentation in my education class. The subject? What she had learned that was worth remembering. She explained that this was nothing that school or teachers had taught her. Her words were simple but profound, forged after a lifetime of participation, taking risks, and growing young. Pearl's WOW, or Words of Wisdom:

1. Fall in love with something, in some way, every day.

2. You've got to have a dream. When you lose your dreams, you die.

3. It doesn't take any great talent or ability to grow older. Stay young by always finding the opportunity in change.

4. The only people who fear death are those with regrets. Seize your day, your chance, your life. Forget your loss, your shortcomings, your failure.

Pearl died one month after her graduation. Hundreds of students attended her funeral to pay tribute to a woman who taught them that you're never too old to become what you want to become. As the title character in *Stuart Little* said, "If a flower blooms once, it goes on blooming somewhere forever—what is changed is never gone unless we let it go." Pearl's wisdom came from a life infused with neoteny, a life celebrated, a life rich in meaning and purpose—the life of a woman who died young, as late as possible. Her contributions, her goals, and her love of life will remain in the heart and mind of each person she encountered.

Pearl's life illustrates the capacities we all possess and what can be achieved by each of us, if we begin now to age in a neotenous way.

The practice and implementation of neoteny requires us to create a mindful state of aging. After all, aging seems to be the only available way to live a long life. To truly transform and transmute our AGE, we must be willing, like Pearl, to become aware of more than one perspective. We must examine our impetus to Act, our decision to Grow, and our need to Evolve.

I designed the following primer to answer two questions: 1) Why should you strive to become young twice? 2) Why are you lucky to be alive? You need special conditions for deep questioning and growth: affirmation, challenge, guidance, stimulation, encouragement, support, emotional nourishment, and permission not to be self-conscious. Indeed, you need permission *to be you*. I've created these techniques with your needs in mind.

You'll begin by taking actions to create the necessary climate for growing young. Then you'll be challenged to deepen your capacity for change. You'll end with a call to personal evolution that will maximize every opportunity of every day.

"The first part of life is for learning, the second for service, and the last is time for oneself," says Gay Gaer Luce in *Your Second Life*. "There is a purpose to old age; a future to be fulfilled." We are all unique and will unfold in our own ways. My suggestions in this book are to be *adapted* for you rather than *adopted* by you. Find things that suit you, and create others that are all your own. Ask yourself why some of the activities are easy for you, while others seem to make no sense. Discover where and why your personal growth should be enhanced.

AGE™

Act

Actions you will take to grow young. These are the daily habits you can incorporate into your life to prime you for the practice of neoteny.

Grow

Growth you will be challenged to encourage in neglected areas of your life. You have the chance to examine and readjust the four capacities (physical, mental, spiritual, and emotional) that nature allows to grow as we age.

Evolve

Evolve a new perspective and purpose for this stage of life. Life doesn't care if you take action or grow; it will go on without you. Your personal evolution is essential to your quality of life, and an example to the people you love. In the final analysis, evolution is critical to our success as a species.

Keep track of your AGE steps forward in your chronicle!

Act

"Go out on a limb. That's where the fruit is."
JIMMY CARTER, THIRTY-NINTH PRESIDENT OF THE UNITED STATES

Unless we pay attention to a quest for meaning and purpose, the gift of a prolonged life is of little benefit to others. If man's (or woman's) main task in life is to give birth to himself, as psychologist Erich Fromm suggested, then later life is the best arena for taking action and using our longer years to live better years. Statesman George Clemenceau said, "When a man asks himself what is meant by action, he proves he isn't a man of action. Action is a lack of balance. In order to act you must be somewhat insane."

Why not change the stereotype of aging you hold now, today? Why not surprise everyone, even yourself, by taking immediate action to become young twice? The five Actions that follow involve a little insanity, a little impropriety, and a lot of life. Read the subsequent checklist, post it on your bathroom mirror, and practice each action daily. The list contains all the daily supplements you need to grow younger. The actions may not replace your vitamins, but you'll find that using them daily is cheaper and more effective.

ACTION 1: Take Attendance

Poet May Sarton noted, "I suppose old age begins when one looks backward rather than forward." It's time to acknowledge that you are getting older, to face it head-on with gusto and grace. As journalist Clare Booth Luce said, "If old age means a crown of thorns, the trick is to wear it jauntily!" Dump the old rules, norms, and assumptions about how you should live. Ask *why* more often, and create your own answers. Restock your life with the music, interests, and intrigues of your youth. Remember, it's not the biological changes of aging, but the way you attend to these changes that has the most impact on you. Look profoundly and lovingly at yourself, and be glad that you have the chance, as many have not, to see a face that has aged. You are among the most fortunate because you are not absent.

ACTION 2: No Cheating

Nothing is sadder than a perfectly fit, healthy, accomplished older person minimizing and masking herself to appear younger. "What I hate most in life," said fashion designer Karl Lagerfeld, "are people who are not really the peach of the day but who want to be young and sexy. You can fool nobody. There is a moment when you have to accept that somebody else is younger and fresher and hotter. Life is not a beauty contest." There's nothing wrong with wanting to look younger, of course, but see what simply smiling does for your face. The day will come when no amount of surgery, hip clothing, or even exercise will camouflage your age. When your spirit, the celebration of your neoteny, reflects your true beauty, people of all ages will be drawn to the power you radiate. Don't cheat yourself by comparing yourself to anyone; your answers are the right answers. The sooner you can accept your passing years by celebrating and enjoying them, the younger—and peachier—you will be.

Action 3: Write Your Own Permission Slip

Musician Arthur Rubenstein reminds us of what's essential in our aging: "During my long life, I have learned one lesson: that the most important thing is to realize why one is alive—and I think it is not only to build bridges or tall buildings or make money, but to do something truly important, to do something for humanity. To bring joy, hope, to make life richer for the spirit because you have been alive, that is the most important thing." Your childhood, young adulthood, and current age are all relevant when embracing your old age. Cut yourself some slack for your mistakes, disappointments, and failures. You no longer need approval from your parents, teachers, friends, or family. Now is your time.

Try the things untried; say the words that need to be said. What have you always wanted to do but were afraid to attempt? Former supermodel Lauren Hutton, now in her sixties but still a magazine cover girl, comments on risk-taking: "The great thing about dangerous situations is that you're so alive. You're totally aware and you're fantastically young. You're five again. Everything is brand new." Risk is a youth-promoting action; it puts a bounce in your step and a flush on your face. Contribute, commune, and continue. By shining big and bright, by allowing yourself to live large, you are giving others permission and power to do the same.

Action 4: Show and Tell

To change the way you feel about aging, to embrace the tough reality of mortality, to try to live younger will be a challenge. But come on. It's nothing compared to what you've already been through just living this long.

"I am perhaps the oldest musician in the world," said Pablo Casals. "I am an old man but in many senses a very young man. And this is what I want you to be, young, young all your life, and to say things to the world that are true." Tell everyone, everywhere, every day that you are learning to grow young. Practice the suggestions in this book and share them with others. Re-ignite your imagination, and share your sense of play and laughter. Show and tell your truth. You only die once, but it lasts a long, long time. Make some noise, make a difference, and make your longer life matter by telling the world the things that are true.

Action 5: Do Your Homework

Study your opportunities, ask life's questions, and relish the answers you have earned. Learn how to create yourself and create your world. How do you greet the day? Which activities will you choose? What's missing, and what can you add?

One day my mother said to me, "I want to be neotenous, but my feet hurt." OK, modifications may be necessary if some of the equipment is a bit worn. How will you adapt? How many times a day can you hug someone, sing, or laugh? I knew a woman of ninety who, when meeting people for the first time, would refuse a handshake and simply say, "These cheeks were meant for kissing." By choosing this action, she avoided discussing the arthritis in her hands and received joy instead. The great thing about getting older is that you don't lose all the other ages you have been. Use your mind, your body, your talents, and your potential every day, everywhere, in every moment, with everyone. If you dole out your energy like a non-renewable resource—it will be! Call upon all that you have been, and allow yourself to become more fully *you*. Start cramming for your final exam in the book of life. Remember, it will be comprehensive, and there are no make-ups.

Copy the Take FIVE Action Checklist or print it out at www.youngtwice.com.

Take FIVE Action Checklist

1. TAKE ATTENDANCE
   "I am lucky to be alive and present. I am looking forward to being young all the days of my life."

2. NO CHEATING
   "I accept and appreciate every year of my life and will not subtract any of them. I am proud of my age."

3. WRITE YOUR OWN PERMISSION SLIP
   "I refuse to be too careful or comfortable. I have permission to keep changing and the capacity to grow young."

4. SHOW AND TELL
   "In my words and deeds, I show everyone why people should grow young twice."

5. DO YOUR HOMEWORK
   "I am an accomplished student of the book of life, and I am prepared to ace my final exam."

Grow

· ·

"Our only purpose in life is growth. There are no accidents."
ELISABETH KÜBLER-ROSS, PSYCHOLOGIST

· ·

Lobsters outgrow their shells. Crowded into their outer casings, they become so uncomfortable that it's eventually impossible for them to go on living in the same shells. In fact, it's crucial to their survival to move on and grow bigger shells. So they do a very dangerous thing. Venturing far out into the ocean, completely unprotected from jagged reefs and predatory fish, in this precarious situation lobsters shed their old shells. They don't do it in groups or hidden in a cave. They do it alone and in the open. The entire tough outer sheath comes off—and the pink membrane inside grows to become a harder, bigger shell.

Like a lobster, if you remain the way you are, you'll become cramped, overgrown, or worse, figuratively dead. Unfortunately, older people tend to become more of what they have always been. They often lack the courage to change, or to face the rough sea ahead. Growth is not an accessory; it must be a continuous process. There's really no need to stay inside a small shell: imagination, playfulness, courage, daring, and constant learning belong to us throughout our lives. And no one but you is responsible for your growth, happiness, or rejuvenation. I know a man who asked his wife of fifty years to make a list of what it would take to make her happy. Every single thing on the list depended on him. How can your life become more fulfilling, how can your life get bigger, if you're always depending on someone else to make the changes necessary to grow a happier and more fulfilling existence?

An explicit message of neoteny is that it's never too late to change, to make old dreams come true, or to dream new ones. At age sixty-five, Laura Ingalls Wilder published *Little House in the Big Woods,* the first of her eight-volume *Little House* series. At sixty-seven, Louise Arner Boyd became the first woman to fly over the North Pole. At ninety, Jenny Wood-Allen of Scotland completed the London Marathon in eleven hours, thirty-four minutes—she had run her first marathon at age seventy-one. Winston Churchill deserved a rest after World War II, but instead took up a pen and won the Nobel Prize for literature at age seventy-nine.

A friend of the late American jurist Oliver Wendell Holmes asked him why he had taken up the study of Greek at the age of ninety-four. Holmes replied, "Well, my good sir, it's now or never." When J. C. Penney was ninety-five years old, he affirmed, "My eyesight may be getting weaker, but my vision is increasing."

Sadly, for many, aging finds us smaller, diminished, and living in cramped shells that we should have abandoned years ago. We become afraid of new places, new people, and new adventures. We avoid discomfort, long lines, foreign travel, or new foods. We protect and overprotect our lives until we have no lives beyond sitting in front of a television wearing our slippers, watching other people live, create, laugh, and love. People who "check out" this way because they think they're too old to participate in the land of the living *become* too old to participate. Remember that being near the top of the hill doesn't mean you've passed your peak.

As missionary and philosopher Albert Schweitzer said, "The tragedy of life is not in the fact of death. The tragedy of life is in what dies inside a man while he lives—the death of genuine feeling, the death of inspired response, the death of awareness that makes it possible to feel the pain or the glory of other men in oneself."

The voluntary loss of our capacity to feel, to notice, and to care shrinks both our world and ourselves as we age. Old age has a purpose, and we can choose to either sacrifice it or actualize it. We have a choice between decay and growth, between a resounding "yes" to life and a feeble, fearful "no." As Bob Dylan said, "If you aren't busy being born you're busy dying."

We all must re-engage our neotenous characteristic of hope: not a hope for immortality or revived youth, and not a hope for a retreat into the past because that's where we are comfortable. Rather, the hope for a continued search, in each and every precious moment, for the source of our better selves.

There is no point at which the laws of nature say *No more writing, No more doing, No more laughter.* Life is more than just a fixed state of reduced tension or a homeostatic condition. Life is a process that is forever changing and developing. We must give meaning to newly initiated values, virtues, and obligations that come with age, and the often increasing intensity of feeling and experiencing that life offers.

So what are your choices? You could choose despair, loneliness, or self-imposed isolation. You could choose to run out of life experiences, to cease your interest in the people around you, in books, in listening. By making this choice, you create a life that makes you boring, makes you tired, makes you old.

Or you could choose to actively participate in what psychologist Abraham Maslow called a time when everything gets piercingly important. "As you get older, you get stabbed by flowers and by babies and by beautiful things." By choosing growth, you choose to feel, see, acknowledge loss, and face fears. You choose to see who you are and what you want to do. You become closer to the center of the universe, you grow a new shell, you become real.

· ·

"Generally, by the time you are Real, most of your hair has been loved off, and your eyes drop out and you get loose in the joints and very shabby. But these things don't matter at all, because once you are Real you can't be ugly, except to people who don't understand."
The Skin Horse in *The Velveteen Rabbit* by Margery Williams

· ·

Jars and Pebbles, Sand, and Water

One of the most frustrating, even frightening, things about being a college professor is looking out at three hundred faces of young men and women in their early twenties—and seeing that for many, their light has already dimmed, their energy has already lessened, their promise has already been squandered. They have already lost all of childhood's best traits in a sad but understandable ploy to be "grown up." They believe that being adult means replacing all the childlike qualities they once possessed. After all, there's only so much room in a person's mind and body, and "being adult" takes it all up.

And they are good at being adults. No one asks questions in class, no one gets excited or shows pleasure when something wonderful happens, no one cries or laughs, and no one acts with the innocence of a boy or girl. That is, until I give them permission: permission to speak up, argue, question, invent, move, sing, and make learning fun. Eventually they figure out that if I'm going to grade them on participation and engagement, they'd better grow *down*!

My students' behavior reminds me of a popular demonstration that highlights personal capacity and time management. Ask someone to fill a glass jar to the brim with pebbles. Is there any room left? You can see that there isn't. Ah, but if you pour in sand, guess what? The jar now holds sand you didn't think would fit, representing time you didn't know you had and energy you hadn't counted on. Now the jar is overflowing with rocks and sand, and you're sure it's filled to capacity, finished, kaput. But you pour in water. What happens? You can fit even more in the jar.

Like that jar, human capacity is greater than we believe. Indeed, we are able to continually make room for the unexpected and for our deepest hopes. In our human vessel, there is always room for more: more fun, more learning, more giving, and more living. We all have an infinite capacity for growth and change and development. We're built for it. We can retain the basic emotional strengths of infancy; the stubborn autonomy of being a toddler; and the capacity for wonder, pleasure, and playfulness of the preschool years. We can keep the capacity for belonging and the intellectual curiosity of the school years, as well as the idealism and passion of adolescence. Then, with determination and diligence, we can incorporate these capacities into a new pattern of development—guided by adult stability, wisdom, knowledge, sensitivity to others, responsibility, strength, and purpose. This growth is a shift of the paradigm "As we get older, we decay." Instead, the model becomes "As we get older, we continue to develop."

We know ourselves better, accept our limitations, and understand what matters in life as we age. But our reactions to the Inventory on Aging in Chapter Two may indicate that we've fallen into a stereotypical judgment of old age that is far more threatening than the reality. We may be setting arbitrary limits on our development, erroneously believing that a certain chronological age equals a certain correlated stage. As author Anais Nin tells us, "We do not grow absolutely chronologically. We grow sometimes in one dimension, and not in another, unevenly. We grow partially. We are relative. We are mature in one realm, childish in another. The past, present, and future mingle and pull us backward, forward, or fix us in the present. We are made up of layers, cells, constellations."

And, I would add, we are made up of capacities that were never intended to diminish. Capacities that can and should grow, alter, adapt, and replenish.

Four Pools of Human Capacity

I believe that as years pass, no one chooses to become less instead of more. Yet most of us share the common fear that aging must equal, at best, a slow diminution of one's capacities. Mark Twain said, "The first half of life consists of the capacity to enjoy without the chance; the last half consists of the chance without the capacity." We assume that more years equal less capacity for life. The best we can do is stand on the helm of our sinking ship with noble stoicism and humble acceptance. Age is to be either denied or dreaded. To become young twice, you'll need to toss the age-equals-decline, the good-old-days-are-gone claims out for good.

Rather, you'll need to understand and, ideally, expand your capacity for life. In fact, one of the central tenets of neoteny is that we must preserve and grow our capacities for life as we age. Following this tenet of growing capacity alone will equal a greater

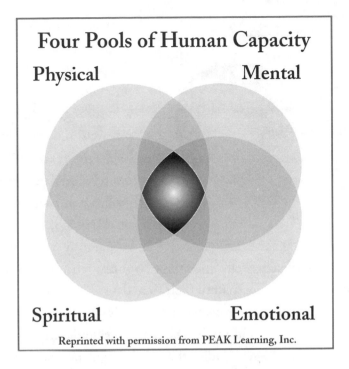

Four Pools of Human Capacity

Physical   Mental

Spiritual   Emotional

Reprinted with permission from PEAK Learning, Inc.

and more fulfilling life. This section introduces the four pools of capacity from which you can draw to optimize the quality and meaning of the years ahead.

Mental capacity is about your brain. It includes your ability to think, imagine, recall, synthesize, create, describe, express, and comprehend. When you enter a casino in Las Vegas, you are instantly besieged by the cacophony of slot machines paying out. You hear only the winners. The losers are silent, leading you to believe mistakenly that there are far more winners than losers. I'll draw a parallel between this and the research done on aging. When it comes to learning about our capacities as we age, particularly in the arena of mental capabilities, we hear about only the losers, not the much more plentiful winners. Alzheimer's disease, strokes, and "senior moments" dominate the age-related headlines. They make all the noise. Meanwhile, mental acuity in one's later years remains a silent victory: a much larger headline that, with rare exceptions, never sees print.

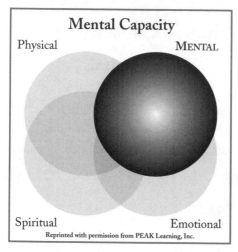

Mental Capacity

Physical   MENTAL

Spiritual   Emotional

Reprinted with permission from PEAK Learning, Inc.

Because many findings aren't publicized, some of the positive research done on aging may seem astounding. In the 1980s, research unveiled in the book *Aging Grace* introduced an exceptional group of nuns in the town of Mankato, Minnesota. Apparently these women not only survived well into their eighties and nineties, but remained mentally sharp until their final days. Through the unusual act of dedicating their post-mortem brains to science, the nuns were able to shatter old myths about the inevitable decline of the human brain as it ages. Rather than shrinking, the brains of these nuns actually showed an increased number of dendrites, or the nerve cells that conduct impulses from adjacent cells. As they aged, their brains grew new neuropathways.

How did these women grow their brains so late in life? By using them. Mental exercises like crossword puzzles, bridge, board games, reading, and music all help expand mental capacity. Challenging the brain in new ways creates new growth. In fact, many of the nuns continued teaching school and leading choir well into their nineties.

Common wisdom has always held that the brain is like a bulb that slowly dims with age. The Mankato nuns enlightened science by proving that the brain is really more like a muscle, which, when properly used, grows in strength and capacity.

Physical capacity is about your body. It's your facility for speed, strength, agility, and stamina. Unquestionably, even under the most rigorous training, these traits will diminish to some degree over the years if you live long enough. Muscle tone, aerobic capacity, speed, quickness, reflexes, and brute strength will all eventually decline

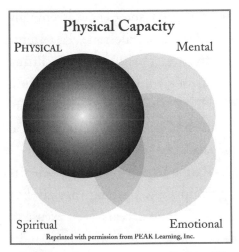

Physical Capacity

PHYSICAL   Mental

Spiritual   Emotional

Reprinted with permission from PEAK Learning, Inc.

from your peak physical potential. But how close have you ever been to your physical potential? In other words, have you reached your outer limits in each of these physical domains? At my fifty-year, 50,000-mile check-up, my doctor told me how I was doing. Then he added, "When most people hit fifty they slow down, modify, and codify. My advice to you is to work out harder, run longer, stay busier, and you'll have an optimum life." Up until the night he died, my father, in his seventies, played tennis at least three times a week, often competing against—and beating—men half his age. I know a woman who didn't start running until she was fifty-four and now, at sixty-two, is running marathons. The human body wants to be well and strong. Your body should be more than a skin bag to get your brain from place to place.

If you're like most people, you've never fully developed your complete physical capacity. If this is the case, you might actually grow to your physical capacity late in life. I recently met a couple in their late seventies at my health club. Every day they lift weights, do the aerobic machines, stretch themselves in yoga classes, and eat a healthy snack at the café. I told them that I was impressed to see them working with such dedication to stay in shape. They both smiled. "Actually, we're in the best shape of our lives. When we were younger, we never had time to work out. Now we have all the time we need. We've never been stronger, faster, more flexible, or more full of energy than we are now!" I stood corrected.

Even if you were once, or are currently, in peak physical condition, and although decline from that peak is eventually inevitable, the speed and degree of decline is largely within your control.

Fitness pioneer Jack LaLanne performs some new, seemingly impossible stunt to celebrate each birthday milestone. Past stunts have included pulling barges in the water with his teeth, lifting weights, and performing thousands of sit-ups. While his physical prowess at ninety certainly isn't what it was in his thirties or forties, Jack is arguably in better shape and possesses greater physical capacity than 90% of the college students I've met.

You don't have to be Jack LaLanne to experience the benefits of stretching, moving, exercising, lifting, and pushing yourself. But the sad fact is that most people use their later years as an excuse to do none of these. Research on the value of regular exercise indicates that benefits extend well beyond the physical and into the other forms of capacity: mental, emotional, and spiritual. As author Carlos Castaneda said, "To be young and vital is nothing. To be old and vital is sorcery."

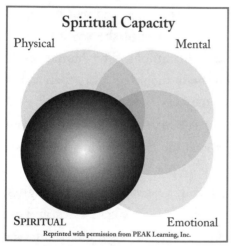

Spiritual Capacity

Physical

Mental

SPIRITUAL

Emotional

Reprinted with permission from PEAK Learning, Inc.

Spiritual capacity is all about your soul. It's your ability to sense, share, connect with, and benefit from a higher power. Spirituality is fed by the neotenous traits of joy, love, play, wonder, awe, and curiosity. It also includes the concepts of flow (being totally consumed by what you're doing) and forgiveness. Spiritual capacity is *age-agnostic*, meaning that there isn't a particular age or path that one must take to be fulfilled spiritually. In fact, for many who live harried lives, spiritual capacity remains the most denied of the four capacities. Only with the gentle easing of life's pace, and the less hurried lifestyle that can accompany the later years, are many people able to reconnect with, explore, and expand this transcendent and often untapped capacity.

Spiritual capacity is more than attending worship services or finding religion. While these remain mainstays of spiritual expression, no matter what belief system you were or were not raised with, spirituality requires no equipment, location, or membership. It's ultimately portable and personal. Even in the heart of a bustling city, you can find opportunities to connect with nature, pray, meditate, or achieve solitude.

You can use your later years as a long-awaited chance to get reacquainted with your spiritual side, and then exercise it daily through any method you prefer. One morning on an all-too-brief holiday in Italy, my husband and I awoke early to take on a challenging hike. We huffed and puffed our way along with our maps, backpacks, and gear, and with a clear goal of the number of miles we wanted to knock off that day, which required an ambitious pace. As we rounded a sharp hairpin curve in the trail, we saw an elderly man about fifty yards off the trail. He was sitting on a rock, taking in the sunrise. His face reflected both the sun and complete inner peace. We, of course, had a schedule, a goal, and a map, and not many days left. So we chugged by, determined to meet our objective. While celebrating our accomplishment later that day, we reflected: Who had experienced the mountain more fully? Was it our peaceful friend—or us?

Emotional capacity is about the heart. It's your power to sense, uncover, and effectively use the full range of human feelings, both within yourself and with others. Today, thanks to the work of psychologist Daniel Goleman and countless others, we often refer to this capacity in terms of the title of his book *Emotional Intelligence*. Most people have considerable room for growth when it comes to their emotions, as with the other capacities. How well do you experience and use the full range of emotion? Have you retreated into the safe haven of a narrowed emotional range? By restricting your opportunities to feel, you can exercise real control over your emotions—but you'll sacrifice some of the richer rewards of human feeling.

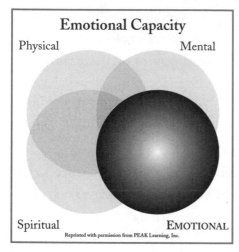

Emotional Capacity

Physical

Mental

Spiritual

EMOTIONAL

Reprinted with permission from PEAK Learning, Inc.

Spiritual teacher Arjuna Ardagh explains, "We constantly resist not only our grief, but also our wild passion and sexuality, our anger, even our exuberance and joy, repressing their free expression. Big feelings overwhelm us. They can easily upset the fragile equilibrium of our lives. We keep a lid on ourselves, till we periodically explode. We don't realize that any deep feeling, pleasurable or painful, can be a wave we surf home into ourselves, into love."

How would others describe your ability to empathize fully, to reflect the full magnitude of emotions, no matter how painful or difficult? How appropriately do you use emotions to connect and relate to others?

Tears and laughter, so natural to children, are often crushed in adults. While you may not suffer the dizzying hormonal swings of a teenager, is there any reason you can't access the full tapestry of your emotions—perhaps more effectively at seventy-one than at seventeen? When you watch a good movie, do you simply detach, or do you become enthralled? Do you observe the movie, or experience it? And what about the moving story that is your life? Are you watching or doing?

Emotional expression is highly cultural, but emotions are also universal. Some cultures are traditionally expressive of emotions, while others are more subdued. But these differences don't imply that subdued people lack emotional capacity, or that people who "let it fly" are emotionally superior.

The point is to strengthen, stretch, improve, and grow your emotional capacity throughout your life. You'll be more complete and evolved than when you started. In the end, emotional capacity comes down to relationships: between yourself and others, and with your world. Improving your capacity can send a positive ripple through all facets of your life.

CAPACITY OVERLAP

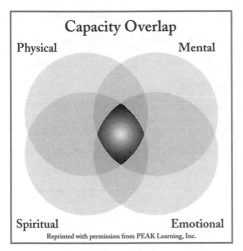

Capacity Overlap

Physical   Mental

Spiritual   Emotional

Reprinted with permission from PEAK Learning, Inc.

As our understanding of humans has evolved over the past fifty years, one of the most important advances has been the realization that all of our systems are integrated. Similarly, all of our capacities overlap and influence each other. An improvement in one capacity generally bolsters the others. That's why many people find spiritual benefits in physical activity, emotional expression, or intellectual challenges. Similarly, through spiritual pursuits our brains are stimulated, our emotions are calmed, and our physiology improves. Positive emotions can also strengthen our immune systems. Any effort to expand and strengthen your capacity in one area is most likely to benefit you in other ways. Truly, one of the gifts of adding years is earning the freedom to focus on and grow all forms of capacity. We can then give more to others, and add meaning to life, helping us to become young twice.

On a page in your Young Twice Chronicle, write *Four Pools of* ✴YTC✴ *Capacity* at the top. Then draw a picture of the four pools of capacity that represent the actual, or current, proportions of your four capacities. Use the diagram above as a guide. For example, if you attend and enjoy worship services every week, but avoid physical exertion at all costs, your spiritual circle would be much larger than your physical one.

Next, draw a picture of the four pools of capacity that represent your *ideal* proportions for each of the four areas.

Then draw a picture that represents the proportions of the four pools of capacity based on what the people who know you best might draw. This picture should be based on others' perceptions of you, your behavior, and your priorities. For example, let's say you drew a large circle for your own emotional capacity, but realize that you haven't said "I love you" to your best friend lately, if ever. How balanced, in comparison to the other four, would your emotional capacity circle be if your friend drew it?

Take a moment to respond in your chronicle to this question: If you could grow only one of these four pools of capacity, which one would you pick? Specifically, what can you do to grow young in your capacity in this chosen area?

Evolve

"Love not what you are but only what you may become."
MIGUEL DE CERVANTES, AUTHOR

To know ourselves, says Mihaly Csikszentmihalyi, author of *The Evolving Self*, is the greatest achievement of our species. "It is for this reason," he explains, "that the fate of humanity in the next millennium depends so closely on the kind of selves we will succeed in creating."

So far in this book, you have been presented with an evolutionary opportunity to grow young. This opportunity is known as neoteny. You've received information debunking many of the misconceptions you may have had about aging. You've learned some steps to begin the process of youthening. And you've examined potential growth areas in multiple facets of your life. By simply reading this book, whether you know it or not, you are evolving. You're beginning to understand that your whole life is a journey toward the fulfillment of childhood promises, toward the fullest expression of the person you want to be. "The thing you are ripening toward is the fruit of your life," said writer Stewart Edward White. "It will make you bright inside, no matter what you are outside. It is a shining thing."

REWIND YOUR CHILDHOOD SELF

I have a Kodak super-8mm movie of my family. (If you don't know what "super-8" is, you should probably put this book away and pull it out again in twenty years.) We're in the backyard of my grandparents' house in Oregon in the early 1960s. It's a normal scene for that era: the barbecue and the adults smoking, my brother throwing a football, my sister sitting in a swing. The camera is panning the activity and passes by me standing alone in the foreground, singing my heart out. The camera continues its pan, then returns; and there I am again, belting out something with drama, passion, gestures—everything but talent. No one is watching. Everyone else, in fact, is oblivious to the major superstar in their midst. But I keep singing, with or without the camera, with or without applause. I was a shining thing.

Until I began my research on neoteny, I never thought of that moment. I never watched that movie as a clue to an essential part of who I am, and who I eventually can become. In retrospect (another gift of aging), there I am in that backyard: the person who always wanted to be something more, something better, something great. Always hoping to be noticed, recognized, and appreciated, I was looking for approval but happy to proceed without it. When I look at my life from that moment until now, from that moment and beyond, I realize that the little girl in the home movie is the big girl sitting here writing this book. I've always done things hoping initially for the recognition and approval of others; but in the final analysis, I did things to the best of my ability and for the ultimate approval of *me*. What I was as a child, I am as an adult. In other words, what made me Ronda yesterday fortifies the Ronda of today, and is the foundation of what Ronda will be tomorrow.

Remember: Your childlike qualities change, hide, deviate, get crushed and denied, but never die. Your childhood self is always waiting to come into focus and be played again. Being young twice is being able to rewind.

Keep Singing

Carl Jung, famous Swiss psychiatrist and colleague of Sigmund Freud, described the curve of a lifetime divided in half. The first half is the time of relationships, and the second half is the time of finding the meaning of the life within. The Hindus call this "following the *marga*." In short, it's the path: The footsteps of your human experience lead to your inner life; then, with no attachment, you move through the last passage of life without anxiety, without fear. Hindus speak of their ideal: "You go to your death singing."

Jung explained it this way: "As a physician I am convinced that it is healthy to discover in death a goal toward which one can strive; and that shrinking away from it is something unhealthy and abnormal which robs the second half of life of its purpose."

In his book *Handbook to a Happier Life*, Jim Donovan tells a wonderful story about purpose. An old priest goes to his doctor because of stomach pains. The doctor informs him that he has a terminal illness, and suggests that he go home and put his affairs in order, as he doesn't have long to live. The priest takes the doctor's advice, and then decides to visit a Mexican church he had always wanted to see. As he approaches the church, he sees a young boy running off with the money in the "poor box." Grabbing the youngster by the scruff of the neck, the priest demands to know why he is stealing from the church. The priest learns that the boy, like many of his friends, is an orphan and has no food. He has stolen the box, explains the boy, to buy something to eat. Moved by the boy's story, the priest goes with him to his village to see conditions for himself. To make a long story short, the priest is so moved by what he sees that he starts an orphanage—and today, *25 years later*, he is still running it.

The priest had found a reason to keep going, to keep "singing." In leaving my university post and becoming an author and life coach, I have also found a way to keep singing. If you create a gripping *why* for your AGE™, then you'll have a compelling reason to take Action, welcome Growth, and choose to Evolve. And you won't rob the second half of your life—because you will have found your *how*.

YOUR EVOLVING SELF

Consider the following questions, and then record your responses in your Young Twice Chronicle:

- What makes you want to jump out of bed and greet the day?

- If you don't have an answer, what *would* make you want to jump out of bed in the morning?

- What's important to you? Why?

- What would you like to be remembered for? Why?

- When you look back, can you see a purpose for your life?

- When you look forward, can you see a purpose for your life?

- Why you? Why did you get to live longer than some others?

As a child, I was often singing: singing for others, performing for applause, singing a tune written by someone else. Evolution of my self has become the structuring energy of my life as I age, without care for achievement, without concern for prestige. I'm now keeping my own beat, not caring who notices or whether anyone applauds. My older age is a replay of my childhood super-8 movie filtered through a lens of experience, development, and choice.

Happy Birthday to *Who*?

When we are born, we are unrealized potential with a thousand possibilities open to us. That's our very first birthday present. We can choose to be born again at any time, and accept the challenges of the selves we've yet to meet. Neoteny infuses our chronological age with the much-needed and often unheeded *why*. In other words, we age because we have the opportunity to fully become. To fully develop. To fully, deeply, and richly live. It's the most astonishing of gifts. Says poet Mary Oliver, "Long life or short, it is amazement we ought to feel."

At each stage of our lives, we are required to make personal adjustments: to engage and re-engage with our changing world, and to acquire or discard things that create our own place in that changing world. Personal evolution calls upon us to regenerate, uncover, and develop our own unique selves—birthday after birthday. In fact, to evolve as we age is to make each day a *birth* day.

Pictures of You: When, Where, How, Why

Like my super-8 movie, you also have photos, tapes, awards, badges, trophies, and trinkets that will uncover your childhood self. Dig them up, bring them out, surround yourself with them, and have a tea party or sleepover. Introduce your current self to your former self. Remember who you were so you can become the person you want to be. Give yourself a few days to display the mementos. After spending some time studying your favorite artifacts, sit quietly, consider the following questions, and record your answers in your chronicle.

- Can you remember what it was like to be very young?

- What's your earliest childhood recollection?

- How old were you? Two, three, four?

- What was your favorite toy?

- Did you have pets?

- Who were your teachers? Your classmates?

- What is life like for you now?

- What makes you laugh?

- What tastes good?

- As you've grown older, have you remained as you always were? For example, were you always shy? Or stubborn?

- Do you avoid situations because of your age?

- What, really, has changed inside you?

- Would you describe your childhood self as happy, smiling, or fun?

- If you could say something to your young self, what would it be? Would it be something to make growing up feel less frightening, less harsh, and more secure?

- What happened to make you feel the way you feel now?

- Is it hard to look at yourself as a youngster?

- Do you feel that you've lost too much and lived too little?

Each of these questions is worthy of an entire week's contemplation, but I want you to begin the process of getting in touch with your childhood self. I want you to reacquaint yourself with some of your best moments, qualities, challenges, and dreams. I want you to arm yourself with tangible ideas to help you youthen.

DREAMS OF RENEWED LIFE

Psychologist Elisabeth Kübler-Ross warned, "There are dreams of love, life and adventure in all of us. But we are also sadly filled with reasons why we shouldn't try. These reasons seem to protect us, but in truth they imprison us. They hold life at a distance. Life will be over sooner than we think. If we have bikes to ride and people to love, now is the time."

Neoteny is an evolutionary advantage that should prompt humans to remember that now is always the time. What bikes are you waiting to ride? Who in your life is waiting to be loved? How can the young boy or girl you once were help you now? What would your young self say to you about your life today?

What kinds of warnings, predictions, or conclusions about growing up might come from this child you used to know? In the movie *The Kid*, Bruce Willis stars as a man who confronts his boyhood self and lives with that child for a summer. Meeting himself as an adult, the younger version releases a tirade about what a loser the older version is. With great disappointment the child moans, "You mean I grow up to be someone who doesn't even own a dog? What kind of person doesn't have a dog? I don't want to grow up to be you!"

To discard former selves for shining new ones requires us to be fully aware, sensitive, and flexible. It also requires the keenest sense of humor. As author Somerset Maugham said to his nephew, "Dying is a very dull, dreary affair. And my advice to you is to have nothing whatever to do with it." Even so, we must have something to do with it.

While personal evolution is not an easy process, it doesn't have to be dreary. "They" can't teach us or change us; only we can do that. "They" can't bring us joy, fully actualize us, or help us grow young. Only we can decide upon the path of our lives, the process of our becoming, or the passion of our future. Only we can embrace ourselves and start anew.

. . . .

"But where to start? The world is so vast. I shall start with the country I know best, my own. But my country is very large; I had better start with my town. But my town, too, is very large. I had better

start with my own street. No: my home. No: my family.
Never mind, I shall start with myself."

ELIE WIESEL, AUTHOR AND CONCENTRATION CAMP SURVIVOR

. . . .

NAYSAYERS AND NORMS

Let's say that we begin to evolve our personal perceptions of aging, that we embrace the child we once were and let him or her come out again to sing, dance, build, question, or play. What might happen? If we employ the full potential of our neoteny, some of our relatives, friends, and lovers may attempt to bind and distort us into their image. For their own convenience and comfort, and usually in the name of love, they will ask, "You aren't wearing that, are you?" Or, "You want to jump out of an airplane! You're too old for that!" Or perhaps, "Please be quiet—you're embarrassing me!"

Once you begin to embrace neoteny, you may discover that society is trying to force you to conform to its own needs, to squeeze you into its narrow mold. Heed the words of author Maeve Binchy, "It's not perfect, but to me on balance Right Now is a lot better than the Good Old Days."

Perhaps you've heard this Oliver Wendell Holmes quote: "Pity for those who have never sung, and having never sung, die with their music still inside them." That thought just takes the wind right out of me; I feel sad, angry, and guilty all at the same time. Too many of us let the naysayers and the norms create the rhythm of our lives. It's a sad thought indeed that at one time, all of us were bright, shining, and unique, but now we're dancing to the same tired old tune and singing the same song. After all, inside each of us is an undiscovered symphony.

Ashley Montagu pointed out, in *Growing Young,* "Open mindedness, receptivity to new ideas, malleability, questing, striving, questioning, seeking, critical testing, and weighing of new ideas as well as old ones; wide eyed curiosity and excitement in the enjoyment of new experiences, the willingness to work hard at making sense of it all, together with a sense of humor and laughter—all these are neotenous traits. Indeed, all these are needs seeking satisfaction in opportunities for growth and development, which it should be the fundamental purpose of every society to provide."

But our society does not provide this. Rather, our society squashes that growth and development, steps on it, wrings it out until it's dry. In fact, studies consistently show that by the fourth grade, when we are only nine years old, mainstream schooling has killed most of our innate creativity. And here's the ripper: A full 90% of us *never get those creative juices back*. Consequently, we spend the rest of our lives squandering our remaining neotenous gifts until we are emotionally bankrupt and our spirits are old and withered.

The Speed of Light

I remember taking my son to visit the middle school he was scheduled to attend the following year. On the way there, my lovely fair-haired boy was singing show tunes, messing with the laces on his high-top Keds, and chewing bubble gum. He was a modern-day Tom Sawyer in his checked shirt and scruffy jeans. But have you been inside a middle school lately? You'll see make-up, push-up bras, tattoos, and hairstyles that look like they belong in any dark bar on the seedy side of any town—except these barflies are thirteen-year-old children. I could not, and did not, let my son go to this holding tank for the soon-to-be jaded, blasé, and bored. Instead, that day we started looking for a school where kids could be kids. Not an easy find.

Our society, our media, and especially our role models and mentors all try to make sure we are in a hurry to grow up. Our culture and our calendar age us and rush us—then push us out to pasture in one very fast and fell swoop. We're admonished, "Act your age, not your shoe size," or "Quit being a crybaby." We're encouraged to fake our IDs and finish our growth stages. We're all waiting to get to the point in our lives when something "big" will happen, and we're always sure it's just around the corner.

Comedian Sid Caesar made an important point: "While people keep waiting and waiting for something big to happen in life, the 'now' is passing them by. Do you know how fast a 'now' passes? At the rate of 186,000 miles per second, the speed of light. So no matter how much you love and enjoy a particular 'now,' that's how fast it becomes a 'was.' That's why I never use the word 'if' anymore. An 'if' is a never was."

Imagine, then, that *now* is the time and you cannot fail. Don't consider your chronological age; instead, recapture your childlike self. What would be the one new thing you would add to your life experience? Write it down in your chronicle, and then answer this question: What are you waiting for?

We are not bodies with souls, but souls with bodies. Leo Tolstoy used a lovely phrase to describe this: "We are," he said, "souls dragging around corpses." That is why, no matter how old our bodies become, our true self never ages. Inwardly, we almost always feel younger than the years indicate. I'm always shocked when I look in my rearview mirror while driving and catch a glimpse of what looks like my mother. *Come on, that face in the mirror can't be me.*

So I guess the remedy for me is to quit looking in the rearview mirror. And that's not bad advice for all of us. We've already seen our childhood pictures. We know who we were. Now, by examining our current thinking about who we are, let's drive ahead. Let's evolve into the people we may become, with the benefit of age. For those seeking to grow young, evolution can be defined in this way:

> *The ability to transcend, through action and growth, the expectations and limitations of being human, and to move toward a deeper level of development and a state of growing young.*

"The deepest human defeat suffered by human beings," said Ashley Montagu, "is constituted by the difference between what one was capable of becoming and what one has in fact become." As long as you continue to grow, age is a matter of insignificance. To be perfectly honest, "old" is a condition that afflicts you, like rheumatism or hardening of the arteries. It happens when you have lost your sense of curiosity, wonder, play, and the potential for learning. "Old" is a hardening of the mind and spirit. Being young twice is knowing there's always something yet to be: a higher hill with a better view, a cup that's never full, a life spent growing up.

PART TWO

How To
Become Young Twice

The world needs
children of all ages.

Re-Introduction

"*I think of life as a good book. The further you get into it,
the more it begins to make sense.*"

HAROLD S. KUSHNER, RABBI AND AUTHOR

In my introduction, I explained that many people are using cosmetic procedures—lifts, peels, and Botox—to turn back time. In the second part of this book, and in the second part of your life, you'll learn to substitute all those quick, superficial fixes for the concept of neoteny to start youthening. Instead of erasing time, neoteny will restore the evidence of living an interesting life. It will reveal the wrinkles that show where you have smiled, wept, loved, and laughed. Neoteny will release your paralyzed facial muscles and give you back you. So long Botox, hello Notox.

We may look and sound like grownups, but we smile, laugh, cry, and fantasize much as we did when we were younger. When does a child cease to be a child? Possibly never. One of the gifts of aging is that we are constantly invited, as Henry David Thoreau said, "to be what we are." And neoteny shows us that we are an extension and amplification of our earlier years. Genetically, we are endowed with a lifetime supply of youthful qualities. We possess everything from ambition to zest.

"*Whether sixty or sixteen, there is in every human being's heart
The lure of wonder,*

81

The unfailing child-like appetite of what's next,
And the joy of living.
In the center of your heart and my heart there is a wireless
Station:
So long as it receives messages of beauty, hope, cheer,
Courage and power
So long are you young..."
SAMUEL ULLMAN

. . . .

Part Two of *You're Only Young Twice* will reintroduce you to ten of your innate childlike qualities. These qualities were with you at birth, and remain in your development for the length of your life. To grow young means to grow in our youthful traits, not to grow out of or abandon them. Part Two dares you to consider how old you would be if you didn't know how old you are.

How "old" are you anyway? Do you remember these things?

- When a 10% tip was excellent?
- When Mom made her own jams and jellies?
- When you played marbles with aggies, peewees, and puries?
- When you loved the smell of a mimeographed piece of paper?
- Fizzies?
- When *Weekly Reader* was your favorite magazine?

To paraphrase American essayist and philosopher Ralph Waldo Emerson, what lies behind us or in front of us is nothing compared to what lies within us. Look at your present age in terms of the three vital behavioral factors of living shown in the OLD chart.

The OLD Survey (pages 83–86) examines these three aspects of living, which together create dexterity of mind, body, and spirit. The survey reveals how much you are using your youthful spirit and capitalizing on your innate neoteny, thus setting the foundation necessary to become young twice.

OLD™

Outlook

Your *Outlook* on life: the attitudes, angles, and lens from which you view life.

Language

The *Language* of your life: the ways in which you talk about your life and living.

Drives

Your *Drives*: the energy, vigor, and ambition that move your life.

Your Outlook, Language, and Drives are just as important as your total years in determining whether you will grow old or become a cheerful, youthful, Notox octogenarian. It's not the years themselves that diminish us, but the way we have learned to live them, perhaps giving up our true selves at each step.

THE OLD™ SURVEY
How old are you today?

Directions

Read and respond to the statements on the next three pages by placing a number (1, 2, 3, 4, or 5) inside the box next to each statement, or use a separate sheet of paper. Each numbered answer will indicate how much you agree and comply, or how much you disagree and do not comply.

How to Score Your Replies

1: Always, or emphatically YES!
2: Most of the time
3: Sometimes
4: Seldom
5: Never, or emphatically NO!

☐ I am in control of my life.

☐ I have friends who are very different from me.

☐ I love physical activity.

☐ I enjoy celebrating my birthday.

☐ I like to meet and talk to younger people.

☐ I am a volunteer for at least one social service, cultural, educational, or religious organization.

☐ I know when to say no.

☐ People say I look younger than I am.

☐ I meditate.

☐ I make plans for things to do next week, or even next year.

☐ I feel considerably younger than my years.

☐ I regularly read a variety of magazines and books.

☐ I don't like to make mistakes and I don't make many.

☐ I enjoy traveling and meeting people from other places.

☐ I like crossword puzzles and other mental games.

☐ I frequently attend concerts, plays, and movies.

☐ I love dogs, cats, and other animals.

☐ I have one or more hobbies for fun.

☐ I have learned something new in the past week.

☐ When in a crowd, I feel like one of the youngest people there.

☐ I like group activities and being with other people.

☐ I make new friends easily.

☐ I believe in the healing power of both laughing and crying.

☐ I rarely let a day go by without calling or writing at least one friend or relative.

☐ I enjoy looking for answers to my questions.

☐ I like to taste new and different foods.

☐ I enjoy painting, writing, or dancing.

☐ I read a daily newspaper.

☐ I have a library card.

☐ I use a computer or word processor.

☐ I frequently fantasize.

☐ I think it's important to earn and receive praise and respect.

☐ I like more than one kind of music.

☐ Before starting to assemble something, I read the directions.

☐ Despite my faults, I like myself.

☐ I believe in speaking openly and frankly about my fears and feelings.

☐ I can relax better doing something than doing nothing.

☐ I am an optimist.

☐ I think everyone has a unique and important mission in life.

☐ I believe in hope.

☐ I am more often lucky than unlucky.

☐ I am not reckless, but I do take chances.

☐ I dream youthful dreams.

☐ I think life is a game that should be played with plenty of love, enthusiasm, confidence, and humor.

☐ I am in love.

☐ I believe that the "good old days" are right now.

☐ I don't expect to ever run out of opportunities.

☐ I look forward to exploring the mysteries of aging.

☐ I laugh easily and often.

☐ I feel meaningful.

Scoring your results—How OLD are you anyway?

Add your subtotals to get your grand total, or OLD Score.

50-75 Exceptionally Youthful. You are much younger than your years and are facing aging with optimism, courage, and common sense. Neoteny will enhance your journey.

76-100 Youthful. You radiate a good balance of youth and maturity as you grow older. You are poised to grow younger.

101-150 Normal. You are at an average level of aging but are growing old faster than necessary. Neoteny will help you release your full powers of self-expression and confidence.

151-200 Aging. You are suppressing your youthful characteristics and inclinations. You lack confidence and self-esteem, and underestimate your intelligence as well as your ability to be neotenous.

201-250 Aged. You are allowing yourself to grow needlessly, unpleasantly, and prematurely old.

. . . .

"With mirth and laughter, let old wrinkles come."
WILLIAM SHAKESPEARE, POET AND PLAYWRIGHT

. . . .

Part Two of *You're Only Young Twice*—and Part Two of your life—are reminders that it's not what we know that brings us the fullness of life, it's how we live. Let's begin. Again.

CHAPTER FOUR

Look Out for Your Outlook

· ·

"I hope I have a young outlook. Since I have an old everything else,
this is my one chance of having a bit of youth as a part of me."
RICHARD ARMOUR, AUTHOR AND TRIATHLON ATHLETE

· ·

The ability to see, manage, apply, and unite what we find meaningful and significant in this world does not diminish as we age. These
abilities actually become more apparent and visible with every year
of our life. Recapturing your neotenous outlook is like putting on
those cool 3-D glasses they used to hand out in theaters or during
special commercials for the Super Bowl. Put them on, and BAM!
New depth, more color. The previously invisible becomes instantly
visible with a different lens and magnified image.

For his book *The View in Winter: Reflections on Old Age*, Ronald
Blythe interviewed English villagers and found compelling evidence of a particular happiness that belongs only to old age. "All I
am sure of is that an unexpected freshness comes to one when one
is old," writes Blythe. The images that we have of ourselves, relat-
ing to both our appearance and the way we feel about ourselves,
can produce a unique stage of happiness in our later years. This
innate, later life happiness indicates that our very outlook on life is
indeed a neotenous trait.

The human ability to create and renew contentment is a trait
that has been barely recognized and certainly not well understood.

I believe that what Blythe discovered means this: All of us carry within ourselves a core, an essence of an eternally youthful spirit, whose inner light warms and illuminates all the days of our lives.

We know that many people harbor negative and harmful stereotypes about aging. But the premise and promise of neoteny is that we age first in our minds, thereby wasting the opulent mental and behavioral opportunities nature provides to stay and grow young. By gaining a fresh insight into your neotenous gifts of resilience, optimism, wonder, and curiosity, you can recover a child-like outlook on the world that will put the "you" back in youth, regardless of your chronological age. So pretend that I have just handed you a special pair of 3-D neoteny glasses. Slip them on, and let's look around.

Resilience

. . . .

"I don't like people who have never fallen or stumbled. Their virtue is lifeless and isn't of much value. Life hasn't revealed its beauty to them."
BORIS PASTERNAK, AUTHOR

. . . .

How did you learn to walk? To run? To do multiplication tables or write your name? You tried, you failed; and you tried again, and again, and again. Remember that feeling of never giving up? Of learning from your mistakes and getting a little better, stronger, or smarter the next time? That's your innate gift of resilience. Children can, and do, take all kinds of tumbles, insults, and deprivations—and rapidly recover.

Just like shock absorbers on a car, this ability to take the bumps in a rough road can wear out over time. As we age, we become more fearful, less daring, more cautious, and less courageous. We have known pain, loss, and unbearable sadness, and we don't want to feel those things again. So we walk instead of run; we hide instead of seek. We lose our rapid recovery ability, and our resilience stalls. But resilience, like all of our neotenous traits, can be replenished, repaired, and even strengthened. In fact, your resilience determines your ability to see past the adversity of aging.

But human beings are not rubber balls. Resilience—the fuel of human evolution—is not just your ability to bounce back from adversity. Instead, resilience is your capacity to be *strengthened and improved by adversity*. Viewed in this way, life's vicissitudes play a vital role in our ability to grow young, and resilience serves as the foundation of all other neotenous traits. In other words, your ability to sustain and grow other neotenous traits late into life is based on your resilience.

I recently moved from a home that was perched on a ridge, and I both enjoyed spectacular views and experienced horrendous winds. Sometimes clocking at hurricane force, these "breezes" would level most common plant species. So when landscaping the edge of my plateau, I asked a local gardening expert for advice. As he paced back and forth across the windswept precipice, he seemed lost in thought, like a child completing a jigsaw puzzle. Finally he announced that he had decided what to plant in such an adversity-rich spot: "We will plant cuttings of those," he declared, pointing at a cluster of Mexican sage, ice plant, and climbing roses growing on the ridge. "But why plant cuttings rather than new plants from the nursery?" I asked, suspicious of any unnecessary cost the added steps might incur. The clarity of his response rang true. "Because new plants would be instantly leveled by the wind. But *those*, those have proven they are resilient. They thrive on the wind. So those," he nodded definitively, "are what we'll plant."

How well do you thrive when planted in adversity? Think back on your life, on the challenges you've faced and the hassles you've wrestled every day. The question isn't the degree to which you eventually recovered, or even if you gained wisdom from your hardships. The question is this: Over time, what effect have life's daily difficulties had on you?

The growing body of research on resilience shows that for most people, the accumulated effect of adversity is detrimental. As adversity builds, the majority of people grow more jaded, cynical, and lifeless. Like many of the plants at the edge of a canyon, many people become worn down by the conditions of life. Consequently, they age in unnecessary and unfortunate ways. How valuable is a strong EKG if the heart has lost its capacity for love, wonder, joy, and play, or if it beats in a shrunken shell?

The accumulated effects of adversity are the reason that many people consider neotenous traits to be the springtime seedlings of a happy childhood—certainly not fit for the harsh winter conditions of the later years. But you've learned that letting these seedlings wither and die is a violation of your biological potential. What, then, does it take to become more resilient, so you don't just survive, you thrive?

The good news is that resilience isn't genetic. On this, scientists are in rare agreement. Based on reports from the Global Resilience Project, directed by Dr. Paul Stoltz, resilience is learned. You can strengthen yours at any age, even thriving in the face of any weather that comes your way. And as you strengthen your resilience, you experience its natural outgrowths of hope, optimism, energy, health, and confidence.

CULTIVATING RESILIENCE

When it comes to cultivating resilience as a source of lifelong youthfulness, we can learn much from the natural world. Because of the profound role resilience plays in our lives, each of the resilience-building suggestions provided in this section are grounded in science, and are known to create abundant and enduring growth.

Stay Rooted, but Bend with the Wind

The most resilient people possess uncommon clarity about what matters most. They know who they are, what they believe in, and the issues on which they will not compromise. They have an unshakeable core, often fed by faith in something grander than themselves. They live a life firmly rooted in their own positive values.

With clarity can come flexibility. One reason that you see more palms than oak trees next to the ocean is that palms bend, while oaks are rigid; yet both thrive when firmly rooted in their natural soil. If you're clear about the issues on which you will not compromise, you have the opportunity to be flexible about everything else. So the next time you dig in your heels, ask yourself, "Is this a root issue? Or could my branches flex a bit more in the breeze?"

Build Some Windbreaks

One of the most powerful and universally accepted ways to strengthen your resilience is through loving relationships. Having someone or something in your life to love—and ideally be loved by—profoundly influences happiness, health, and overall resilience. The good news is that you don't have to be surrounded by soul mates to gain these benefits. Studies done in nursing homes, including those designed for the Eden Alternative by Dr. William Thomas (author of *What Are Old People For?*), have shown time and again that residents who are given plants to tend, live an average of two to three years longer than residents without plants. Pets, friends, community, neighbors, and even plant care can provide loving connections, strengthen your natural resilience, and protect you from some of life's harshest winds.

Welcome the Rain

One of the most detrimental but common tendencies of people as they age is to seek more and more comfort, and less and less adversity. If you are successful at removing all struggles and suffering from your life, you will shrink your capacity to deal with those challenges. Eventually, you'll be ill equipped to take on the big challenges life is sure to provide. Instead, seek adversity by taking on small challenges every day. Build them into your life.

Park a little farther away from the store. Delve into, rather than dive under, the messiness of life. In measured doses, let yourself experience cold, heat, wet, dry, loud, busy, and frenetic. Do something because it's tough, uncomfortable, or daunting. In proper doses, taking on challenges builds your sense of mastery and prevents you from accumulating misery. And with mastery comes a stronger sense of resilience.

Create Your Own Ecosystem

As you age, one of the more disconcerting trends can be a growing sense of victimization, or a feeling that the world happens to *you*—you don't happen to *it*. One of the more insidious forces feeding this perceptual cancer can be unfiltered television. As people slow down, many replace personal control with the remote control. A recent national study conducted by the Annenberg School of Communication revealed that 77% of stories on the evening news were about "helplessness inducing or significant adversities over which it is clear you have no control." Be careful of the seeds you allow someone else to plant. They just might grow.

Instead of letting the media contaminate your world, take control of your own soil. Oak trees (another species that thrived on my ridge) have a subtle but wise power. As they age, their power grows. These noble trees chemically alter the soil surrounding them such that only helpful plants can grow under their proud canopy. Enemies cannot take root. Don't let outside influences tell you how to view the world. You own your response to life. Like the mighty and wise oak, you can create your own ecosystem.

Endure Winter, Live for Spring

One of the barriers to harnessing your resilience can come from confusing resilience with positive thinking. While thinking happy thoughts is delightful, it doesn't make you resilient, any more than pruning leaves can strengthen roots. But strengthening your resilience does result in more authentic optimism.

· ·

*"In the depth of winter, I finally learned that within me
there lay an invincible summer."*

ALBERT CAMUS, AUTHOR AND PHILOSOPHER

· ·

In reality, a life fully lived usually includes plenty of adversity. This can crush you or make you stronger. We're taught that life goes on, but at what cost? Adversity is sometimes brutally heavy, dark, huge, and protracted. Life can throw you into what seems like interminable winter, during which anything you have planted may appear dead.

Yet people who show the most amazing resilience have an uncanny propensity to see past even the darkest days. They hold the inherent belief that spring will once again unleash its brilliance and life will bloom forth. Studies of pessimists have found that simple exercises, including describing, painting, or visualizing life *beyond* the most unspeakable hardships, can have a dramatically positive effect on energy, vitality, and hope.

YOUR RESILIENT YOUNG LIFE

Remember that a resilient outlook is learned. If you didn't learn resiliency in childhood, now is your chance. By taking the lessons of our natural world to heart, you can regain your mental agility, suppleness, mastery, and fortitude. Use these youthful qualities to help you lean into the wind, harness its power, and continue growing young, strong, and proud.

═══ **Do-Over: LIVE™ in Resilience** ═══

A Do-Over is a second chance and a current challenge. Every Do-Over in the remaining chapters of this book is an activity designed to refresh your Outlook, Language, and Drives. Do-Overs are designed to teach you how to grow young. Experiment with the suggestions presented in each Do-Over, and create new

LIVE™

Look

Take a realistic view of any challenge you face. Look realistically—not idealistically—at your own thoughts, feelings, and behavior. Rather than looking at what isn't working, what isn't right, or what could be better, look at things from another angle: What is working and what is right? And don't forget this one: What could be worse? You may ask, "Why me?" when something bad happens; but do you ask, "Why me?" when good things happen, too? Understand that everything is temporary, and that there really is a bright side if you look hard enough. And to do that, you must...

Inquire

What is the cause of your adversity? Is it permanent? What can you change or control to make it better? Will it compromise other areas of your life? Don't spend valuable time and energy digging trenches, and then crawling in to defend them. Once you truthfully look at the adverse situation, and ask what you can do about it, you're already twice as resilient as you were when you reacted only with surrender, anger, terror, or tears. Speaking of which...

Vent

Go ahead. Scream, cry, eat chocolate. In fact, do whatever makes you feel better at the moment, but make sure it isn't a longer-than-necessary moment. Adversity is real, and although it's tough, it's usually not the end of the world. No, you don't have to fool yourself. You don't have to tell yourself that you enjoy surrendering a former capability, interest, or occupation. You can even *hate* the loss or curtailment. But you can't pretend. Instead, you can vent sensibly, and then reinvent what you can and will do from this point forward. Acknowledge the difficulty, and then use your childlike resilience to find ways to...

Enjoy

You can enjoy the challenge of living with restrictions, repairs, and renewal. You can find meaning and purpose in the struggle: That's how spiritual transformation and growth take place. Be willing to grow through the adversity, not just go through it. When confronted with unavoidable adversity, make your anti-whining campaign a fascinating project. Take pride in refusing to kvetch and complain when conditions force you to settle for less than you want. Whatever the passing years may take away, there's something new waiting for you. Find new involvements. Instead of jogging, you can speed walk. Instead of playing active sports, you can learn to paint, or play a musical instrument. Give alternative hobbies and interests some real thought. Find a vital, absorbing interest—something big, ongoing, and personally important to you. Champion a cause worth fighting for or against. Begin a project that you'll never completely finish. Do anything that you find engrossing and enjoyable.

circumstances—new habits of mind and heart—that will produce a climate to nurture and re-engage your neotenous traits.

Resilience research shows a direct relationship between hardiness and a person's *explanatory style*. In other words, the first step a resilient person takes when confronted with adversity is to explain the tough circumstance in a positive *and* realistic way. By altering your outlook and response to hardships, you can alter your reaction to adversity.

. . . .

"Eighty years old! No eyes left, no ears, no teeth, no legs,
no wind. And when all is said and done, how
astonishingly well one does without them."
PAUL CAUDEL, POET AND PLAYWRIGHT

. . . .

Growing older inevitably means having to modify some of your lifelong habits. Some physical things aren't going to work as well; you may need to learn to walk again, this time with a cane. **You might need bigger, bolder print to read.** Learning to accept any large or small loss, any unfortunate situation, and all the things you cannot change is an accomplishment that can benefit anyone. You can consciously choose not to be disturbed by these limitations. In other words, you can choose to be neotenous and rebuild your resilience. Plenty of things in my life have aimed at breaking my spirit, and I know the same is true for you. It's all part of the human experience. When something, anything, happens to compromise your resilience, your Do-Over challenge is to automatically think this: "I have lived this long, and I can LIVE through this." The chart on pages 94–95 explains how.

When you LIVE through adversity, you have a chance to "do over" the negative responses and unproductive reactions that have crept in during the years. You can gain fresh perspective on the moving power of your life. Opportunities to find a deeper power within us often come when life seems most challenging. Now that you know you're only young twice, you can create a robust resilience and a renewed optimism.

Optimism

· ·

"Believe that life is worth living, and your belief will help create the fact."

WILLIAM JAMES, NINETEENTH CENTURY PHILOSOPHER

· ·

"Are you *still* running?" "*Still* writing, I see." "Are you *still* teaching?" "*Still* enjoying life?" The Still Syndrome is yet another negative stereotype of aging, one that requires us to rejuvenate our optimism. Once we do so, we can honestly and emphatically reply, "Yes, I am *still* happy," "Yes, I *still* have love," and "Yes, I'm *still* very much alive." Research cited throughout this book and elsewhere shows repeatedly that, despite our aging, we can still look forward to lots of improvements.

Ashley Montagu believed that optimism as a neotenous trait serves a real biological and social function. "Most children carry with them the feeling that whatever the state of things now, they can only improve with time," he said. "The child lives in a world of rising expectations and because he does so he puts the self-fulfilling prophecy to constant use." And in his book *Optimism*, author Lionel Tiger contends that optimism is not an optional trait; it's as natural to humans as our eyes or ears, and as irreplaceable as the air we breathe. Unfortunately, as we get older and the world makes us weary and wary, we tend to think of optimism as an attitude that one puts on like a new layer of makeup or a pair of rose-colored glasses. We associate optimism with disconnection from reality—in fact, haven't we all heard the terms "blind optimism" and "pie-eyed optimist"?

Yet we know that optimistic people are happier, so we assume that optimism must involve simply saying happy things and wearing a happy face, no matter how you *really* feel. Many people think that optimism means seeing—or at least talking about—only the upside, and walking a wide circle around any potential downside. Optimism is walking through only the good neighborhoods on the sunniest days.

You can probably guess that I'm a raging optimist. And I have paid a price for it. For people who prefer stereotypes, because I am blonde, my being optimistic goes right along with my being dumb. But let me point this out: Anyone can see what's wrong in the world. Anyone can complain about its inequities, and live in fear of losing love or life. Being a critic is the easy way out. But to see what's wrong and ache because of the inequities, to face fear while still firmly believing you can change things and make life a little better—that takes strength, resilience, intelligence, and optimism. Living is, or should be, an optimistic endeavor.

In fact, having relationships on any level is an act of optimism. To change, to learn, to wish, and to dream all demand hopefulness. To be young twice will be a Herculean test of your optimism, but as I've suggested, what's the alternative? Living in pessimism; waiting for the sky to fall and the rent to rise; expecting people to disappoint you; and knowing "It will never work." Does that sound like a fun way to spend your time? You'll be on everyone's "avoid like the plague" list. I'd rather take the slings and arrows of being a happy blonde!

Landmark research in recent decades, including the seminal work by Martin Seligman, author of *Learned Optimism*, reveals that optimism has much greater depth, importance, and power than traditionally believed. Optimism isn't a superficial paint job, or just a stroll through the daisies. We now know that optimism fuels health, vitality, spontaneity, hope, and, yes, longevity. Optimists tend to live longer. More important, they tend to live *better*, and even as their bodies slow, their happiness can grow. Here's the best news: Seligman discloses that while genetics plays a minor role, optimism is developed and can be learned.

OPTIMISM AND HEALTH

Among the most powerful findings of research on optimism are these two revelations:

1. Compared to their pessimistic counterparts, optimists actually experience fewer incidences of most forms of catastrophic illness, and they recover faster from most surgeries.

2. Keeping a positive attitude about aging can extend life by up to a decade, which is longer than gains made by not smoking and by exercising regularly.

As mentioned throughout this book, often it is the perceptions of aging and the feeling of control with which we face aging that most affect both the quality and the length of our lives.

LEARNING TO FLY

The late Israeli prime minister Golda Meier said, "Old age is like flying through a storm. Once you are aboard, there is nothing you can do." Recall the times when you've sat on the tarmac at an airport when your plane is already late. Your natural response might have been to feel stressed about the situation. But there's another choice. You can choose not to get upset. You can spend your time thinking about how you'll deal with this new circumstance. Optimism engages the positive life-force propeller. The more optimistic you are, the more life force you enjoy. The more life force you enjoy, the more optimistic you feel, and so on. Once in motion, the propeller gains considerable momentum, giving us considerable immunity against many of life's diseases and much of life's dis-ease. We can soar through the storms and glide into the sunset.

Optimism is the capacity to see the good in the bad, the lesson in the hardship, the higher good, and even the most buried hope. It's the ability to unearth possibilities, opportunities, lessons, and advantages. Optimism is what keeps some prisoners of war alive while others perish. It's the jet fuel of goodness. Sometimes, optimism is the one thing you can muster in order to put one foot in front of the other. It's the one thing that helps you face another unpredictable day.

There's No Such Thing as a Bad Landing

One way of telling how optimistic you are is to figure out how big, bad, and long-lasting you expect specific events to be. The more pessimistic you are, the more natural it is for you to predict that any given situation will be big, bad, and likely to get worse. Pessimists view bad things as lasting and good things as fleeting. They predict that the good fortune they are enjoying will quickly pass, but misfortune can last a lifetime. If they predict a dire result and are wrong, then they become even more convinced that the next situation will prove them right. One of the satisfactions that pessimists reportedly enjoy is the ability to predict some sort of negative consequence and then say, "See, I told you so."

Optimists tend to predict that the same events will be smaller, shorter-lived, and far less serious. For them, catastrophes are rare but challenges may be plentiful. Any misfortune they face is temporary, to be replaced by better times if they work hard enough. Life can and will improve. They truly believe that most people are inherently good. And despite its harsh side, they believe that life is inherently good.

Pessimists notice only rough weather, turbulence, skid marks, and sudden stops. Optimists are pleased by any landing, and find multiple ways to kiss the ground.

Soar with Your Strengths

How can you enjoy the health- and life-enhancing benefits of optimism without being viewed as the village idiot? You must employ *realistic* optimism. Life is hard, but it can be good. Most people mean well most of the time. Even good people do bad things, but that doesn't make them bad people. Even if your best friend is the pilot of the plane, wear a seat belt. Prepare for the worst, but strive for, and believe in, the best.

A neotenous and optimistic person would never claim that aging is without challenges. However, this kind of person would look at added years through a positive and realistic lens, believing that...

- Inspired living causes brain cells to grow more branches throughout the lifespan.

- Our ability to cope increases with age, while our stress level decreases with age.

- We take more responsibility for our health as we age.

- We understand ourselves with an improved perspective.

- We are more confident, caring less what other people think.

- We are sexually more relaxed.

- Our capacity to love increases with age.

- Our gratitude deepens.

- Our capacity for curiosity and altruism increases.

As a life philosophy, *You're Only Young Twice* concentrates your efforts and energy on a realistic but optimistic approach to aging. This simple rule of thumb applies: The more serious the potential consequences of adverse situations, the more vigorously you must protect yourself. Protect yourself from the downside, but at the same time, continue to focus on and believe in the upside. If retiring penniless would be a nightmare, then put in place every possible safeguard to ensure that doesn't happen. Make sure your safety nets have safety nets. Ask yourself, "What would a champion pessimist do?" Once you've protected the downside, you can build on and believe in the upside. That leads to a happy, youthful, strong life.

TIME FOR A FLIGHT PLAN

Some of us are born optimists, but most of us have to work at it. Recent breakthroughs in psychology, neurology, and chemistry—also supported by Eastern practices like meditation—reveal that optimism can be learned. The brain can change, and it can change throughout a lifetime. But if you really want to be happier than your grandparents may have provided for in your genes, you'll need to learn what you can do, day by day, to let your life take off and fly. And it may not involve what you expect.

A 1978 study examined two groups of diverse people: lottery winners and patients with spinal cord injuries. Results showed that neither event—lottery or injury—changed people's lives as much as observers expected. In fact, another study revealed that major events, happy or unhappy, lose their impact on optimism levels in fewer than three months. What does this teach us? We're better off if we aim for happiness from moment to moment, instead of trying to engineer our happiness through long-term planning. While you can't make winning the lottery happen, you can adjust your attitude and look at the wealth of experiences, friends, family, or good health that you do have—all of which makes your ultimate destination a trip worth taking.

Do-Over:
Count Your Frequent Flier Smiles

Nothing is more pitiful than aging pessimists. They complain and grumble about getting older, and live in fear of loss and insignificance, but they never do anything about it. These are the people who give aging a bad rap, and truth be known, they probably gave childhood, marriage, and apple pie a bad rap, too. Think of all of that wasted time. We're already on a tight schedule, so now is the time to chart our final course to an optimistic destination.

This Do-Over asks you to think about moments in your current life when your plans, ideas, or dreams were cancelled. But when one opportunity is grounded, a new plan almost always takes off. Consider these cancellations and write about them in your Young Twice Chronicle.

- Think of a specific change in plans you recently faced. Because of this change, what else happened or took flight?

- What's the most important thing in your life that was cancelled or changed? What took flight because of that change?

- Name something that was cancelled because of bad luck or a missed opportunity. What opportunity took flight instead?

- Name a cancellation due to loss, rejection, or death. What took flight instead?

- In all of these cases, did you *immediately* see the opportunity that could take flight instead?

- Does it take you a while to get over changes and cancellations?

- How do cancellations, losses, and rejections affect your ability to take flight?

- When a cancellation occurs, what can you do to get yourself into take-off mode more readily?

The next time you're faced with a change in plans, a cancelled opportunity, or a re-routing of goals, look for things that could take off as a result of unexpected changes. If you want to travel far and fast, then travel light. Lose your envies, jealousies, selfishness, and fears. This is baggage you don't need in the coming years. Search for the positive moment, and let your life, dreams, and hopes take wings. Optimism needs to be planned and practiced. It weighs less than a guilt trip, doesn't come with excess baggage, and is a first-class way to go. Once you make optimism part of your everyday travel through life, you'll wonder how you ever got along without it.

Wonder

· ·

"The world will never starve for want of wonders,
but for want of wonder."

G. K. Chesterton, author

· ·

Wonder is an encounter with the mysteries of life. It is amazed admiration, or awe, especially at something beautiful or new. If you allow yourself to youthen, you can't help but adjust your outlook to see every day as beautiful and new. Fortunately, we never lose the *quality* of wonder, but in our world, we do lose the extent to which we wonder.

One morning I decided to take a break from writing and walk by the local creek. I gave myself forty-five minutes to see how far and fast I could go before getting back to work. Headphones? Check. Baseball hat? Check. Sunblock, check…and I'm off. As I was heading into the home stretch, picking it up a little to stay on pace, I glanced down and saw a furry, fuzzy, black caterpillar. To be honest, I only noticed this creature because I was thinking about writing this section on renewing wonder. You've heard the old adage, "You teach what you most need to learn." So instead of racing by, I stopped. I got down on my hands and knees and looked at this marvel, this movement, this miracle. And then it hit me like a ton of bricks: a memory I hadn't thought of in many decades.

I used to spend summers in Portland, Oregon, with my grandparents Meme and Daddy Bob. Each summer I was there, we collected caterpillars from the lawn and created habitats for them. Meme would give me a coffee can, and I'd create a caterpillar castle. I'd paint the can, add a tall twig for climbing, and put in fresh leaves, lettuce, and bottle caps full of water. My caterpillars were living large. I didn't know the term *metamorphosis*, and I couldn't explain why or how the change happened; but I watched in wonder as the little fur ball would spin and weave and sleep…to become a butterfly. Once the butterfly appeared, it would flit and fly around that castle. As its "mother," I really thought that for a few minutes, the tiny insect was waving good-bye and thanking me for its wonderful home.

Wonder is the natural astonishment that, as a child, you felt about the world around you. As adults, we often allow our spontaneous response of wonder to be stifled. We have deadlines, we have to keep pace, and we now understand metamorphosis. Neoteny anthropologist Ashley Montagu said that wonder is "the beginning of all knowledge and philosophy. It is a kind of exaltation of interest to which a certain excitement attaches, and which is accompanied by an expectation of 'more to come,' 'more to do,' the power of perceptual participation in the known and unknown."

At one time, most of us have lain in the grass, staring up at a starry night and wondering how far the universe goes. *Wonder* can be a verb: "I wonder how far it goes?" It's also an emotional experience: "Wow! It goes on forever!" Wonder is a neotenous characteristic that both reveals the depths of our minds and deepens the meaning of anything that occurs.

Like many of us, my wonder has wandered. I had to make myself notice that caterpillar during my walk, but in my yesterdays, I sought the caterpillars. I am mired in the mundane and have ceased to marvel. Too many of us have decided that we already know everything, or we believe that everything has been discovered and answered. We've lost the joy of wondering just for the sake of wondering. In adding years, we have subtracted surprise.

· ·

> *"To be astonished is one of the surest ways*
> *of not growing old too quickly."*
> COLLETTE, WRITER, DANCER, AND MIME

· ·

To wonder is to allow your mind to roam with no particular place to go. By seeking wonder, we see the world anew and increase the chance of evolving our outlook.

REBUILD AN INFINITY OF INTEREST

The original gift of wonder is the awe and astonishment that comes from seeing something for the first time. As we age, we can become afflicted with the "been there, done that" syndrome.

Life should be filled with mystery, not mastery. The world offers you infinite possibilities: things to explore, dream, and do. You must intentionally keep your sense of wonder about life. On a trip to San Francisco, we took our children to a spectacular place called the Exploratorium. It was filled with gadgets, noises, inventions, and invitations to explore the new and unfamiliar. Everything in the Exploratorium was designed to instill wonder. Well, so is everything in your backyard, library, newspaper, body, and just about everywhere else. Create wonder as an intention; find the new and unusual in the familiar; dare to inspect and invent. Be bold in accepting new ideas and adventures. Search for the extraordinary. The world is the most remarkable exploratorium of all, or haven't you noticed lately?

THE SEVEN WONDERS OF THE WORLD

In their inspirational book *Chicken Soup for the Soul*, writers Jack Canfield and Mark Victor Hansen tell the story of a group of junior high school students who were asked to list what they thought were the present Seven Wonders of the World. Before I tell you what the students said, pause and wonder: What do you think they are?

Despite some disagreement, the following wonders received the most votes:

1. Egypt's Great Pyramids

2. Taj Mahal

3. Grand Canyon

4. Panama Canal

5. Empire State Building

6. St. Peter's Basilica

7. China's Great Wall

The students were happy with their answers—except for one student who didn't turn in a paper. When the teacher asked if she was having trouble with her list, the girl replied, "Yes, a little. I couldn't quite make up my mind because there were so many." The teacher said, "Well, tell us what you have and maybe we can help."

The girl hesitated and then read, "I think the Seven Wonders of the World are to see, to hear, to touch, to taste, to feel, to laugh, and to love."

The room was so quiet you could have heard a pin drop. Clearly, this young girl knew that the things we overlook as simple and ordinary, the things we often take for granted, are truly the greatest wonders.

"I still look at the world," wrote Walt Disney, "with uncontaminated wonder." Think of wonder as nurturing your inner four-year-old child. If you can retain the distinctive qualities of openness, fearlessness, and wonder, you'll have little time to mourn what age may take away. The quality of utter engagement with the world is as attractive in an eighty-year-old as in a preschooler.

Do-Over: Wander with Wonder

Wonder doesn't show up as a skill on any test, or as a competency to be measured. In fact, to measure wonder would be to destroy it. The feeling of wonder implies innocence, openness, freshness, sublime pleasure, and admiration. Wonder often comes with adventurousness, eagerness to explore the unknown, love of living, and deep appreciation for creation. What did you do as a child that made you forget all about time passing? Therein lies the wonder-full mystery to guide you in living a young-twice life.

When I was ten or eleven years old, a trip to the beach would find me marveling at things like the rainbow colors inside a clamshell, the shapes and sizes of clouds, and the curve of a wave. Now that I live near the beach, I find myself wondering instead where all the tourists are coming from. I certainly need to recharge my sense of awe and admiration. Take a moment to remember what once amazed you, and make a list of those childhood wonders in your Young Twice Chronicle.

I was more exhilarated finding that caterpillar on my recent walk than I am on a normal day when I don't look around. It rekindled fond memories, began a chain of wonder and musing—and it was fun. Keep writing in your chronicle, this time about the present: What do you wonder about today? What catches your attention? What is yet to be explored?

Now check your past and present lists of wonders. Are there any similarities between the two lists? Can you see how and why some of your wonder power was diminished or squandered? What's one action you can take to help you push the reset button on your sense of wonder?

People who wonder do not burn out. As writer Maurice Goudeket tells us, "It is really something of a feat to have lived seventy-five years, in spite of illness, germs, accidents, disasters, and wars. And now every fresh day finds me more filled with wonder and better qualified to draw the last drop of delight from it."

Your Do-Over is to begin wandering through wonder, keeping a keen eye open to the strange and different. As you go through your day, keep an ongoing list in your Young Twice Chronicle. Note the things that catch your eye, make you pause, or leave you speechless. Search for the outstandingly good; stare with awe at the beautiful trees on your street; admire the flowers in your garden. Really *look* at the faces of people you love. Take a walk through the maternity ward at your local hospital, and stand mute in that moment that fractures everyone: a human birth.

In other words, replace the 3-D glasses I gave you earlier with a microscope or telescope, and look closely at the world around and above you. Make yourself notice. Pay attention. Taste something strange, listen to different music, explore new territory. Fully use your seven wonders. Then, like Alice in Wonderland, the world around you—and most of all, *you*—will become not just younger, but "curiouser and curiouser."

Curiosity

- -

"Do not grow old, no matter how long you live. Never cease to stand like curious children before the Great Mystery into which we were born."
ALBERT EINSTEIN, SCIENTIST AND NOBEL PRIZE WINNER

- -

Curiosity follows wonder. First you find something worthy of wonder, and then you become curious. Curiosity is eagerness to gain information about something. It may have killed the cat, but it's a breath of fresh air to a tired mind or an old soul. Curiosity works on a continuum: First, we experience wonder and awe; then comes an insatiable inquisitiveness, or curiosity about the subject of the wonder. This leads to questioning and discovery, which heads us back to wonder. The pattern continues. Although wonder and curiosity often work in tandem, the two are separate neotenous traits. In fact, both are developed and used very differently in the pursuit of growing young.

Curiosity is lust of the mind, and it can keep us young. New interests give us new life, offer an infusion of vital spirits, and safeguard us against boredom. Ashley Montagu warned, "If there ever was a neotenous trait more, almost more than any other, that must be kept alive and constantly exercised, it is curiosity." In children, curiosity leads to intellectual and emotional development. This remains true for adults, but it plays an additional role in longevity.

In fact, a recent study conducted at the Stanford Research

Institute concluded that curiosity in older adults is directly correlated to overall health. In a five-year study, older adults who scored high on the trait of curiosity lived 30% longer than low-scoring adults. The study also found that higher levels of curiosity represented an improved ability to respond to challenges. Curious older adults had "active coping" mechanisms; they sought new experiences, new friends, and new ways to solve problems. According to lead researcher Dr. Gary Swain, "Shrinking curiosity may be one of the earliest signs of an abnormal aging of the central nervous system, an added health risk, and a possible contributor to a shortened lifespan."

If we have filled up the beaker of life and ignited everything that needs to be consumed; if we have asked all the questions and lived all the answers; then we won't fear old age. But if too much life remains unlived, we approach the threshold of old age with unsatisfied demands that turn our glances backward. Curiosity encourages us to look to the future instead of the past. Exercising a lively curiosity not only keeps our brains working, it lends spice to the wonder we feel when encountering the new and strange. And as we get older, spice can be in short supply.

I have a friend named Chet who has an apartment in an assisted-living home. I met him during my visits there with students from the college public speaking class I teach. On one of our visits, my students did a presentation on past and present sex symbols. They gave hints like "She was in *Gentlemen Prefer Blondes* and *Some Like It Hot*, and married a famous baseball player." The audience of residents yelled out "Marilyn Monroe!" My students weren't surprised that the residents got that one right.

But next the students said, "She was on the new *Mickey Mouse Club*, she does Pepsi commercials, and she…" Chet's was the lone and loud voice: "Britney Spears!" I don't know who was more flabbergasted, the other residents or my students. Everyone looked at Chet and asked, "How did you know that?" He calmly replied, "I saw her on Jay Leno last night with the band Foo Fighters. I was curious about her so I Googled her information on the Web."

Why should it be so incongruous, both to his contemporaries and to those younger, to hear an eighty-year-old man even *say* Foo Fighters? And he surfs the Web? Upon further discussion, we discovered that Chet reads the Sunday *New York Times* from cover to cover, corresponds with people all around the world, and was currently learning to use a digital camera.

My students were impressed, I was impressed, and so were a few of the residents. But some residents felt threatened. Chet had something they had given away. Not the right answer, but the right use of the neotenous trait of curiosity. Chet wanted to know what was going on in the world. He had questions about politics, technology, movies, and music. To this day, many of my students continue to visit Chet because they want to learn from—and with—him. Chet has used his curiosity to create a new community. He's someone who understands what actress Ethel Barrymore meant when she said, "You must learn day by day, year by year, to broaden your horizon. The more things you love, the more you are curious about, the more you enjoy, the more you are indignant about, the more you have left when anything happens."

REMAIN INTELLECTUALLY FIT

Neurosurgeon Emmett Fox uses the term *apoptosis* to describe the unnecessary loss of flexibility, reaction, and ability that occurs when any portion of a human brain is not used. When you give up daydreaming, for example, your brain begins to behave like a brain that *cannot* daydream. Apoptosis, the worst kind of self-fulfilling prophecy, is the malady that strikes us as we age and give away our neotenous traits. We spend so much time not thinking young that, *presto*, we can't think young.

But there's a way to reclaim your youth. Shake off predictability, familiarity, and routine. Being intellectually curious makes you interesting to be around, and virtually guarantees you an enjoyable life. As literary giant Samuel Johnson said, "Curiosity is one of the permanent and certain characteristics of a vigorous mind." And it's a sure-fire antidote to apoptosis.

Focus on the most mundane, the flattest circumstance, and then make yourself scratch a sense of newness and potential out of that circumstance. Make a trip to the library a weekly scavenger hunt for things you've always planned to read someday. Look for lectures, meetings, and movies that will stretch your mind. Take up Scrabble, do the daily crossword puzzle, do the build-your-vocabulary exercise in Reader's Digest. As your self-appointed mental fitness trainer, I am emphatically telling you to use it…or lose it.

Jump Out of Your Own Skin

I believe that there are two types of curiosity. Both are about getting out of your own way, immersing yourself in something outside yourself, and growing more interesting, vital, and vibrant.

Extradermal Curiosity

This is curiosity about things in the world and how they work. It means wondering about the science and technology of life. People with extradermal curiosity take clocks apart, love looking under the hood, ask for the recipe, and actually read the owner's manual.

Interdermal Curiosity

This is curiosity about people, including yourself. What makes people tick? Who are they? Why do they like or dislike something? People with interdermal curiosity read *People* magazine, love to watch the Oscars to see the clothes, check out biographies, and wonder why we have to read the owner's manual.

Here's the important thing: No matter what piques your curiosity, pique your curiosity!

Whether you're mainly extradermal or mainly interdermal, be interested in big things. You'll be the oldest, saddest, loneliest person if you're interested only in yourself. Concentrating only on your own comfort, your own pain, and your own days will be your loss. You'll create a small world and a self-fulfilling prophecy of isolation and fear—because your curiosity was crushed, and your interests were stingy and only skin deep.

Being curious could lead you to join a club, listen to other points of view, or visit new places. Find out where old classmates are, and write letters to them. Make daily discoveries by writing in your Young Twice Chronicle, or start that short story you've had in your head for years. Discover the species of birds at your backyard feeder. Unearth some new preference or idea each day, and then give something of yourself away every day. By engaging yourself in this way, you'll get out of your own skin and back into the young experience of extradermal and interdermal curiosity.

DON'T FORGET YOUR SECOND WIND

Most people give up when initial fatigue sets in. Writer Harriet Beecher Stowe told us, "When you get into a tight place and everything goes against you until it seems that you cannot hold on for a minute longer, never give up then, for that is just the place and time when the tide will turn." The phenomenon of second wind reassures us that if we persevere, we'll get a little boost just when we need it to cross the finish line or turn that tide. Curiosity is the boost, the kick in the pants—or the head—that we need. Life can make us tired, and getting older has its losses and gains. But in searching for new interests, seeking unknown vistas, and discovering unlikely answers, a curious thing happens: We become more alive.

It's important for you to advance through the desire to retreat, and learn to ask instead of tell. Move forward, fueled by the quest for the depth, meaning, and knowledge that are yours for the taking in the second half of your life. "Never, never, never surrender," said Winston Churchill. Curiosity will get you to the end of your race with the energy, grace, and life force that was yours at the beginning.

═══ **Do-Over:** Create Curiosity ═══

We now know that curiosity seems to be innate in children, and also remains alive in a small circle of older adults, including scientists, writers, and artists. The rest of us must make an effort to keep this very important neotenous trait alive and kicking.

In his book *Conceptual Blocking*, Stanford University professor James Adams writes, "Everyone has a questioning attitude as a young child because of the need to assimilate an incredible amount of information in a few years. The knowledge that you acquire between birth and the age of six, for instance, enormously exceeds what has been consciously taught. A great amount is obtained through observation and questioning. Unfortunately, as we grow older, many of us lose our questioning attitude."

Can we regain that questioning attitude and re-create our curiosity? Adams is convinced that we can. "You merely need to start questioning," he writes. "An emotional block is often involved here, since you seem to be laying your ignorance out in the open. However, it is a block that will rapidly disappear once you discover the low degree of omniscience present in the human race. No one has all the answers and the questioner, instead of appearing stupid, will often show his insight."

The key to creating curiosity about something we don't understand can be found in an anomaly—a deviation or departure from the common order or rule. For instance, we've all seen those children's puzzles that ask for the number of things wrong with a picture. With great glee, a child will start counting upside-down cows, pigs in dresses, and so on. That's a simple example of spotting anomalies. In his book *The Right Attitude: Learning to Ask and Answer Questions*, author Robert Shank says, "We can decide to see nearly everything as anomalous." If you are able to find anomalies in everything instead of just seeing daily routine, you'll experience life in a richer and more rewarding way, while building a stronger and more fluid curiosity.

Spotting Anomalies

1. Assume that everything is anomalous until proven otherwise. Ask questions.
    - "What makes spicy Mexican food different from spicy Thai food?"
    - "Why would someone open a restaurant on that corner?"
    - "How is that TV commercial trying to get me to buy this product?"

2. Propose alternatives to everything.
    - "What if I used Asian hot peppers in a Mexican salsa?"
    - "Where would I open a restaurant in this area?"
    - "What information in a commercial would get me to buy a particular product?"

3. Reject standard explanations. The goal isn't simply to criticize everything (that's the domain of the old), but to come up with new alternatives. Something "everybody knows" is a great target for your own developing curiosity.

4. Pretend you're talking to a foreigner or a person from another planet. How would you explain traffic jams, for instance, or soap operas?

Shank presents four tools to help us spot anomalies. First, select any three things that happened to you during the course of your day. They can be perfectly normal events that you might not think to mention. Using the tools in the chart above, describe each of these events as if they were anomalies.

New research continues to prove that your brain is wired to be used. Rather than lose brain cells, as was previously thought, you can build and add new cells, new dendrites, and new connections by taking on a new challenge. This Do-Over will create curiosity by taking your mind to interesting places. If you don't give your mind a little freedom every now and then, it may stop wanting to go anywhere.

The practice of neoteny insists that you re-engage your curiosity at any time, any place. Make it a daily practice to hunt for anomalies and ask questions. Curiosity repays you with a longer life, a facile brain, and a youth-full quest.

CAN WE TALK?

In the play *Camelot*, King Arthur discovers that "Merlin doesn't age, he youthens—he remembers tomorrow so he can help you today."

You've learned that becoming young twice is really the difference between growing older and being old. If you continue to Act, Grow, and Evolve, you can youthen just like Merlin. How did you score on the OLD Survey? By now you've discovered that by adjusting your Outlook, you can obliterate many of the stereotypes of aging. I hope that by now, resilience, optimism, wonder, and curiosity are really beginning to youthen your outlook on age.

Next may I have a word with you about your Language?

Chapter Five

The Language of Your Life

What you are about to read is true. Only the names have been omitted to protect the not-so-innocent. One of our dearest friends was dating a much younger (chronologically speaking) woman, and we were about to meet her for the first time. On the drive to the restaurant, my husband said, and I am quoting here, "I think tonight we should talk young."

My immediate response doesn't need to be included, as it was not very literary, poetic, or intelligent. But after calming down, I asked, "What, exactly, do you mean, 'talk young'?" His reply: "Anything that most of our friends talk about all the time should be out. Mortgages, IRAs, the most recent medicines, plastic surgery, food allergies—you know, all the older people topics. We should concentrate on things that will make her feel more comfortable being around us." I confess to this sarcastic reply: "Like what kind of candy she likes, or what kind of wine goes with peanut butter sandwiches?"

I don't think I managed to "talk young" on our dinner date that evening. I was too stunned and resentful. After all, I am the neoteny guru! I don't talk old. But I thought about that conversation for weeks afterward, and I realized that my husband did have a point, poor timing aside.

The current language of aging is like a virus that invades our lives. It's contagious, spreading throughout an entire population and preying on us at our most vulnerable moments. Instead of discussing "young topics," we substitute the excuses and explanations of "old topics," which undermines and demeans our development. We have become familiar with the downside of aging, and seemingly immune to the upside. How often do you hear people talk about possibility, spontaneity, new dreams, or fresh undertakings? The answer: not nearly as much as they talk about undertakers, I'm afraid.

The implicit understanding we have permitted is that we never talk out loud about tomorrow's possibilities. The explicit expectation is that as we age, we can talk about what hurts, what's wrong with the young, our limitations—and we can complain about almost everything. It's always too hot, too cold, too noisy, too spicy, too much. We communicate these negative notions not just to others, but more destructively, we communicate these negatives to ourselves.

Listen to yourself for a day. Do you say, "Oh gosh, I feel really old today," or "Well, what can you expect after forty?" or "I'm just too old for that"? These and many other beliefs and expressions create a language of age that diminishes the power of your internal immune system and accelerates aging. What's in your mind is constantly sending influences throughout your body. Through the limbus area at the base of your brain, impulses are carried down to every muscle, organ, and gland. Your life force is determined by the exercise you get, by what you eat and drink, by the air you breathe, and by your state of mind.

The language of our lives can have a positive or negative effect on all other factors of our well-being. How we use vocabulary, how we choose words, can either enhance or weaken the effect of any experience.

Language can be transformational. By changing the words we use to define a situation, we can change its effect on our lives. If you want to prove it to yourself, try this: The next time someone asks you how you are, instead of saying "Fine," try saying "Young!"

with enthusiasm and feeling. You know the old saying "Fake it 'til you make it." You'll be surprised how good a joyous, humorous, loving reply will make you (and the other person) feel.

The words we live by contribute to bad feelings about our age. I recently had dinner with an over-fifty friend who was upset by a book her sister had sent her. "It's some awful thing about being a crone," she said with disgust. "I mean *crone*. Yecch, who would ever want to be called that?" I agree: It's a nasty little word for a truly beautiful and important part of a woman's life. While we're at it, how wonderful is the term *geezer?*

This chapter is about using of the power of talking to others with joy and humor. It's about moving toward positive thinking, which results in positive actions like laughter and learning. Learning a new language of life means re-creating the aging self as an active being. You'll be engaging your available strengths, putting meaning into things rather than taking the meaning out, and staying positively connected with others. In the previous chapter, you planted the seeds of a resilient, optimistic, wondering, and curious self. Now you'll find that the way you speak can help those seeds take root. The neotenous traits in this chapter will grow a "verb garden" from which you can select and savor the fresh choices that belong to the young at heart.

MEME AND MEMES

. . . .

"Don't complain about old age. How much good it has brought
me that was unexpected and beautiful. I concluded then that
the end of life will be just as unexpectedly beautiful."

LEO TOLSTOY, AUTHOR

. . . .

Meme was my grandmother. She was elegant, tall, funny, and kind. She taught me about growing up and, as it turns out, growing old.

I never heard her complain. When I went swimming, she went swimming. If I tried ice skating, she tried ice skating. We picked peaches, colored pictures, rode in wagons, and pretended we were princesses. Meme always took care of herself. She never went anywhere without lipstick on, and she smiled at everyone. I didn't even realize she was old, and I don't think she did, either. Meme laughed easily. She encouraged me to put on talent shows in the basement or organize neighborhood parades. She put sugar on my cottage cheese, and had me listen to my Cheerios whisper, "Eat me, eat me." She made me a chocolate milkshake every night. Meme taught me about art, music, and manners. She was my favorite playmate.

Memes, on the other hand, are defined as units of behavior, values, and language that evolve and are passed on through imitation and learning. When you learn the words to Lincoln's Gettysburg Address, or the way to tie your shoelaces, or how to face your changing face, you're part of the process of selection that transmits memes over time. One could even argue that language is the ultimate meme. Proponents of the meme theory, known as memeticists, regard humans as creatures of our memes. You've heard these expressions: "The concept took on a life of its own" and "Never underestimate the power of an idea whose time has come." To memeticists, these aren't just axioms, but reflections of the true state of affairs. In fact, many memeticists believe that memes play a vital role in our biology and are responsible for our seemingly built-in faculty for language acquisition.

Memeticists say that language offered an advantage to our early ancestors because it could transmit memes: for instance, how to make a stone ax. Memes thus tipped the evolutionary balance in favor of individuals with language skills.

In her everyday behavior, love of life, and energy, my grandmother Meme transferred information, beliefs, and language—or memes—about aging. Television, movies, music, advertising, friends, and family continue to do this, too, but not as positively or productively as my grandmother did.

A person can select information contained in memes to follow a positive evolutionary direction. Neoteny is, ultimately, a meme. It's all about desirable behaviors inherent in our biological make-up that, until now, haven't been available to many of us to select and pass along. Sadly, a person can also select negative information contained in memes, like the movie stereotypes of older people, the "youth is king" attitude in music, or the idea that we must wear certain clothes at certain ages. I believe that these values and beliefs, these negative memes, have been passed on too often and for too long.

Mihaly Csikszentmihalyi, author of *The Evolving Self*, argues, "The evolution of memes is now probably much more critical than genetic evolution in determining our future." If we choose negative, unproductive, or harmful memes about growing older, we harm not only ourselves; we harm the potential development of future generations. By selecting negative memes of aging, we become directly responsible for devolving the human spirit and continuing the degradation of old age.

You can consciously choose positive over negative memes. You can focus on the positive Outlook, Language, and Drives that inform and incite your awareness and actions about aging. Memes require only your mind to feed on, and will replicate images of themselves in your consciousness. Altering the language of your life through the neotenous characteristics of joy, humor, and music can be an important evolutionary contribution to altering the understanding and acceptance of the real beauty inherent in aging.

Who benefits from the current negative memes regarding aging? Snake-oil sellers (sometimes in the guise of healthcare companies and cosmetic retailers) prey on our fear and revulsion. By exploiting our weakness and inattention to truth, they drain our lives in order to enrich their own.

Joy, humor, and music are the anti-viruses to parasitic memes. By integrating them into the language of your life, you will spread positive values and beliefs throughout your system. These anti-viruses will create what communications professor and researcher Dr. Elisabeth Noelle-Neumann calls strong personalities. These people are "curious, try many new things, enjoy influencing others, are less selfish and more concerned with helping others, and are especially well equipped to affect the positive evolution of memes." Like my grandmother Meme, we can all pass on positive and accurate memes about the aging process, and create for future generations a new and improved translation of old age. We have the exciting opportunity to change forever the language of living longer.

Joy

· ·

"What would make you happy? It's a simple question,
but one with profound consequences. Asking and answering
that question, and then acting on it,
is often our path—a path that will lead to the next step, a path
that is in our best interests. We will be choosing our destiny.
And the destiny we're choosing is joy."
MELODY BEATTIE, BEST-SELLING AUTHOR AND JOURNALIST

· ·

A letter from an old friend, or a present for no special reason. An unexpected phone call, or a $20 bill in an old coat pocket. Fireflies in June, a rose you grew, a birthday cake with candles. The human capacity for joy is extraordinary, and often stems from the ordinary. My own official definition of joy is "the passion or emotion excited by the acquisition or expectation of something good; pleasurable feelings or emotions caused by success, good fortune, and the like, or by a rational prospect of possessing what we love or desire; gladness, exhilaration of spirits; delight." Just reading some of the synonyms of joy can help you feel it: pleasure, delight, exultation, rapture, bliss, merriment, festivity, and hilarity.

Joy in all its guises can be the root word for the language of our lives as we age, but we must make an effort to create the circumstances necessary to find it. Renaissance English author Sir Thomas Moore wrote, "We are a society that finds it difficult to discover the exuberant joy and spontaneity of childhood." Unfortunately, things haven't changed too much in the past five hundred years. Once we had the joy of running through puddles or being tickled; now it's our turn to find joy in taking other children through the puddles and laughing as someone else gets tickled. This can be a challenge for most people as they age. Many of us are so bereft about what we have lost, we cannot look at what has replaced it. But the purposeful practice of neoteny guides us to harvest and savor the joy we have accumulated throughout our lives, and helps us make the effort to refresh it.

"I celebrate myself," wrote poet Walt Whitman. Stop and repeat that phrase. The language in Whitman's statement is so provocative. Imagine the joy that would come with celebrating yourself: your achievements, your experiences, and your existence. Imagine what it would be like to look in the mirror each morning and say with honesty, "You. It is you I celebrate."

Joyfully journal in your Young Twice Chronicle while you ponder the following:

- Can you still find joy in the small things? Do you remember to look?

- What makes you happy?

- What about your life *right now* produces spontaneous joy?

- Define your joy(s).

As I write, I see a family portrait above my fireplace and a bouquet of sunflowers on my desk; I am drinking a mug of hot tea. These things bring me joy. It's not the things themselves, but the meaning they hold. They create a joy library: a daily reminder that every day is special, that every moment holds joy. Elaine Dembe, author of *Use the Good Dishes: Finding Joy in Everyday Life*, reminds us, "Joy is in the temporary, in the moments that don't last, the day that is gone before we know it, in the life that is gone before we know it."

Our challenge at this age is to remember to look for joy and to continually replenish its appearance. Allow yourself to make a "joyful noise" when greeting friends, to laugh out loud at finding money in your pockets, to smile and sigh at a rose you grew, and to give a jolly, joyous performance of "Happy Birthday to You" next time you get to sing it. You'll be creating a personal thesaurus for joy in your life. I once had a girlfriend who pleaded joy to get out of serving on the jury of a murder trial. When the lawyers asked who should not be retained as a juror, my friend proudly stood up and said, "My life is about joy, and taking part in these proceedings would certainly diminish my daily joy in living and my pleasure in the small graces of life." She was promptly excused. I'm sure the lawyers thought she was a kook. I think she was brave and sincere. She knew what we are all, I hope, finding out: Life is too short to spend on things that take from you rather than give to you. (And no, I'm not recommending we all try to get excused from jury duty!)

Think of the words you choose to define your life. Do you think that people who talk to you come away from the experience happier? Or might they come away heavier? What kind of influence are you exerting? How often do you have a conversation with a friend about something that brings you joy? A friend of mine refused to leave people with a hackneyed "Have a nice day," saying instead, "Remember, every day above ground is a good one." It was fun to see the varied—mainly amused and delighted—reactions to that statement. Are merriment, hilarity, or festivity in your current vocabulary? Have you lost the ability to squeal or giggle with delight? When you defined your joy, did you first think of things, or feelings?

For a number of years, I was a single mother of two boys. I was teaching five courses as a tenure-track university professor, working on my doctorate, and teaching aerobics classes five days a week.

But my top priority, and most time-intensive commitment, was to my children. While I was exhausted and struggling to hold it all together, I still hoped I was giving them an amazing childhood. All of their friends had high-end bikes, the best sports equipment, vacations to special places—and two parents. Many nights we had "celebrate cereal dinners," trying to make a party from my food budget panic. Our vacations were Saturday trips to the neighboring town for a fast food lunch and maybe roller-skating. Yet the contrast was palpable between my inventive, creative, and thoughtful sons and the wealthier children numbed by video games, remote controlled cars, and catered parties.

One afternoon I went for a run with my younger son, Sean, who was riding his garage sale bike alongside me. We were talking about the fact that it was my responsibility to give him and his brother a good childhood; it was something I cared deeply about and worried about, especially because I knew what the other kids had and did. My little six-year-old son lifted his feet off the pedals of his bike and glided right past me, yelling, "Mother, I am having a wonderful boyhood!" There lived joy. My sons' days were filled with imagination, creativity, friends, and love. Plus, none of the other kids ever got to have cereal night! Joy is found in activities, not possessions. And even the smallest children will tell you that joy is not found in a trouble-free life, but found in *spite of trouble*.

Joy is made up of small things that are big enough to fill a heart. And joy is capable of reaching many other hearts. Sean felt the joy of boyhood, and his reply flamed my joy of motherhood. Words like Sean's, so filled with joy, move us. Indeed, they are the language of our moments and memories.

There is something in joy that does not die. Neotenist Ashley Montagu said, "All joy is young and age sets no boundaries to it." While we may no longer have the sheer joy of childhood bike riding, joy can now be the fulfillment of the delight and pleasure that rides with abandon through our remaining days.

Finding Joy

You can find joy at 1500 Marsh Street in San Luis Obispo, California. Really. Okay, Joy is my friend and a massage therapist. I thought I'd take a shortcut, and send you straight to her to find joy—because she lives up to her name!

Our human urge is to search for joy, pursuing it down long and twisting paths. But joy isn't a cause to be followed. It's a consequence. When you do a thing well, you're happy. Joy is the result, the reward. The more you search for it, the more it eludes you. You don't find joy—it finds you. Where? In a massage, in a mall, in a memory.

Through the ages, joy has found wise and inspired people in just one place: themselves. As Nobel Prize winner George Bernard Shaw wrote, "This is the true joy in life, the being used for a purpose recognized by yourself as a mighty one. The being thoroughly worn out before you are thrown on the scrap heap, the being a force of nature rather than a feverish selfish little clod of ailments and grievances complaining that the world will not devote itself to making you happy." Read that quote again. Now think of the positive role models of aging you listed in your chronicle early on. Did their lives have a purpose? Did they contribute? Think of the negative role models. Were they selfish clods? Bingo.

Maggie Kuhn was forced to retire in 1970 at age sixty-five. As a parting gift, colleagues gave her a sewing machine. She never unpacked it, instead rebelling against everything she believed it stood for. She led marches and staged guerilla theater to protest widespread discrimination against the elderly. She founded the Gray Panthers and radicalized older Americans to fight the image of the old as useless, infirm, and withdrawn. "Old age is an excellent time for outrage," said Kuhn. "I plan to say or do one outrageous thing every week." And she did. The inscription on her headstone reads, "This is the only stone Maggie Kuhn left unturned."

There is joy in outrage: in overcoming, surviving, and thriving. Contented people are rarely idle. They always seem to have something to do. "There is not half so much danger of overwork as underwork," wrote Sir William Robertson Nicholl in *The Day Book of Claudius Clear*. "There are four of my friends who might be fairly described as work drunken...they are generally hopeful, they have little relaxation, but what they have is relished with an intensity of joy. They are people who keep young in the true sense of the word."

Sitting around doing nothing is stressful, and stress doesn't lead to joy. The antidote to anxiety is action. Having something to do, someone to love, and something to seek makes joy the language of your life.

. . . .

"How good is man's life, the mere living! How fit to employ all the heart and the soul and the senses forever in joy."
ROBERT BROWNING, POET

. . . .

Do-Over: JOY (Just Obey Yourself) Jar

Each day brings new adventures, new struggles, and new chances to work at reviving our joy. Think of what childhood joy really is: a delight in looking at something, head cocked, eyes wide; noticing an insect, a rainbow, a puppy. Joy is seeing everything as freshly painted, something to be explored, something full of wonder. It's studying all the surfaces of a rock in the sun, or staring at the ripples from a pebble thrown in a pond. Joy is knowing that you don't know, and then looking for the answer. The answer will be wonderful to know, not something to be feared or dismissed as irrelevant.

It would be presumptuous of me to tell you, "This is the way to manifest your joy." But I am suggesting that you make a concerted effort to name—not numb—your joy.

So choose to not lose it. Dig up some joy every day, in your own way and in your own words, as you did when you were a child. Invite joy into your life by staging celebrations to mark transitions and changes in your life. Life is yours to celebrate. After I became a mother-in-law (which sounds so much "older" than being just a mother), I had a party for friends who were all destined to become mothers-in-law. We watched my son's wedding video, ate cake, and drank champagne. The occasion became more joyful when shared with friends.

Toast your own moments of happiness as you go through your day. You don't need champagne. I've made it a habit to place my hands in a prayer gesture and say *Namaste* when I finish a workout, eat a good meal, or see a beautiful moment—wherever in the world I am. *Namaste* translates as "the God within me honors the God within you." By uttering that word each time I finish running on my local roads, eating chocolate, or seeing a butterfly (and in as big a way as after I climbed mountains in New Zealand), I feel the joy of being healthy, thankful, and alive. If you want joy to furnish you with the words and meaning of your life; if you want to grow young, discover new joy, and live in the language of joy, you'll have to exercise your joy every day.

When my children were growing up, a "job jar" sat on the kitchen counter. I wrote on slips of paper the jobs that needed to be done, and stuck the slips in the jar. Wash dogs. Scrub trash cans. Sweep garage… You get the picture. Each day, my sons picked one job from the jar to complete before their free time. Just for fun, I also wrote on slips of paper, "Eat some ice cream," "Kiss your mother," or "Sing for your supper." They never knew what they would get, but they always knew they were expected to do whatever it was.

Your Joy Do-Over is based on this job jar approach. Get yourself a really cool-looking jar, or a favorite old hat, shoe box, or anything that will hold at least 30 slips of paper. Next, print this quote from writer William James in large letters on your container: "To miss the joy is to miss it all." During the next few days, write out activities, ideas, suggestions, and mandates on separate pieces of paper—list all the things that "speak joy" to you.

. . . .

"Write it in your head that every day is the best day of the year."
RALPH WALDO EMERSON, ESSAYIST AND PHILOSOPHER

. . . .

Here's what the little pieces of paper in my jar say:

- Hug a child, preferably one you know or won't scare.

- Sit for at least fifteen minutes and listen to the birds in the yard.

- Smile at someone you don't know.

- Stargaze at night while drinking hot cocoa (with marshmallows).

- Call your friend Cindy.

- Eat chocolate.

- Dance to at least one song from the 1980s.

You get the idea. Each day, pull out a piece of paper. Each week, renew your jargon on joy. It's okay to put the same things back into the jar, but once you get going, I guarantee that you'll find new ways and new activities to create joy. Once you pull out that piece of paper, JOY, or Just Obey Yourself. Commit yourself to re-activating joy. These simple pleasures, the things you've selected, can bring you closer to finding the joy in your life. Joy wants to see you smile at the everyday graces that flow your way. When you experience joy, the natural result is gratitude. You'll become more and more thankful for every year of growing young. And there will be no wrinkles on your face, only laugh lines.

Humor

. . . .

"I've always been aware of the child in me. Humor, especially the best of it, is very childish. It can be wise, philosophically

valuable, or helpful to the world. But childishness is one
of the marvelous things about being human."
STEVE ALLEN, COMIC AND HUMORIST

· ·

Humor is a special kind of joy. Humor often results from a peculiar and unexpected insight, a cleverness that takes us by surprise. Humor creates laughter, which is immediate, explosive, and brief. Laughter is often a sudden release of tension between the mind and the emotions, which may be artificially set up by telling a joke.

Here's an example from comic George Carlin. "The most unfair thing about life," he says, "is the way it ends. I mean, life is tough. It takes up a lot of your time. What do you get at the end of it all? A death! What's that, a bonus? I think the life cycle is all backwards. You should die first; get it out of the way. Then you live in an old age home. You get kicked out when you are too young, you get a gold watch, and you go to work. You work forty years until you are young enough to reach your retirement. You do drugs, alcohol, you party and you get ready for high school. You go to grade school, you become a kid, you play, have no responsibilities, you become a little baby, you go back into the womb, you spend your last nine months…and you finish off as an orgasm."

WHAT IS HUMOR?

Some of you will laugh at George Carlin, and some of you won't. Some think Jerry Lewis's brand of humor makes him a comic genius (okay, only if you are French), and some prefer Steve Martin. No neotenous trait has a simple definition. Each is unique to a person, place, and circumstance. So it is, too, with humor.

Experts say that several obvious differences among people affect what they find humorous. Research confirms what neoteny teaches: The most significant difference between what's funny to one person and what's funny to another seems to be age.

For instance, infants and children are constantly surprised by the things that go on around them, and they find these things funny. What's funny to a toddler consists of short and simple concepts. The pre-teen and teenage years are, almost universally, awkward and tense. When you are dissatisfied with being older and would like to go back to your teens, just think of algebra and you'll snap out of it! Lots of adolescents and teens laugh at jokes that focus on sex, food, and authority figures. Adolescence is a time when people use humor to protect themselves.

As we mature, both our physical bodies and our mental outlooks grow and change. There's a new language to our humor by the time we have grown up. We have experienced more life, more tragedy, and more success. Along with the language, our sense of humor has also grown and changed; it's now more subtle, more tolerant, and less judgmental.

. . . .

"You don't stop laughing because you grow old,
you grow old because you stop laughing."
MICHELLE PRITCHARD, ACTRESS AND DANCER

. . . .

Laughter is triggered by something we find humorous. There are three traditional theories about what people find humorous:

1. Humor is the experience of *incongruity*. Someone falls down in a situation where a fall is not expected. Or the incongruity may relate to concepts or thoughts, often illustrated by the punch line of a joke or a cartoon caption. When a joke begins, our minds and bodies anticipate what's going to happen and how it's going to end. That anticipation takes the form of logical thought intertwined with emotion, and is influenced by our past experiences and our thought processes. When the joke goes in an unexpected direction, our thoughts and emotions suddenly switch gears. We now have

new emotions, backing up a different line of thought. In other words, we experience two sets of incompatible thoughts and emotions simultaneously. We experience this incongruity between the different parts of the joke as humorous.

2. The *superiority* theory of humor relates to jokes that focus on someone else's mistake, stupidity, or misfortune. We feel superior to this unfortunate person, and experience a certain detachment from the situation. So we are able to laugh about it.

3. Moviemakers have effectively used the *relief* theory of humor for a long time. In action films or thrillers where tension is high, directors use comic relief at just the right moments. A director builds the tension or suspense as much as possible, and then breaks it down slightly with a side comment or funny moment, relieving the audience of pent-up emotions.

Laughter is a way to cleanse our systems of built-up tension and incongruity. According to psychologist Dr. Lisa Rosenberg, "The act of producing humor, of making a joke, gives us a mental break and increases our objectivity in the face of overwhelming stress."

. . . .

"I don't feel old. In fact, I don't feel anything until noon.
Then it's time for my nap."
Bob Hope, comic, on turning 100

. . . .

Steve Sultanoff, PhD, director of the Association for Applied and Therapeutic Humor, sums it up this way: "For me, humor is comprised of three components: wit, mirth, and laughter. Wit is the cognitive experience, mirth the emotional experience, and laughter the physiological experience. We often equate humor with laughter, but you do not need to laugh to experience humor."

The most important definition of humor, however, is *your* definition. What do you find funny? If beauty is in the eye of the beholder, then humor is in the funny bone of the receiver. And we all have a funny bone.

HE (OR SHE) WHO LAUGHS LASTS

Appreciating humor can keep you mentally fit, adding enjoyment and fun to your life. Few activities are as mentally demanding and intellectually stimulating as humor. It's no accident that in one section of the world's most respected IQ test, exam takers are asked to arrange cartoon pictures to tell a story.

Humor and laughter may even help protect you against a heart attack. A recent study by cardiologists at the University of Maryland Medical Center in Baltimore found that people with heart disease were 40% less likely to laugh in a variety of situations than people of the same age without heart disease. "The ability to laugh—either naturally or as a learned behavior—may have important implications in societies such as the U.S. where heart disease remains the number one killer," says Michael Miller, director of the Center for Preventive Cardiology at the University of Maryland Medical Center. "We know that exercising, not smoking, and eating foods low in saturated fat will reduce the risk of heart disease. Perhaps regular, hearty laughter should be added to the list."

WATCH A FUNNY MOVIE AND CALL ME IN THE MORNING

Humor and laughter may have other benefits besides helping to fight heart disease. Doctors Lee Berk and Stanley Tan of Loma Linda University in California have conducted research showing that laughing lowers blood pressure, reduces stress hormones, and increases muscle flexion. Laughter, they say, boosts immune function by raising levels of infection-fighting cells. There's more: Laughter also triggers the release of endorphins, the body's natural painkillers, and produces a general sense of well-being. Laughter is an easy pill to swallow; it's free and has only positive side effects.

· ·

"As I got older, I developed furniture disease.
My chest fell into my drawers."
LORETTA LAROCHE, STRESS EXPERT AND HUMORIST

· ·

Laughter can be a great workout for your diaphragm, facial, leg, and back muscles. It massages abdominal organs, tones intestinal functioning, and strengthens abdominal muscles. As if all that weren't enough, it's estimated that hearty laughter can burn calories equivalent to several minutes on the rowing machine or exercise bike. Think of all those runners hitting the pavement, expressions of grim resolve and miles of strain on their drawn faces. (If anyone made running look fun, then more of us would do it.) Laughing at one Marx Brothers movie could cut that running time in half.

And there's even more. Further studies from Loma Linda University show that laughter stimulates both sides of the brain to enhance learning. Laughter keeps the brain alert and allows people to retain more information. An alert, active brain is a good piece of equipment at any age.

According to the Geriatric Psychiatry Alliance, depression affects 15% of older Americans, or about six million people. Suicide is always a risk for those who are depressed, and in fact, 25% of suicides occur with people who are more than fifty years old. Study after study confirms that laughing elevates moods. In fact, many psychologists now use humor as a therapeutic tool to battle depression.

Striving—and often it does take striving—to see the humor in life, and attempting to laugh at situations rather than bemoan them, will help your disposition and the disposition of those around you. Do family and friends leave your home with smiles on their faces? Is it a pleasant experience to visit you?

Many of us used to dread visits to our grandparents' homes: old grumpy people with sour dispositions and too many things you couldn't touch. Always being told to keep the noise down and weird mushy stuff to eat. It was torture. (If this sounds like what your grandchildren experience at your house, thank goodness you are reading this book.) But I was lucky. Besides my grandmother Meme, I also had Grandma Echo. She was a lively redhead who was witty with words and wrote poems to make us laugh. Like this one:

. . . .

A Good Bit of Advice

There is nothing the matter with me,
I'm as healthy as I can be.
I have arthritis in both of my knees
And when I talk, I talk with a wheeze!
My pulse is weak, my blood is thin
But I'm awfully well for the shape I'm in!
My teeth are bad and they have to come out
And my diet I hate to think about.
I am overweight and I can't get thin
But I'm awfully well for the shape I'm in!
The moral is, as this tale we unfold,
That for you and me who are growing old
It's better to say "I'm fine" with a grin
Than to let them know the shape we're in!

ECHO ROSE CLARK

. . . .

Echo lived in almost constant pain from a botched spinal surgery, gangrene in the knee, and a condition that made too much scar tissue grow inside her body. But she was always ready and willing to have some fun, saying, "I'll be in pain and feel rotten if I sit home, and I'll be in pain if I go out and have some fun, so I'm going out to have some fun." Not only is that statement applicable to all of us, it's a perfect example of the way the language of life affects the living of life.

Answer the following questions in your Young Twice Chronicle:

- What do you do just for fun?

- What's the last fun thing you did just for *you*?

Echo was great at one-liners, too. One day when she was in her eighties, we went out to lunch. As we approached the restaurant, an older gentleman smiled, winked, and held the door open for her. "Hey Grandma," I said, "You've still got it." Without missing a beat she replied, "Yeah, but at my age, who needs it?"

Your ability to laugh at yourself is a valuable accomplishment. It gives you enjoyment, connection, and good cheer as a defense against the bores and the boring, the sedate and the solemn, the dreary and the dull. The ability to perceive what's amusing in the somber and serious, as well as in the comic, adds greatly to the language of your life.

. . . .

"The Doctor says, 'You'll live to be eighty!'
'I am eighty!'
'See, what did I tell you?'"
HENNY YOUNGMAN, COMIC

. . . .

TAKING HUMOR SERIOUSLY

Babies as young as six weeks respond positively to smiling faces—and avoid frowning faces. I'm still prone to do that, aren't you? When a baby is twelve weeks old, laughter emerges. In listing humor as a neotenous trait, Ashley Montagu explained, "The development of a sense of humor is important for without it, life becomes dreary business. It is the sense of humor that renders life a great deal more endurable than it would otherwise be, and much more amusing." Clearly humor is one of our greatest and earliest natural resources. Every day provides lots of material for amusing others and ourselves. People are drawn to a smile, even if that smile is on a well-worn face.

Human laughter is a defining trait of our species; we are the only creatures on earth who have the neurophysiologic mechanisms to do it. Humor is essential to our mental health. When taken seriously, it can help us grow young in five ways:

Humor...

1. helps us connect with others.

2. reduces stress by giving us perspective.

3. replaces distressing emotions with pleasurable feelings.

4. changes our behavior and increases energy.

5. keeps us young because it just feels good.

To create a neoteny-rich life, may I suggest that we take the practice and planning of humor seriously, and that we laugh often to live well?

WHAT'S SO FUNNY?

Writer Edward Hoaglund said, "Life is moments, day by day, not a chronometer or contractual commitment by God. The digits of one's age do not correspond to the arrhythmia of one's heart or to the secret chemistry in our lymph nodes that, mysteriously going rancid, can betray us despite all the surgery, dentistry, and other codger-friendly amenities that money buys. Nor do good works keep you off the undertaker's slab. But cheeriness, yes maybe. Cheery, lean little guys do seem to squeeze an extra decade out of the miser above."

The following survey will help you determine if you're as funny and prone to laughter as you think you are or ought to be.

Last Laugh Survey

In this questionnaire, you're going to measure your cheeriness, sense of humor, and habits of laughter. You'll find scenarios that you may have faced at some time. Imagine what you would do in each scenario, or take a moment to recall a similar scenario. Then record the number of the phrase that best reflects your response.

A. You are on vacation and you see someone you know from college or high school. How would you respond?

   1. I would probably not bother speaking to the person.

   2. I would talk to the person but avoid using much humor.

   3. I would find something to smile about as we reminisce.

   4. I would find something to laugh about with the person.

   5. I would laugh heartily with the person.

B. You're awakened from a deep sleep in the middle of the night by your grandchild running into your room to tell you his or her silly dream. What would you do?

   1. I wouldn't be particularly amused.

   2. I would be somewhat amused, but I would not laugh.

   3. I would be able to laugh at something funny my grandchild said.

   4. I would be able to laugh and say something funny to my grandchild.

   5. My grandchild and I would laugh together.

C. You accidentally hurt yourself and have to spend a few days in the hospital. During that time, how would you behave?

   1. People would have to draw the short stick to be the visitor, because I am not amused.

   2. I would ask for any magazine or book to read.

   3. I would request funny movies or reading material.

4. I would find the situation funny.

5. I would laugh heartily much of the time with my visitors.

D. One day when you're bored and have no commitments, you decide to do something you enjoy with friends. To what extent would you respond with humor that day?

1. The activity we'd choose wouldn't involve much smiling or laughter.

2. I would smile sometimes but wouldn't find an occasion to laugh out loud.

3. I would smile frequently and laugh at times.

4. I would laugh aloud quite frequently.

5. I would laugh heartily much of the time.

E. You are watching a movie or TV program with some friends, and you find one scene particularly funny, but no one else seems to find it humorous. How would you most likely react?

1. I would think that I must have misunderstood something, or that it wasn't really funny.

2. I would smile to myself but wouldn't show outward amusement.

3. I would smile visibly.

4. I would laugh out loud.

5. I would laugh heartily.

F. You have a romantic evening with someone you care for deeply. How would you behave?

1. I would probably tend to be quite serious in my conversation.

2. I would smile occasionally but probably wouldn't laugh much.

3. I would smile frequently and laugh from time to time.

4. I would laugh aloud quite frequently.

5. I would laugh heartily much of the time.

G. You are eating at a fine restaurant and the waiter accidentally spills a drink on you.

1. I would not be particularly amused.

2. I would be amused but not show it outwardly.

3. I would smile.

4. I would laugh.

5. I would laugh heartily.

H. In choosing your friends, how desirable is it for them to be easily amused and able to laugh in a variety of situations?

1. Not very desirable.

2. Neither desirable nor undesirable.

3. Quite desirable.

4. Very desirable, but not the most important characteristic.

5. It's the most important characteristic I look for in a friend.

I. How would you rate your likelihood of being amused and laughing in a wide variety of situations?

1. Very little.

2. Less than average.

3. About average.

4. Above average.

5. My most outstanding characteristic.

Add up the numbers you recorded. A score of 27 or higher may mean that you have the added longevity and youthening of the neotenous traits of humor and laughter; you may indeed have the last laugh. If you scored less than 27, it may be time for you to add a laugh track to the background of your life.

Do You Have Humor Impairment?

"Humor," said comic Mel Brooks, "keeps the elderly rolling along, singing a song. When you laugh, it's an involuntary explosion of the lungs. The lungs need to replenish themselves with oxygen. So you laugh, you breathe, the blood runs, and everything is circulating. If you don't laugh, you'll die."

Sometimes it's not easy to lighten up. For most people, using humor effectively requires practice and planning. You need to build your humor repertoire so you can access it when you need it. Collect cartoons, one-liners, jokes, anecdotes, and the like. Why not memorize one joke a day, building your memory while making others laugh? Develop your own sense of humor: Take a stand-up comedy class, or use humor every chance you get. Remind yourself to have fun. It's okay to be foolish on occasion, and it's good for you, too.

"Unfortunately, many people do not consider fun an important item on their daily agenda," notes test pilot Chuck Yeager, perhaps best known as the first test pilot to break the sound barrier. "For me, that was always the highest priority in whatever I was doing." Take a laugh break instead of a coffee break. When something bad happens, pretend to be your favorite comedian—how would you react? Spend time with people who help you smile, laugh, and look at the bright side. Get together regularly with these people. Start with a *tee-hee*, build up to a chuckle, and then go for it: A BIG BELLY LAUGH! Pretty soon you're laughing, your endorphins are rushing, and you begin to feel better. To laugh or not to laugh is not even a question. You know what a young spirit would choose. You are that young spirit, and it's always your choice.

Do-Over: Start a Comedy Club

Unless you exercise your sense of humor on a regular basis, your ability to use humor declines with age. Instead of a book club, or a cooking club, or even a Red Hat club, I suggest you start your very own comedy club. Get a package of party favor noisemakers, and attach an invitation to each to join in monthly wit, mirth, and laughter. Send invitations to people in your life who are already funny, and to the not-so-funny. Pick a monthly standing date, and call your get-together something like *Live from My Living Room, It's Wednesday Night!* At your first meeting, read this mission statement adapted from Sam Walton, the founder of Wal-Mart:

. . . .

"Celebrate your success and find humor in your failures.
Don't take yourself too seriously. Loosen up and everyone around you
will loosen up. Have fun and always show enthusiasm. When all else
fails, put on a costume and sing a silly song."

. . . .

The chart on the text two pages presents some ideas to get you started.

Wearing big nose glasses at a service station will do more than fill up your tank; it will fuel your funny side. On a recent bumpy plane ride to Cody, Wyoming, I was lucky enough to have a flight attendant who donned a tiny, glittery cowboy hat and galloped down the aisle tossing us peanuts and pretzels. We were laughing so hard that we all forgot to get airsick!

Humor calls into play your beliefs about the world. Humor is a way to break out of your rigidity, a gentle way to alter the language of your life. Daily doses of humor and laughter bring you—in the immortalized words of Chuckles the Clown on the *Mary Tyler Moore Show*—"a little song, a little dance, a little seltzer down your pants."

Comedy Club Ground Rules

1. Figure out what makes you laugh and decide to do it, watch it, and read it more often. When you find something really funny, bring it to the next meeting to share.

2. Subscribe to a joke-a-day Web site. Just type into a search engine the word "jokes" or the name of your favorite comedian(s), and you'll have plenty of choices.

3. Memorize one joke each month to deliver at the meeting.

4. Every member brings a cartoon to each meeting to share and swap.

5. A different member of the club serves as host for each meeting and determines the theme, costumes, and activities.

6. Invite guest speakers: local comics, singing telegram performers, and community theater actors. You'll be surprised at the number of funny people in your community who will welcome the chance to talk about their work.

7. Hold your own Comedy Revue once a year. Invite spouses and friends, and feature the funniest jokes you've found during the year. Tell stories of humorous things that happened in meetings, and enlarge and post some of the best cartoons. In short, celebrate the laughs.

8. Do something fun, something outrageous, and something to make you laugh at every meeting. Rent funny movies: *Arsenic and Old Lace* with Cary Grant or *Harvey* with Jimmy Stewart. Introduce your club to the comedy of Monty Python. Visit the library to find

old books by humorist Robert Benchley. Listen to old-time radio program tapes by satirist Stan Freberg.

9. Between meetings, challenge yourself to practice humor. Start writing your own jokes, and swap knock-knock jokes with kids.

10. Put together a Comedy Club First Aid Kit. Fill it with comedy cassettes, joke books, and various disguises like red clown noses or big nose glasses. Keep the kit in your car to pull out immediately when something happens that challenges humor—like getting stuck in traffic or seeing the outrageous price of gas!

Music
(Song and Dance)

"Look, I really don't want to wax philosophic, but I will say that if you're alive, you got to flap your arms and legs, you got to jump around a lot, you got to make a lot of noise, because life is the very opposite of death. And, therefore, as I see it, if you're quiet, you're not living. You've got to be noisy, or at least your thoughts should be noisy, and colorful and lively."

MEL BROOKS, COMIC, SCREENWRITER, AND ACTOR

Although it's often said that humans are the only primates able to talk, it's rarely noted that humans are also the only primates who can sing. In fact, since singing is a simpler system than speech, with only a pitch as a distinguishing feature, many anthropologists suggest that singing was a prerequisite to speech, and thus to language. However, a distinguished line of scholars has also supported the notion that the first human language was primarily gestural, carried on with hand and arm signals instead of vocal sounds. A few decades ago, Danish philologist Otto Jespersen speculated that early human courting sounds, "simulating the melodious love-songs of the nightingale," stimulated the evolution of language. These early love songs, according to Jespersen, led to courtship rhythms, which led to the body synchrony that is a "universal stage of the human courting process: we become attracted to each other, we begin to keep a common beat."

Historian William Wundt perhaps best expresses these theories about early vocal and movement development. "For a long time before the evolutionary emergence of articulate vocal language," he says, "early hominids probably communicated propositionally by means of hand and arm gestures. [These were] supplemented by vocal calls not yet deserving to be called speech." While it's a beginning, this "gesturing" language doesn't fully or easily explain the essential youthening tendency of song and dance. And to better understand growing young, you need to learn more about your musicality.

LIVE OUT LOUD

. . . .

"If you ask me what I came into the world to do,
I will tell you I came to live out loud."
EMILE ZOLA, JOURNALIST AND NOVELIST

. . . .

Whether singing, speaking, crying, shouting, or even humming, our voices tell the world who we are. Too often life seems to throttle our natural voices, or worse, steal them. When my grandparents were children, everyone would gather around the piano and sing. During my Girl Scout days, the most anticipated event of summer camp was the nightly sing-along by the fire. Almost fifteen years later, I even taught my sons some of the songs I learned at Pine

Tree Camp. But who is doing all the singing these days? Tipsy people at karaoke machines?

Children are natural singers, hummers, and dancers. At the airport recently, I saw a little girl twirling, sliding, and moving—while the rest of us stood in line listlessly, with sourpuss faces. No matter where you are these days, in elevators or grocery stores, on the phone or on hold, background music is always piped in. We could be singing and dancing fools all day long! But no, we have all grown old, so we stand still. I considered asking the man in front of me in the airport ticket line if he wanted to dance, but with airport security the way it is, I thought I'd better just watch the little girl. And so often, that's how it goes: We decide to watch, our songs are stifled, and our dancing is over.

When I was in third grade, I decided to try out for *The Lew King Ranger Show*, a local television talent show. It was the Phoenix, Arizona, version of *The Mickey Mouse Club* with a decidedly lower budget. I had no vocal training, but as you may recall, I loved to sing. I practiced a song I learned in my elementary school music class, and asked my father to take me to the auditions. With visions of becoming the next Annette Funicello dancing in my head, and with all the lyrics to "I Never Get the Blues in Arizona" in my heart, off we went.

I signed in as number seven on the audition list, took my seat, and watched in mounting horror as the first six well-trained, talented child performers tapped, twirled, and tenored their way around the sound stage. I begged my father to take me home. "I'm no match for these kids. I don't know what I'm doing!" I was thinking, *Please get me out of here. How embarrassing, how humiliating, puhleeze don't make me do this!* My father calmly replied, "We'll leave after you sing your song."

From the soundstage came the call: "Number seven!" In tears, I asked for another moment. As more singers and dancers arrived confidently at their scheduled audition times, I sat—a crumbled and tear-soaked shadow of my former self. Finally, after everyone had gone, I walked up to the piano. In which key would I like to sing? "Which key?" I asked. "What's a key? I guess a black one?" I sang my little song in my little voice, and knew it had all been a big mistake. I vowed I would never sing in public again. My voice had been stolen by fear of rejection, terror of comparison, and lack of self-confidence.

The voice, wrote world-renowned psychiatrist Carl Jung, is "the ring of fear." Voices can get lost in childhood. We get shushed, told to raise our hands to speak, ridiculed, and finally silenced. Eventually a pattern sets in, and we stop sharing our songs, our joys, our places in the world. In short, we stop living out loud.

My older son, Chase, decided on a career as a pilot in the United States Air Force. But then, as a college ROTC student, Chase was told by a superior, "You have the worst military bearing I have ever seen. You must stop singing and whistling in the halls." I'm happy to report that my son's singing, smiling, upbeat self found a better fit when he joined the Peace Corps. He teaches in South Africa, a place that thrives on song and dance.

Judgment—our own or others'—makes us silent, steals our songs, and cages our souls.

Biologist and author Loren Eiseley recalls a moment when he saw a "Judgment of Birds." He had been hiking and decided to sit down in a clearing to rest. A commotion and an outcry of anguish awakened him. He looked into the field ahead and saw a huge black raven devouring a small baby bird. The sound that had awakened him was the screaming of the baby bird's parents, two small birds circling, trying to save their nestling. The raven paid no heed and carried on. It was only playing its role, notes Eiseley, as the "black bird at the heart of life."

Eiseley watched as a flock of small birds suddenly appeared: a half dozen varieties, all congregated above the raven, all joining in the cries of the baby bird's parents. They cried in a common misery, sighed, and swooped, seeming to point their wings at this tragedy as the raven flew away with the carcass of the baby bird.

It was then, believes Eiseley, that he saw the judgment. "It was the judgment of life against death. I will never see it again so forcefully presented. I will never hear it again in notes so tragically prolonged. For in the midst of mourning and silence, the small birds forgot the violence. There, in that clearing, the crystal note of a song sparrow lifted hesitantly in the hush. And finally, after the painful fluttering, another took the song, then another, the song passing from one bird to another, doubtfully at first, as though some evil thing was being slowly forgotten."

Eiseley continues, "Suddenly they took heart and sang from many throats joyously together as birds are known to sing. They sing because life is sweet and sunlight is beautiful. They sang under the brooding shadow of the raven, for they were the singers of life, not of death."

Birds don't sing because they have an answer. They sing because they have a song. To be young twice is to forgo the critics, judges, upsets, and obstacles—to sing our song of life. We must write our own lyrics, create our own music, and increase the intensity of our voices until our ultimate, inevitable crescendo.

FOLLOW THE BOUNCING BREATH

When I was a little girl, I used to watch Mitch Miller's television sing-along show. Do you remember it? The words appeared on the screen; and with a chorus of wholesome singers behind him, Mitch would say, "Follow the bouncing ball." A little white ball would mark the words and the beat of the song, and everyone watching in America could sing, "She'll Be Coming 'Round the Mountain" or "Mares Eat Oats." That little bouncing ball gave us permission to sing as if we knew what we were doing, as if we were in Mitch's chorus, and we belonged. In the comfort of our living rooms, without being judged, not caring about tune or key, we were free to sing.

Vocal specialists agree that when people can sing their songs, bottled-up voices are set free. This song of yours has nothing to do with memorizing lyrics, carrying a tune, following a bouncing ball, or even having a "good" voice. "Standing with who you are and offering the song of your life is a sacred act," says noted vocalist Susan Osborn. Here's an exercise she suggests to help you begin singing the song that's still inside you.

"If a person stands relaxed and centered, and then allows the sound to emerge on the exhale and follows it wherever it leads," explains Osborn, "an amazingly direct experience of human essence can be felt and heard. All the emotions that arise can be used to fuel the song, and the whole body will sing and listen."

Try that now. Just take a deep breath and let out a note—a sound, your sound.

To sing life's praise, you must set your voice free. Begin with a breath, and then move to a hum. When my husband returned from a visit with his ninety-seven-year-old grandmother, the first thing he told me was this: As she went to water aerobics, fixed lunch, called friends, played bridge, and moved through her neotenous day, she hummed. In the morning making tea, she hummed. Driving to the market—more humming. "Grandmum always," said my husband, "has a song inside of her."

And so do you.

SOAK IT UP

"Take a music bath once or twice a week for a few seasons," suggested author and physician Oliver Wendell Holmes. "You will find that it is to the soul what the water bath is to the body."

Where there is song, there is music. And where there is music, there is magic. I've always wondered why aging rock stars who lived on the road and abused drugs look, for the most part, so good (not counting Keith Richards of the Rolling Stones). The answer? They have another, more powerful, drug coursing through their veins.

The ancient Greeks were aware of the positive effects of music. Democritus was noted for prescribing the music of the flute for various ills. Galen believed that music could be used as an antidote to scorpion and viper bites. And from the sixteenth through eighteenth centuries, music was considered a treatment for gout, sciatica, epilepsy, convulsions, delirium, and even plague.

Both King Phillip V of Spain and King George III of England reportedly used music as a cure for their severe depression. Even an 1880 study showed that a person's blood pressure and pulse rate varied according to the type of music being played.

A modern study was conducted showing the effect of music on vasoconstriction as reflected in finger temperature, an established measure of stress. Results showed that subjects listening to the works of French composer Claude Debussy experienced warming of the fingers, indicating lowered stress. And there's more: The National Association for Music Therapy, which has more than 3,000 members working in hospitals, nursing homes, and other facilities, wants the U.S. government to allow Medicare to pay for music therapy. The association also wants federal support for research into the effectiveness and possible uses of music therapy.

Violinist Yehudi Menuhin said, "I can only think of music as something inherent in every human being—a birthright. Music coordinates mind, body, and spirit. The greatest service to the population would be if every school day began with singing. If people sing together, they have a feeling of individual coordination as well as within the body of the group. I have never met a member of a choir who was depressed."

The time may come when your doctor will prescribe an hour of Debussy, or an evening of The Beatles. But why wait for that prescription? Music is a moral law. It gives a soul to the universe, wings to the mind, flight to the imagination, comfort to sadness, and life to everything.

"For the past eighty years," notes musician Pablo Casals, "I have started each day in the same manner. It is not a mechanical routine, but something essential to my daily life. I go to the piano, and I play two preludes and fugues of Bach. I cannot think of doing otherwise.

It is a sort of benediction on the house. But this is not its only meaning to me. It is a rediscovery of the world of which I have the joy of being a part. It fills me with awareness of the wonder of life, with a feeling of the incredible marvel of being a human being."

Like me, you may not play a musical instrument. But as I mentioned in Chapter Three, you can pull out the old records (even those eight-tracks and cassettes that I know are in your garage) and play the music of your youth. You can fill this new prescription by going to the local music store and buying some current music; perhaps music your children, grandchildren, friends, and family might also like to hear. Or listen to the radio while you're in the car, and sing along. Music is the language of imagination and rhythm. And we are immersed in a sea of rhythm.

HAPPY FEET

Rhythm is inherent in nature, and therefore in humans. The beat of our body is the beat of the earth. The cycles of day and night, the moon, and the seasons were instrumental in forming the ancient psyche. In his book *The Dance of Life*, Edward Hall claims that today's rhythms are hidden from everyday experience, yet compose "the unspoken and implicit rules of behavior and thought that control everything we do."

Hall believes that "this hidden cultural grammar defines the way in which people view the world, determines their values, and establishes the basic tempo and rhythms of life." But we aren't tuned in—and in many cases, have been turned away from—these basic rhythms of life. "If I had my life to live over again," wrote naturalist Charles Darwin, "I would have made it a rule to read some poetry and listen to some music at least once a week. Perhaps the parts of my brain now atrophied would thus have been kept active through use. The loss of these tastes is a loss of happiness, and may possibly be injurious to the intellect, and more probably the moral character, by enfeebling the emotional part of our nature."

The language of your life without neoteny is too often the enfeebling language of less: less hope, less possibility, less humor, and less noise. Neoteny urges more: more optimism, more wonder, more laughter, more song, and more movement.

In the middle of comic Steve Martin's original stand-up comedy routine, he was often struck with "Happy Feet," causing him to dance uncontrollably. The audience's laughter of acknowledgment and familiarity meant, "That's exactly what I feel like doing sometimes!" Yet the unspoken and implicit rules noted by Edward Hall often stop us, control us, and give us feet of clay.

But when we saw Steve Martin dance, it gave us permission. Around water coolers and in hallways throughout America, lots of people were getting happy feet. Martin broke the rules, so we could, too. There are wonderful people who always march to the beat of their own drummers, and from those people we can learn. In his best-selling book *Tuesdays with Morrie*, Mitch Albom describes his beloved professor: "He had always been a dancer, my old professor. The music didn't matter. Rock and roll, big band, the blues. He loved them all. He would close his eyes and with a blissful smile begin to move to his own sense of rhythm. It wasn't always pretty. But then, he didn't worry about a partner. Morrie danced by himself."

Going Through the Motions

Most of us don't dance; in fact, we don't move. Most of us don't even fully breathe. Now is your chance to regain your childhood love of motion. Make movement a priority. It isn't about "just do it." We are at the stage of life when we *must* do it. It doesn't have to be planned, and it doesn't have to be perfect, but the dance must be performed. The late dancer and choreographer Martha Graham summed it up this way: "Dancing lasts longer than sex. It's prettier, more graceful, and unlike sex it's more fun as you get older."

Slowdance

Have you ever watched kids
On a merry-go-round?
Or listened to the rain
Lapping on the ground?
Ever followed a butterfly's erratic flight
Or gazed at the sun into the fading night?
You better slow down
Don't dance so fast
Time is short
The music won't last.

Do you run through each day on the fly?
When you ask, "How are you?"
Do you hear the reply?
When the day is done,
Do you lie in your bed
With the next hundred chores
Running through your head?
You'd better slow down
Don't dance so fast
Time is short
The music won't last.

Ever told your child,
We'll do it tomorrow
And in your haste, not see his sorrow?
Ever lost touch,
Let a good friendship die
'Cause you never had time
To call and say "Hi?"
You'd better slow down
Don't dance so fast
Time is short
The music won't last.

Slowdance (continued)

When you run so fast to get somewhere
You miss half the fun of getting there.
When you worry and hurry through your day,
It is like an unopened gift...
Thrown away...
Life is not a race.
Do take it slower
Hear the music
Before the song is over.

David Weatherford

· ·

At the end of each semester of my university teacher education class, I bring in some very special guests. These people serve as models to my students, showing them the power of full engagement, lifelong learning, and neoteny. After all, who needs these role models more than the people who will become our teachers?

The Foxy Fillies is a chorus line of women, age fifty-five and older, in sequined costumes. They tap dance their way into my students' hearts and minds. Many of these women had never danced before retiring, and most are in their sixties and seventies. They're vivacious, energetic, and exuberant. After a standing ovation following one of their routines, the Fillies told my students, "Dancing is good exercise. I had always wanted to try it and it was now or never!" And, "With dancing, I don't seize up like a lot of seniors do. They sit too long and they don't do anything because their knees hurt or their backs hurt or their ankles hurt. I've moved past that."

These women instinctively know what one recent study conducted by The Aerobic Research Center in Dallas, Texas, indicated: Dancing protects against dementia better than activities such as walking, swimming, and cycling. Why? Researchers think that moving your feet to the beat may require more concentration than doing rote exercise.

Dance in any guise is infectious. I asked students to do dance presentations at an assisted-living center. They taught wheelchair-bound couples a dance called the Macarena, using hand and arm movements. The residents and my students had so much fun that now the center holds weekly dances. If your feet don't dance, move your arms. No arm movement? Nod your head, wink your eye, and listen to the dancing beat of your heart.

STEPPING UP AND OUT

. . . .

"I know I am going to be eighty years old, so I don't take the steps two at a time, although I would like to. I go down steps a little more gingerly than I used to. But that's not my fault. That's nature's fault! Mentally, I'm going up two and a half steps at a time!"

SAMMY CAHN, SONGWRITER

. . . .

Your mind is always where the limitations start *and* finish. Neoteny is the practice of reawakening and refurbishing your mind with the gifts of a youthful spirit. Of course, you can ignore neoteny, refuse its invitation, and allow your dance to remain still. Are you afraid to die, or are you afraid to live?

International dance expert Gabrielle Roth, author of *Sweat Your Prayers*, says that dance "can change our lives completely." She explains, "First, a person's energy becomes more fluid, and second, a person would be able to name the energy. Like I'm feeling very inert or edgy. You get a language with which you can transverse your inner worlds and name things so you can move through them and let go of them. In the dance, most people gain access to deeper emotions and how to express them."

Go dancing with your partner or friends. Take classes. Rent any Fred Astaire movie, or a film about ballet, flamenco, or ballroom dancing. South African activist Nelson Mandela and many others were imprisoned for decades because of their stand against apartheid. In their Robbins Island prison, there were no cots and no furniture, bars on every door and window, cement walls, and constant threats of beatings or death. How did the prisoners get through it? "Sometimes," said Mandela, "to pass the time, we taught each other ballroom dancing."

Whether in your head or your heart, on the dance floor or living room rug, it's time to break out of your cramped, self-imposed cell and "dance with the one that brung 'ya'."

Do-Over: Fill Your Dance Card

Songs, dances, chants, cheers, rhythm, or rhymes: "What we really play," said Louis Armstrong, "is life." To fully participate in the neoteny potential of our second half of life, we need to find the way back to what makes our spirits sing and our bodies dance.

When I was about nine, I desperately wanted dance lessons. My parents suggested I find some way to earn them. I looked longingly at the Jeri Johnson School of Dance as I passed by on my daily bike ride home from school. The school was located in a strip mall next to a hair salon. I finally worked up my nerve and went to the salon owner. I asked if I could sweep up hair for ten cents a day, thus affording me one dance class a month (I really needed a bargaining agent). But no takers, so no tap shoes.

That should never have stopped me, but it did. Whatever squelched your happy feet is also in the past. To make up for my lack of formal dance training, but with loads of enthusiasm, I became a cheerleader and then an aerobics instructor, and I continue teaching aerobics to this day.

Following are some ways to fill your Second Chance Dance Card.

Second Chance Dance Card

1. *Trust Your Body*
2. *Notice the Melodies*
3. *Move to Your Own Rhythm*
4. *Give a Live Performance*
5. *Look for the Grace Notes*

1. Trust Your Body

Evolution has given us neoteny and an intrinsic knowledge of our bodies. But most people don't feel at all connected with their own flesh. "If they're not controlling it, drugging it, putting it in exercise machines—if they're not in charge of it, then they think they'll fall apart," says dance professor Andrea Olson. "It's totally the opposite. The more we can trust our bodies, nourishing basic needs of the human nervous system for safety and emotional integration, the less we have to do through conscious thought processing. Then we can attend to the moment at hand with joy, contentment, and ease."

I once took Cindy, a friend of mine in her late seventies, to one of my aerobics classes. I was concerned because we were moving too fast for her, and she seemed unable to keep the beat. I kept going over to her, giving her encouragement and support. Cindy finally said to me, "Look, these wrinkles mean I have had lots of time to get used to not knowing what I am doing, not being perfect, and not caring, so you dance your way, and I'll dance mine." 'Nuff said!

2. Notice the Melodies

Huston Smith, a scholar of world religions, notes that every spiritual tradition includes practices for paying attention. Throughout our lives, we have been trained to produce, not to pay attention, but now is the time to become discerning. Pay attention to your voice; it's the blueprint of your soul. Begin with Susan Osborn's voice exercise mentioned earlier. Look for opportunities to cheer, to sigh, to free your voice.

. . . .

"Anything too stupid to say is sung."
Voltaire, author and philosopher

. . . .

My children and I used to perform lunchtime operas. We'd sing at the top of our lungs about what we'd like for lunch: "Peanut butter, peanut butter, *peanut butter!*" It was silly, it was stupid, and it was *fun*. Try singing "I love you" or "Did you pick up the mail?" and see what happens!

Birds do it, bees do it, even syncopated fleas do it, and so can you. Find the beat and pulse of daily activities. Begin a humming meditation. Pay attention to the beautiful unchained melodies that have been waiting for so many years to be noticed. Before long, you'll find yourself joining in.

3. Move to Your Own Rhythm

Environmental philosopher Thomas Berry once said that our senses were developed to function at "foot speed." As much as possible, get out of the car and travel the way you were meant to travel: on foot. Walk. Dance. Move. You're slower than others. So what? You have a quick pace? Use it. Our innate sense of rhythm can be seen in the way we strum our fingers on the desk, play drums with our pencils, or fold laundry at therapeutic pace. Some of us are runners; others like skating or swimming. And some of us will not be hurried as we stroll with our dogs. Your body knows how it wants to move, knows that it must move. So honor your individual pace and your real rhythm because you have places to go and people to see.

4. Give a Live Performance

Instead of listening to music, play it. Besides singing and dancing lessons, I also wanted to play an instrument, with pretty much the same results as my other musical endeavors. Finally, by the eighth grade, my parents got tired of hearing me whine about all my unused talent. For my birthday that year they gave me…a tambourine. Hey, it was one step up from a kazoo, and it was something tangible. I loved it. It was fun, it was real, and it was mine. Get a drum or harmonica; play spoons. There are great "family band" kits at toy stores. Buy one and create a neighborhood parade. Whatever you do, make it hands-on.

5. Look for the Grace Notes

In music, a grace note is an extra note—a tiny, little note. In life, grace notes are the little touches. "What is life? It is the flash of a firefly in the night. It is the breath of the buffalo in the wintertime. It is the little shadow which runs across the grass and loses itself in the sunset." These, the last words of Blackfoot warrior Crowfoot, reflect his grace notes. Sometimes it's a kind gesture, or hearing a remembered lullaby. Perhaps it's seeing a kitten dance with yarn, or hearing a child sing the ABCs. To live a long life, to have a chance to sing and dance one more day, is to truly live in grace.

YOU'VE GOT THE MUSIC AND PROBABLY A LOT MORE IN YOU!

A man played piano in a bar. He was a good piano player. People came out just to hear him play. But one night, a customer told the piano player that he didn't want to hear him just play anymore. The customer wanted him to sing a song.

The piano player said, "I don't sing."

But the customer was persistent. He told the bartender, "I'm tired of listening to the piano. I want that guy to sing."

The bartender shouted across the room, "Hey, buddy! If you want to get paid, sing a song. The customers are asking you to sing!"

So he did. He sang a song. A piano player who had never sung in public did so for the very first time. And nobody had ever heard the song "Mona Lisa" sung the way it was sung that night by Nat King Cole.

As motivational speaker Les Brown says about Cole, "He had talent he was sitting on." He may have lived the rest of his life as a no-name piano player in a no-name bar, but because life circumstances made him sing, he went on to become one of the best-known entertainers in America.

You, too, have skills and abilities. You may not think your talent is particularly great, but it's probably better than you think. Besides, if you sit on any talent you possess, you might as well have no ability at all. The question isn't "What ability do I have that is useful?" The question should be "How will I use the ability I have?"

Some musicology graduate students at Amherst College performed an experiment at a playground. The students filmed children at play, with no accompanying audio recording. The students then tracked these visual events with a sequence of pre-recorded music. The result? A nearly complete synchronization of the musical beat with the movements of the children. The children appeared to be dancing to the beat of a common, underlying rhythm.

Joy, humor, and music give us the Language lesson of the OLD Survey. Working in concert with neoteny, they release the rhythm already inside us, give us back our music, and provide the score for the motivations that Drive us to our ultimate destination. Read on!

CHAPTER SIX

Your Drive to Thrive

Imagine the picture you want to see of yourself when you are older. Is it a picture of love, self-confidence, high self-esteem, flexibility, strong bones, and prosperity in mind, body, and soul? If the outlook or language I've supplied doesn't describe what you want, then substitute the view and words that do.

Now consider the thoughts that go through your mind about being older. Take them one at a time. Do these thoughts help you to be your picture?

Your mind does the thinking. Your mind is in charge of your brain. Your brain is in charge of your nerves. If your mind tells your brain that it's getting old—in other words, if you're thinking or saying these thoughts—your brain will relay to your nerves the process of getting "old."

Unfortunately, a lot of people unwittingly encourage the reactions they think are caused by growing old. "I know when so-and-so reached forty [or fifty, or sixty, or seventy...] years old, her body just plain broke down. She got arthritis, she had a hysterectomy, her stomach kept getting upset [and on and on]. The same thing happened to so-and-so," and so on. People reach what they feel is the logical conclusion: When they turn forty, or fifty, or sixty, or seventy, all that stuff will happen to them, too. You know the progression, you invite the progression, and you encourage the progression. The progression begins to be *you*. And this unwarranted, unwise, unhealthy progression can also stop with you.

There's a huge difference between growing older and growing up. No matter what you do, if you live another year, you have only grown a year older. If you haven't been driven to learn something, improve something, contribute, or love, you haven't really lived.

The philosophy of being young twice suggests this: As long as you're alive, why not live life to the fullest? Don't just survive—thrive.

THE SECOND LAW OF THERMODYNAMICS

I'm sure I have pieces of metal on the left side of my brain where physics and geometry were supposed to happen. These were never my best subjects in school. But I do know a valuable hard science idea when I see one, and that's where the Second Law of Thermodynamics comes in. Essentially, this law says that every system tends to decay into simpler forms. To keep itself in an ordered state, every system needs energy. Energy cannot be created, but it can be dispersed. In other words, you can forestall *entropy*, or the dissolution of order into redundant randomness. Organisms that successfully find ways to extract more energy from the environment for their own use tend to—you guessed it—live longer and avoid chaotic disarray.

How does all this relate to growing young twice? This chapter presents the energizing traits of neoteny: work, play, and learning. These are the drives designed not only to extract energy from our systems, but to provide the power and force that can steer us away from entropy, and move us toward meaning and mattering in our later years. "Unlike physical energy, which tends to run down as we get older, emotional energy can increase the more you learn about what works best for you," notes Mira Kirshenbaum, author of *The*

Emotional Energy Factor. "Imagine getting more and more energy every day of your life." We can begin purposefully cultivating the seasoned energies of our longer lives to drive our destinies, rather than to diminish ourselves.

. . . .

"A musician must make music, an artist must paint, a poet must write, if he is to be ultimately at peace with himself."
ABRAHAM MASLOW, TEACHER AND PSYCHOLOGIST

. . . .

Maslow's Hierarchy of Needs

Self-Actualization
(fulfillment)

Esteem
(self-respect, achievement, recognition)

Social
(affection, acceptance, friendship)

Safety
(security, protection from harm)

Physiological
(hunger, thirst, shelter)

Psychologist Abraham Maslow is perhaps most famous for his "Hierarchy of Needs" theory. The basic premise of this hierarchy, which looks like a pyramid, is that before you can care about security or safety needs, your basic needs for food and shelter must be met. Before you can garner self-esteem, your need for emotional attachment must be met. The pyramid rises in this step-by-step progression.

In reality, Maslow's hierarchy theory represents a complete life cycle. A newborn baby's needs are almost entirely physiological. As the baby grows, it needs safety and then love. Toddlers are eager for social interaction. Teenagers are also anxious about social needs, while young adults are concerned with self-esteem. Those of us in the second half of life may be fortunate enough to transcend these first four levels, enabling us to spend time self-actualizing. Maslow called self-actualization the highest drive, one that can be achieved only when the lower four are satisfied. Think of the many blessings brought by older age: the gift of knowing your *self*, having time to do things you choose, and not caring so much what other people think. This stage of our lives must surely be an apex.

If you read the "About the Author" section at the end of this book, you'll note that I am a driven, accomplished, and—some would say—anal-retentive person. I am the quintessential first-born overachiever. I believed that it didn't matter if you won or lost, as long as you won. I had it so bad that I once stole a blue ribbon from a swim meet rather than bring home the third-place ribbon I had won honestly. I spent a great deal of the first half of my life worrying about offending or disappointing people, making people like me, being nice, doing what others expected, and just getting along. I worked overtime worrying about what other people thought of me.

I'm not saying that all of a sudden on my fiftieth birthday I decided that I would offend people, not care who liked me, and become difficult. (Although, come to think of it, that does sound like the behavior of a lot of older people I know.)

Instead, I have gradually discovered a lessening drive to please everyone at the cost of displeasing myself. I find myself less competitive and more relaxed; and if someone doesn't like me, okay, that still bugs me, but I'm getting better. I find myself more driven to spend my time wisely, to surround myself with things that bring me joy, and to wear the world like a loose garment. If it took me fifty years to get to this level of Maslow's hierarchy, I'm determined to spend the next fifty years enjoying it.

At some time you must choose to face your own mortality. You can relish your own shift of gears then, and grow into the self-actualized you. Being you is when the real fun begins, because that will make you young again. Author George Sand said, "The day I buried my youth, I grew twenty years younger."

TEST DRIVE

. . . .

"Any life, no matter how long and complex it may be,
is made of a single moment—the moment in which
a man finds out, once and for all, who he is."
JORGE LUIS BORGES, AUTHOR

. . . .

Giving yourself the right to become your full self is the most important thing you can do, but some of us keep making wrong turns. Being careless with your life at this stage isn't just sad; it's simply wrong. Ask yourself the following questions, and record your answers in your Young Twice Chronicle.

- Have you ever dreamed of running away with the circus or hitting the open highway, for instance?

- What did you imagine the experience would give you?

- What would you pack on your drive of escape?

- What would you leave behind?

- If you moved to a new place, what would change about you?

- When and where did you last feel like a wide-eyed child?

- What changes would it take to describe your life as an adventure?

- Are you surprised by any of your answers so far?

- Based on your answers, are you driven to change anything about your life now?

Young people don't have the liberties we now possess. They have careers to build, families to raise, and mortgages to pay. They're preoccupied with the things we have already done. Have you begun to nourish your new freedoms, or do you remain locked inside the person you were yesterday?

Our newfound freedom can be exhilarating. Life is again full of options, as it was when we were very young.

THE OPTION THEORY

Humans are motivated and driven to maximize their options in life. By this I mean that the human psyche feels good when the circumstances of life are under its control. The self wants assurance that in any given situation, it has choices, or options, to do what it truly fancies. The need for options can drive people to make many sacrifices, even risking death rather than living a life deprived of choice.

Prior to considering neoteny as a life philosophy, you may have feared aging because it was portrayed as a loss of control, or a loss of options in life. But in linking our biology to our emotional evolution, we can reclaim and rename our options, choices, and aging. Consider this:

- In how many ways are you downshifting your drives because of your age?

- How are you currently forfeiting your right to your life?

- How many options have you released because of other people's expectations?

There is, and always has been, someone extraordinary inside you. And now that you understand how finite your time is, you should be driven to discover and delight in yourself once again. Options are available to you, work is left to be done by you, and life is waiting to play with you.

. . . .

"The great secret of life that all old people share is that you haven't really changed in seventy or eighty years. Your body changes, but you don't change at all. And that, of course, causes great confusion."

DORIS LESSING, AUTHOR AND NOBEL PRIZE NOMINEE

. . . .

It would take longer than one lifetime to live all the lives inside of you. Don't confuse time passing with time over. Choose not to live in the past lane. This is your opportunity to be driven to the full magnitude of your possibilities. Consider this time, and your choices, as the road map to new options and opportunities found only in age.

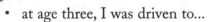

- at age three, I was driven to...

- at nine, I was driven to...

- at fifteen, I was driven to...

- at eighteen, I was driven to...

- at twenty-one, I was driven to...

- at thirty-seven, I was (am) driven to...

- at forty-five, I was (am) driven to...

Time is Flying By

The Option is Yours

TIME FLIES

Think of the directions your life took in the past, and then think of the things that you once were driven to accomplish. Next, create a "road map" in your Young Twice Chronicle that incorporates the ideas shown in the diagram on the previous page. Then write about what's driving you today. Is it compelling? What routes are available to help you locate a worthwhile drive? Examine your list. What's consistent? What has evolved? What options have you ruled out? What options are still available to you? What are you waiting for?

Please read the posted road signs carefully. "Do you think it is a small thing," asked French theologian St. Bernard of Clairvaux, "to know how to live?" You are in the driver's seat, and you've traveled a long way already, but the best part of the journey awaits you. There is more work to be done.

Work

. . . .

"The man who works and is never bored is never old. Work and interest in things are the best remedy for age. Each day I am reborn. Each day I must begin again."

PABLO CASALS, CELLIST AND CONDUCTOR

. . . .

In three days, I will no longer have the job I have called my life's work. More than twenty-five years ago, I went to graduate school and spent eleven years earning my masters and doctoral degrees while raising my family. I taught more than ten thousand students in my twenty years at major universities, and I felt humbled and honored by what I considered my calling. Because I am leaving this position, I have been given a plaque for exemplary service and a theme dinner informing me, "You Made a Difference." (Good thing I work for intrinsic rewards.)

Although I chose to retire early to expand my life-coaching and consulting business, I must admit that I had a hard time saying the "R" word. There is such a sense of expiration and ennui surrounding the term *retirement*. In fact, when my girlfriend Peggy received the invitation to my retirement dinner, she sent me an e-mail: "My friend Ronda is too young, too vibrant, and has too many things going on to be called retired. Someone should think of a new and better word that fits her." I love Peggy for that. She's a good friend, and clearly astute in her assessment—not just of me, but of the word *retirement*!

Work, whether paid or unpaid, is basic to our sense of social and personal identity. After many years of study and research into the human condition, Sigmund Freud concluded that work and love are the two essential ingredients of a happy, well-adjusted personality. A recent study conducted at the University of Texas Health Science Center confirmed that doing something meaningful is the key to longevity, not to mention happiness. So if this is true, why do we complain so much about work, and then hate the term that celebrates leaving it? How in the world could something like work be a childlike or neotenous characteristic?

THE NEED TO WORK

. . . .

"I don't like work, no man does. But what I really like is in work. The chance to find yourself. Your own reality for yourself, not for others, what no man can ever know."

JOSEPH CONRAD, AUTHOR AND ESSAYIST

. . . .

There is labor involved from the moment we are born. It takes a great deal of relentless effort to be a human being, and it's work that never ends. It has been said that we never work harder than during the first five years of life: breathing, crying, walking, talking, eating, spilling, falling, and constantly learning. To survive and become a functioning human is no easy task; it's both physical and emotional labor that results in being able to *do* something. "The baby is soon confirmed in his drive that work can be pleasurable," said neotenist Ashley Montagu, "and it is a pleasure that is renewed in other forms of work throughout one's life."

At a very early age, children love to work. I had to buy small plastic replicas of lawnmowers, workbenches, brooms, and ladders when my sons were small because they demanded to "work" alongside me. As their capacities increased, so did their responsibilities. They saw pleasure in work; we had fun doing these things. Real lawnmowers and hammers eventually replaced the toys. Jobs were assigned, allowances given, and the freedom and responsibility that can come from work were established.

In one way or another, we all have been exposed to the character and discipline involved in work. Work is neotenous because through its routine, the disciplined development of all our traits is most effectively achieved.

Work is any purposeful activity designed to produce a result. At times, even the best work can be burdensome and boring, requiring extraordinary effort; but a life without work would be empty and depressing.

I know a lot of older people who do not work, and who find themselves totally immersed in that nasty, conceited, small world of "I." They're examples of the old proverb "The devil finds work for those who do not make it for themselves." They ruminate about the past, complain about the present, and dread the future. They are so wrapped up in producing evidence of their petty problems that they seem unable to contribute to anything positive. They fail to employ their health, education, and leisure time to serve a greater purpose. This is what I call wasting away. "Don't stay in bed," warned seasoned comic George Burns, "unless you make money in bed."

Work drives away the care and small troubles of life. The busy person has little time to brood or fret. Work brings the prizes in life. The reward of a thing well done isn't a plaque or a watch, or even a paycheck: It's the fact that you did it. You can see that reward when your child finishes mowing the lawn with his plastic mower. You can feel it in the sweat on your brow after a physical challenge. You can hear it in your voice when you say, and mean it, "Job well done."

SO MUCH TO DO, SO MUCH TO HOPE FOR, SO MANY THINGS TO BE

Most people fear retirement because they will no longer know how to define themselves. If I am no longer a professor, what am I? If I no longer have gainful employment, what will happen to my sense of independence? Why do so many people who retire die within a year?

Your attitude toward work affects not only your self-identity, but also your journey toward realizing your full potential as you age. If you base your assumptions about the future on a fear of loss, you will compromise new identities, miss out on alternate callings, and become more frightened with each passing year. Consequently, you will have created the retirement of your nightmares.

As I have stressed throughout this book, the true gift of a richer life is to become the person you most fully and joyfully can be, using neoteny to help you. It takes work to become young twice.

Whether you are currently employed or retired, or have never had a paid position, being young twice means transforming your future work into a creative process. If you simply continue to put in your time, watch the clock, or wait for the whistle, you're wasting many of the best years of your life. It's time to prepare yourself to do what you find enjoyable, affirming, and transcending—as a vocation or an avocation.

There is no single definition or use for any word, or for any person. You may have had a great job, but that doesn't sum you up. Projects are waiting to be done, new businesses to create, and worlds to explore. I know a fifty-three-year-old woman who raised five children, and when the last one went off to college, she started her first business, a consignment house. It took her only two weeks to recruit enough consignors to open. She has twice moved into a bigger location. One sixty-eight-year-old man I know started traveling around the world, biking and climbing. Now he talks about his adventures in grade schools throughout his community. Nobel laureate Linus Pauling, when interviewed at age eighty-nine, said, "I don't think I ever sat down and asked myself, 'Now what am I going to do in life?' I just went ahead doing what I like to do."

Of all the people *ever* who have reached age sixty-five (the standard retirement age), half are alive today. By contrast, if you lived to age thirty-six or forty during the Middle Ages, you were very, very old. For 99.999% of human history, our lifespan was between eighteen and twenty years. As our reward for being born nearer the middle or toward the end instead of the beginning of the twentieth century, we'll most likely have another thirty years of life. What are you going to do with it?

Neoteny beckons each of us to listen to our childhood self, to someone who wasn't afraid; to someone who ran and cycled, letting the body and mind roam. We were funny, inquisitive, and spirited. We had little use for money and even less patience for pain and sickness. It's time to recapture that spirit, find that creative center, and build our new work from it. The burden of our job years can be traded, or at least supplemented, by regaining control of our sense of self. We can renew our hope for tomorrow, and restore our drive to be someone significant.

YOUR ACHIEVEMENTS COUNT

"I will work in my own way, according to the light that is in me."
LYDIA MARIA CHILD, NINETEENTH CENTURY WRITER, EDITOR, AND ACTIVIST

If we could sell our experience for what it cost us, there's hardly anyone alive who couldn't retire very comfortably at a ripe old age.

As a life coach, I'm continually surprised by how little credit people give themselves for most of their authentic accomplishments. My sister's lousy husband cheated on her. She lost her home, and was thrust into single motherhood with three hurt, angry, confused boys. Yet she went on to create an entrepreneurial venture, and eventually became an event coordinator at one of the world's leading technology corporations. At least, that's how I see it. But in a recent phone conversation, my sister told me that she had nothing to show for her life. I mentioned the obvious: providing a home and college education for her children, her deep love and respect for others, the friends she has nursed through terminal illness, and on and on. Her reply? "Those don't count."

EVERYTHING counts! If your life's work involved making just one person happy every day, with a simple gesture, kind word, or gentle touch, by now you would have made approximately 14,600 humans happy. What we have done for ourselves alone dies with us. What we have done for others and the world truly adds up. If you look at it this way, we aren't just young twice. We are immortal.

Look back at the first half of your life. Make a list of what you consider your most important contributions, in order of their importance to you. After these contributions, list your other achievements, followed by your activities, also ranked in terms of importance to you. For each noted item, list the skills you developed or strengthened as a result of those contributions, achieve-

Contributions	Skills Developed	How These Skills Drive New Work
Achievements	Skills Developed	How These Skills Drive New Work
Activities	Skills Developed	How These Skills Drive New Work

ments, and activities. Finally, list the ways that your skills may help drive your new work for the second half of your life. You may want to re-create the chart on page 173 in your chronicle.

Next, describe yourself as you are now and as you have been in the past. Compare these descriptions with what you may become in your second half of life.

What am I now?	What have I been?	What may I become?

Continue to work along these lines by providing the following information:

- What terms would an objective person use to describe me today?
- What terms no longer apply to me?
- What new terms would I like people to use about me in the second half of my life?

Finally, list ten traits that would add worth and significance to your second half of life.

All these skills, strengths, terms, and traits are the resources that you bring to your work as a developing person in the second half of life. Look how much you have going for you, and look what you've accomplished! Do you want to know a secret? Younger people look at you and hope to have a life like yours: a house, a job, and a family. You have done all those things, and more. The first part of your life was really the toil and trouble, the noise and sweat to get you ready for the second half of your life, which will be a real work of art.

YOU'RE FIRED...UP!

. . . .

"I was smoking in my forties, but I am on fire in my fifties."
OPRAH WINFREY, TALK SHOW HOST, MAGAZINE PUBLISHER, AND ENTREPRENEUR

. . . .

Author Jim Gambone suggests that we get rid of the word *retirement* altogether. Like my friend Peggy, Dr. Gambone thinks we need a word with a larger vision for the future: one with a beneficial impact that leaves a permanent legacy for future generations. His term *refire*ment fits the bill.

Refirement is a positive, optimistic vision of the way to live a meaningful, youthful life. The word suggests energy, recommitment, anticipation, risk, nerve, verve, and drive. It says, "I've just begun" instead of "I guess I'm done." Say it out loud: "I'm going into refirement." Feel the difference?

When I announced my refirement to my class of three hundred college students, they all broke into spontaneous smiles of acknowledgment and respect. My sons were delighted with my refirement: "Mom, that's so you." And it's so you, too. Retirement sounds like loss and acceptance. Refirement sounds like rockets and thrust and lift-off! Let's give up retirement forever and concentrate on our own refirement.

To create the work of your refirement, ask yourself the following questions:

Retire or Refire?

What work would I do if money were no object?
What career do I wish I had explored?
What kinds of work do I find meaningful?
Time flies when I...?

You may not be ready, physically or financially, to leave your job; but refirement is the new work of your neotenous life. You can refire your current employment, relationships, and health. And as I suggested earlier, you can refire your wonder, curiosity, humor, and joy. Your soul is combustible, and your life's work is calling you to blaze a new trail.

Do-Over: Work Out

At this point in your life, you have a warehouse of talent and an inventory stocked with skills. To create your life as a work of art, you need to get out more, or in this case, to work out more. To discover your hidden genius and find meaningful work for the second half of life, you need to grow young—with your boots on. Your challenge is to refire your work with love. How? By loving your work.

As anthropologist Desmond Morris reminds us, "If our work does not feel like play, then we should ask ourselves whether we are in the right job. Our zest for life may have been suppressed, but genetically it is still there inside us, smoldering away beneath heavy layers of negative thinking. It is not easy to strip off those layers—we are all so sensitive, especially when younger, to criticism, mockery, and punishment—but it can be done."

Morris continues, "If we can find one area of activity where we feel the throb of uncrushed enthusiasm, we may be able to intensify it and expand it, until it blossoms into an exciting form of personal expression. It is there, lying dormant, waiting to be developed, because it is an essential part of what it means to be a human being."

Regardless of your current employment status, your second half of life is the time to take inventory of your talents and skills, and then rekindle an activity that you can do with enthusiasm. Let go of the criticism and punishments of yesterday. Get outside yourself, and find new passion in the work of helping others. This work, said octogenarian author Ethel Percy Andrus, "is the new image of aging, growth in self and service to all mankind."

Volunteering, in any capacity for any task, can be a rewarding way to make the transition from full-time employment to refirement. Abundant opportunities await you. Look around: How about your neighborhood churches, synagogues, hospitals, and schools? Researchers at Johns Hopkins University studied a group of 128 volunteers, aged sixty to eighty-six, who were involved in a program called Experience Corps, which placed them as tutors in urban schools. The study included a control group of similar adults who did no volunteering.

The benefits to the volunteer group were clear: 44% reported feeling stronger after the experience, and many reported an increase in social activity. By contrast, members of the control group showed an overall decline. The volunteer group experienced fewer falls than the control group. They were also more active mentally, which may help preserve their cerebral abilities as they age.

The National Senior Service Corps is a network that places older volunteers in assignments within their communities. The Peace Corps welcomes anyone with your experience and maturity; President Carter's mother, Lillian, joined when she was seventy-seven years old. Chicago resident Tim Kelley, seventy-four, a former Jesuit priest, and J. R. Phillips, a fourteen-year-old African American, have been together every weekend for three years through the Big Brothers Big Sisters program. Every Friday evening, sixty-five-year-old Claire Fitzgerald, who has nine grandchildren, opens her arms to comfort infants in the "cuddling center" of a nearby hospital in Palo Alto, California.

The decision to work in any capacity is the decision to stay active, mentally alert, and productive. As you grow in age, you'll discover that you have two hands—one for helping yourself and one for helping someone else. Now is your time to start new activities and set new goals. Your Do-Over is to volunteer in some new capacity for at least three hours a week. Regardless of your current schedule, you can probably make the time to do this. Work—volunteering, learning, or refiring—serves as a vehicle to drive your life not to the stop sign, but into the passing lane. Buckle your seat belt: If you're on the downhill side of years, you'll be picking up more speed. You'll pass the stereotypes, negative judgments, and people who have chosen to grow old instead of young. And best of all, if you become young twice, it won't be all work and no play.

Play

"If life doesn't offer a game worth playing, then invent a new one."
Anthony D'Angelo, inspirational author

. . . .

Did you know that when animals don't learn to play, they don't survive? Play is transformative. It creates a socialization that reaches across generations to encourage not simply survival, but friendship.

Children know instinctively how to play. A child's delight in play is too contagious to resist. Watch any schoolyard at recess, and you'll see children hurling themselves into the yard, bumping, tripping, bouncing, and laughing. I remember wanting to be the first third grader out of the room to capture a tetherball court and take on all comers. What do you remember? Four-square, kickball, jacks, marbles? We all felt trial, disappointment, belonging, and not belonging. We won some, and we lost some.

People of any age who are young at heart continue to play throughout their lives. There will always be playgrounds, recess, toys, and games for anyone who is driven to find them. The universe is one big playground, and our lives are made of the noises and games of the recess we choose to create. Desmond Morris puts it clearly: "How has evolution managed to give us such a powerful drive to explore the world in which we live? The answer is that we became neotenous apes. A neotenous animal is one that retains its juvenile characteristics into adulthood. In one sense, it is an animal that never grows up. We are like that, we never grow up. We retain the playfulness of childhood all through our lives. And playfulness is the quality that is essential for high levels of curiosity and inquisitiveness. Like children, we are always ready to try out something new, to develop it, to tame it, control it, and finally, using it to our advantage. So the secret to our motivation is that the human being is the ape that never stopped playing."

Humans need to be curious and playful, to explore the world, and to learn. We play practical jokes. We invent things throughout our lives. As we get older, play may be called by different names: science, art, dance, sport, or music. No matter what we call it, this drive to participate in playful activities exists because of our childhood desire to explore new toys, enjoy new games, and create new rhythms. After all, what is a vacation? It's a chance to recapture our traits of exploration, fun, and play.

THERAPLAY

Too many of us think of play as an indulgence. Even worse, we believe that people who play lack responsibility. But play is crucial to our mental health and happiness. Play lifts stress, refreshes and recharges us, restores our optimism, changes our perspective, and stimulates our creativity. But even more important, play may be the highest expression of our humanity: Play appears to allow our brains to exercise flexibility and maintain, perhaps even renew, the neural connections that embody our human potential to adapt. With adaptation, we are able to meet any set of environmental conditions, including aging.

Play is difficult to define because it encompasses so much variety, individual taste, and talent. In her book *Beyond Love and Work: Why Adults Need to Play*, physician Lenore Terr argues that play is an opening to our very existence. "It permits us emotional discharge without too much risk." According to play studies expert Brian Sutton-Smith, PhD, play is more than an attitude and more than an action. He considers play an alternative cultural form. "Like art and music," he says, "play has a verbal and body language all its own."

Studies continue to show that adults who have played the most throughout their lives have also lived the longest. But longevity is only half the story. In a recent groundbreaking study on aging, researchers from the Center on Aging, Health, and Humanities at George Washington University found that older adults who partic-ipate in playful activities like art or lawn bowling actually see their health improve. A group of seventy-five adults, aged sixty-five to one hundred years, who all engaged in playful activities at least once a week, reported that they took fewer medications, were less depressed, less lonely, and more active than a peer group of seven-ty-five similar seniors. Dutch researchers, citing a series of studies of video game playing, found that adults who play have better memories. They are cognitively more capable, and they're happier.

Play has been shown to be key in achieving lives of mastery, eminence, and joy in adulthood. Play can offer access to the gift-edness we all possess.

PICK YOUR PLAYGROUND

. . . .

"It is a happy talent to know how to play."
RALPH WALDO EMERSON, ESSAYIST AND PHILOSOPHER

. . . .

When something has wiggle room, we say it has play. It isn't rigid or fixed. You can't play unless you can move, figuratively or literal-ly. If you're stuck in the rut of growing old, then play will help you wiggle away from your fear, your loss, and your pain. Play can get us all off our duffs, away from our sad stories, and out of our bad habits. Play can redirect us into fresh thinking, feeling, and experi-encing. When you forget to play, you can lose your love of life. And loving every remaining day of your life is rule number one in the game of growing young.

I just bought a set of giant plastic jacks with a multi-colored rubber ball, which I keep in the kitchen. I play one game every time I have to do dishes. This activity keeps me coordinated, makes me smile, and almost makes me want to do dishes, although I tell my husband that two people can also play jacks and do dishes. Then he reminds me that we don't all play the same way. His idea of a playground is different from mine, and mine is probably different from yours.

We also differ significantly in play style. In studies of tic-tac-toe players, researchers at Pennsylvania State University observed differences along several dimensions. First, researchers noticed the high-velocity players: For them, the fewer the strokes, the better. On the other hand, low-velocity players engaged in the play of the play: They simply enjoyed making the moves. Researchers found that players also differ by strategy. Some play to win. Others play to not lose. For these players, a draw is as pleasurable as a win.

Some of us like to play in ways that test our physical skills, while some of us prefer pure strategy play, as in a game of chess. Others opt for word games and puzzles. And some of us—the very lucky ones—get to play for our work.

Whatever playground you choose, play is an exercise in self-definition. It drives us to the core of self. It reveals what we choose to do, not what we have to do. We not only play because we are, we play the way we are, and the way we could be.

RECESS

. . . .

"You can discover more about a person in an hour of play
than in a year of conversation."
PLATO, GREEK PHILOSOPHER

. . . .

Sometimes we lose sight of the fact that just being, just having the ability to inhale another breath, is fun. Do you remember recess? Not only did recess relieve the tension and tedium of school, it also provided fresh air, stories with friends, a snack, a slide, and a swing.

Why People Don't Play

As we age, we make all kinds of excuses (notice I did not say reasons) not to play.

"I never played much as a child."

"I feel silly."

"Playing is a waste of time."

"I don't have the energy."

"Kids play and adults work—that's just the way things are."

"Life is so hard right now that I just don't feel playful."

Giving us time to play and get our ya-yas out was one way to insure that we would have the control to work on math or spelling when we returned to class—or so the teachers hoped. We played by instinct, not even questioning whether we should have fun. Consequently, we just had fun.

Begin now to schedule daily recess for yourself. My friend Monica's idea of recess from a demanding real estate career is throwing a tea party for her grandchildren. Another friend, Carol, likes to "fluff" and redecorate her home. Whatever you do, relieve yourself of today's tension, tedium, homework, and assignments. Get some fresh air. Remember what you liked to do as a child? Go back as far as you can. If you can't remember, phone your siblings or old friends and ask them what you used to play. Then do it. Or hop on a swing and see how high you can go. I started skipping instead of running during my workouts. Getting there wasn't half the fun; it was *all* the fun. Isn't it great to be older and not care how silly you look?

As I was skipping back to my car the other day, an older man smoking a cigar was watching me. As I approached, he chuckled and asked, "You're going to live forever, aren't you?" I shamelessly plugged, "No, I'm just young twice." I thought that after seeing me, he might move a little more, or smoke a little less the next day. Play can be contagious, and by simply playing, you may help others to do the same.

Checkout Receipt

Aram Public Library

Renew your items online:
www.sharelibraries.info

Title: You're Only Young Twice : 10
Do-overs To Reaw...
Call Number: 155.66 BEA
Item ID: 33111005858507
Date Due: 11/27/2018

Eat breakfast for dinner, play on the floor, don't clean up, play with your food, and buy a comic book. Or write down the names of four friends who really know how to have fun, and schedule a play date with each one. Your recess can also be a chance to learn some playful skill you've always wanted to master, like magic tricks or juggling. Use your play to release your inhibitions and constrictions. "In every real man, a child is hidden that wants to play," said German philosopher Friedrich Nietzsche. Let him—or her—out!

Do-Over: Exercise Your Right to Play

A long time before I ever thought about writing this book, a friend of mine recruited me into the Society of Childlike Persons. I would like to add you to this elite group of folks who are going to prove, once and for all, that *you're only young twice.*

On page 184 is the official Right to Play checklist of the Society of Childlike Persons. Each day pick at least one thing from this list and do it during a daily recess.

No matter how old we are, we are still that little boy or girl who played catch, skipped rope, roller-skated on the sidewalk, flew a kite, skinned knees, and raced to buy popsicles from the ice-cream man. Your need to play doesn't diminish with age. No self-help book, life coach, or well-meaning friend can tell you what will give you pleasure and feel like play. You have to find this out for yourself. Each day ask yourself, "Have I done anything fun yet?"

The founder of Motorola, Bob Galvin, is a windsurfer. Former Securities and Exchange Commission Chairman Arthur Leavitt Jr. leads Outward Bound expeditions. Both architect Frank Gehry and former Los Angeles Mayor Richard Riordan play hockey. All are charter members of the Society for Childlike Persons, and now you are a member, too. You support the vision that while you cannot deny the aging process, it doesn't have to define you.

Society of Childlike Persons
Right to Play

walk in the rain
jump in mud puddles
collect rainbows
smell flowers
blow bubbles
stop along the way
build sand castles
watch the moon and stars come out
say hello to everyone
go barefoot
go on an adventure
sing in the shower
have a merry heart
read children's books
act silly
take a bubble bath
get new sneakers
hold hands and hug and kiss
dance
fly kites
laugh and cry for the health of it
climb trees
take naps

birthday parties
wonder around
feel scared
feel mad
feel sad
feel happy
give up worry, guilt and shame
stay innocent
say yes
say no
say the magic words
ask lots of questions
ride bicycles
draw and paint
see things differently
fall down and get up again
talk with the animals
trust the universe
stay up late
do nothing
daydream
play with toys
play under the covers
have fights
learn new stuff pillow
get excited about everything
be a clown
enjoy having a body

picnic areas
beaches
listen to music
playgrounds
find out how things work
make up new rules
tell stories
save the world
make friends with the other kids on the block
see the first light of dawn
write in a journal
leave a telephone hug
frequent amusement parks
meadows
mountain tops
swimming pools
forests
summer camps
circuses
cookie shops
ice cream parlors
theaters
aquariums
zoos
museums
planetariums
toy stores
festivals
OTHER...

...and do anything else that brings more happiness, celebration, relaxation, communication, health, love, joy, creativity, pleasure, abundance, grace, self-esteem, courage, balance, spontaneity, passion, beauty, peace, and life energy to you and other humans and beings on this planet. Presented with celebration and joy!

Dr. Ronda Ann Beaman, vice chairperson
Society for Childlike Persons

Learning

· ·

"Anyone who stops learning is old,
whether at twenty or eighty.
Anyone who keeps learning stays young.
The greatest thing in life is to keep your mind young."
HENRY FORD, FORD MOTOR COMPANY FOUNDER

· ·

As I know you have learned by now, *You're Only Young Twice* is not about medically prolonging life. Rather, it introduces the concept of neoteny as a viable means to insure that a longer life is worth living.

Growing young can be accomplished on many fronts, most of which we've already discussed. But none of these age-defiant characteristics is more practical, or more easily integrated, than the quality of lifelong learning. "It is cognitive capacity, more than any physical disability, that most often determines whether people can attain extreme old age while remaining active," explains Margery Silver, EdD, a Harvard University neuropsychologist. Psychologists like Silver are proving almost daily that humans in their later years have far more physical and mental strength than previously imagined.

In fact, according to Peter Martin, PhD, a professor of human development at Iowa State University, "No matter what your age, the brain is still trainable. You can teach an old dog new tricks." The mental decline that most people experience isn't due to the steady death of nerve cells; rather, it's caused by the gradual atrophy of brain cell connections. This atrophy is caused by engaging only in routine behaviors—the things we do day in and day out with no imagination, change, or drive. Many of these behaviors are subconscious and require little brainpower.

PSYCHOSCLEROSIS

We spend most of our lives protecting ourselves from surprises, risks, and setbacks. What's the end result? A predictable life, free of surprises, that produces a "hardening" of the mind. This hardening keeps us a long distance away from the flexibility, acceptance, and open-mindedness of our original childlike brain. More than anything, this protection of the status quo ages us, makes us bores, and creates in us a reluctance to expand or extend ourselves. What then? Our lives pass us by, and we are old too soon.

Education and learning don't impose an age limit on those who pursue it. Why bother learning something new at ninety-three, or for that matter, at twenty-three? It's simple: Learning makes you viable, vibrant, and vital. You grow young with each new thing you learn. Have you ever noticed that when you're driving to an unfamiliar destination, it seems to take a surprisingly long time to get there? And once you know how to get there, does the trip seem shorter? It's the same thing with life. If you drive the same road of life over and over again, decades will speed by unnoticed. Take new roads by implementing your Do-Overs, learning Italian, taking up tennis, or playing harmonica. My friend Nancy and I are sharing a horse named Lucy who "schools" us every day.

As time slows down, your brain becomes less nimble. You must continue to try new things to prevent the number one killer of youth: what I call *psychosclerosis*, or a hardening of the categories. Never be satisfied with knowing how to get there, or with what you can already do. If you've never done a crossword puzzle, try one. If you do jigsaw puzzles, advance to a 3-D version. If you play bingo, try something that uses more brainpower, such as bridge. My mother-in-law Sandra plays bridge three or four times a week, calling it "mental aerobics." Educate yourself about local or international history, music, and art.

"The pursuit of truth and beauty is a sphere of activity in which we are permitted to remain children all our lives," said Albert Einstein. The contest is to do something that challenges and engages your mind, not because it's difficult, but because it's different from what you normally do. Al Siebert, PhD, who has studied resilient seniors, discovered that they have a "childlike curiosity and a lifelong love of learning." By contrast, Siebert found that people who die in their fifties and sixties often have this life trajectory: school, then work, and then leisure. Resilient seniors who live well into their eighties and nineties combine all three variables throughout their lifetimes.

UNIVERSITY OF LIFE

Life itself provides all the learning experiences we need. Everyone is granted admission, everyone is entitled to study, and everyone will be graded on their own merits. We are all responsible for our own destinies, our own definitions of success, and our own graduations. We choose our own teachers and create our own curricula. By choosing this book and reading this far, you have already learned some new ideas, confirmed some old ideas, and been challenged to discover and learn more. You're ahead of most people.

Now I suggest that while you're at it, you continue to apply the youth-boosting Live and Learn Guidelines on the next page, which will create additional learning opportunities as you grow young.

Last year I decided that I would learn to knit. It was an honoring gesture to both of my grandmothers, and I also thought it would be good for my coordination, patience, and holiday gift list. But I was terrible at knitting. I was trying so hard to make the best mitten in the class, do it the fastest, and be the teacher's pet—I gave myself a backache and headache from so much concentration and effort. It turns out that knitting is not meant to be a contact sport or Mensa challenge. Like you, most of my prior learning experiences were about having the right answer, being on the upper end of the bell curve, and not making errors in grammar or

Live and Learn Guidelines

- Become childlike in your curiosity.

- Look ahead to what can be, not back at what was.

- Gather information from many sources.

- Find people to play with you.

- Experiment again and again.

- Take chances at every chance.

- Make many mistakes.

spelling. I unconsciously transported all those rules and expectations to knit one, purl one, and that took all of the fun out of it. School was rote, but it wasn't right.

Instead of rote learning, it's vital that we look ahead to the joy of learning for our own interests and involvement, rather than dwell on the negative aspects that formal schooling often brings. After the knitting fiasco, I looked for a way to blow off my pent-up frustration at being so very bad at it. I discovered a fitness regimen called Pilates, something new to learn and test myself. My coach, Ardy, helps me keep it all in perspective. I'm not the best at it, and I'm not competing with anyone, but I'm doing what's most valuable: I'm learning.

I am going to share with you a mantra that focuses on the pursuit of lifelong learning. While simple, it is truly effective and should be chanted on a daily basis: *"There is no right answer, there is no wrong answer."*

That's it.

When I am giving presentations or workshops (or even when I'm alone, still attempting to knit), I ask everyone in the room to close their eyes and repeat this mantra with me. At first, people laugh or feel a little uncomfortable; but by the third time through, I can feel palpable relaxation in the room. People let down their performance anxiety, their previous rigidity about having to know the answers. They begin to enjoy the session, and they're more open to learning. Try making this your mantra the next time you take on a new challenge. You'll be surprised how much more fun your learning will be.

I always remind my students that my classroom is a "mistake-making place." If they knew all the material, and always had the right answers, then they wouldn't need me or my class. By now you have discovered that life itself is a mistake-making place. And it never gets any easier. Maybe you're afraid to learn something new, afraid of feeling or looking stupid. I have a little piece of advice that may help you: GET OVER IT. Age brings you more freedom to experiment, less concern about judgment, and more leeway to be carefree. Making mistakes, trying new things, falling, and then dusting yourself off is hard work. Failure in any venue is messy, troubling, and often defeating.

Remember the words of poet and Nobel Prize winner Rudyard Kipling: "Gardens are not made by singing 'Oh how beautiful,' and sitting in the shade." What you may lose by not sowing and growing your mind will cost you a lot more than the criticism of some negative people. It will cost you the chance to create, enhance, and embellish your own garden of ideas, hopes, and dreams. Choosing to stagnate rather than cogitate will really cost you the chance to be young twice.

YOUR MIND CAN TAKE YOU ANYWHERE

When I left for college, my father sat me down and gave me an incredible piece of advice. Most of my fellow students, he said, will finish their homework, complete their assignments, and do only what it takes to get the grade and move on. My dad suggested a different approach. "This is your chance to read books no one assigns, and find out about things that interest you—just because they interest you." He advised, "Don't come home to us every weekend. Go visit your friends' families and see how they live.

Then question your beliefs and ideas in comparison to theirs." Dad went on to say that all the collected knowledge of humankind would be housed in the libraries of my campus, within walking distance of my dorm. He encouraged me to talk to professors outside of class about their choice of discipline and study, and go to foreign movies and student-written plays. "Have an intimate encounter with this golden time and make the most of it," he said. "Doing this will serve you well the rest of your life."

I'm happy to report that this was one piece of parental advice I really followed. My brain was in overdrive throughout college. But this four-year opportunity flew by. When it ended, I got busy with my career, raising my family, getting ahead, and building a life. My brain was marinated in the information it needed to raise babies and write advertising slogans, but got pretty mushy in the disciplines I couldn't "use" on a daily basis.

Now, thanks to the gift of living many years beyond my college days, I have an increasingly less structured schedule and more discretionary income. Just as important, all the collected knowledge of humankind is still available. In fact, it's even more available now to you and me. We have a second chance at a curriculum of our choosing, based on our interests and applicable to our needs. Enrollment in lifelong learning offers us more years in our life and more life in our years. Besides, we've already paid the tuition!

We've moved from the strivings of our youth, with its test scores and rank standings, to the knowledge, integration, and perhaps even wisdom of our later years. As comic Tom Wilson reminds us, "Wisdom doesn't necessarily come with age. Sometimes age just shows up all by itself." It was wise of me to follow my father's college advice to make the most of my chance to learn; and it would be wise of us all to follow it now.

Many colleges and universities serve older adults by offering discounted tuition, counseling, and financial aid for seniors who want to earn a degree. Many offer specially designed continuing education courses for people in retirement, and most campuses host Elderhostel programs.

A young student of mine said that he always thought Elderhostel was a group of angry old people. In truth, Elderhostel is a program that brings students, mainly age sixty and older, from all parts of the world to a college campus to spend a week or longer. Students take short, intensive courses, usually taught by regular university faculty. Courses range in interest from local history to international cooking. In 2002 more than 500,000 people registered for this experience. Faculty members describe Elderhostel students as challenging, independent, curious, self-directed, and motivated by intrinsic rewards like self-esteem and creative expression. Not one commented that students were old or hostile!

Recultivate faith in yourself as a learner. Your community probably has a Parks and Recreation Department. One of its purposes is to offer classes on everything from pottery to salsa dancing to Thai cooking—just so you can have a chance to learn. Educational television programs probably broadcast to your home. And there's a library in your neighborhood. So you have no excuse to stop learning, stop growing, or stop at all. Adult learning theory shows that adults are better learners than children; we shouldn't be stalled in the drive to re-engage our brains.

I AM STILL LEARNING

. . . .

"Intellectual blemishes, like facial ones, grow more prominent with age."
FRANCOIS DE LA ROUCHEFOUCAULD, CATHOLIC BISHOP AND
FRENCH REVOLUTION MARTYR

. . . .

Spanish artist Francisco de Goya is known for his self-portraits. In 1826, at age eighty, he created one of his most famous works, a black chalk drawing titled *Aún Aprendo*. At this stage of his life,

Goya was also experimenting with the new technology of lithography, a method of producing signed and numbered copies of a limited edition. Copies? Today, these limited edition copies can make a few wealthy owners feel very special indeed. Goya's late-in-life drawing translates as "I am still learning."

A friend of mine told me she didn't want to go back to school because she would be sixty-two years old by the time she got her bachelor's degree. I said, "You're going to be sixty-two anyway, so you might as well be sixty-two with a diploma." You see, we are all special limited editions, and we are the artists of our own lives. We are designed to continue learning and adapting throughout our lifetimes. But the only due dates, late assignments, or failing grades we have now are the arbitrary ones we impose upon ourselves. *Learn* is an active verb. Your continuing education is something you must tailor to yourself, not something you can get ready-made. You've already received an education from your teachers. Now it's time for your second education, the more important and personal one—the one you give yourself.

In terms of neoteny, adults and children do learn in different ways. As adults, we should now have a deeper sense of ourselves, our time, and what's worth learning. Take a moment and ask yourself what's worth learning, and why. Consider these questions, and add your thoughts about them to your Young Twice Chronicle.

What are your hobbies?

Do you like to travel? Where have you traveled?

Have you learned anything new in the past two years?

Do you plan to try anything new or different in the future?

Could you answer those questions? Why or why not? Imagine being asked the same questions by a young person in your life.

What picture would your answers draw? What could your answers teach a younger person about who you are and about the value of a long life?

Perhaps you've never thought about it this way, but you are really pursuing a terminal degree that will take your whole life to complete. Your answers to the questions above are a good place to begin your course work. You can avoid the class, forget the homework, never study, and ignore your results; but come on—you already did all that in high school or college. You now have a chance to graduate with honors in living and learning.

Learning isn't something we can see externally, yet too often we make corrections to our lives only on the outside. Of course, if it makes you feel better, carve up your face: remove blemishes, bags, spots, and signs of time passing. But look inside as well: Did you respond negatively, or not at all, to the questions I asked above? Worse, have you no questions of your own to ask? Then you're failing your comprehensive exams. Do you have plenty of excuses for not developing your mind, spirit, or potential by learning about yourself, others, and the world? Then it doesn't matter how few wrinkles you have or how many push-ups you can do. You'll be old for the remaining days of your life.

"With age comes the inner, the higher life," said Elizabeth Cady Stanton, nineteenth century women's rights leader. "Who would be forever young, to dwell always in externals?" Surely, the greatest tragedy of any life isn't the growing old; it's the failure to learn who you are and what you're capable of doing. Lifelong learning can give you the colorful lessons, knowledge, and materials to create an extraordinary self-portrait.

Do-Over: Back to School

Colleges and universities have orientation programs for incoming freshmen. One of the orientation activities requires new students to write down all possible major areas of study that might appeal to them. While this is just an exercise, and no one has to sign up for a specific major yet, the activity helps students get to know themselves.

To get into the college of your choice, you don't have to score 1600 on the SAT college admissions exam, or write an extraordinary essay, or even pay tuition. You can write to any college or university in the country and ask for a catalog of courses; once they arrive, you are ready to mentally enroll.

. . . .

"Sixty years ago I knew everything; now I know nothing. Education is a progressive discovery of our own ignorance."

WILL DURANT, PULITZER PRIZE–WINNING WRITER AND HISTORIAN

. . . .

As an incoming freshman in the Young Twice program, it's now your challenge to find an area of interest. You're not restricted to prerequisites or class standing, so you can take all the courses that interest and excite you. You'll probably see courses that were unavailable when you were in school. Make a list of all the courses that sound interesting, intriguing, or challenging. Do you see any patterns? Do people, things, or ideas interest you? Do you prefer hands-on classes? Lectures? What do your choices reveal about your interests? Your personality? What are you driven to learn at this point in your life?

Once you've identified some things you would like to learn, your homework, due yesterday, is in the chart on the next page.

On his seventieth birthday, American poet and educator Henry Wadsworth Longfellow wrote a letter to a friend, in which he compared his life and career to climbing a mountain. Having climbed to the summit, wrote Longfellow, he could look back with some degree of pride at all the peaks he had scaled. Yet on the horizon were ever more mountains, higher and more difficult, that he might or might not have the strength to climb. "That is the whole

Homework

- Choose your own learning goals: You don't have to get a degree or an A. You can decide how far or how long to pursue the learning.

- Choose your topics wisely: This learning isn't compulsory. No one will subtract points if you don't show up. But by giving it your all, you are guaranteed the health and emotional benefits of learning. Make sure it's something that turns you on.

- Give yourself credit: Take advantage of things you already know and enjoy so you can start out with confidence.

- Use every available resource: You can draw from a wide variety of people, organizations, media, and meetings. Videotapes, cassettes, and local college professors can all be valuable sources for your pursuits and interests.

- Final Exam: Determine the results you want from your learning, and measure them in ways that are most meaningful to you.

story," he concluded. "Amplify it as you may. All that one can say is life is opportunity."

Whether you choose to learn knitting or a new language, or to take on formal training in a new field, there will always be mountains of opportunity looming on your horizon. It's been said that a mind is a terrible thing to waste; and so is a day, an hour, or even a single moment. Learn something new every day, think a new thought, read a new book, dream a new dream. Dr. Seuss told us, "You're only old once." But through constant, never-ending learning, you can become young twice.

CHAPTER SEVEN

The Child Inside

. . . .

"Part of me is dying, maybe to let the rest of me come to life."
STEPHEN LEVINE, POET AND TEACHER

. . . .

Living is no different at the end of life than at the beginning. Light one of the leftover birthday candles from your last celebration. Watch the flame and notice its brightness. Although it gets smaller and smaller, the flame is as bright at the end of the candle's life as at the beginning. So it is with life; it has no age. It can shine brightly at any and every moment.

Human beings are both wise and foolish at any age. We're filled with optimism or soured by setbacks. We're alive and kicking or silenced and numb. Some people in their sixties and seventies feel or fear abandonment and loneliness. They're sure that they'll get sick, and no one will show any interest in them. But look closer: Chances are these adults also felt this way as children. Many people feel "old" at age twenty or eighty, yet others retain their zest for living at any age. These zestful people have decided, often unconsciously, to capture and treasure their neoteny despite the turbulence life can bring.

Most of our fears about aging are really childhood memories that we haven't addressed. Fear is what keeps our character rigid; it's derived from the past and projected into the future by our thoughts. I believe that most of us direct our attention to what the outside world is doing to us, instead of what our inner world looks like. I've asked you to look more deeply within, to relinquish your surface in favor of your depth.

What are your concerns about aging, retirement, inactivity, isolation, economics, illness, disability, and death? I believe that people die of disease, not of old age. What makes us feel old, lonely, and fearful is the accumulation and fixation of past emotions that have no relevance to our present lives. As a life force, being young twice focuses on how our psychosocial attitudes can allay the fear and denial of aging. The practice of neoteny reminds us that it's never too late to have a happy childhood. While it's true that you can't go back and make a new start, you can start now to create a brand new ending.

The ideas and information about neoteny presented throughout this book are reminders of where your journey began, and visions of where it can and should end. Make a decision to incorporate the ten traits of neoteny into the practice of your living. By doing so, you will virtually be turning back time and giving birth to the Outlook, Language, and Drives that you need to youthen.

The Ten Traits of Young Twice
1. Resilience
2. Optimism
3. Wonder
4. Curiosity
5. Joy
6. Humor
7. Music
8. Work
9. Play
10. Learning

Think for a moment. How will you ignite each neotenous trait? What can you rebuild, what are you willing to try, and what can you look forward to adding or subtracting in your daily life? Once more, write those reflections in your Young Twice Chronicle.

The rest of this chapter will describe how the ten neotenous traits are all encouraged and enlivened by a single other quality. It's a part of each trait, a part of each promise, and a part of each person. To engage this final trait, there is not so much a do-over as a do-always. Although you change a great deal as you get older, deep within you, you carry certain clearly recognizable styles, traits, and attitudes belonging to the child inside. That child lives on in your heart and loves you.

The Youngest of These Is Love

"Age does not protect you from love, but love to some extent protects you from age."

Jeanne Moreau, actress and producer

Above and beyond each childlike trait I've presented as a way to grow young, the most central and centering is *love*. A child is born with the need to be loved and the need to love others. These needs remain with us throughout our lives. I've saved this final neotenous trait for last because it's the trait that beyond all others makes us human, makes us whole, and makes us young. Love is the power behind our resilience and optimism, the fuel for our wonder and curiosity, the essence of our joy, the core of our humor, the energy behind our music, the motivation for our work and play, and the penultimate lesson in our learning. Ashley Montagu described love as "the most perfect of all conservers of mental and physical health, the highest form of intelligence, and the most effective of disciplines."

Some people are happier and healthier giving love, while others need to feel loved to remain healthy. Numerous studies show that love does indeed improve our health. These studies look at love not only in the context of primary relationships, such as marriage, but also in the context of a person's general social support and connection to others.

Researchers from the University of California at Los Angeles analyzed data from the MacArthur Successful Aging Study, a seven-year look at the physical and mental health of 18,189 people in their seventies. They found that a strong network of loving family and friends actually helped slow cognitive decline among the long-lived. "We looked at the degree to which you have ties," said lead researcher Teresa Seeman, "and also the quality of those ties. What we found was that the more emotional support and satisfaction you perceived you had from loved ones, the better your brain functioned as you aged."

You can make great progress by starting the comedy club suggested in Chapter Four, by volunteering, or by enrolling in Elderhostel or a similar learning opportunity. These activities will help you build a deeper and broader base of emotional support, and perhaps even meet new people to love. In fact, each neotenous trait and its matching Do-Over is intended to build a bulging bank account of emotional support, affection, and love for you on your path to becoming young twice.

Love and Survival author and physician Dean Ornish conducted a study at Yale University that involved 119 men and 40 women undergoing coronary angiography. Those who felt the most love and support had substantially fewer blockages in their heart arteries compared to the other subjects. In a related study, researchers looked at almost 10,000 married men with no prior history of angina. These men had high-level risk factors, such as elevated cholesterol, high blood pressure, and diabetes. The men who felt that their wives didn't show them love experienced almost twice as much angina as the men who felt that their wives did show them love. Love makes more than the world go'round.

While feeling loved appears to benefit health and longevity, giving love seems to do the same. The results of a study of more than 700 elderly adults showed that the effects of aging were influenced more by what the participants contributed to their social support network than by what they received from it. In other words, the more love and support they gave, the more they benefited. Studies conducted at the Institute for HeartMath in Boulder Creek, California, confirm the health-improving and life-affirming effects of love on the human body. By studying the heart's rhythms, researchers have discovered that when we feel love—or any positive emotion such as caring, compassion, or gratitude—the heart sends messages to the brain and secretes hormones that positively affect our health.

With all that we know about love, hear about it in music, see it in movies, and read about it in books, why can't we express it more in the day-to-day world? When I'm working with a group of teachers, I often ask them to pair up, look into each other's eyes, and take turns saying, "I love you." Considering the uncomfortable grimaces, giggles, glances, and refusals I get, you'd think I had asked them to say, "You're ugly." I try to make the point that a teacher is really saying "I love you" every day, implicitly and explicitly, to strangers in a classroom. This is a revelatory exercise for everyone: teachers, CEOs, mid-life boomers, and older zoomers. In the real world, when we reach out for love, we are shut down and out so often that by the time we're about thirty, we don't want to risk getting hurt anymore. Consequently, we don't love as much anymore. But we must take that risk. In growing young, love is the definitive, driving force.

Love as a neotenous trait is not limited to or narrowed by roles, expectations, or definitions. A neotenous love can be the love you feel for your dog, cat, fish, or plants. It can be love for a co-worker, parent, child, sibling—or even unknown children on a playground. Neotenous love can also be the regard you feel for the checker at the grocery store, or even the grouch at the dry cleaners. Ultimately, love, like life, begins and ends with you.

FALLING IN LOVE AGAIN

"You, yourself, as much as anybody in the entire universe, deserve your love and affection."

THE BUDDHA, MYSTIC AND FOUNDER OF BUDDHISM

As you have learned, you are aging most fully when you are aging within your spirit. What if you are without love, and unable to feel? What if you've lost your inner resilience, and feel burdened with the past and afraid of the future? Then a large part of you is already dead. *You're Only Young Twice* encourages you to turn away from your old convictions about aging, turn away from deception and cover-ups, and rekindle your bright and burning flame. Learn to love yourself. Fall in love again with the innocence, hope, magic, and purity of your childlike self. Through this love, we all may feel what author Anne Lamott felt: "Age has given me what I was looking for my entire life—it has given me, me." Think of the following as a set of bonus do-overs to help you do-always.

Falling in ∨ Love Again

- *What I like about me*
- *Think it, believe it, achieve it*
- *Be your own best friend*
- *Collect love letters*
- *Have compassion for yourself*
- *It's all about you*

What I Like About Me

Make a list of things you like about yourself. Don't concentrate on externals; look instead at who you are, what you believe, what you cherish, and what you value. How do you contribute? Be as honest and immodest as you can be. It's important to blow your own horn, or at least toot it. As we get older, we often forfeit the very things we liked best about ourselves. Why? Because we—or others—think we should have outgrown them. We quiet down and fade away.

If you're having trouble thinking of things you like about you, try thinking of things you value in your friends. These people are probably your friends because they are like you—so add their qualities to your list. Create a special notebook for your "What I Like About Me" list that makes you happy, and keep adding to your list. Look at the notebook any time you're feeling down, or every day if you can. Give that child inside at least one truly loving piece of feedback daily to hold on to and build upon.

Think It, Believe It, Achieve It

Make it a daily habit to think about all the things you like about yourself. Because of the self-help movement and the backlash of self-esteem programs, being kind to ourselves has gotten a bad rap. If we lose the habit of praising ourselves, we may also stop praising others. Our kindness gene shrivels. That's why so many young people think of older people as mean. But praising ourselves is healthy and helps create more acceptance of others. When we love and approve of ourselves, we are happier and freer, and we can spread love to others.

Be Your Own Best Friend

Think of a person you love and admire: someone who loves you. Think about why you love and appreciate that person. Notice how the love feels inside, and then turn it around and imagine that person feeling the same love for you. See yourself the way your friend does. Why would someone love you? Feel it, relish it, and let yourself see yourself through that friend's love.

Collect Love Letters

Every time someone says something nice about you, or when you receive any kind of positive feedback, write it down in your "What I Like About Me" notebook. If someone writes something nice in a card, save it. Look at these notes when you need a reminder of what makes you lovable. I started a collection like this when I began teaching. Whenever I felt that I was in the wrong line of work, looking at those cards and letters really encouraged me. You'll be continually delighted when you look at the thoughts and good wishes of people who care for you.

Have Compassion for Yourself

When you're feeling old or ugly, or think that life has passed you by, try to understand the source of that "noise." Look for an answer deep down inside. What's making you fearful? Why are you feeling insecure? Have you ever wondered why we can often remember the terrible and foul things written on bathroom walls, but have trouble memorizing a sonnet or love letter? That's our reptilian brain for you. We vividly remember the criticisms of others, our failures, and our shortcomings. Try to connect to the child inside who recalls those wounds, and really notice what he or she is feeling. Then put it into perspective: Consider the source of the pain or judgment, and release it. Feel compassion for the child who was hurt or criticized, love that child, and then love you.

It's All About You

Some of the ideas in this book will work for you, and others may not. Take a quiet moment to sit and ask yourself what you can do to feel more loving, more compassionate, and less judgmental. You know best what works for you and what feels natural. Know that you have great wisdom inside you. Your loving, childlike qualities are waiting to re-emerge and help you enjoy all that the rest of your life has to offer.

Beauty Is as Beauty Does

. . . .

"Try to keep your soul young and quivering right up to old age,
and to imagine right up to the brink of death that life is only beginning.
I think that is the only way to keep adding to one's talent,
to one's affection, and to one's inner happiness."

George Sand, novelist and feminist

. . . .

After a certain age, youth can come only from your loving heart. You've heard it said that in order to be loved, you must be lovable. It follows then, that in order to be young, you must be "youngable." People with neotenous traits don't seem to age. They retain their youthful characteristics and become more beautiful every day; their faces seem to shine.

When I first met my husband, who is seven years younger than I, I told him that I'd consider plastic surgery if I ever started looking too much older. He replied, "Do you know who is always the most beautiful woman in a room? It's certainly not the youngest, or most perfect, or even best dressed. It is always, without a doubt, the woman with a smile on her face and a kind word for everyone. It's the woman who feels comfortable in her own skin and radiates love and joy. No amount of plastic surgery can do that for anyone." I thought, *I could marry a man like that*—and I did! Since that conversation, I've never even considered plastic surgery. I've chosen instead to have "work done" on my resilience, joy, curiosity, and humor.

Wrinkles may show on your face, but lack of enthusiasm wrinkles your soul. You can decide how your wrinkles will develop. Will they be laugh lines or frowns, wide-eyed optimism or suspicious squints? You can fall in love with the wonders of this world, or sleepwalk through each day. You can build powerful muscles by reaching out to help carry others' burdens, or develop rounded shoulders from carrying only your own. Your feet can be tired from dancing or withered from waste. You can develop a more loving countenance every day, or you can avoid the mirror's reflection of what you've allowed yourself to become.

"If you are beautiful when you get older," says actor John Cleese, co-author of *The Human Face*, "it's not a free gift. It's because your face shows qualities that are timeless—strength, kindness, dedication, wisdom, enthusiasm, and humor, intelligence, compassion."

I know you believe in life, not death. If you're interested in living a long and youthful life; and if you are finding ways to show, by your eagerness, vitality, and enthusiasm, that you love living; then you have every right to expect and enjoy every one of your young-twice years. And those years will be deeply rooted in what matters most.

LOG OF LIFE

. . . .

"I asked myself the question, 'What do you want of your life?'
and I realized with a start of recognition and terror, 'Exactly what
I have—but to be commensurate, to handle it all better.'"

MAY SARTON, POET AND NOVELIST

. . . .

As I mentioned earlier, I have lived on top of a mountain where winds are blustery and inhospitable many days of the year. It takes a tremendous amount of resilience on the part of plants and trees to thrive in such an environment.

Not long ago I hiked up one of the hills. I felt my knees creak a little more than usual, noticed my slower pace, and generally felt wistful about my advancing age. Then I noticed a tall, spreading oak tree at the summit of the hill. The winds were howling, and the smaller, younger trees were buffeted and bent. But the regal old oak stood its ground with grace, pride, and power. The wide branches of this aged tree held nests and resting birds, and gave me shade. I could stand behind its trunk and protect myself from the wind. As I stood by this tree, I looked closely at its trunk, which was weathered, bumpy, wrinkled, and worn—not smooth, fresh, and pretty like the trunks of the younger trees around it.

I also noticed that the younger trees lacked purpose. They were too small to hold nests or give shade and protection. Nature holds many lessons for us, and as I stood close to this sturdy and weathered tree, I realized that it's not about the outside form of something, it's about the function. In other words, it's not how smooth or pretty we are, but how we are helping others, contributing, and making the world a better, safer, less threatening place. Life isn't about living forever; it's about living well and doing good things today.

Your future can be exciting, fulfilling, youthful, and vigorous. By branching out through the gifts of neoteny, you can determine and define a full life that you love living.

We begin to feel old when we perceive others' reactions to us; they agree that our face is that of an older person. When I got my first "ma'am" at the grocery store, when a stranger at the airport asked me if I had grandchildren, and when someone offered a senior discount at a movie, I was flabbergasted. I can see how other people my age look—but I look younger, I'm different. And so are you...or so we think.

Sooner or later, we all have to face the facts and the mirror. Yet we can interpret our mirrors cheerfully, angrily, or with indifference, depending on how much we love our lives and ourselves. If we are sure of ourselves, we stand steady through the winds of adversity, feeling content with what we have planted and reaped. If we love others and ourselves, we are planted joyfully in the gift of our future, and the misunderstandings and myths of aging are, at last, uprooted.

THE TITHONUS WISH

. . . .

"I think my present age, although it is very advanced, is my pleasantest and the finest of my life. I would not exchange my age and my life for the most flourishing youthfulness."

LUIGI CORNARO, *DISCOURSES ON THE SOBER LIFE*

. . . .

Humanity's longing for immortality is embodied in Greek mythology and the legend of Tithonus. When his wife mistakenly asked the gods to grant him eternal life instead of eternal youth, Tithonus wound up in an endless purgatory of decrepitude. To live a longer life, to merely achieve longevity, is a wrong and wretched wish. The myth of a fountain of youth has been part of human longing for at least two millennia. The legend of Tithonus gave our human longing a cautionary quality.

Ancient cultures, notably the Egyptians and Chinese, gave immortality an aura of quackery: More than 2,000 years ago, Chinese alchemists known as *thermatugists* devoted considerable energy to creating a "drinkable gold" as a means of prolonging life. Spanish explorer Juan Ponce de Leon's search for a mythical "Fountain of Youth" gave the quest an enduring ethos of futility. The search for immortality took a pseudoscientific turn in 1889, when respected scientist Charles Sequard claimed that he could rejuvenate old men with an injection containing crushed dog testicles. Sounds absurd, doesn't it? But how is it different from today's Botox or collagen injections?

Biologists, molecular scientists, and even etymologists (people who study the origin of words) are working around the clock, spending billions of dollars to help us stay younger longer. A recent study from Case Western Reserve University revealed that cockroaches do not age gracefully. After about sixty weeks of adulthood, roaches get stiff joints, which inhibits climbing, and hardened footpads, which prevents sticking to vertical surfaces. One of the researchers, noticing that the aged roaches seemed to have lost the ability to escape from predators, hypothesized that this loss was brain-based. He tested his hypothesis by removing the roach's head—and brain. Sure enough, for a short time the roach was once again able to flee like a youngster.

Would you remove a part of your brain to become more youthful? If you could make a wish or sip a magic potion to erase or extend your years, would you do it? Would you liberate yourself from your past memories, possibly surrendering your personality?

And which years would you subtract? The year you fell in love? What about the years your children were born? Would you take away the grief-filled year that was spent saying goodbye to someone you cared about? In removing painful memories, would you also remove the small section of your brain that recalls the smell of the lawns you mowed, or the memories of the first time you saw Paris?

Or can you, because you have chosen to be young twice, see the value and victory of each precious year? Can you be grateful for the years that have passed, and graceful in each promising year ahead?

There is no cure, no potion, and no possibility of not aging—except death. Death is inevitable; but you can die feeling old or die feeling young, and as late as possible.

In the movie *Shirley Valentine*, the main character is a middle-aged wife and mother of two grown children who finds herself talking to the kitchen wall while cooking dinner for her husband. She decides to travel in order to engage her curiosity and wonder, and to ignite her love and laughter. She doesn't want to wait until it's too late, believing, "Most of us die long before we're dead. And what kills us is the terrible weight of all this unused life that we carry around."

RE-BIRTHDAY

. . . .

"He is the most fortunate man who can bring the end of his life
round to its beginning again."

JOHANN WOLFGANG VON GOETHE, NOVELIST AND PLAYWRIGHT

. . . .

Because he feels so young at heart, my father-in-law Gary believes he's entitled to a discount on his real age. On his seventieth birthday last year, he claimed that with the discount he was actually fifty-six. This year, he added some travel and learning to his life, so now he has upped the discount, and is currently fifty-four. Gary is living proof that mere physiology, biology, and chronology do not govern age. As I have consistently pointed out, there is another more poetic and precise premise of age—it's your state of soul.

Inside you are all the exceptional neotenous qualities of humankind, given to you at birth as gifts to be cherished, developed, and enhanced, not discounted or denied. Neoteny is not immortality; it is *immutability*. Life may bring surrender, and you may succumb, but because you still have those birthday gifts of neoteny, you don't really change. What you were as a child, you are now. Your birthday candle is still burning bright.

There is unused life inside you. Don't extinguish it, don't let it weigh you down, and don't let it make you old. We can all be so much more than we are. Our greatness, our beauty, our extraordinary humanity is as individual as it is universal. Take the lessons, ideas, and suggestions in this book to heart. Re-read, review, and then renew your life. Live in neoteny. Catch yourself: Are you reacting to life as a *has-been* or a *will-be*? Youthen your mind, your spirit, and your tomorrows.

Play on the floor, climb a tree, and jump at any chance. Ask questions and share stories. Get out of your house, your chair, your way. *Grow young.* Center your days in optimism, romp in childlike joy, and delight in work and play. Learn, laugh, and do it every day, everywhere, with everything you've got. Make your own happy ending. The persistent practice of neoteny, of becoming young twice, allows you to redeem and revive all that was original and good and true within you, once upon a time.

And once is never, ever enough.

Acknowledgments

. . . .

*"At times our own light goes out and is rekindled by a spark
from another person. Each of us has cause to think with deep gratitude
of those who have lighted the flame within us."*

ALBERT SCHWEITZER, PHYSICIAN AND NOBEL PEACE PRIZE WINNER

. . . .

I am thankful for the ideas and illumination of Ashley Montagu
and Stephen Jay Gould. I value Martin Seligman and John
Hillman for taking life to a more positive place, and Mihaly
Csikszentmihalyi for evolving the concept. Credit is due to my
partners at PEAK Learning, Inc., for being my climbing team.

Deep and everlasting thanks to Ken and Carol Lorek for
encouragement and a place to call home; Karen, David, and Lauren
Mueller for the joy and support; Gaye Luna for the strength and
sisterhood; Peggy Rittmann for the royal treatment; Monica King
for a roof over my head and a place for my heart to land; Stephen
Stern for wise counsel and care; Angie Logan for making me look
good; Ardy Janku for making me feel good; Lydia and Ed
Heinbockel for advice and assurance; Sherri Buvick and Ana Bass
for being there from the beginning; Jeff Thompson for being my
big brother; Tina Shultz for really fixing me up; Gary Stoltz for
keeping me covered; Mike and Cindy Pimental for enhancing
decades and denying distance; Al Mason and family for giving me
my real start; all my friends in Shippensburg, Pennsylvania, for
becoming my hometown; Katie Martin for joining the clan; Sandra
Stoltz for being the first one who knew all my students, and
STARS for their example; Tim O'Hearn for the anticipation and
acceptance; Bruce and Teresa Lovelin for the home sweet cabin;
Eugene Hughes for believing in me; Mildred Haniford for being
everyone's role model; Susan Schmit for finding it all; Geraldine
Champion for naming it; Beverly Baltz for unending encourage-

ment; Sam and Nancy Mancino for always doing the neighborly thing; Hilary Grant for cleaning it up; and all my past and present childhood friends who came out to play with me. Lastly, my three boys: Chase for the light, Sean for the laughter, and Paul for the love. We *will* be forever young.

Selected Reading and Resources

Buford, Bob. *Halftime: Changing Your Game Plan from Success to Significance*. Chicago: Zondervan, 1997.

Chopra, Deepak. *Ageless Body, Timeless Mind*. New York: Harmony, 1993.

Chopra, Deepak. *Grow Younger, Live Longer*. New York: Harmony, 2001.

Cooper, Kenneth H. *Regaining the Power of Youth at Any Age*. New York: Nelson Books, 2005.

Cohen, Gene D. *The Mature Mind*. New York: Basic Books, 2005.

Csikszentmihalyi, Mihaly. *Finding Flow*. New York: Basic Books, 1997.

Dembe, Elaine. *Passionate Longevity*. New York: John Wiley and Sons, 2004.

Dychtwald, Ken. *Age Power: How the 21st Century Will Be Ruled by the New Old*. New York: Jeremy P. Tarcher/Putnam, 2000.

Gambone, Jim. *Refirement: A Guide to Midlife and Beyond*. Minneapolis: Kirk House Publishers, 2000.

Gerzon, Mark. *Listening to Midlife: Turning Your Crisis into a Quest*. Boston: Shambhala, 1992.

Jamison, Kay Redfield. *Exuberance: The Passion for Life*. New York: Knopf, 2004.

Langer, Ellen J. *Mindfulness*. New York: Addison Wesley, 1990.

Livingston, Gordon. *And Never Stop Dancing*. New York: Marlowe and Company, 2006.

Leider, Richard, and David Shapiro. *Claiming Your Place at the Fire: Living the Second Half of Your Life On Purpose*. San Francisco: Berrett-Koehler Publishers, 2004.

Montagu, Ashley. *Growing Young.* New York: McGraw-Hill, 1981.

Moran, Victoria. *Younger By the Day: 365 Ways to Rejuvenate Your Body and Revitalize Your Spirit.* San Francisco: HarperSanFrancisco, 2004.

Roizen, Michael F. *The RealAge Makeover.* New York: HarperCollins, 2004.

Rowe, John W., and Robert L. Kahn. *Successful Aging.* New York: Dell Books, 1999.

Sadler, William A. *The Third Age: Six Principles for Personal Growth and Rejuvenation after Forty.* New York: Perseus, 2001.

Sarton, May. *At Seventy: A Journal.* New York: W. W. Norton & Company, 1993 (reissue).

Scott-Maxwell, Florida. *The Measure of My Days.* New York: Penguin Books, 2000.

Seligman, Martin E. P. *Authentic Happiness.* New York: Simon & Schuster, 2002.

Sher, Barbara. *It's Only Late If You Don't Start Now.* New York: Delacorte Press, 1998.

Stoltz, Paul G. *Adversity Quotient: Turning Obstacles into Opportunities.* New York: John Wiley and Sons, 1997.

Stone, Marika and Howard. *Too Young to Retire.* New York: Plume, 2004.

Snowdon, David. *Aging with Grace.* New York: Bantam, 2001.

Thomas, William H. *What Are Old People For? How Elders Will Save the World.* Acton, MA: VanderWyk and Burnham, 2004.

Vaillant, George E. *Aging Well.* New York: Little, Brown, 2003.

Viorst, Judith. *Suddenly Sixty and Other Shocks of Later Life.* New York: Simon & Schuster, 2000.

Index

1/07

About the Author

Dr. Ronda Beaman is president of Second Wind, Inc., a midlife coaching center, and vice president of PEAK Learning, Inc., an international research and consulting firm. She is also an adjunct faculty member at California Polytechnic University in San Luis Obispo, California, where she teaches honors courses. Dr. Beaman also serves on the board of directors of the National Pay It Forward Foundation, a nonprofit organization that seeks to promote good deeds worldwide. She earned her doctorate in leadership at Arizona State University following a career in advertising and broadcasting. Additionally, Dr. Beaman is a certified life coach and personal trainer, and a wife and mother of two sons. Both *USA Today* and American Greetings named Dr. Beaman's family "America's Most Creative Family."

Dr. Beaman is a nationally recognized expert on leadership, health and wellness, education, psychosocial development, and communication. She has won numerous awards for her work, including being named the first recipient of the National Education Association's "Excellence in the Academy: Art of Teaching" award. She has conducted research in a host of arenas, and is author of a book on student development and many articles. She has extensive and international expertise in public speaking, and is described as a dynamic, inspiring, and thought-provoking presenter.

For information on *You're Only Young Twice* programs and workshops or Second Wind Life Coaching, please contact Dr. Beaman at www.youngtwice.com or call 1-800-255-5572.

MY HIDDEN
JOURNEY

My Hidden Journey

Sanjay Patel

To order additional copies of this book, contact:
Xlibris
844-714-8691
www.Xlibris.com
Orders@Xlibris.com
826433

CONTENTS

SPECIAL THANKS

My journey has had its ups and downs. I was only able to keep moving forward and stay positive with the help of some incredibly special people in my life. I would like to say thank you to all these important people who understood me, had my interests at heart, and lifted me up when I felt I was at a dead end.

To my parents, my late father Sureshbhai Motibhai Patel and my mother Savitaben Patel,

You are the reason I am here, and you taught me many qualities of life. You never showed your stress in front of us. You always smiled, even though you had hundreds of things going through your minds. Thank you for making me the person I am today.

To my wife, Jayshree (Jay) Patel,

I could not have found a better person to have next to me throughout this journey. You felt what I felt on every bumpy ride. You supported me unconditionally and worked hard to bring in income when we were in financial hardship. You supported me throughout our lives together. You challenged all my crazy ideas, which helped me realize that I may have overlooked or underestimated my calculations. Thank you for being my backbone and fighting for me when I showed my weakness.

To my son, Jaime Patel,

You have brought me joy every day. Even on difficult days, seeing you relieved my stress. As you grew into your late teens, we competed against each other in all sports and challenged each other. Now that you have become a man, our talks have become more mature. You are my right-hand man.

To my sister, Sadhana Patel,

We were always close in Uganda and in our early years in Britain. We supported each other and looked out for each other. We did the duties of adults when we were very young and learned a lot from each other. We were always a great team.

To my brother, Sandip Patel,

As you become older, you became more than a brother. We played sports together, we did household DIY projects together, and we partied hard with our East London friends and came home in the early hours of the morning together. You are someone whom I can trust with my life. Thank you for being the person I can call anytime because I know that if I need you, you'll be there.

To my Uncle Pravin and Auntie Ranjan,

You have been in my life ever since I was born, and you have given us courage and support in every way. We spent many weekends at your home and built up the strength for the week ahead. Thank you for being by our side through our journey.

To my cousins, Ajay and Bobby,

I will never forget each day that we have been together. You have been my breath of fresh air, and I couldn't live without you. You've made my life fun. We shared lots of laughter and got up to lots of mischief in our younger years. To this day we reminisce about all of our shared memories as if they happened yesterday.

To my friend, John Young,

You got me through my toughest time in my schooldays. You made me stronger and more assertive. You helped me build confidence just by being a friend, which I desperately needed. You understood my hardship and never belittled me. Thank you also for sending me a Christmas card every year without fail for over forty years.

To Xlibris,

Thank you to the publishers who gave me the opportunity to fulfill my dream of writing my book.

To Adrienne Stallings,

Thank you for your help in editing my story without compromising my vision.

And to everyone else,

I'd like to thank anyone who has been part of my life, cheered me on, given me moral support, encouraged me, and believed in me.

PROLOGUE

August 4, 2022 will be an important day for many Ugandans, Britons, Canadians, Indians, and countless others across the globe. It will mark the fiftieth anniversary of the day Idi Amin, the former president of Uganda, expelled Ugandan Asians from Uganda.

On August 4, 1972, Amin forced approximately eighty thousand Ugandan Asians to leave Uganda within ninety days. They were not allowed to take anything with them, having been ordered to walk out empty handed.

Most Ugandan Asians had British passports; therefore, they went to either Britain or Canada. Others went to South Asia, and some ended up elsewhere in Europe. Some did not make it anywhere at all and were left unaccounted for.

Apart from those who settled in South Asia, Ugandan Asians found it difficult to assimilate in their new countries. They were faced with multiple setbacks—language barriers, poverty, and racism. Even minor inconveniences like climate, cuisine, and clothing became gigantic hurdles. It took years, even decades, to get back on their feet, but they persisted and found a way forward through hard work, determination, will power, and sacrifice.

Having found peace and settled into their new lives, many Ugandan Asians now accept what happened fifty years ago. They look back at the fantastic life they had in Uganda and remember their journey through those fifty years. My journey is only one out of tens of thousands. And while I don't claim my story as the universal experience, the hardships we all had faced are ubiquitous.

IDI AMIN

General Amin, the seven years heavyweight boxing champion of Uganda, spent most of his army career as a sergeant. Dr. Milton Obote, who led Uganda gain independence from Britain in October 9th 1962, became the president, Amin was rapidly promoted to Chief of the Armed Forces.

On January 25th 1971, General Idi Amin seized power from President Obote, enacting a military coup while the president was attending the Commonwealth Conference in Singapore. Ugandan troops sealed off Entebbe Airport. Tanks and soldiers swarmed the streets of the capital, Kampala. The Obote's residence was surrounded, and all major roads blocked.

Amin declared himself President.

Life in Uganda

Something was happening in Uganda. The tension had been rising since Idi Amin came to power and Amin's behavior became increasingly violent. We heard stories of his brutality—that he had killed or ordered others to kill thousands of people. We worried yet thought nothing of it. We had hoped that we would be fine.

Before Amin came to power, we felt free. We loved Uganda. It was rare to hear a Ugandan Asian say that they did not enjoy their life in Uganda with its opportunities for business and adventure. Some even said there was no better place in Africa than Uganda. The weather was perfect all year round; the fruits and vegetables always tasted delicious and fresh; the land was filled with mountains, lakes, and wildlife. Why would anyone want to live anywhere else?

In the late 1800s and early 1900s, South Asians settled in Uganda after the British recruited nearly thirty-two thousand of them from South Asian countries to build the Ugandan railroads. Once the railroads were complete, most of the South Asians went back. Only about seven thousand stayed behind. By the 1970s, the number of Ugandan Asians had grown to around eighty thousand. Over a quarter of the Ugandan Asians were Gujaratis, just like my family.

My grandfather first came to Uganda and worked as a manager in a cotton factory after he was married. He retired in India in 1964. My dad was born in Uganda but went to India for four years to study accounting. To travel to India, they traveled by ship, which could take fifteen to twenty-one days depending on the weather. Passengers would pack their own food before boarding. I had the experience of making this journey once with my family when I was three years old. It was fun at the beginning, but quickly grew boring. Many people fell sick as the ship was jostled by the waves. I felt as though the ship would never reach the shore.

My family lived in Kampala, which capital of Uganda. Kampala sits on the northern side of the largest lake in Africa—Lake Victoria. We initially shared an apartment with my Uncle Pravin and Aunt Ranjan in the Market Mansion on Market Street, they moved into the unit next door after I was born. Their two sons, Ajay and Bobby were born few years after I was born.

The apartment we lived in was near a fruit and vegetable market and a huge taxi park. There was also a Hindu temple— the Shree Sanatan Dharma Mandir—a few minutes' walk away that we frequented. The slightly off-white surface and magnificent architecture of the temple stood out from far away. This was an extremely popular temple that was used by many Indians for their prayers and religious ceremonies.

Our apartment was comfortable with one bedroom, a kitchen, a bathroom, and a large living room. My parents slept on a double bed in the living room with my baby brother, Sandip, while my sister, Sadhana, and I slept on bunk beds in the bedroom. Being the smaller of the two, I slept on the lower bunk and Sadhana, who is two years older than me, slept on the upper one. When I was still very young, Mom would often sleep with me until I fell asleep before returning to her own bed.

Market Mansion was located above a row of shops. My family's apartment was directly above a bicycle store. The owners of the store were nice—they always greeted us as we entered the big doors on the right side of their store, which led into our community.

There were eleven apartments: one at the bottom of the stairs, five on the second floor, and five on the third floor. There was a very large terrace at the very top, which is where we gathered and socialized in the evenings. It was a wonderful place to take pictures. We'd dress up and let Dad take our pictures with his 35 mm Canon. "Stand here. Look there. Smile." He'd say.

We lived on the second floor. There were no elevators, just stairs that we climbed to get to our apartments. In the center, there was a communal area. Everyone knew everyone and treated each other like a big family. We welcomed each other into our houses, sharing food and cooking together. All the ladies would meet in one open communal area and the men in another while the children played anywhere they could. The men played badminton once a week in the communal area underneath the floodlights. We watched them from our balconies, clapping and cheering them on. This community was the best part of our lives.

In my very early years, I cried a lot. I had an unknown illness, and since I couldn't talk, I cried instead. I drove everyone mad. Even at night, I cried nonstop. Many times, Dad took me in the car and drove around until I fell asleep. When I was about three years old, Mom grew frustrated with not knowing why I cried. In her anger, she snapped a black string that had been tied around my wrist by a holy person. I stopped crying almost instantly. For some reason, that black string had something to do with why I cried. Some thought it was black magic.

Mom didn't want us children to play outside in the sun because our skin would turn dark. I didn't want to be dark. If I had to walk in the sun, I would run to the nearest shaded area. My cousins, Ajay and Bobby, were much fairer than me, almost as white as the British. People compared me to them. They always got the attention while I was ignored. I wanted to be fairer so people would like me, too.

Sadhana and I went to Nakivubo Primary School, which was about a ten-minute walk from our home. There, I had made many friends and we would eat lunch together and share our food. I liked school. Although I wasn't the brightest child, I loved to learn and did all my homework on time. I was very observant and preferred listening.

After school, Mom would teach me how to read and write Gujarati and Dad would help me with mathematics. I learned some

Swahili—Uganda's official language—as well. Most of the words I learned were for kitchen and food items since I learned from my mother's communication with the African boys who worked mainly in the kitchen for us. Most Ugandan Asians had servants. Some only had one or two, but the wealthier Ugandan Asians could have several. Our boys were hardworking and very punctual. We paid them a reasonable amount and gave them food, clothes, and extra money on some occasions. They seemed to be happy with our treatment and never complained or discriminated against us, and we felt we treated them well in return.

Our apartment didn't have air-conditioning, but we never felt overly uncomfortable. The temperature in Uganda hovered between 77- and 84-degrees Fahrenheit throughout the year with occasional heavy rainfalls. The evenings were simply perfect—not too hot nor too cold.

Because of the fair weather, Dad frequently drove us to the park, where we dressed up and took photographs. The park had a large clock imbedded in a flower bed, making the perfect backdrop for Dad's pictures.

I loved looking like Dad. His shirts and pants were always perfectly ironed, and he was always well groomed with his hair oiled to keep his head cool in the heat. Once, I tried to groom my hair like Rajesh Khanna, who was my favorite Bollywood actor, but Mom cut my hair so short I could never get the same style. Instead, Mom oiled my hair and parted it on the side, combing it like how Dad combed his hair.

Dad wore cuff links to work every day. I saw how professional and handsome they made him look and told Mom that I wanted some too. Since I was about five years old, my family laughed at me. However, Mom got me a white shirt and made holes in the cuffs so that I could have cuff links. She used Dad's cuff links since they did not make child-sized pairs, which were very heavy. I thought I looked smart. She tucked my shirt into my shorts (which I had outgrown but still wore for comfort purposes) and took me to the park to have photos done.

Mom, who was four feet ten inches tall, slim, and the sweetest lady you'd ever meet, would wear a nice sari, sit in the garden, and pose for the camera with the fabric fanned out on the ground around her. Dad never told Mom to smile, as she was always smiling anyway. He would just adjust the focus and capture the moment.

THE ANNOUNCEMENT

Things changed in early 1972. Idi Amin did not like Ugandan Asians running all the businesses and sending money overseas to their loved ones. He saw too many stores with Ugandan Asian names and felt that the Africans should own these stores instead. Uganda's economy was healthy, but it was run by Ugandan Asians, who were less than 1 percent of the population.

It was said that Idi Amin had a dream that God had talked to him regarding Ugandan Asians controlling the economy and leaving nothing for the Africans. Following this dream, he made the decision to expel the Ugandan Asians from Uganda.

On the morning of August 4th, 1972, Amin gave a speech wherein he decried the actions of the Ugandan Asians. He claimed they have refused to properly assimilate into Ugandan society and accused them of exploiting Uganda's economy for their own benefit, calling upon the British government to claim responsibility for this population.

He claimed the decision was for the economy of Uganda. In his eyes, though Uganda had been independent from Britain since 1962, they did not have control over their own economy since it was run by the Ugandan Asians. This expulsion, he believed, would be the key to wholly reclaiming Uganda for the Ugandan Africans.

When a reporter inquired about the consequences of the Ugandan Asians ignoring the order and remaining in Uganda, Amin responded vaguely, but with a heavy undercurrent of threat.

There were also rumors that Amin had wanted to marry an Indian woman; however, she and her family refused. For her safety, she went to India. Amin was outraged, so he decided to expel all Ugandan Asians. Regardless, this was one of his many acts of madness.

There were mixed messages about the expulsions. Headlines stated, "Some will stay, some will go." First it was said that all those who had Ugandan citizenship may stay. Then he announced that only certain professions could stay. A few weeks later he said that all Ugandan Asians must go. Despite this indecisiveness, the ninety-day deadline was firm.

Ugandan Asians were confused about what to do and where to go. India and Britain initially didn't want to take them. They tried to negotiate with Amin and his government, but Amin was firm in his decision.

Some Ugandan Asians initially didn't take Amin seriously. They thought he was asking for the impossible and would never be able to pull this off. However, Amin grew irate a few weeks after his announcement. Ugandan Asians didn't want to take a chance. They knew what he was capable of and no one dared to go against him. He would not hesitate to murder a person, a family, or an entire community.

Amin felt he was doing the right thing for his people, the Ugandan Africans. Even though most Ugandan Asians had Ugandan citizenship, they felt they didn't belong in Uganda anymore after Amin made his threats.

At that time, I was too young to understand whether leaving Uganda was a good thing or a bad thing. All I cared about was that I would be separated from my friends. Would I see them again? It was hard to let go of everything that we had lived for over all those years.

Amin's military were everywhere, and they freely did as they pleased. The Africans laughed in our faces; they felt they had the power now. We were scared that at any time they would assault us and steal our possessions. There was not much police protection. We had no choice but to give in and let them take whatever they wanted. The Ugandan Africans felt that whatever they could get their hands on was theirs. They hovered like vultures waiting for us to leave and so they could swoop in and claim their reward.

Soon there was no one in the streets. It was unsafe to go out. Dad stopped sending us to school. We had heard lots of stories about people being kidnapped, raped, tortured, and murdered—about Ugandan Africans going around with razor blades, slicing any Ugandan Asian they saw walking in the streets. They were ready to take over.

Ugandan Asians started to think seriously and panicked as the deadline closed in. Sixty days were left.

In the first thirty days after the announcement, the flights to Britain were half empty. Most Ugandan Asians thought Amin would withdraw his threat. As people realized the urgency, planes began to fill up quickly. There was chaos at the travel agency and total confusion. Many Ugandan Asians had British passports; however, they still needed entry permits. To receive these, they had to queue outside the British High Commission in Kampala. The lines were very long and moved slowly. They had to go back every day until they managed to get their paperwork sorted out, and many times they were turned away and asked to bring other documents. Some had to go there several times before they managed to get bookings.

The ninety-day deadline was too short, but we did what we had to. Some had to travel from far away just to get to Kampala. On the way, there were numerous roadblocks. Ugandan Asians were stopped by the army and asked to show what they were taking. The army took almost everything. By the time travelers arrived in Kampala, they had nothing. All their possessions were gone. Some said that they heard Ugandan Asian women were being harassed and raped. The men were powerless. We were on our own.

Uganda had given the South Asian community happiness. Most had been born there and had started families. Made countless great memories.

South Asians have an ability to unite and help each other. The family bond is strong. We had had everything we wanted, and within ninety days of Idi Amin's announcement we lost it all, including our friends and neighbors from whom we were separated. We lost touch with almost all of them, as communication in those days was limited. We had to stay strong. Idi Amin could not take away our experience, knowledge, qualifications, culture, and ability to work hard. We did what we had to because that was the only way.

THE TIME HAS COME

In our community, we saw families packing and saying their goodbyes to each other. They had been like family for many years, but the time had come for them to separate. Tears and uncontrollable emotions were shared amongst all. No one knew where they would end up or if they would ever see each other again. They didn't even know if they would get to the airport safely, given the rate of violence and looting on the way.

The women gathered and prayed together for the final time and helped each other pack hoping that that ever makes it to Britain will be a blessing, knowing that we were not allowed to take anything. From here on everything is left up to God.

The men had a final gathering at our house, which Dad hosted. They had whiskey, some Indian snacks, and hot, battered, fried potatoes called *bhajia*, made Kenyan style. They talked about all their memories and laughed and joked. Some were going to Britain, and they talked about their vision of what Britain would be like— the weather, the pretty British women, the history, the business opportunities, and the civilized manners. They would all experience it very soon.

Sadhana and I were not allowed in the room. We lay in bed as the chatter drifted over from the living room. Looking around, I noticed the small window above our bedroom door. "Sadhana, let's see what's going on in there."

"No." She said, "We'll get caught."

A round of laughter rang in my ears. My body buzzed with energy, so I grabbed the bunkbed ladder and leaned it against the door.

Sadhana scrambled up from her bed, "Stop! Don't do it! Get down from the ladder—you'll fall!"

I paused my ascent to peer at her, "Can you hold the ladder for me?" She hesitated but anxious to know what was going on in the room. She jumped from the bunk bed and ran towards the ladder, then curled her fingers around the side rails. Rung-by-rung, I climbed until I could peer over the windowsill into the living room.

"What do you see?" Sadhana whispered looking up at me from the bottom of the ladder.

"They're all just talking." I whispered back.

"About what?"

"About Britain." I replied, and then it hit me. We are going to leave Uganda. I clutched the ladder tighter as I thought about the friends I'd leave behind. She frowned, "I want to see. It's my turn."

I shook my head, "No, you will fall." I looked back in time to see one of the men getting up. My heart leaped into my throat and I slid back down the ladder.

"What is it?" Sadhana asked.

"I think one of the men saw me. Let's put the ladder back."

Ladder stowed away, Sadhana and I resorted to placing our ears against our bedroom door.

"So how cold does it get in Britain?" Came the muffled question.

A reply boomed through the wood. "Well, if you go for a pee on the open ground, your pee will freeze. While you are peeing, it will become hard, like a stick, so you can just snap it off and throw it away." A new round of laughter followed.

Sadhana and I shared a look, both of us imagining the scene. Laughter began to spill from our lips, growing louder and louder with each second. Soon, we were collapsed on the floor, holding our stomachs to ease the cramps from our joy.

The door opened. "What are you doing awake? You better go to sleep now." Dad scolded us as we quickly scrambled into our beds.

After Dad left, I lay awake and listened to Dad and his friends talk the night away. I imagine they all knew this was the last time they would meet. In a few days, our new lives would begin in Britain. Amin was taking away our possessions and our friends. We would start with absolutely nothing.

The next day, I awoke to empty alcohol bottles strew around the living room. Dirty plates were stacked on every surface. Our boy started to clean the mess. Dad was highly organized and normally did not allow such a mess, but this was not a normal time.

We were lucky. Dad applied for British passports and received them just two months before Idi Amin's announcement. Had we not had British passports, we most likely would have had to go to India. Dad had managed to get plane tickets for the day after the gathering. We wanted to get out quickly. Others were waiting until the last minute, hoping that Amin would change his mind, or the British would be able to convince him to extend the deadline.

However, Amin said he wanted to teach the British a lesson. He said that the British should have employed Africans and taught them how to build railroads. It was Britain's responsibility to take in the Ugandan Asians since the British were the ones who brought South Asians to Africa and gave them British passports.

Britain was not ready for us, but they started setting up temporary accommodations, using army barracks scattered mainly in south Britain. There was a lot of work to be done in a short time. Close to 27,000 Ugandan Asians entered Britain through the Uganda Resettlement Program.

Amin's army were everywhere. They stopped cars and stole whatever we had. Married women wore a necklace called the *mangalsutra*, given to them by their husbands during the marriage ceremony. It was a very sentimental item—irreplaceable, like a wedding ring. These were all stolen. At that stage, all we could hope for was to leave Uganda alive and not think of our possessions.

Amin's reason for making us leave everything behind was that he felt that Ugandan Asians were milking the economy. He believed that since we came with nothing, we should leave with nothing. He saw us making money in Uganda and sending it overseas to our families back in India or other home countries to support poorer family. Yes, we did that, and no one denied it. A lot of money, however, was spent in Uganda to buy cars, homes, businesses, everyday items, and luxury items. This stimulus was why the economy was always good.

We were stripped of our wealth, which had been accumulated over generations. Amin was a hero to the Ugandan Africans, who had been waiting for this for a long time. They couldn't wait for the expulsion to be completed and were ready to take over all our belongings. They felt that now they truly had their independence.

Amin wanted some key professionals to stay longer. Dad was one of them. We saw everyone from our community leaving, but we were ordered to stay. Dad's profession was not allowed to leave immediately, but we knew what type of a person Amin was. If we stayed any longer, we didn't know if we would live or die. Amin had killed many of former president Milton Obote's supporters. These people were civilians. It should not have been a crime to support the opposition, but Amin had taken the law into his own hands. With that type of personality, he would surely have us killed if we stayed.

"We must leave immediately."

The ride to the airport was tense. We were all praying we wouldn't be stopped, but luckily, we made it without trouble.

The airport was a battle ground. Amin's soldiers patrolled with loaded guns. The Ugandan Asian men showed strength; however, the women broke down with emotions. We waited in long lines to be taken into a cubicle and thoroughly searched. The adults forfeit their jewelry—no... it wasn't theirs anymore. Not even children and babies were spared. I emptied my pockets and put the contents into a container as instructed.

Once we got passed security, I let the situation sink in.

This was it. We were at Entebbe Airport. We were going to leave Uganda.

I looked around at all the people waiting for their flights. Men wore suits and ties on the flight, still looking professional even in those challenging times. Some people had lost family members in one way or the another, but they still held their heads up high.

I wondered what they were thinking. Not all Ugandan Asians were well off. I imagine the ones who were poorer were looking forward to starting fresh. However, most of them had comfortable lives—such as my family.

What was going through my parents' minds? They were starting a new life with three young children, no money, no home, and no jobs. How would we survive?

The announcement that our flight would begin boarding broke through my thoughts. Soon, we were finally on the plane—a first for many people. They were excited to be there. Their chatter followed us as we moved with the crowd. We found our seats, settled down, and buckled up.

I stared out the window as the plane took off. It was night, so I could only see lights. I tried to take a last glimpse of the beautiful country. It was an end of one lifetime.

The flight was long and tiring. It was very silent on the flight, apart from babies crying. My family nodded off around me. I stayed awake, though, wondering who would live in our home. Who would sleep on my bed? Who would drive our car? Who would wear Dad's watch?

We eventually landed in Britain to start a new life from scratch. I was almost eight years old. Sadhana was ten. Sandip was a year and a half. Mom was thirty and Dad was thirty-six.

A new chapter has arrived.

Our New Life Begins

We landed at Stanstead Airport on October 9th, 1972, coincidently this was exactly 10 years from Uganda's independence. I looked outside the plane's window, it was cloudy, and the ground was wet. As we stepped outside, the cold nipped at my face in a way that was not entirely unpleasant. I had never experienced wintry weather like this before.

This was the start of our new lives.

We had all heard about Britain, and in a way, we were excited to start this journey. Britain had history and wealth. It was more organized than Uganda. Even though we had nothing, there was potential to make our lives better.

We were welcomed by the Ugandan Resettlement Board. The volunteers were very kind and escorted us to our bus to take us to our designated camp.

Once on the bus, I just stared out the window, trying to take it all in. The rain was rolling down the window, which steamed up. I kept on wiping the glass with my hands and the sleeves of my coat. I frowned as the sky grew dark when it wasn't yet evening. In Uganda we had around twelve hours of daylight throughout the year. Eventually, the rumble of the bus lulled me to sleep.

Mom woke me up. We had finally arrived at the Heathfield army camp, which was in Honiton, Devon. We were checked in, and a volunteer took us to our small camp.

"Welcome to Britain." The volunteer smiled at Dad, "Please make yourself comfortable. I will check back with you in an hour."

Dad smiled back, "Thank you." Dad was the only one in our family who understood English.

We had packed several suitcases in the hope that some would come through. Only two suitcases reached us. We were lucky to have those since other families arrived with nothing. In those suitcases were clean clothes for us to wear.

In our camp room there were two beds—a bunk bed and another bed—and a small table. We sat staring at each other. I felt we were each thinking many things; however, we kept our thoughts to ourselves.

My eyes scanned the room in wake of the silence. Seeing an unfamiliar device attached to the wall, I got up to investigate. Warmth enveloped my body. I placed my frigid hands against it.

"That's a heater." Dad said after watching me for a beat.

Heater. This was the first word I learned after landing in Britain. "Heater." I said. *Whenever I get cold, I will ask for a heater.*

The organizers came back after an hour. "There is a tent set up where they have prepared dinner." She told us, pointing in the direction of the tent.

We were all hungry, so we rushed out, but were met with a lengthy line. It seemed like wherever we went, there were long lines.

While waiting in the line, Mom and Dad talked to the other Ugandan Indians and introduced themselves. They talked about their experiences and their journey. Their voices waivered as they spoke, and when I looked up, I caught a glimpse of watery eyes.

Ugandan Indians came from all over India, particularly the state of Gujarat. Gujarat is on the west coast, about 350 miles north of Mumbai and 670 miles southwest of Delhi. Within Gujarat there are numerous villages called *gams*. At the time, there was a caste system in Gujarat. One was only allowed to marry within one's caste or gam. That was many years ago; it's certainly changed now.

Because of the system of castes and gams, when a Gujarati meets another Gujarati, they will be able to find some sort of connection.

A typical conversation involves a formal introduction, followed by a discussion of their names, their fathers' names, and which gam the speaker comes from. It might go like this: "Oh! So you are the son of the uncle who owned the shoe factory that my neighbor owned and sold to his cousin, who was married to the nephew of an accountant who had a Mercedes and later sold it to your father?"

"Yes, that's me! I'm Akash."

Within a few minutes, they will connect other relatives, and soon they'll be able to talk for hours about other people. At the time, it was boring for me to listen to that sort of conversation, which happened frequently.

As I stood in the queue, I could smell the food, but didn't recognize any of the scents. I bounced on my feet, straining to see what was being served. When we finally approached the table, I felt my stomach turn. There was some kind of meat and boiled vegetables. Most of us were vegetarians, so hardly anyone touched the meat. We were starving, so we piled our plates high and ate the tasteless vegetables. There was watered-down juice set aside on the separate table, from which we filled small plastic cups.

After eating, we went back to our camp and slept on an extremely uncomfortable bed. I was asleep the moment I closed my eyes.

In the morning we walked to the dining area. The breakfast that was served consisted of cereal, milk, bread, butter, and tea. The tea was hot water poured over a tea bag, with a drop of milk added. This was different from how Mom made tea.

(An Indian tea, chai, is made with water heated on a stove and few teaspoons of tea granules. For flavor, Mom added tea masala, consisting mainly of dried ginger, cardamom, black pepper, and cloves. This mixture is left to boil. Milk is then added and is also brought to a boil. The heat is turned up and reduced repeatedly, alternating between simmer and boil several times. Sugar is added to taste. Chai is much sweeter than British tea. Making chai is a much longer process, but it tastes much better.)

After breakfast, we went to another area, where I saw several large containers. Each held gloves, hats, and coats, with the sizes shown on the outside: large, medium, and small. The bins with the small and medium sizes sat empty, so only large were left. We got there too late. Nothing fit us, so we took whatever was available, even though it was two sizes too big.

For lunchtime, we had bread with cheese, sliced tomato, and cucumber laid between the slices. There was a bag of crisps and diluted orange juice. We weren't used to this bland food, but it was food regardless and we were hungry. Ultimately, we were grateful to have something to eat. In the evening we had tomato soup and buns. The soup was nice because it was hot. We added salt and plenty of pepper to everything, which made it much tastier.

I felt sleepy during the day and wakeful during the night. I couldn't figure it out. I heard other people talking in the middle of the night. I guess they couldn't sleep either.

"It's jet lag." Dad explained when I asked. "Because you're used to Uganda's time, you're having trouble adjusting to Britain's."

"Oh…how long will it last?"

"A few days should be enough."

I didn't mind it too much though since there wasn't much to do at the camp.

One day, I was looking out the window and listening to two British people speaking. Their words jumbled around in my head. I only knew how to say simple phrases such as "hello," "goodbye," "please," and "thank you." This was complete gibberish to me. Even Dad (who learned English from his father, who was an English teacher) would have trouble understanding them given the strength of their accent and speed of speech.

I noticed once again that it got dark quickly. We hardly saw the sun. In Uganda, it was sunny almost every day. In Britain, the gray clouds hung low and blocked the light. The daylight lasted barely seven hours. It felt like suffocation. Like a punishment.

We all had to get acclimated. This was our new home, and it would take time to adjust. Not knowing what was ahead of us, we stayed optimistic. We needed time to explore this wonderful country that was talked about by people from all over the world.

I often thought of my friends in Uganda. I didn't know if I would ever meet them again. I didn't know where they had ended up and if they were safe. I felt sad; I missed them a lot. I wondered if I would find similar friends here.

We saw families coming in each day and some leaving. The people who left were picked up by friends and relatives who were already living in Britain. They looked pleased to see each other and hugged each other tightly for a good fifteen to thirty seconds. Then they put their suitcases in the trunks of cars and left. I wondered what their destination was and what their lives would turn out to be like.

It was like a mission or a game for all of us, a question of survival. The mission started by stripping away everything we owned. We were given £50 and a suitcase of clothes. We were then dropped in an unknown territory with obstacles put in front of us, just like in a film. We had to use our knowledge, experience, and creativity to dodge the obstacles and move to the next checkpoint. In this game, you only had one life. In short, this was how I felt.

Dad's sister lived in Britain; however, Uncle Pravin had already moved in with her. We had nowhere to go to. We were at a dead end even before the game started. After ten days, there was no hope for us.

An article was printed in the local paper, asking if anyone could take in a family of Ugandan Asians, as the camps could not keep us for long. Virtually everyone had found places to go except us. Mom prayed that someone would accept us. We didn't want to stay at a stranger's place, but we needed a roof over our heads. It felt shameful, as though we were begging. In reality, we were—we became beggars overnight. Our luck was running out. Who would take in a family of five strangers from another country? Salvation was impossible.

An Angel Reached Out

The newspaper article explained that Dad was an accountant and that we came from a respectable background. Eventually our prayers were answered. A lady interviewed Dad to make sure we would be a good fit. He was well-spoken and looked professional, as always. The lady, Zelie, accepted us and invited us to live with her rent free for six months.

Zelie was elderly, maybe in her sixties. She was a widow living in a large farmhouse in the countryside. Her well-manicured garden contained all sorts of flowers and plants. The house was old but very well kept. I had never seen a more beautiful house. It was just like you'd see on a postcard. I wondered if we'd ever live in a house of our own. We were very lucky and honored that someone with a good heart welcomed us into her home.

We weren't allowed in certain areas of the house. We accepted that and were happy just staying in our bedroom. The evenings got cold, and the homeowner gave us a small electric heater as a backup. It was a lifesaver. I was happy in some ways but very curious, and I couldn't understand how our lives could have changed so much in a matter of two months.

One day, early in the morning, the chill had settled more soundly in my body, but I always felt it the most in my feet. As I was putting on my socks, I looked at the heater and had an idea.

A little while later while I was brushing my teeth, the sharp tang of burning cotton tickled my nose. I looked around the room, sniffing, only to find my socks smoldering. My heart leaped into my throat and my head went light. I rushed to pick them up, threw them in the sink, and ran the water. I could have burned the house down.

Luckily, while I did get a good telling off, I didn't get a spanking. Zelie fumed for a bit but simmered just as quick.

"You couldn't have known the implications of what you had done." She sighed. "Really, I should've been the one who was more careful."

Now I had to wear socks with holes.

Sadhana and I were admitted to the local school. It was very strange to see all white faces. We were the only nonwhite people. The other kids were the same age as I was but much bigger and stronger. They ate meat and we ate vegetables. They stared blankly at us wherever we went. I couldn't work out whether they liked us or not. I was very confused. I had been one of the most popular students at my school in Uganda. I was liked by all my peers and teachers. I was the leader of the pack.

Here?

Here I was a nobody, a stranger. I couldn't even communicate in English.

Soon, the other kids began to make fun of me. I was weakened by emotions and went numb at the taunts. I normally made friends easily, but now my tongue felt like lead. I couldn't say a word; if I tried to speak in English, the kids would laugh at me and mock my speech. I stayed strong though and never cried in front of them. I couldn't show my weakness. I was, as they say, "Billy no mates." I tried to be kind to people. Why were they not kind back to me?

Back in Uganda, Amin had become extremely popular with his people. For the first time, the Africans felt that Uganda was theirs. With the Ugandan Asians gone, they claimed our possessions and enjoyed everything that the Ugandan Asians had worked hard for. Indirectly, they stole it from us. All the Ugandan Asian properties, businesses, cars, jewelry, and bank accounts were taken, and no one was arrested. Why wouldn't they like Amin? Without him, they would have been serving Ugandan Asians for an indefinite period. Amin was a hero to his people.

For Africans to claim Ugandan Asian businesses, they had to prove that they were a right fit for a particular business. They were interviewed, and the business was only passed to them if they had the experience, knowledge, or qualifications. However, there were few Africans who were as experienced as Ugandan Asians. Within a short time, Uganda realized that it could not run without the Ugandan Asians as Africans lacked knowledge in business, finance, medicine, teaching, and economics. When they needed medical attention or business advice, who could the Africans turn to?

The Africans who were given our businesses started to trade with shops full of the inventory Ugandan Asians left behind. They made money and were happy to get something for free. However, they didn't know about supply chains or how to reorder stock when goods needed replenishing. Their success only lasted a brief time, and then the economy began to collapse.

Amin realized that he needed the Ugandan Asians and started to call them back. He said they would be able to retrieve their homes and businesses. Bitterly, most Ugandan Asians refused. Life would not be the same. They did not trust Amin and felt safe in in their new homes. Some, however, did go back. They saw that there would be no competition and realized they could capitalize on this unique opportunity. The ones who went back became successful and continued with the life they had left.

Amin also offered to allow us to pick up our luggage two years after we left. No one knew what luggage was left—and if they found their luggage, what would have been looted and what would remain? All those memories—photographs, sentimental items, and valuable possessions—were lost and could never be regained.

Comparing Life

Though Zelie had welcomed us for six months, we knew this situation could not last for the long term. Dad began applying everywhere for accountancy jobs since he was an expert in that field.

In Uganda, Dad had been an accountant working for Ford Co. where he made enough money for us to live comfortably: we had a car—a white Peugeot 504—and good savings. In Uganda, Ugandan Asian ladies didn't need work; they were housewives. We had two African boys to help with housework. One cleaned the house and the other did odd jobs, which included washing dishes and cleaning clothes. They ironed Dad's shirts and polished Dad's shoes every day before he went to work.

This was a normal life for Ugandan Asians. There were others who were much richer than us and had several servants to help with gardening and cooking. Some even had security guards at the entrances of their houses, we were incredibly happy with our lives. We had many friends living in our community; it was like one big extended family.

We learned from reading the papers and listening on the news that most Indians went to Leicester, which was about one hundred miles north of London. Indians wanted to live with their own people and build a community. They would squeeze as many of their friends and family into a house as they could. Eight, ten, even twelve people living in a three-bedroom house was not uncommon. They understood each other's hardships and united. Indians were not welcome, however. There were many protests and violence against us. Eventually, the Leicester council stated that Leicester was already overcrowded and could not offer more Indians housing or jobs and that other cities should take them instead.

Most Indians would not claim unemployment benefit or apply for council housing, believing this to be shameful. They took any jobs offered to them at any wage, despite the fact that they may have been in management or professional positions in Uganda. Many Indian businessmen already established in Britain employed Indians since they knew many Indians were hardworking, educated, and reliable.

Eventually Dad found an accounting role in Wellington, Somerset. They understood our situation and offered Dad a salary that included a bridge loan of £1,200 toward a deposit on a house. Dad was thrilled with their generosity and jumped at the opportunity. We ended up buying a house on Springfield Road. It was on the outskirts of Wellington, so it was much cheaper than living near the town center. It cost £6,000. It was no Leicester, but we weren't fussed with where we lived so long as there was roof over our heads.

For the first time we felt what poverty meant. It was something we had never thought would happen to us, as our position in Uganda was stable. We had everything one could want.

From Uganda to Britain, overnight we lost everything—car, house, money, community, and security—and gained hardships in return. We fell victim to the biting, frigid weather. We struggled with basic English speech. Outside our four walls was hatred. Though we had been treated well by the refugee organizers and Zelie, the general British public didn't want us there. They worried we would take their jobs and housing and set up National Front organizations and protests throughout the country. We were unsafe and confused.

In less than ninety days, 80,000 other Ugandan Asians faced similar issues. Most faced unimaginable hardship. How would we survive? Where do we go from here?

OUR HOME

Wellington is in the southwest of Britain. Our home was on Springfield Road. Our home sat near the bottom of the road. There was a nursery school on that corner at the bottom of the road, which my brother attended. After we had lived there a few years, a sports center was built. It had a large swimming pool and a synthetic ski slope. It was very odd to see an artificial ski slope in our small town whose residents were mainly older people. The admission was two pence, which we couldn't afford. As a result, we only went there if we had visitors to entertain from London.

Once, when an uncle visited us, he used the showers at the sports center since we didn't have any in our home. He was a rich businessman and had lived in Britain for many years. He owned a burgundy-colored Mercedes-Benz. When he visited us, people stared at the car. Some even took pictures since no one had a Mercedes where we lived. It embarrassed us. We had no status in Britain, yet we had been wealthy in Uganda. Would we ever get back to where we had been before? At the time, we were lucky just to have our own roof over our heads.

Before we moved into our home, a charity asked for our house key. We had no idea why, but we gave it to them regardless.

Walking in after Dad opened the front door, I saw a lot of items. Used cutlery lay on the table. An odd nightstand, two chairs, some clothes, and an armchair sat scattered around the living room.

We later found out that the charity had taken a truck around Wellington and asked if anyone would donate to us, people gave what they could.

We were grateful for their kindness. It was, however, shameful. We never accepted charity. Rather, we were the ones *giving* to charity. We were the ones who gave our worn clothes and old household items to a worthy cause. We never thought we would one day be using someone else's belongings. To be almost homeless and accepting donations caused a pit to settle in my stomach. We hadn't committed any crime, yet we received an unimaginable punishment.

Our home was very small. It had three levels. The ground floor had a living room, a dining room, and a kitchen. The living room was small, only fitting to place a couple of chairs. There was a fireplace that took up lot of space. The dining room was only slightly bigger as it was wider.

The kitchen was small and narrow. We did not have a full bathroom; the bathtub was under the Formica countertop, which was on hinges. To have a wash, we had to close the curtains in the kitchen, lift the countertop, and hold it up with a stopper. Next, we locked the kitchen door and boiled water on a heating element. Once the water heated up, we poured it in a bucket and mixed it with cold water. We got undressed, sat in the tub, and, using a tumbler, washed ourselves. Even though this was a big task, we came from a place where we washed every day, so we maintained that habit. Mom bathed my little brother in the kitchen sink. At times it was hard to tell if someone was having a wash or was cooking. Therefore, Dad purchased a lock that when turned counterclockwise showed "vacant" and when turned clockwise showed "engaged."

There was one toilet outside the kitchen in an enclosed room that had corrugated plastic roof. If someone was bathing, it was nearly impossible for someone else to use the toilet. The only way was to go out of the front door, run down the street, double back along the path at the back garden, then enter through the back door to get to the toilet. This proved very difficult when it was cold, which was most days.

The second floor had two bedrooms, one slightly bigger than the other. The top floor had a loft room with slanted roofline on both sides. It had a window with a view of the back garden we shared with the neighbors. In the distance, you could see a railway line. I spent much time looking out of this window and gathering my thoughts. There was something magical about looking out of this window. It brought me peace. Anytime I was sad, I went up to the loft and stood by the window—watching the trains, the sky, and the birds flying past—protected and looking down from above. When it snowed, it was a winter wonderland. The snowflakes floated to the ground and slowly came to rest, piling up into a soft, smooth surface. It formed a beautiful white finish and curved around the edges of roofs, walls, and cars.

Since we had nothing except the walls of our home and some clothes, we felt empty, worthless, and lost. We prayed every day. Would our prayers be heard? So many Ugandan Asians left the same way we did. I'm sure they are praying too. There probably are people around the world much worse off than we are. Why would God listen to our prayers over theirs? *Where are we in the line? When will it be our turn for God to listen to our prayers?*

We were in a country that was significantly colder than Uganda. None of us could speak any English except Dad. The food we ate was mainly chapati, curry, and rice, which was much different to what the British people ate. They hated the smell of our food. The smell got into our clothes and the whole house, so we often opened windows. The neighborhood houses were small and close together, so the smell got everywhere. Because we were the only Indians for miles around, they knew we were the cause.

We faced racism virtually every day. I couldn't understand why since the British had ruled India for more than 150 years. We had no money except the £50 per person that Amin had allowed us to take. We didn't understand soccer; our main sport was cricket. The clothes we wore were different, especially the ladies. They wore saris, which were suited for hot climates.

Some British people, however, understood our hardship. Since we seemed to be educated and from the middle class, they didn't want us to be embarrassed by their donations. They would place small items in a black bag and leave the bag outside our front door. Each morning when we opened the door, we found items like spoons, plates, old clothes, and other small items. That was a great start. One couple gave a sofa that had a broken seat. We propped it up with a plank of wood. At least it was better than sitting on the floor—our butts hurt after sitting on the floor for a long time. The arms of the sofa were also broken, so we tied rope around them to hold them up. It wasn't much, but it would do.

One day, someone told us that he had a mattress that he would like to give us. The only caveat was that we would have to pick it up from his house at the top of the hill. Since we had no means of transportation, Dad went to our neighbor.

"Do you have an idea of how we can go about this?"

The neighbor pursed his lip and gazed at his house. "Wait here." We waited for ten minutes when he popped his head out the front door, "Alright, come around to the back garden."

Dad and I looked at each other. *What does he have?*

When we arrived at his garden, he was standing there with a wheelbarrow." I can lend this to you." He said with a sheepish smile, "That's all I have, though. You'll need to figure out the rest yourself."

Dad and I shared another look, eyebrows knit tightly, but didn't linger for long. "Thank you." My dad said to our neighbor as we left with the wheelbarrow. Even empty, we struggled to keep it straight. *How are we going to get a mattress home using this?* Still, no other option presented itself, so we made do.

We went at night to collect the mattress. Our ears burnt at the thought of anyone seeing us pushing a mattress-laden wheelbarrow down the road.

Once we got to the man's house, he already had the mattress ready. "Here you go.' He said with a flourish, "It's all yours. Would you like me to help you load it in your car?"

Dad stuttered, "I'll...I'll be fine! My son and I can manage, thank you."

We waited until the door clicked behind him to pick up the mattress. I was (admittedly) not much help but cheered him on as we trekked back to our house. Our difficulty managing the wheelbarrow increased tenfold with the added weight. Every two feet, the mattress would topple over, forcing us to reposition it and try again. After several attempts, I walked alongside the wheelbarrow with my hands on the mattress to keep it upright while Dad served as the engine.

Dad was an accountant who had worn suits all his adult life. Seeing him pushing a wheelbarrow in the middle of the road, it made my insides churn. Still, I pushed my feelings to the side. I couldn't burden him any further. After thirty or forty minutes of this agony, we arrived, limbs rendered to lead by the effort.

The next day, we gave the mattress a thorough cleaning. It was hard to sleep on someone else's mattress. What if someone may have peed on it? Or maybe kids jumped on it with dirty shoes. Dogs may have shed their hair. There may even have been sexual activities on that mattress. We forced ourselves to suppress these worries and appreciate what people gave us.

Cold Weather

When the cold crept in, drafts came from everywhere—under the doors, between gaps in the windows, through the roof. At night I slept curled up into a fetal position, knees drawn to my chest and arms clutching my legs. I slept in my socks and sweaters, but they did nothing to protect my face. I hardly slept.

Someone donated a small paraffin heater to us, which was our only source of heat. We would sit around it, holding our hands near the fire to warm them up. It was our own personal campfire. It ran out of paraffin very frequently. Sadhana and I had the job of taking the empty one-gallon paraffin container to the gas station, having it filled, and bringing it home. By now, Sadhana was eleven years old and I was nine.

The gas station was about a half mile away. The attendant filled the container and handed it back. My arms shook under the weight as the thin looped handle cut into my little fingers. We struggled to carry it, so we took turns. I went first and carried the gallon maybe a hundred feet. The cold didn't help. Instead of easing the pain, it exacerbated it. Once the ache in my fingers turned into a bite, Sadhana took over for the next hundred feet, and so on until we reached home. We switched the gallon between us about twenty times before we got home. Our job was complete when Dad filled the paraffin bottle and lit up the heater.

Someone else gave us a hot water bottle. Dad slowly poured hot water into the bottle and gave it to Sadhana, whose body was often racked with chills. Once she warmed, she passed it on to me. My feet were usually the coldest, so I placed it between my feet. Mom was always worried that we would be sick if we didn't keep warm, so Dad later purchased a hot water bottle for each of us. We couldn't keep the heater on all night, so this was an excellent alternative.

Winters were extremely cold in Wellington. It snowed almost every winter. We had never seen snow before and were excited. One day we heard from a neighbor that it was going to snow that night, and the weatherman confirmed it, saying to expect an inch.

I rose early and bounded to the window to see the snow, my family close behind. We looked out and, while there was snow, it barely covered the ground. I grabbed a ruler as we began making our way outside. Kneeling, I dipped the ruler in the snow. It didn't even clear 1 centimeter. I frowned deeply.

Though the cheer ebbed away, we were still curious and prodded at the snow. It was white and soft but cold and melted almost immediately.

I ran back into the house to put my shoes on, marveling at the footprints I left behind. I ran and skid suddenly, trying to slide, but there wasn't enough snow to achieve the effect.

"Sadhana! Come join me!" I called to her through the window.

She shook her head and drew her coat tighter around herself, "No, thank you. I'll watch you from here."

As I ran around, Mom carried Sandip in her arms. When he reached towards the snow, she bent down and allowed him to touch it. He reached out and got a little on his finger. He put it straight into his mouth. Mom pulled his hands out of his mouth and wiped his hand with her sari as we all laughed at his actions.

The next day there was heavy snowfall. I got my ruler out again and measured it. This time, there was three inches! A white, smooth layer covered gardens, roofs, and roads. It was still early in the morning, and no one had been walking outside, so it looked just like a picture on a postcard.

"Mom, can I play outside?" I asked with a wide smile.

Mom frowned, "No... it's too cold. We don't want you get sick. And what if you fall and hurt yourself. I'm sorry, but we really can't afford either of those happening."

As such, I spent the day at the window and watched the snow fall, mesmerized by how it danced with the wind.

We quickly found out that although the snowflakes were soft and looked harmless, they had the potential to create a lot of problems. The snow piled up on the polycarbonate roof of our outer building. Over the years, it had cracked. As the snow melted from this roof, water seeped through the cracks. We placed buckets under all the drips, which filled up within the hour. We took turns emptying them. The snow kept on falling and melting. We were at a loss. We tried to scrape off the roof with a broom and a spade, but the snow just kept on building up. Dad got some thick tape to seal the cracks, which slowed the leaks down, but the solution wasn't permanent. We had no money for a new roof, and for many years we struggled with the same issue.

One winter years later, a foot of snow piled up on the roofs in the neighborhood. When people put the heating on, the bottom layer of snow melted. This loosened the entire pile, and all the snow came crashing down like an avalanche. We would hear a loud rumble, and when we ran to the window, the snow would already have fallen.

Mom went to work one evening when there was very little snow. Then almost two feet fell while she was out.

"Mom should be coming home soon." Sadhana commented while looking at the clock. "Let's watch her walk down the street."

So, we took to the window. We waited and waited until we saw her figure appear in the distance. She kept slipping as she walked on the thick snow with her flimsy work shoes.

"We should go help her." Sadhana said to me as Mom slipped yet again.

"Yeah." I nodded.

"Dad!" Sadhana called.

"Yes?" Dad came to the room.

"We're going to help Mom!"

Dad cast a glance out the window, "Okay, but make sure you're wrapped up before you go out."

We quickly ran to our rooms to put on sweaters and coats. As we ran out of the house, we heard the rumble. We whipped our heads around. *That could be coming from any roof.* Then we saw the snow on a roof adjacent to where Mom was walking start to slide.

"Mom! Mom! *Mom!*" We started sprinting towards her. However, it was impossible to run on fresh snow that was two feet deep. The snow came crashing down, luckily missing Mom by a few inches.

We hurried as best we could, shouting, "Mom, wait! We are coming!"

Mom struggled to get up on her own. Her shoes were buried as we tried to pull her up. It was difficult, but somehow, we managed. We got home and told Dad what happened as Mom warmed up. He was shocked that we had managed to pull her out and grateful we had seen her.

It felt like something bad was happening one thing after another. We were being hit with so many roadblocks. We were trying to get up, but something always came along to kick us down again.

During another winter, every day brought extreme weather, especially where we lived. We listened to the nine o'clock news every evening to see what the weather would be like the next day. One day, the weatherman forecast snowstorms and chilly winds. We loved the white and fluffy snow, but we didn't like the disasters it brought with it.

Our windows were single pane, the ones you had to lift to open. The frames were made of rotting wood with paint that was flaking off. In the wintertime, the frame shrank so you could not close the window tightly. It left a slight gap through which you could feel a cold draft. It didn't take long before the house got freezing cold. We stuffed pieces of cloth into the gaps to stop the draft, but the wooden frame was so thin that the cold seemed to come through the wood.

Our blankets were light and provided no insulation. We slept with our pajamas tucked into socks. I put my blanket over my head to stop the cold. Mom rubbed our hands and tried her best to keep them warm.

Dad later found a better solution. He bought each of us a sleeping bag, so the cold would not enter from the sides. The bags were quilted, and our body heat kept us warm during the night. We loved our sleeping bags. We slept peacefully on the floor, and in the morning, we rolled up the sleeping bags and put them on the side.

One winter the snow was at least three feet deep. It looked beautiful outside. All the schools were closed. We played outside for a few minutes but came inside because it was too cold. We didn't have proper shoes, so the cold got to our feet. We saw other children fully wrapped in thick coats, hoods, gloves, and boots. We thought one day we would have winter clothes and be able to play in the snow. We later bought rubber boots called "Wellington boots." Was it a coincidence that the boots were called Wellington boots and we lived in Wellington? Those boots were waterproof.

We saw men clearing snow with shovels to make a path. We even saw an old lady a few doors down the street who was moving snow with a spoon. Each home cleared their own. Dad cleared ours. I helped for few minutes but got cold and came in to get warm. Once warm, I went out again to help Dad. It was challenging work; we could barely clear our own path. At least we could get out of our home. This allowed us to get to the main road, where the snow had been flattened by cars driving up and down.

Dad and I put on a few layers of sweaters and coats. Mom made a shopping list of basic items—bread, milk, and butter. We asked our elderly neighbors if they needed shopping, knowing the mile-long journey to the shop would be tough for them. Their list was much longer than ours. Walking in the snow for that distance was tiring. The shops had lines, and most of the shelves were empty. We could have survived on chapati, potato curry, and rice, but we had to get food for our neighbors. It felt like the entire day was spent getting food.

It usually took two weeks for the snow to melt since winter temperatures were below freezing most days. The most dangerous times were when the snow turned into slush and then froze over. When the slush melted, it left a layer of water. When that froze, it was even worse—a sheet of ice. It was hard to walk. Many times, we fell and hurt ourselves. This was all new to us, and without the right shoes, it felt impossible to walk on ice.

DAILY LIFE

Mom started to look for work. She had never worked in her life, as was customary for Ugandan Asian women, but she wanted to help earn money. Dad insisted she stay home and look after us. We needed her, especially my baby brother. But she knew that on Dad's pay alone, we would continue to struggle. Therefore, for the first time, she defied Dad.

Eventually, Dad conceded that we needed a second income and helped Mom look for work. She applied to many places; however, with no experience and no fluency in English, who would employ her? She finally found a night shift job at an aerosol factory. She worked from 6:00 p.m. to 10:00 p.m. as an assembly worker on a conveyer belt.

She was not allowed to wear her sari. For safety reasons, she had to wear a top and pants like Western people. Mom had never worn anything apart from a sari. Her employer said that if she wanted the job, she had to wear pants and a top.

Mom was extremely embarrassed and cried for days. She didn't want to wear pants and a top; this was a Western thing. She was slightly overweight and felt ashamed to expose her body in this way.

However, Mom was not a weak person. She thought positively. She had to help with the bills. She also found that one of the privileges of her work was that the company sold damaged goods for pennies to the workers. All antiperspirants, shaving gels, air fresheners, and similar items were usually five pence. We saved a lot of money on consumables as a result.

Mom's first workplace was about a mile from our house. We didn't have a car, so she walked to work. Mom only worked night shifts. She waited for Dad to come home. Then we'd eat, and Mom would go to work while Sadhana and I cleaned up. I took all the dirty dishes and the food from the table to the kitchen while Sadhana washed the dishes. I put all the leftover food in containers and placed them in the fridge while Sadhana continued washing the dishes and instructed me to wipe the countertop and the dining table.

My sister and I looked after Sandip in the evenings. Dad was often tired from a hard day at work, so he didn't have the energy to play with us. He rested and caught up with the news, often retiring early. It was impossible for him to balance work and family time.

Our food was very consistent; we had no choice of what to eat. Almost every day it was chapati, dal, rice, and sautéed vegetables mixed with spices or gravy. This was not the most nutritious meal, but it was the cheapest since we bought the flour, rice, and oil in bulk. This was the typical food that Gujarati people ate. Gujarati food was not suitable for the cold weather. We didn't eat meat apart from Dad and I, who ate chicken. Chicken was not in our budget, so we only had it occasionally.

We had a large, overgrown garden. Dad tried growing some vegetables so we could eat fresh for free. We mainly grew potatoes and tomatoes. Dad had never did gardening before, so he learned from the neighbors.

We had an area of overgrown grass. We didn't have a lawnmower, so one day I cut the grass with household scissors. It was ridiculous, but I wanted to play in the garden. My neighbor saw me and gave me his old pair of shears. They didn't cut well and were rusty and blunt. Dad saw me struggling and finished cutting it.

A few months passed. The neighbor had an old manual grass cutter with a rotating blade. It cut the grass as you rolled the mower back and forth. It took some time to get the hang of it, but once we got into a rhythm, we finished the job quickly. It looked good, and now I was able to play.

THE MILKMAN

When I was ten, I wanted to help my parents earn money.

Every day, I would watch the milkman deliver milk. He always came up with three or four bottles of milk in one hand and a couple of empty bottles in the other. We didn't have this service in Uganda, so I was fascinated. He came in a small, open van filled with crates of milk bottles and had a little book which held records of how many bottles to deliver to which house. At the end of each week, he collected the payments.

He always noticed me looking out of the window waiting for him to come. I smiled at him; he just looked at me and did his job. I suppose he's too busy to smile back.

One day, I waited at the doorstep. When he came up with the milk bottles, I sprang up. "Can I help you?" I asked with my limited English.

He stared at me for a bit before he nodded slightly, "Okay, son, I'll give you a try. This ought to cut my delivery time in half."

A grin broke out on my face, and warmth spread throughout my body.

He continued, "I won't be able to pay much, though." He pointed down the road. "Meet me at the end of the road at exactly six o'clock every morning. I'll drop you off back home at 7:30 when we finish." He put the milk bottles down and picked up our empty ones, "All you need to do is pick up the empty bottles while I deliver the full ones. Think you can do that?"

I nodded fast. "Yes!"

He rubbed my head before walking off, "See you tomorrow, then."

When he was gone, I ran inside to tell my family about my first job.

When I finished, my parents had deep frowns on their faces. My own smile began ebbing away.

"You're too young." Mom shook her head. "You don't need to have a job yet."

Dad nodded, "Your mother's right. You shouldn't do it."

"But we need the money!" I argued, "This could help us out!"

Dad hesitated.

"Every penny counts right?"

Dad sighed. "Yes, it does." He waved me off, "You have my blessing."

The smile returned full force. I thanked them and rushed off.

I went to bed super early that night so I wouldn't be late the next morning. I set the manual alarm clock for 5:30 a.m. Despite this, I couldn't sleep. All I could think about was my first job. The night seemed to stretch for an eternity before my lids fell heavy enough to not open back up.

I jolted up and looked at the time, dread creeping into my bones. It was 5:45 a.m. I hadn't pulled the button up on top of the clock.

I rushed to put on my long socks and tucked my pajama bottoms into them. I pulled my pants over my pajamas, so I had insulation. I quickly brushed my teeth and put on two layers of sweaters and a coat. The clock read six o'clock.

I ran out the door as fast as I could. The cold wind slapped me in the face. Tears rolled down my cheeks. I frantically ran my sleeve over my face so I would not be blinded, though it ultimately didn't matter. A thick fog had settled low overnight. I couldn't see if the milkman was at the end of the road, waiting for me.

Coming out of the fog, I saw him about thirty feet away. He said nothing and had a deep scowl on his face.

I ran behind his van. "I'm sorry! I'm sorry I'm late! Please, wait!"

He stopped the van and waited for me to catch up. I brightened. *He's giving me a second chance!*

Once I caught up, huffing and puffing, he looked down at me for few seconds, "If you can't wake up early, then I can't give you this job."

I froze at those words as he got in the driver's seat. He drove off, leaving me standing in the middle of the road.

My heart sank. I watched the van disappear into the fog. What had I done? I had an opportunity to help the family and I let it slip away. I had begged Dad to let me help and had taken this job against his will. Now what would I tell him? I had failed. How could anyone trust me now?

I shuffled back home but couldn't bring myself to go inside. I cried and cried. I didn't want to face my family. Thoughts of how useless I was swirled in my head. Eventually, my shaking hand reached for the door.

Dad heard me come in and came out to greet me. "What happened?" He asked, "I thought you wouldn't be back until later."

A million excuses ran through my head, but the truth spilled from my mouth, "I was late, and he wouldn't let me help him anymore."

His eyes softened and he knelt to wrap his arms around me. He leaned back, "Look, son, you will learn many lessons in life. You will make mistakes, like any human being. The lesson you must learn from today is to prepare everything the day before, so you don't have to rush at the last minute and be able to be there either ten minutes early or exactly on time." He pat my head, "This is a big lesson that you have learned at a small cost."

I took Dad's words to heart. I promised from that day forward I would never be late for anything, and I would be prepared the day before. To this day I remember this lesson.

After that I couldn't look at the milkman through the window. When I saw him, I was ashamed of myself. My days of watching him were over.

LEARNING TO SAVE

One day, while walking in the high street, Mom went into a ladies' clothing shop to buy some Western clothes for work. The owner spotted her. He was an Indian gentleman. He approached Mom and asked her if she was Indian. She said yes. There weren't any other Indians living in Wellington, so they clicked straight away. They talked for ages as neither had seen other Indians for a long time. Mom shared our story, and he introduced his family to her.

The shop was a family-run business. The owner offered Mom a job straight away and Mom accepted without hesitation. They exchanged information. He asked Dad to check his accounts, which Dad did. Dad found some errors straight away, so the owner asked Dad to do his accounts permanently. Dad accepted and did them in the evenings. We were not allowed to make any noise while he was working since he needed full concentration.

We got along very well with their family. They shared stories of their background. The owner told us that he started his business by selling clothes door to door on his bicycle before opening his first store. As of 2020, he has hundreds of stores worldwide. The family loved Indian food, so Mom frequently made them traditional dishes. They were the inspiration and lifeline we had been looking for. They could relate to us and understood our hardship.

Dad was primarily a bookkeeper, but he understood various aspects of the accountant's role. He loved what he did and was very good at it. He sometimes did odd jobs for other people and brought the account books home. In those days accounting was all manual entry, so everything was written in special bookkeeping books that were wide with lots of columns. Dad always had a calculator next to him, crunching numbers all day long and entering them in the books. He was like a computer. I was amazed that he hardly looked at the calculator while tapping in the numbers at an extraordinary speed with his fingers jumping up and down at the buttons.

Dad taught us how to save and not to spend on unnecessary things. I watched Dad save all his pennies. He made a note of each expense in a book. The book had rows and columns. He inserted figures according to what the money was spent on. His earnings were recorded in the income column. He used a pencil. His writing was very neat and readable. He always watched what he was doing, and he asked me not to interrupt him while he concentrated. Dad was very accurate with his figures and rarely made mistakes. I sometimes looked through the book when he was at work and tried to work out what he did. Since I was good at math, it started to make some sense. I never understood why he wrote in pencil though.

Dad wanted silence when he was working, so we couldn't watch TV. I loved cars, so I played with my toy cars while Sadhana helped Mom in the kitchen.

On the news we listened to a lady from Bangladesh who was a math genius. Her name was Shakuntala Devi. They called her the human computer. She could do long math problems in her head and never made mistakes. On one occasion, in front of a live audience, she challenged a computer. Before the operators could even enter the numbers on the computer, she had the answer. She got it wrong. She said the numbers given in the question were wrong—and she was right. People were shocked by her talent.

Dad was amazed by her and bought her book, which helped us with some of our math. I understood math and felt that it was a great weapon to have. I watched Dad negotiate with people simply by doing the arithmetic in his head. The other party usually was not as sharp. I learned how to negotiate at a young age. At school, I could do math very quickly and get the right answers. However, the teacher marked my solution incorrect, and I got zero marks. I could not understand why, as the answer was correct. The teacher said the way I worked out the question was not right. The teacher wanted me to use the way she had taught us. I had used Shakuntala Devi's method, which I found much easier. I wanted the teacher to use this method. She got mad. I got really upset and confused.

I told Dad and he was furious. He went to the school, and the teacher explained the school's system. She said the students must follow the system. Dad told me to use Shakuntala Devi's system to double check the answers I got using the school's system.

One day, Dad determined we were using too much toilet paper. In Uganda we used a bidet, so we never had toilet paper. Water is much cleaner than toilet paper, so I guess someone was using more toilet paper to be cleaner. Dad cracked down on this and decided we had to learn the value of consumable items. He gave each of us an individual roll. We took our own rolls to the toilet and put them back in our drawers once we finished our jobs.

We tightened up with every consumable item. We had no luxuries like sweets, chocolates, or ice cream. For a treat we had jelly, custard, and tinned fruit for dessert. My favorite was Dream topping, which was light and fluffy like whipped cream. It came as powder in a packet. We just needed to add a little milk and whisk it. I always volunteered to make it and wash up. I didn't allow anyone in the kitchen while I was making it. The reason I did this was so that I could lick off the excess stuck to the whisk and the bowl. This was my reward for making the dessert. I had a sweet tooth, and this treat satisfied it.

We knew that we had to live on a day-to-day basis. One day I saw Mom scraping every bit of butter from the wrapper so there was no wastage. All our jars and tubes were scraped so every bit was used.

Our diet was very consistent. Every day for breakfast we ate the same thing—cornflakes and milk or buttered bread and tea. Dal was our only consistent source of protein. We got vitamins from vegetables and calcium from milk, which we had with our cornflakes every morning. Mom cooked rice and chapati almost every day. We bought a large sack of rice, a sack of flour for the chapati, and a drum of cooking oil. Buying in bulk worked out much cheaper in the long run. Fruit was rarely purchased, and usually only apples and bananas.

We did have our indulgences (albeit rarely). Typically, we ate whatever Mom made and never requested anything else unless it was our birthday. While we never had birthday cakes or blew out candles (those were luxury items), Mom made our favorite vegetarian dish. Mine always was mango pulp (*ras*) which was straight out of a tin and mixed with milk. Mom added a little salt and ginger powder. She said that in the cold, *ras* was bad for the throat, and the ginger powder saved us from getting ill. We ate *ras* with chapati and spicy dry potato *shak*. We dipped the chapati in the *ras*. It was delicious—the perfect blend of sweet and spicy.

Dad realized we were going through cereal very quickly. It got expensive. We were still young and needed the cereal, so he thought to buy it in bulk. Dad went to the local supermarket and asked for the manager. He explained our situation and asked if the manager would give him a discount if he bought three boxes of cereal at a time. The manager said that since the supermarket was a large company, they could not accommodate the request. However, the manager promised to contact his head office to see how they could help.

Eventually they came up with a solution. They contacted the manufacturer, who said that they could sell a large sack of cornflakes that would last for two or three months. They offered us a special price and had it delivered to our house. The cereal was almost half the price of individual boxes.

We stored this sack of cornflakes in the loft on the third floor of our house. We scooped cornflakes from it using a tumbler and filled a small container, which took about five scoops. This lasted us a week. It was our standard breakfast for many years. We occasionally had bread and butter, which we dipped in tea. It was soggy but tasted so good.

Christmas was something we weren't familiar with. We learned about it from the adverts on TV and newspaper. Apparently, people gave gifts to each other. With my birthday money, I wanted to buy Dad a gift. I only had a few pounds, so I couldn't give a gift to everyone.

I went to the high street and looked for something. Everything was too expensive. However, there was a rubber stamp maker on sale that I could afford. I had seen Dad hand-writing our address on envelopes, so I thought this could save him time.

On Christmas, I gave him his present. I didn't have money to wrap it, so I just gave it to him. "Here, Dad, a Christmas present for you."

He looked at it, turning it around in his hands with a frown on his face. He didn't seem impressed. "What is this?"

"I thought it ... it ..." I couldn't finish the sentence. Whatever I said would not make sense to him. I shivered and knew he would lose his temper. I had thought it was a good idea at the time, but in hindsight, my justification was not strong enough to validate my purchase.

"We can't afford presents. You must take it back."

"Don't be too harsh with him." Mom's scolding echoed behind me as I ran off to my room, tears welling up.

I took the present back the next day.

After a few Christmases, Dad realized that we were missing out on giving gifts. He bought a small gift for each of us. Sadhana and I started to argue about who got the better gift. We raised the issues of unfairness and favoritism with Dad.

He looked at us, frown deep on his face. We stopped talking. Voice level, he said, "That's it. From now on, no more presents for anybody. You don't deserve it."

From then on, we received no gifts except for a little bit of money for our birthdays. Dad felt that if we thought he was playing favorites, he had no time to explain. The easiest option was no gifts for anyone. We had not appreciated that he worked hard to give us gifts—had not valued the gesture. "I'm teaching you that if you don't appreciate what you are given, then the other person's hard work to earn the money to buy you a gift is wasted. Understood?"

FAMILY TIME

We knew that our parents were trying to keep a good balance among many things. Sadhana and I never gave them trouble and helped where we could.

We didn't have washer or dryer, so Mom washed clothes in the sink. She wrung the clothes out and hung them on a clothesline outside to dry. The clothesline ran alongside the garden path from one end to the other. Many neighbors dried their clothes this way. In winter, though, that was not possible.

There were five people in our family. Mom couldn't cope with washing that many clothes in the sink. We had no choice but to take them to the laundromat. The closest one was in the high street, which was about a mile away. It was my job to take the clothes to the laundromat.

Mom put the dirty clothes in a carry-on bag and gave me coins for the washing and drying. I put on some thick sweaters and a coat and started my journey. As I pushed the carry-on bag, which was almost the same size as me, people stared. It looked as if I had left home and taken my belongings in the carry-on bag. People may have been thinking, *Should I call the police? This small boy may be lost*. I shrunk under the attention, but I had to do it. I had no choice.

Halfway along, there was a clock outside a house. I timed how long it took me to get from there to the laundromat and back, including of course the time it took to wash and dry the clothes. It took around two and a half hours.

Once I reached the laundromat, I gave the carry-on bag to a nice lady who always helped me. She looked like she was as old as my Mom, in her early thirties. She wore a red-and-white apron with flowers and a pocket in the front, where she hung a small napkin. She constantly wiped her hands on this napkin.

I'd approach her, and she would take care of me. I gave her the money for the washing and drying. I couldn't speak much English we spoke to each other through eye contact and actions. Once she took all the clothes out of the carry-on bag, she placed them into a huge washer. She put in the washing powder, closed the door, selected the correct wash setting, put the money in the slots, and turned on the machine.

I sat on a bench, watching people come in and out or walk on the street. I studied what they wore and how they looked and wondered where they were going. Almost everyone who came into the laundromat looked at me for few seconds. I could almost hear their thoughts. I was shy and didn't look them in the eyes. I stared at the floor, hoping they would leave soon. I felt ashamed. *This is not how life should be for a ten-year-old. In Uganda, we had had boys to clean our clothes. Now, I've taken their place.* I shook my head. *No, I should be thankful to all the people who have helped us since the day we landed in Britain.*

The washing took about an hour, depending on what setting the lady selected. The lady then put the clothes into the dryer, which was on the opposite side of the washing machine. Mom packed a small snack in my pocket, and once the lady put the clothes in the dryer, I could eat my snack. It was usually something sweet, because Mom knew I had a sweet tooth. The dryer took another forty-five minutes.

Once the clothes were dry, the lady folded them and placed them neatly in the carry-on bag. Then the lady would wave goodbye and smile, saying, "See you next week."

I'd wave back and reply, "Thank you."

I walked back home, taking note of the time on the clock halfway. At home, I gave the carry-on bag to Mom. "Thank you, Beta." She'd smile as she passed the carry-on bag to Sadhana, who sorted out the clothes and put them away in the assigned drawers since Mom was too busy looking after Sandip.

Sadhana was like a second mother to Sandip. She was twelve years old and Sandip was three. She'd keep my brother entertained while my Mom silently cooked in the kitchen. Often, the only sound we heard was running water from the tap, the opening and closing of cabinet doors, or cutlery clinking.

Mom was a great cook. I knew she was thinking all the time as she cooked. We didn't disturb her. I believe she was usually thinking about what life had been like in Uganda compared to Britain.

In Uganda, she had sung Hindi songs while cooking. She had a lovely, soft voice. Mom and Dad had watched Indian movies every week in Uganda. They often went to a drive-in cinema. They gave my sister and I a shilling each to stay at home while they went to watch a movie. Our neighbors looked after us. In Britain, we were cut off from all Indian activities, so they hadn't watched an Indian film for many years.

If Mom needed help in the kitchen, Sadhana would assist her. She learned to cook basic items. When Mom went to work, she gave detailed instructions to Sadhana. She cautioned her about being careful of hot surfaces since my sister had got burned when she was seven years old. Mom told me that she had been running and bumped into someone carrying a boiling-hot pot of tea. The tea spilled on Sadhana's forearm. She was hospitalized for a couple of days so nurses could change the dressing. The scar is still there.

Since then, Mom was always worried about us running and reminded us to be careful. We were kids, so we buzzed with energy. Our house was small, so there wasn't much room to run around. Our main living area was about fourteen feet by ten feet and had a small but tall window. It was the room where we played, ate, watched TV, did our homework, and shared each other's activities for the day.

We bought an old, secondhand, twelve-inch black-and-white TV. There were three channels to choose from: ITV, BBC 1, and BBC 2. There was a knob to turn the channels and an aerial that you had to move to get the best reception. We sat the TV on a crate. Mom and Dad sat on the sofa, and Sadhana and I sat on the floor most of the time. We loved watching comedy shows together as we needed to laugh in those tough times. Dad had a great sense of humor and always laughed the most since he understood English better than us. Mom just smiled. She enjoyed watching Dad laugh more than what was on TV.

Dad loved watching wrestling and really got into it; it was as though he were in the ring. We watched him make faces and movements with his arms as though he were one of the wrestlers. Sometimes we couldn't help laughing out loud. But his mind was blocked from the outside world, and he just concentrated on the wrestlers' moves. He did not hear us laughing. We could see anger on his face. Dad was a very simple and shy man. He wouldn't hurt anyone. To see his angry face was scary but funny.

We loved cricket and watched a lot of it. However, we never played it ourselves. We didn't have a cricket bat, stumps, or a cricket ball. When the cricket test matches came on, Dad turned the tv volume all the way down and listened to the commentary on the radio. It was more detailed than the commentary on the TV. We closed all the curtains and sat around the screen. Dad even allowed us not to go to school if it was a very important match, especially between India and Pakistan. The two countries were longstanding rivals. If India won against Pakistan, it was like we had won the World Cup. It may sound strange, but if India and England were playing, we always supported India, even though we lived in Britain.

TV time was great family time, and we enjoyed each other's company. That made it difficult to go into the outside world, as it was always unpredictable what a day out there would be like. Our home was our comfort zone, a safe haven, a place where we understood each other and supported one another. It was the place where we united and openly shared our stories. We only talked about the good things. Individually, we may have had bad times, but we didn't share those.

Once we stepped outside our home, we were individuals who worked out issues and problems on our own. Even though we only knew a few English words, we could read people's expressions and know they were making racist remarks. Some were more obvious than others. We only made a few friends among our neighbors. It was hard to communicate with them. They had difficulty understanding us and we had difficulty understanding them. Many people felt sorry for us. We were not the same people in Britain as we had been in Uganda.

One day we received an unexpected call from Zelie.

"Hello." She greeted Dad, "Would Savita mind helping me out with something. I am organizing a children's charity event and was wondering if you could make your delicious food for it. I love your cooking, and I know they will too." Dad conveyed the message to Mom.

Mom smiled wide and nodded an affirmative to Dad, "Of course. She'd be honored."

"Great! Just tell me what ingredients you will need, and I'll buy them."

Unfortunately, a lot of Indian spices were not available, but Mom made do with what she had. The dishes she made were simple, but tasty. Once finished, we took them to the fundraiser.

Mom arrived dressed in her best sari. "I'm going to be introduced to many people, so I want to look my best" She told Dad". However, she didn't know the mayor would be attending.

The mayor approached her with a smile, and Dad, sporting his most professional suit, stepped forward to translate.

After a few minutes of talking, the mayor gestured to the food, "May I try it?"

"Of course!"

He leaned over one of the dishes and opened his mouth. Mom fed him a spoonful of Indian curry. The photographers caught the shot, and the next day it was in the newspapers.

The event was a great success. Zelie was pleased with the turnout and wanted to pay Mom for her hard work. Even though we desperately needed the money more than ever, Mom refused to take it. She communicated with Dad to tell Zelie to give it to the children's charity. Her work had been for a good cause, and Mom felt good giving the money to the charity. Zelie teared up and gave Mom a big hug, insisting Mom take the money. Mom stood her ground and refused.

SCHOOL DAYS

I went to Beech Grove Primary School, about three-quarters of a mile from my house. Students there wore a school uniform. The uniform was expensive; however, Dad's company generously covered the cost as part of Dad's compensation package. We bought it a size bigger so it would last longer. Mom hemmed up my pants and, as I got taller, she re-hemmed them.

At school, we played with marbles in the gutters. If you won, you received a bigger marble. I became an expert as we had played a similar game in Uganda. With some negotiating skills, I won many uniquely different marbles and had a great collection. I held the marbles up to the light and lost myself in the contorting colors as I rolled the marble between my fingers. It gave me peace.

I was the person of color at the school. It was easy to feel that I didn't belong there. This was nothing like Uganda. I wished I were back in Uganda.

I didn't have many friends. Most of the time I kept to myself and just observed other kids. They often played soccer with a tennis ball. Their laughter echoed across the field while I watched from the sidelines, just trying to understand the game.

One day, a boy in my class ran up to me. "Hey man!" He gestured to the other kids, "We're short of a player. Do you wanna play?"

I shied away, "No."

"You don't wanna play?"

"No."

"It'll be fun!"

"No."

"Are you *sure* you're sure, man?"

"I'm sure."

"Oi! Can't you see he doesn't know how to play." One of the boys interjected with a shout, echoed by the laughs of the others.

The first boy rolled his eyes, "Yeah, but come on, we're desperate." He turned back to me, "Look, man, all you gotta do is this" he kicked his leg out a few times to the ball. "Got it?"

I hesitated, "Okay."

He beamed, tugging my arm to the field, "Great! Let's play!"

Anytime the ball came to me, I kicked my leg out just like he had showed me but missed every time. Eventually, the other boys stopped passing to me. We ran about until one of the boys called for a break.

They gathered in a circle, poking fun at how each other played. I crept over to them but hovered at a distance. Surely, they would say I was a horrible player.

One boy saw me and waved me over, "What's your name?"

"Sanjay." I whispered out.

"What did you say?" He said.

"I don't understand." Another added.

"SAN-jay."

"Samhay?"

"San-JAY"

One of the boys huffed, "Let's just call him John." They all nodded in agreement

"Which soccer team do you support?" The same boy asked.

My mind blanked and my mouth moved on its own accord, "Which team you like?"

"Leeds United are the best team, hands down!"

Who are Leeds United? "I like Leeds United, too."

"He has good taste!" They cheered, flashing me thumbs up and toothy smiles.

I smiled back shyly and gave a thumbs up back, heart racing in my chest.

I had done it. I had found the secret formula to making others like me—I just had to be like them.

Easier said than done.

I played with them several times and honed my skills. On the school playground, though, a much older boy always kicked the ball far away from us and laughed with his friends. He was a slim but tall kid with a long face and short hair. He looked like a gang leader as other kids followed him around. This happened every time a ball came near him. Every time it happened, we would whine, and some of the boys would stomp their feet, but nobody dared to say anything to him.

One day he kicked the ball away and laughed, as usual. I was so furious that, without thinking, I lunged forward.

I was much smaller and weaker than him. I didn't know how to fight and swung my arms blindly, but once I started it, I couldn't back out. I had to keep fighting back. I couldn't show him I was scared. The other kids circled us, chanting, "Fight! Fight! Fight!"

A playground monitor ran over and yanked us apart. He was one of my teachers. "Break it up, now! Break it up! That's enough."

We both stared wide-eyed at him, covered in scratches (and luckily no blood). We were escorted to the headmaster's office and got away with a good telling-off. That boy never touched our ball again, but he always gave me a dirty look as if to say *I'm going to get you one of these days, so watch out*. It did scare me because he was always in a gang. There was no chance that I'd fight him again. I stayed well away from him.

After seeing the headmaster, I went to my next class looking all beaten up. Part of my shirt was hanging out and my hair was mussed up. I opened the door grazed hands. When I walked into the classroom, all the kids cheered and clapped.

"Here comes Muhammad Ali." My teacher laughed.

I straightened, warmth blooming across my chest. I was liked!

When I got home, I put on soccer shorts and a sporty top and practiced kicking a ball against our door. I began to withdraw slightly from my family. Soccer wasn't our game. We never watched soccer and I was the only one with any remote interest in it. All the warmth that had stayed with me slowly ebbed away. *Why should I change myself to please others?*

Because it's the only solution.

Slowly, the other boys began excluding me again. I knew too little about soccer to talk with them, so they moved on. I found myself in this great divide—do I stay true to my current way of living or assimilate completely into the culture in which these white people lived?

ME AND MY BIKE

From the front gate of our house, I watched the boys who lived a few doors away riding their bicycles. It looked like so much fun. In Uganda, the kids rode their bicycles in the common area. At the time, I had been too young to ride a bike and couldn't wait to grow up so I could join them. I followed them in a pedal car. I would speed up and and then slam the brakes, so it would skid. I thought I was a rally driver. I drove fast in a straight line and suddenly took a sharp turn, causing the car to go on two wheels for a few seconds. Other people clapped when they saw me doing that. It was so much fun. Back then, I couldn't wait to have my own bike. Little did I know I would get my first bike in Britain.

One day we heard a knock. Mom went to the door and I followed her. It was the boy from across the street with his bicycle.

"Does Sanjay want to play with us?" He asked politely.

Mom looked at me with drawn eyebrows. I stared back at her with a barely concealed smile, "He does." She spoke slowly. Once the words left her mouth, I ran to put on my shoes.

I said goodbye to Mom and bounded outside with him.

He pointed up the hill, "I'm going to go up the street to meet my friend."

"Okay!" I nodded, "I'll be right behind you!"

He started pedaling, but since I didn't have a bicycle, I just ran behind him. I grew tired quickly and started lagging.

"Come on, run faster!" He cheered, slowing down so I could keep up. "You can do it!"

My lungs burned when we finally reached our destination. He went up to his friend's house as I tried to catch my breath.

"So where do you want to go?" I looked up as they walked back.

"Do you want to just go up and down the street?"

"No, that doesn't seem too fun." My neighbor scrunched up his nose, "What about the Recreation Center?"

His friend shook his head, "There's not enough space there."

"The playground, then?"

"Sure."

They mounted their bikes and turned to me, "Are you ready?"

Lungs stuttering (but functional), I nodded.

Again, my legs were no match for wheels. They stopped every so often and waited for me to catch up, both sporting pinched expressions. "This isn't any fun." I heard as I stumbled to them once. "He's really being a burden." I heard a few stops later.

The moment we reached the playground, the two boys abandoned their bikes and ran to a grassy area. "Do you want to play?" My neighbor pointed to a ball his friend held.

I shook my head, "I'll watch from here." I lowered myself on Jell-o knees to rest on the ground.

They shrugged and began to kick the ball around. An hour or so later, we went home. The boys never asked me to join them again.

There was always something—I didn't know soccer; I couldn't ride a bike. Kids at school had stopped talking to me entirely once they figured out I couldn't talk about soccer. I tried talking about cricket, but they didn't like cricket and didn't want to talk about exciting cricket matches. I really was trying, but no matter my efforts, I couldn't make friends.

Dad saw how much I wanted a bike, but if he bought me a bike, he would also have to buy Sadhana one, which he could not afford.

One day Dad brought a beaten-up bike home. He smiled at Sadhana and I and said, "Here you go—your bike, Sanjay can share it too. Someone gave it to me for five pounds."

I looked at it with disappointment. It was too big—an adult's bike. I couldn't even sit on the seat. Sadhana was taller than me, and she could barely sit on it herself. We didn't know how to ride a bike and would hardly be able to learn with these conditions. I felt Dad got it for my sister and not me, despite the fact that I was the one who wanted a bike.

"Thank you." I said to Dad regardless. He had to have worked hard for this, after all,

I tried riding it. I tried for several days but fell off before I could move an inch. I gave up and didn't touch it again. I cried for many days for a bike, but I know Dad could not afford it.

For days I cried silently in my bedroom not allowing anyone to notice or hear my cries, as I knew Dad could not afford to buy me a bicycle. However, one day Dad heard me crying in my bedroom. He opened the door, "Sanjay?"

I sniffed, refusing to lift my face from the pillow.

"Come downstairs." The door closed.

I'm in trouble. I clutched the pillow tighter and burrowed further into the blanket. After some time, Mom came to the door, "Sanjay? Come downstairs." I stayed silent. My mother's footsteps pad away from the door.

Sadhana was next, "Come downstairs."

"No." Came my muffled reply.

Finally, Mom came up again. "Sanjay, can you please come downstairs?"

I took a breath and wiped my eyes. Slowly, I made my way downstairs.

Opening the living room door, I saw a perfectly sized brand-new bike. It was called the Raleigh Budgie chopper. It was purple and had tall handlebars and a long seat. It had removable stabilizers to stop me from falling over until I learned how to ride. I stared at it and couldn't stop smiling.

"Thank you!" I beamed at my parents.

Though we didn't show our love by hugs or saying, "I love you," they didn't need any of those things to show me their love. We showed our love in other ways.

Dad laughed, "Okay, but we have a problem. Where are we going to keep it?"

I thought of all the areas we could store it in so it wouldn't get in the way. The perfect idea came to me: "I can keep it in my room next to my bed!"

Mom and Dad looked at each other and laughed, "Okay."

I carried my bike upstairs and stood it right against my bed. In the middle of the night as the moonlight shone through window, I peeped at my bike. It was like a dream.

Every day after school, I went home and quickly did my homework. Then I brought the bike downstairs and rode it for an hour or so until dinner time. The other boys were envious of my new bike.

An older boy lived up the street from us, appearing about twenty years old. On his way home, he stopped and watched me struggle to ride. He did this for several days. One day I saw him enter his home. He came out after putting his bag in the house and rolled his sleeves. He came toward me. I thought he was going to beat me up or steal my bike. I froze. I looked around for help, but there was no one there to protect me.

He stopped next to me and put both his hands on his hips. "Right, let's do this."

I stared at him, wide-eyed. I was only ten years old. Why did he want to fight me?

He looked at me. "Come on, get off the bike."

Tears began welling up in my eyes as I complied. Why would he steal my bike? I know where he lives and it's way too small for him.

He bent down and began taking my stabilizers off. Once he finished, he put them down on the side of the road. "Okay, you can get on again." I shied away. He gestured to the bike. "Go on, then. Do you want to learn to ride a bike or not?"

It finally clicked in my mind and a smile stretched across my face. A stranger was going to teach me how to ride a bike.

We were at the top of the road, which had a slight downhill gradient. There were no cars. He pushed the bike and I pedaled. A quarter of the way along, I was starting to get my balance. I pedaled faster and faster.

"Okay, let go." I said.

No response. "Okay, let go." I repeated.

Again, no response. "Let go, please."

This time, when he didn't respond, I turned my head to see why—and realized he already had a long time ago. I had ridden most of the way on my own.

I braked and turned the bike around. In the distance, he was waving at me. I waved back. I couldn't say thank you as he was too far away. I knew what time he came home, so I found him and said thank you the next day.

I felt like this was a new beginning. My life had changed. I could ride my bike anywhere I wanted; it would be my best friend. My family joked with me because I slept with the bike next to my bed, but there was no maliciousness behind their words. They knew what it meant to me.

One day I took the bike to a nearby playground. I was with Sadhana.

"Can you watch my bike while I play?" I asked her.

She nodded, "Yeah."

I leaned the bike against a post and ran to play on the swings. I kept my eyes on it as I was swinging, and from a distance, I saw an older boy approach my sister. He started talking to her. *Does she know him from school?* But we came from a culture in which one shouldn't be seen to talk to the opposite sex, so why was she talking to this boy? Then I saw that Sadhana got on the bike and realized he was harassing her. He wanted to take my bike.

I jumped off the swing and ran toward them. He pulled her hair hard and she fell off the bike, which tumbled to the ground. I saw red. I ran faster.

The boy laughed as my sister fell. He grabbed the bike and got on it. His back was to me, so he didn't see me running toward him. As he started to pedal, I grabbed him by the neck in a choke hold and pulled him down. The front of the bike went up, as his hands were still grasping the handlebars.

I couldn't let go of him, otherwise he would really beat me up. He struggled and I had to tighten my grip. I glanced up and saw lots of people watching us. There must have been about a dozen. My sister was crying.

The boy wrenched himself from my hold and looked at me. He was a couple years older than me. He charged at me. A much older boy stepped in his path and broke up the fight. I was frozen to my spot

The older boy looked familiar—he was the one who had taught me how to ride the bike. He sighed, "Okay, come on. Let's get you home." He was my guardian angel. He took us home safely. I didn't want to go back to the playground anymore in case the thieving boy came back.

When we got home, I told Mom what had happened. She felt that people would start to judge us and question how we could afford a new bike. It was another lesson for me. People can become jealous of nice things. Nice things can attract the wrong people. That day I didn't want to clean my bike; I wanted to make it look old.

WELCOMING GUESTS

In Wellington, we were the only Indian family and could not make friends very easily. The British people did not want us there. "Go back home!" They shouted when we walked by.

I was confused. What home? I am an Indian who had been born in Uganda and then moved to Britain, as was my right with a British passport. How could I explain that to the British people who were fuming at our entry? The only thing I could do was put my head down, walk along, and ignore them.

Dad told us not to mind them. "We have a roof over our heads. We are protected by our four walls and have food on the table. That's what matters." Mom and Dad both worked hard and saved to build our lives up again. There were no get-rich-quick schemes. The only way forward was to focus and stay focused.

When we had reached a financial stability, Dad said that the first thing we needed to do was have a proper bathroom built. Using the bathtub under the kitchen worktop was too inconvenient. There were two bedrooms on the first floor. One of them was made smaller so a bathroom could be squeezed in. This was our first step in making our house a home.

For the next, Dad went to a local wallpaper shop. "Excuse me," Dad caught the shopkeeper's attention, "I will buy wallpaper from you if you give me instructions and all the items I need. We have never done this type of work before."

The shopkeeper provided Dad with the items and said, "I have everything you need except one, which no one sells. But you must have it before you can do DIY work."

Dad was confused. "What is it I need?"

The shopkeeper laughed and said, "Patience."

Dad laughed back, "I will always remember your wise advice."

Dad was brave. He had never done any type of manual work before, so this was going to be interesting. At that time, I was about twelve years old and Sadhana fourteen. Dad said we all had to help. I was excited to get going.

Dad instructed us to wet the walls a section at a time and let it soak in, so the old wallpaper would peel off easily. Sadhana wet the walls and I picked up all the old paper that Dad threw on the floor. It took a whole day to take off the old wallpaper and clean up the walls.

"Let's put up the new wallpaper now!" I cheered when the walls were bare.

Dad remembered the shopkeeper's advice and said, "No, son, let's take a rest and let the walls dry."

When he deemed the moment right, he got an empty bucket and followed the instructions on the glue packet to make glue for the wallpaper. However, Dad was not happy with the outcome. It was lumpy and not smooth. He was upset that we had wasted a whole packet of glue—money down the literal drain. We had to pour it away. We were all unhappy, and Dad felt that he had failed.

He went to the store next day and told the shopkeeper what had happened. "Where did I go wrong?" He asked.

The shopkeeper shifted his weight, "Sprinkle the powder very slowly and stir at the same time. That should do the trick."

"Thank you." Dad smiled, handing him money for a new glue packet.

We tried again the next day. My sister slowly sprinkled the glue powder while Dad stirred. We all knew this could not go wrong; we could not waste another packet of glue. This time it was perfect. We looked at each other and I felt warmth bloom in my chest.

Dad had already calculated how many rolls we needed, including some extra to cover odd areas. We got all the tools ready, including scissors, tape measure, pencil, Stanley knife, and plunger. We had a ladder as well, but it was very old and unstable.

Dad applied the glue in a systematic fashion. Sadhana and I held the ladder steady and watched, helping him when asked.

We eventually got a system going where we took turns coating the walls. It was fun for us. We spent the whole day applying a layer of paste to the bare walls.

"Let's put the wallpaper up!" I cheered at the end of the day.

However, Dad remembered the shopkeeper's advice to be patient. "We shouldn't work if we are tired or we'll make mistakes. Let's get some rest and let the paste dry a little. We will start again tomorrow."

The next day Dad marked up the wall with the plunger. When he was finished, Dad stared blankly at the wall. Finally, he balanced himself on the ladder, "Pass me the roll."

I ran, got the roll, and gave it to Dad. Dad measured the top part and slowly came down the ladder to mark the bottom part, leaving about an inch extra for errors.

We laid the roll on the table, and Dad cut the top and bottom. We had our first piece. Once the paste was applied, Dad got to work applying pressure to the top part and slowly work his way down to the bottom, using a dry, wide brush to take out the bubbles while aligning the side of the paper along the plumb line.

There were lots of bubbles on the first attempt. Dad peeled the paper off slightly and tried again, but the bubbles were still there. Dad looked really upset. He just aligned the wallpaper to the plumb line and left the bubbles. "Let's stop here," he sighed, "Tomorrow I will ask the shopkeeper where I went wrong."

When we woke up the bubbles were gone. It seemed that when the paper dried, it let the air out. Dad was happy. However, Dad still went to the shopkeeper and told him what had happened. The shopkeeper advised him not to put the glue on too thickly since we had already put thin layer of paste on the wall.

We went home and repeated the papering procedure with a much thinner layer of paste. It took a long time to figure out a system. We learned by our errors. Dad had problems cutting around light switches, windows, door frames, and corners. The mistakes were noticeable. Still, we were happy. It was new wallpaper and looked clean and fresh. It brightened a dull room into a happy place.

We had the chimney taken down in the front room to allow for more space, then wallpapered that room. Dad found out that due to the cold, damp weather, he got asthma. It was severe. The old carpet was smelly. We changed it, thinking it could be part of the cause of Dad's asthma. The new carpet was the cheapest kind, but it was new.

Over a few years, we ended up wallpapering the whole house. Dad became an expert. Our process grew faster, and we made fewer errors.

We saved all the unused wallpaper and stored it in the loft on the third floor, which was a scary place. We rarely went there as we thought it was haunted. We kept the door locked. No one dared to go there on their own. We occasionally heard the windows slamming and creaking.

Dad braved to check on the loft to see if we could make it habitable since we were expecting visitors from London. Many relatives who lived in London wanted to visit us and tour around our town. There were many local areas worth visiting. Dad said to accommodate them, we needed to use the loft. The loft was large; however, it had awkward roof angles. I was short, so that aspect didn't bother me.

Even though it was creepy, we tidied it up to make it habitable. Dad fixed the creaking window and put on new hinges. From the window, I had almost a 180-degree clear view. You could see the back gardens and, in the distance, train tracks. Occasionally trains would pass. It was a very peaceful room and became my favorite part of the house. I was no longer scared of it. We didn't put any beds in it, as the ceiling height was low. We just had mattresses.

While cleaning up, I asked Dad, "What should we do with all this wallpaper? It seems a waste to throw it out."

He thought about it. "Since the loft is a bonus room, we'll use all the leftover wallpaper in it."

That plan seemed weird to me. Nevertheless, I went along with it. Once we hung up all the leftover wallpaper, I was reminded of every room in the house. It was great!

We did other work around the house as well. I always wanted to see how things were done, but I ended up doing with the boring jobs since I was still too young to handle power tools. My job was mainly to clean up after Dad did the work. I hated cleaning up since Dad made so much mess, but I learned a lot. I learned to be perfect. Mistakes just weren't affordable.

We bought polystyrene tiles with an embossed pattern to put on the ceiling, which we painted gold to make them look royal. As they dried, Dad got up on the ladder. One person applied glue, and another person passed the glued tile to Dad. He placed each tile in a strategic way and applied pressure until the tile was almost stuck. Then he adjusted the tile until it touched the tile next to it. It took a long time to get going, but we eventually developed a process. Working with each other like an assembly line, we managed to get the tiles done in two days. It looked clean and fresh. We were slowly making a house into a home.

Before the next winter arrived, Dad asked the shopkeeper what the most cost-effective way was to prevent drafts from seeping in through doors and windows so we could reduce our heating bill. The shopkeeper sold him a ten-foot long roll with foam on one side and adhesive on the other.

"Just peel the paper off here and apply it to your windows and doors." He explained.

At that point, we had just been jamming old rags and newspapers into the gaps. It was unsightly, but it was free.

We got home and tried one window. However, we made the mistake of not cleaning the surface before applying the strip. The dust rendered it ineffective. Luckily, we didn't waste a big strip. Dad gave me the job of using a damp cloth to wipe the window frame, then drying them with a dry cloth.

Dad was like a surgeon, and I was his assistant. He put his hand out. "Scissors." I gave him scissors. When he had snipped the strip, he gave me back the scissors. We worked well together (though I still hated the cleanup). Before the day ended, we had completed all the windows.

We waited excitedly for the cold weather to test our work. Lo-and-behold, the strip stopped the drafts. It was amazing. A small bit of cold, however, continued coming in due to the rotting window frame. It was too expensive to replace the windows entirely, so we learned about filler. We went around the whole house, filling in gaps and sanding it down to get a smooth finish.

We bought paint next. The window frames were thin, only about an inch wide. We couldn't paint them well. The paint got on the glass and looked terrible. We tried to wipe the paint off with a wet rag, but it didn't come off cleanly.

I found a thin paintbrush in a painting set someone had bought for me. We tried to use that for the edges, but it took forever. Finally, we tried letting the paint dry, then removing the excess from the glass with a razor blade. This also took a long time.

Dad asked the shopkeeper for advice. The shopkeeper sold him a roll of masking tape. It got used very quickly and was expensive. It seemed a waste to apply the masking tape only to throw it away after using it once. We didn't buy another roll.

We experimented and slowly worked out a technique by not having too much paint on the paint brush and keeping the hand steady with one smooth stroke to avoid paint getting on the glass. This saved us the cost of masking tape. It also saved time because we did not have to apply the tape or clean the glass. We painted the window frames blue and white. Blue was Dad's favorite color.

Now our house felt new and clean, we could now invite family. Our home was complete.

We wanted to show it off to our friends and family who visited. We were proud of our achievements so far. Dad had never had to do any of this in Uganda; that has been a different life. My parents, however, showed happiness wherever we were or whatever we had.

We visited Dad's sister in Forest Gate to stay with them for a week. From Wellington to Forest Gate was about 170 miles, so we went by train. We packed two suitcases and took turns carrying them since they were heavy.

As we walked to get to their home, everyone in the cars driving past stared at us. The cars would slow down. The people inside wound down their windows and looked as if they were going to come out of the car and beat us up. Often, we got shouted at: "Pakis, go home!" We just put our heads down and carried on walking as their laughed echoed behind us.

We finally finished the long, hard journey after 40 minutes. My aunt's house was like a palace compared to our home.

Inside their house was a big, wide foyer. The stairs were almost double the size of ours. There were plenty of rooms downstairs. The upstairs had five bedrooms, all large. Their back garden had pear trees. They had lived in Britain for many years and were well established. The family was big and all of them were very nice. They tried to make us feel welcome. They were always laughing and happy. My cousins all introduced themselves. They were all girls though, so I was shy talking to them. Sadhana had great time with them despite her own shyness.

Though we enjoyed the trip, it was a reminder of how far we had fallen.

We had lived very comfortably in Uganda. In Britain, we felt we had been beaten to the ground with no chance of getting up. We felt lower than low. We didn't want anyone to see us this way. Over the years we saved, compromised, and worked together to keep moving. Now we could have family and friends visit us. We had enough room to sleep up to eight people in the loft. It was the brightest room in the house and safest, as it was on the third floor.

When guests came, we spread out and played Monopoly, which was my favorite game. One of our uncles taught us the game, and we played for hours. He was a jolly man. We all loved him because he was so much fun. Monopoly gave me insight into buying, investing, and negotiating. I wasn't very good at first but became better the more I played.

This uncle had also lived in London for many years. We often went to his house and stayed with him for a few months. He played with us, taught us a little English, and took my sister and I to the library and the local parks. My sister and I would laugh when he burped and said, "Pardon me," because in Gujarati those words sounded like *pad on me*, which means "Fart on me."

When friends and family visited us, they brought a lot of Indian food that we could not get in Wellington—for example, large bags of flour and rice, drums of oil, fresh Indian vegetables, and sweets. We went on day trips to sightsee and go to the seaside. However, we never went in the water. We walked on the beach fully dressed, while others were in their swimwear. The British people would stare at us. I was always embarrassed in front of them. In Uganda, no one cared how you looked. It felt very free. In Britain, we walked with our heads down, ignoring the racist comments and laughter behind our backs. We felt unsafe, but we had to keep going and face what came. We couldn't give up; we had to continue living.

Our visitors came during the summer months. We were always excited to have them. We got to the stage where each group had to book days with us so they wouldn't overlap. Sometimes it got too much for Mom since she was working. Mom and Dad couldn't take time off work, so the guests did a lot of sightseeing on their own. They came home in the evening, and Mom prepared the evening meal. She had to make the food for our guests, who felt they were on vacation and didn't help.

For five months of the year, guests came and went. My two favorite cousins—Ajay and Bobby— often came with my Aunt Ranjan during summer vacation. They were a couple years younger than me and very fair-complected. We had grown up together in Uganda, where they lived next door to us. They were also part of the Ugandan Asian expulsion. We got along well and were very close.

Evel Knievel was someone I admired. He was a motorcycle stuntman who jumped over cars and buses and through fire. I had an Evel Knievel toy that was my favorite plaything. My cousins and I wanted to be like him.

One day in the back garden, we took a plank of wood, placed it on the ground, and put three bricks under one side to make a ramp. We had Sandip lie down sideways, so his body was touching the ramp. Ajay and I took turns on my bike to take a run up and jump, clearing my brother by inches. We had a lot of fun.

Mom saw us and ran out. We got a good telling-off. After thinking about it, I realized it was a dumb idea. Things could have turned ugly if either of us had fallen off the bike or if the ramp had given way. I was the eldest, so I was held responsible.

As we used the bike more and more, it needed new tires and brake pads. Occasionally the chain would come off. Uncle Pravin loved fixing cars and anything mechanical. He visited us often with Aunt Rangan, Ajay and Bobby. Uncle Pravin replaced the bike's brake pads, tightened the chain, and repaired a puncture in the tire. We watched carefully and with a lot of interest. We were amazed at his skills. In India and Uganda, bikes were used very often, so these were small repairs for him.

As I got older, I learned how to repair bikes. I liked it. I was not scared to use the tools my uncle used. I learned their names and what they did.

I grew out of the bike I had, so my cousins and I decided to experiment on it. We bounced ideas around. We remembered seeing motor bikers riding in the high street. There were lots of them in a gang; they called themselves Hell's Angels. Most had heavy tattoos and piercings. They wore chains in their pockets, big boots, and leather jackets with lots of designs. The bikes made loud noises and looked a little bit like my Budgie; however, their front wheel was angled much farther out.

I had an idea, "Let's do something to make the front of the bike longer."

After thinking about how to do it and analyzing the mechanism, I found the answer. It was simple. We had to replace the short front fork with a large fork. We had to find the right equipment, but then how could we afford it?

Then, in the distance, I saw my sister's bigger bike. She never used it. I asked her if I could experiment with it. She hesitated but finally said yes. I was happy and ready to experiment.

Ajay, Bobby, and I took the front forks off both bikes, installed the large fork on the Budgie, and put the bike back together. It worked! The Budgie looked like those bikers' motorbikes. The front fork was long and looked very cool and unique. Everyone I showed it to couldn't believe it. The only problem was that it was hard to turn corners since the wheels were too small. We could only ride straight. We laughed at the discovery but still felt it was an achievement.

DAD HAS A CAR

Dad eventually bought a car—a small white Austin. Dad liked clean cars. In Uganda we had people to clean our car, but in Britain we did it ourselves. I didn't mind helping Dad with a bucket and water.

One day we were all dressed up for an event. When we were almost ready to go, Dad saw the car was a little dirty, so he asked me to wash it. I refused as it was about to rain. He was adamant that he wanted the car clean. Finally, he huffed, "If you are not going to do it, then I will." He marched to the kitchen dressed in his dress shirt and clean pants and filled the bucket with water.

I wasn't going to help because it didn't make sense. "Go and help him." Mom urged. We finally got the car washed, it started to rain as we just finished washing it.

Having a car after several years of walking or riding a scooter seemed like a weight off our shoulders. We could finally venture out of Wellington. The next main town was Taunton. It was about fourteen miles away from Wellington. We went there quite often as it was bigger than Wellington and had more shops.

Eventually we bumped into an Indian family. They had a small Indian group in Taunton. We met with them almost every weekend. It was a breath of fresh air to see Indian people who understood us. We invited them to our home, and they invited us to theirs. One of the families had two boys and one girl. They were similar in age to Sadhana and I, and we got along really well.

We cooked chicken curry for them and ate it with bread instead of naan, as we had done in Uganda. Neither family had a big dining table, so we placed a sheet on the floor. Everyone sat around it in a circle.

The men and boys ate first. I watched the men scraping all the meat off the bone. I was new at this and tried to do what they did, but I left some meat on the bone. Dad said, "Scrape off all the meat. You mustn't waste any food." I did what I could, but I didn't like it.

We ate with our hands. The food seemed to taste better that way. We never used knives and forks in Uganda, only spoons. When we came to Britain, we had to learn to use knives and forks.

Dad didn't buy alcohol as it was too expensive. It was a luxury he didn't need. In Uganda, he would have friends come to visit him, and so they often opened a bottle of whiskey for the occasion. One of his friends told him that, since British winters were cold, Dad should buy cider and occasionally have a small cup before going to sleep—it would warm him up.

On our next visit to Taunton, we found a great cider place. Dad bought a small bottle and had a sip when he felt cold. On particularly cold nights, he would give us a small sip too and say it was apple juice. We loved it. Dad bought a gallon the next time we went. He kept an eye on it and marked the bottle so he would know if we drank it. He was the only one allowed to touch it.

Our Life Continues

Since we didn't go out much, we spent a lot of time together. In the evenings, we planned what programs to watch on TV based on the advertisements in the local papers. We circled all our favorite shows. Most of the time, they were comedy shows—we loved British humor. It kept us laughing and we forgot about the outside world. Every day Dad watched the nine o'clock news. Sadhana and I weren't into news; it was boring for us. He often nodded off halfway through but woke up if we changed the channel. We all loved cricket, which we watched every opportunity we got. Dad wanted to record all the big matches, so he bought a video recorder with a corded remote control (the cordless cost more). We were just happy to have a video recorder.

Once Dad came home positively beaming.

"What happened?" My mom was the first to ask.

"I won a bet on horse racing." He said with a puffed out chest.

"You were gambling?" Mom recoiled, "What if you had lost?"

"It was a major race and everyone at work placed a bet." He explained. "I didn't want to be left out, so I just placed a small one.'

"How much did you win?" Sadhana asked with wide eyes.

"I bet it was thousands of pounds!" I cheered.

He laughed, shaking his head, "Nope. I just won one pound."

I deflated instantly. There goes that dream.

The next day, he bought a projector screen for eleven pounds. "I think I deserve a treat for winning." He explained. It didn't make sense to us, but if it made sense to him, it was fine with us.

Dad started to spend more money from there. We asked him where he got the money from, and he showed us a card. "This is a credit card. You can buy whatever you want with it until you reach the credit limit so long as you pay it back before the deadline." He said.

We were worried that he might overspend. However, he was an accountant, so we trusted him. We tried to economize wherever we could, but at the same time we wanted to spend wisely.

Dad told us that he had taken lots of photos in Uganda. Using the projector, we spent an evening looking through all the slides. It brought back many memories of how we had enjoyed our lives in Uganda. I often thought how we got to Britain and wished we were back in Uganda. In Britain we had to start life over with the bare minimum and survive against all odds. Dad's investment in the projector and the screen was worth it. Being able to reminisce on our Ugandan lives was priceless.

The labeled slides were stacked in a yellow case. Dad asked us what we'd like to see and displayed the corresponding slide. I liked the safari pictures. The community we lived in organized a safari for its families to take in their cars. There were eleven families. The women got together and arranged food. The men got the cars ready. We went in a convoy.

We stopped at a large open ground and had a picnic, eating spicy rice called *khichdi* and cold lassi and spicy potato curry. The men played cricket. The children ran around and kicked a ball. We were all so carefree.

The safari sometimes got challenging. We drove through shallow rivers and sometimes water entered through the floor of the car. We were scared the car would sink, but everyone got through safely. We saw lots of wild animals—lions, rhinos, gazelles. My favorite were the elephants. They were big and powerful. We weren't afraid so long as we watched them from a distance.

When we were looking at the slides, I glanced over at Mom. She was tearing up. Dad stayed silent. Sadhana and I commented on each slide and sometimes giggled at our memories.

The slide machine stacked thirty-six photos slotted into the machine, which projected the image onto the screen. After we viewed a photo, Dad manually changed to the next image by sliding a mechanism back and forth. Once we saw all thirty-six photos, Dad emptied the tray and inserted new slides while my sister replaced the old ones back into the yellow case. It was a long process but worth the wait.

The slides were negatives, cut and placed in a thick card like a small picture frame. When the slide was placed in the projector, a light shone through the negative and passed through a lens, which enlarged the positive image on a screen. Initially, when we couldn't afford a screen, we used a white sheet. It was far from perfect, but we were so desperate to look back through our memories that anything would work for us, even a bare wall covered in wallpaper.

When friends and family visited us, they all wanted to see our photos. After dinner, Dad set everything up. We looked at those photos many, many times, but we never got bored. That had been our real lives—so much fun and ease, with great friends and culture. We had been lucky that those photos made it to Britain, or we would have lost the chance to share our memories with others.

When friends and family came to visit us, we went on day trips and saw many places. We lived in a county called Somerset, which is in the southwest of Britain. There were many great places to visit nearby, including Devon and Cornwall. When we went, we were always on the lookout for people who might give us trouble. There were many people who didn't want us there. We often heard comments like "Go back home" and "Pakis, go home." We didn't understand the latter slur because we were Indian, not Pakistani.

We feared bigger groups of racists. They were often members of the National Front. Skinheads had shaved heads and usually wore black steel-capped boots and green Harrington jackets. It was rare to see them alone. We never initiated any trouble and always minded our own business. Even so, skinheads would come close and use abusive language. Luckily, we always got away without them assaulting us. However, the words they spewed spread like poison through our bodies and clamped down on our hearts. In tourist places, at least, we were not the only ones who were not white.

The school my sister and I went to was mostly white. We were the only two Indians. We stuck out like sore thumbs. I got comments like "You look dirty—did you not have a wash today?" The other kids laughed. I couldn't say anything. When I washed, I rubbed vigorously with soap, thinking that if I could remove the top layer of my dark brown skin, the skin underneath would be lighter, just like theirs. Sometimes I scrubbed so hard that I bled.

In Uganda, I had been one of the more popular students. In Wellington, that assertiveness disappeared. I was quiet and shy; I hardly spoke out. I lacked motivation for my studies. In class my chest felt hollow, and I often found myself wondering how my sister was doing. I'm sure she also got nasty comments. We didn't share our experiences, or else we'd have nothing else to talk about. We didn't tell our parents either, as it would upset them. What would they be able to do? Absolutely nothing! *Bear the language. Learn to ignore what they say.* I would tell myself.

The worst times came in my physical education class. I hated going to the changing rooms. They made fun of me. No one seemed to understand how I got there and what we had suffered. They just saw a brown, small boy who didn't belong there. "Paki, go home!" They kept yelling.

I was not the most fit nor the strongest child. My education went downhill. I couldn't see a light at the end of the tunnel. There was darkness all around.

Dad thought he needed to get more income, so he looked for ways to earn more money. He found a guy who sold animal-shaped, battery-operated novelty clocks. They were about eight inches by six inches in size and hung on the wall. The animals were like cartoon characters, very colorful and cute. There was a pendulum at the bottom of the clock that was connected to the eyes of the character, so when the pendulum moved left to right, the eyes did the same.

"I'll take a box of one hundred." Dad declared, thinking he could sell them for five pounds apiece as Christmas gifts. "I'm willing to pay three pounds for each."

"I have fifty now and I'll get you more in couple of days—but I need the money in advance." The guy replied, "I'm even willing to do £2.50 each, as a sign of good faith."

Dad hesitated.

"Two pounds each." The guy amended when Dad didn't respond. "But that's as low as I'll go."

Dad sighed, pulling out the money, "Okay."

"Thanks for the business" The guy winked as the he handed Dad the receipt,

We checked all fifty clocks. Most of them didn't work for long. We waited for the guy to return, but he never showed up. We felt that Dad had got cheated, but we wouldn't say anything. He still had hope that the guy would come. "Once he comes, I'm going to ask for my money back." He declared.

After five days, the guy still had not turned up. He was a con man, and Dad fell for it. We didn't say anything to pressure Dad because it might bring on his asthma, but we all hoped he learned from the experience.

"Can I try fixing one?" I asked Dad one day, holding a clock up.

Dad looked tired, "Yes, go ahead."

I loved fixing things. I took the clock apart and noticed that one of the connectors was loose. I tightened it, and after several attempts I managed to fix it. All the clocks had a similar issue. It looked like a design fault.

We managed to get most of them working and started to sell them for £7.50 to try to recover some losses. Mom took them to the factory she worked at. Dad took them to his work as well. We passed them around our friends in Taunton. After several months, though, we had only sold ten. People found them too expensive. We reduced the price to five pounds to break even, but still they didn't sell. We had about half left. We stored them away once we ran out of ideas and counted it as a loss. It was an expensive mistake, but we learned from it and watched who we did business with.

Trip to India

When I was eleven years old and my sister was thirteen, my parents wanted to send us to India to visit our grandparents. The last time I had been to India was when I was two, and my grandparents missed us. We didn't have enough money for the whole family to go, but since my grandparents were getting old, Dad decided to send Sadhana and I. He had just enough saved to send us. Mom was not happy sending us since India was a dangerous place and we were vulnerable because we were so young.

Even after Dad justified to Mom how important it was to send us, Mom was still discontent. Dad, however, did his own thing (as he always did). He booked our flight. My sister and I were excited to meet our grandparents, and they were anxious to see us too.

My parents took us to the airport in a silent car. Dad had luckily found a good friend who was going on the same flight as we were. Dad asked him and his family to keep an eye on us. They gladly said yes. In those days, people dressed up to fly, so I wore a suit and a tie. I wanted to look smart like Dad. Sadhana wore a nice, comfortable dress.

The air hostess looked after us as well and woke us up when food was served. I ate the food because it was a change from the food we usually ate. However, Sadhana was fussy and hardly ate. I wore my suit throughout the whole flight, which seemed to last a lifetime. It was hard to sleep upright, especially in a suit. I didn't want to crease the suit, so I sat stiff as a board throughout the flight.

Just before we landed, I went to the restroom to comb my hair and straighten my tie. I woke my sister and told her that we were about to land so she could go to the bathroom and comb her hair, as instructed by my Mom.

Once we landed, my heart beat a rhythm in my chest. Thoughts raced through my mind. I was excited to see my grandparents, but I wondered what my parents were doing. I didn't know what to expect. *We'll have to take it as it comes, I suppose.*

Dad's friends and the air hostess guided us to the exit of the plane. The humid heat and acrid smell slapped me in the face as the plane doors opened. I started sweating straight away, causing the suit to chafe. Nevertheless, I didn't want to take my suit off. I wanted my grandparents to see me all grown-up.

There was an airport assistant who looked after us since we were underage and helped us find our luggage. They took us through immigration. My dad's friend also made sure we got through customs and stayed with us until we saw our grandparents.

At first, I looked around and couldn't see them anywhere in the crowd of people. My sister and I got worried. We kept whipping our heads around, tears pooling in our eyes.

"Sanjay! Sadhana!"

"Sanjay! Sadhana!"

"Sanjay! Sadhana!"

Our heads shot up. We followed the repeated calling of our name until, in the distance, we saw our grandparents wearing great big smiles. Sadhana sighed beside me and waved back.

We weaved our way through the crowd until we reached them. We hugged them very tight. They wouldn't let us go.

"Are you two hungry?" My grandmother asked.

Sadhana and I shared a look. "Yes!"

We got into a taxi. All I saw out of the window was poverty. It wasn't clean like Britain. The homes were old looking, with faded paintwork and rusted metal roofs. It was again a different world compared to Uganda and Britain. The taxi's radio was playing Hindi music. I recognized some of the songs as ones Mom sang. I missed her.

We got to an old building. I had thought we were going to a restaurant. This building just had empty rooms with no tables or chairs. My granddad asked a little boy, who must have been about ten years old, to wipe the floor. With a dirty rag, the boy wiped the floor and then wiped his hands on his stained shirt.

Granddad sat on the floor, "Come, sit down next to me." Still dressed in my suit and tie, I sat next to him and my sister next to my grandmother.

Granddad ordered *khichdi* and *lassi*. The little boy brought four glasses of water. To carry them all in one hand, he put his fingers in the glasses. I was horrified. *He just wiped the floor with those hands and didn't clean them.* Sadhana and I didn't drink the water even though we were thirsty. The food came on one large plate. We divided it and ate with our hands. There was so much for me to take in. Sadhana and I found it unhygienic to eat there, so we ate little and stayed hungry.

We got back in the taxi. The driver took us to a train station. My grandparents' home was an eight-hour train ride to Gujarat. Beggars walked up and down the streets in droves. Even though we had had nothing when we first landed in Britain, that was still better than the situation of some of the people I saw in India. My thoughts were mixed. I believed my family was poor, yet beggars came to me to ask for money, thinking I was rich because I wore a suit.

As we sat in the taxi, I wound the window down and pulled out a single rupee to give to a beggar. Within a few seconds the taxi was swamped. They reached out their hands, hoping I would give them all some money. My grandmother saw what was going on and quickly wound up my window.

"There are many beggars here. Are you that rich that you will give everyone money?" She scolded. At that moment I realized there were people in much worse situations than mine.

The train station was crowded. My granddad held my hand tightly and pushed people away to get on the train. There was no system or lines. Everyone pushed and squeezed and sat anywhere they could find space. We had a seat; it was a wooden bench. We sat tightly against each other.

I looked at the other travelers and they stared back at me. I wondered what they were thinking. I felt uncomfortable, so I just looked out of the window. I could feel people staring at me. It was a different stare from the ones I got in Britain.

The train journey from Mumbai to Ahmedabad was about three hundred miles and took eight hours, stopping at several stations. It was more tiring than the plane journey and very uncomfortable. I looked out of the window almost the entire journey to take it all in. The scenery was vastly different from both Uganda and Britain.

We finally got to our Ahmedabad, where a car was waiting to take us home to my grandparents' village. My grandparents' home was one of the largest. It was three stories tall and situated on a corner. The house next door was made of mud and had a buffalo next to the entrance. I was stunned.

"Why do they have a buffalo?"

"Oh," My grandmother smiled, "It produces milk, which that family sells for their income."

I looked at the house in different light. Even though we were poor in Britain compared to others, seeing how some people lived in India made me feel rich.

These neighbors invited us over the next day for tea and snacks. They were very hospitable and offered us a variety of snacks to try. They looked happy. Visiting them made me realize that people find happiness in different forms.

What I noticed is that Indians living in their own country walked freely around without listening to racist comments. They could leave their windows open and make spicy curries, and people walking by complimented the aroma. People didn't consider me different. They accepted me regardless of what I wore or how I looked or how I spoke. Everyone was the same. They understood the culture and got along with each other. I looked like a foreigner, so I didn't fit in completely. Regardless of this, they looked after me and took me to places and treated me like royalty.

I made many friends. The children my age sat around me and asked me questions. They were interested to hear about my life in Britain as everyone's dream was to go to Britain. I only told them the good things because I didn't want to shatter their dreams. I felt free in India. I played cricket with them, flew kites on the terrace, and watched Hindi movies. The kids my age were shorter than me, so I felt taller. I looked more educated. Coming from Britain, I stood out like a sore thumb in India. As I walked along the streets, people looked at me, though not unkindly. I looked fairer than most people in India, unlike in Britain, where I looked darker than most. I was loving the attention for once.

Everything was cheap compared to British prices and money went a long way. However, there were many things that I didn't like. I liked our home in Wellington; I liked the cleanliness in Britain. Everything was organized in specific systems. The flies and mosquitos in India bothered me, and it was too hot to sleep at night. In Britain, it was too cold to sleep. If we had stayed in Uganda, then we would have had the best of India and Britain.

After staying with my grandparents for a month, I was ready to go back. When the day came, there was a car to take us to the train station. We were escorted by a family member. We said our goodbyes to our grandparents and hugged them. They didn't want to let us go. Who knew when we would see them again?

The driver spoke up, "We better leave now, otherwise we'll miss the train." We all cried as we parted and continued waving goodbye as the car pulled away, heart sinking as they faded out of sight contrasting the anticipation zipping through my body as we reached the airport.

My grandmother had given me instructions on how to tip people who helped us along our journey. I remember discreetly giving ten rupees to the person who checked my bag at the airport so they wouldn't harass us. In India, people negotiated in everything. I saw bribery everywhere. I guess it was a way of life, and everyone knew the system.

Coming back home felt good. I was glad to see the clean streets and breathe the fresh air. I hadn't realized the good things about Britain until I went to India. I learned that wherever you go, you must focus on the positive points. There were people much worse off than we were, and yet they had smiles on their faces. At that point I decided I must be satisfied with what we had and be grateful for it. I felt like a changed person after the visit to India.

I told stories to my parents. "The trip was worth it." I declared to their smiling faces.

I think my parents had needed a break from us, since we were still young and needed looking after. But going to India on our own changed the way I felt and thought. I felt more mature and responsible. It seemed I had grown up faster than other children in my year at school, since I had experienced so many things, good and bad, and learned as I went along.

GONE FISHING

My parents didn't buy any toys for us, but family and friends often brought something for us every time they came, so I was satisfied. I accumulated enough toys to keep me entertained for hours. My parents were busy making ends meet, so all the school homework I did was on my own. They had no time to read books to me or sing songs to put me to sleep. When they had time, though, we loved watching *Starsky and Hutch* as a family. The main characters drove a red car with a white arrowlike stripe on each side and a thick white strip on the roof. It was an iconic look. I loved that car. I took a red car from my collection and painted white stripes on it.

I loved the shapes of cars. I collected flash cards that gave information about different cars. After watching the East African Safari Rally, I was crazy about cars—their speed, the sound of their exhaust, and their sporty looks.

I didn't see any nice cars where we lived. People drove older cars. I liked sports cars. All I could do was play with my toy cars and hope that one day I would have a sports car of my own.

One of my uncles visited us and bought us presents to thank us for our hospitality. He bought me a car set with yellow track pieces. I slotted the pieces together immediately and put the car on the track. Raising one end of the track enabled the car to roll. The track had a loop in the middle. There was a springlike mechanism at the beginning of the track that you could pull. A lever whacked the car when let go. The car was pushed forward by the force and ran along the track, making the loop.

Another relative bought me a Meccano set. The system consists of reusable metal strips, plates, angle girders, wheels, axles, and gears. It also had plastic parts that were connected using nuts and bolts. I experimented with different combinations to make working models. I realized that I loved figuring out how things worked.

Since it rained or was cold most days, I spent most of my time playing with my cars and the Meccano set. The set had a small motor that revolved when connected to a battery. I was fascinated with this small motor and thought of how I could use it to make things work. I attached rubber bands, cogs, and gears to it and watched it rotate. I tried to make a car from it by attaching wheels to it. I tried to make a helicopter too. My experiments usually failed, but I loved trying anyway. It kept me busy.

I learned how to use a lot of small tools like screwdrivers, spanners, and the Alan key—a hexagonal tool that fitted into some small screws. I always got confused which way to turn to tighten the screw until I memorized "Close is clockwise." This helped me a lot, and I never got it wrong again.

Dad decided that our English-speaking abilities were lacking. Therefore, he made a rule that when we were at home, we were only allowed to speak in English. We found the language ridiculously difficult, so we ended up hardly speaking. We made fun of some English words—it was a way of remembering words and phrases.

English was my worst subject in school. I kept translating it to Gujarati, so I often made grammatical errors. This made me a slow reader. Kids made fun of me when I had to read a passage out loud to the class. The more they laughed, the more nervous I got. I lost concentration and made mistakes, especially when a word had one spelling but two meanings. The words swam viciously in my head. I lost interest in learning English because of this.

I didn't quite like PE either. Since I was the only nonwhite person, I was picked on a lot. The teacher liked me, though, so I felt somewhat protected. He knew that I was being bullied, so he let me get away with things he normally wouldn't allow. The other kids didn't like that. They detested me for being the teacher's pet.

I was much smaller than the other boys and much weaker. I wasn't good at sports, nor did I attempt to become better. I wouldn't be picked for anyone's team if I improved anyway.

I did, however, make one friend at school. His name was Paul. He was very bright and studied constantly. We became good friends, walking to school together and coming home together. It was about a half mile walk, which took us fifteen minutes. On the way back from school, we picked up conkers, which are a seed of a horse chestnut tree. We enjoyed playing games with them. We would each thread strings through the conkers and take turns striking each other's conker until one broke. When it was autumn, we went through a small, wooded area with trees, and tried to catch the falling leaves. I looked up at the tall trees with the light showering down through the leaves. The quiet chirping of birds blanketed the area. Other kids often avoided the area. If we heard other kids coming, we hid behind the trees until they had gone.

One day, Paul asked me to go fishing. Paul wasn't one to make fun of me, so I could ask him anything and he would help me. I accepted since I didn't know what fishing was and wanted to experience it.

Paul smiled, "Okay, be sure to bring a packed lunch."

I blinked, "What do you mean?" He cocked his head to the side, "What's a packed lunched?" I amended.

He let out a quiet "ah." "It can be anything." He explained, "A sandwich, crisps, fruit, a chocolate bar, a drink—make sense?"

"What's a sandwich?"

"You don't know what a sandwich is?"

"No. Please explain."

He laughed, though not unkindly, "A sandwich is two slices of bread with stuff inside it."

"What sort of stuff?"

"Anything you want."

I was still confused, but I didn't want to bother him further. "Oh. I see. Thank you."

When I got home, I asked Mom to help me make a sandwich.

"What's a sandwich?" I told her what Paul told me. She blinked and began buttering two slices of white bread. "Okay, now what do you want in your sandwich?"

I had no idea.

"How about banana?" I said. So, Mom peeled a ripe banana, cut it evenly into slices, and placed them neatly between the bread slices. She packed the lunch and placed it in a small plastic container.

Paul and I left early in the morning. Our breath clouded in the air and mingled with the fog. We walked to a place called The Basins. I had heard rumors that there were ghosts there. I was frightened to go.

Paul noticed my trepidation. "It's fine. There are no ghosts." He reassured.

Despite this, as we walked, I swear I saw a ghostly figure dancing in the fog. I moved closer to Paul, wearily watching our surroundings as we walked to the pond.

Paul carried his fishing rod, and I carried our chairs and a small cool box. As I sat down, Paul organized his fishing rod and put worms on the hook. This was all new to me, and it felt strange—like I was watching a ritual. The fog lifted and the sky slowly appeared. We must have sat there for three hours without catching anything. I squirmed in my seat. *Why do they find this fun?*

Finally, Paul caught a fish and reeled it in. It was a very small fish. I was amazed until he unhooked it and threw it back in the pond. I sunk back into my chair. *This really isn't any fun.* I wanted to tell him "Let's go home," but I waited for few more hours. He didn't catch any more.

Finally, he said, "Let's pack up." He glanced at the sky, "And let's eat our lunch before we go."

I straightened in my chair and pulled out my sandwich. My stomach had been grumbling for a bit. He reached for his bag and took out his. His had meat and was double the size of mine.

I was embarrassed but started to eat.

After a few bites, he looked at me, "What's in your sandwich?"

I said, "Banana."

He smiled but didn't say anything, so I thought it was fine.

After lunch, we sat for another hour and just talked. I wanted to talk as much as possible to get better at English. He corrected me many times and helped me with my pronunciation, but he never made fun of me. In fact, he asked me many questions about my background. He was a genuine friend.

We walked home, and I was very happy to finally get there. Sadhana heard me come through the front door and ran up as I was taking off my shoes, "So? How was it?"

"It was boring."

She giggled, "Aw, and you were so excited to go too." She poked at my arm, "Only to find out it was *boring*."

Our Diet

Dad knew that we were lacking nutrition in our diet. A friend at work asked him if we ate meat. When Dad answered that we didn't, his friend advised that to survive cold weather, we'd need meat in our diet.

British people were big and looked much stronger than we did. They seemed to have thicker skin. Their hands looked swollen and large. Our hands were small and thin. When we stretched out our fingers, you could see the bones and veins. The cold weather bit through our bodies no matter how much clothing we wore.

One British man suggested we try fish. However, just the thought of eating fish put my siblings and I off. My parents went to the grocery store and found fish coated with breadcrumbs about an inch wide and three inches long. They came in different quantities. Dad bought a small pack of six to try since these "fish fingers" were very expensive.

He made them later that night.

"Try these." He set the plate down in front of us. "They're like potato chips, but thicker."

Despite the fishy smell, I liked them.

Sadhana took one bite and spat it out, "Yuck." She scowled.

Sandip chewed on the fish finger for a while but couldn't swallow it. Eventually, he too spat it out.

Dad didn't buy fish fingers again.

I ate school meals at lunchtime. We lined up in an organized fashion and chose a meal and a dessert. The meal always had some sort of meat—fish, beef, chicken, pork, luncheon meat, or even steak on special days. There was an area to collect veggies and an area for dessert. The teachers sat with the children to eat lunch.

I always sat at a table where there was a teacher so I wouldn't have anyone bullying me. At first it was difficult for me to use a knife and fork. At home we ate with our hands. You cannot eat Gujarati food with a knife and fork, and it tasted better eaten with one's hands. I picked up my food, and one boy saw me. "That's disgusting." He said then turned to tell the other boys.

In Britain, it was indecent to eat with your hands. Dad taught us how to use a knife and fork. We tried to eat our chapati and curried vegetables and pickles that way but had a hard time. It felt very awkward. Mom didn't want to try and continued eating with her hands, but Dad forced Sadhana and I to learn.

"Hold the knife and fork as though you were holding a pen." Dad demonstrated, "Dig the fork into the food. Put the knife alongside the fork, making sure the knife touches the fork. Saw back and forth. Make sure you cut only bite-size pieces. Never speak with food in your mouth."

It felt like there were too many rules about eating food the British way. In Uganda, we never ate our food that way. Why were there so many rules? Food didn't taste right when using a knife and fork, but we had to learn to be part of British society.

Once I sat at a lunch table, I just ate my vegetables. I tried a little piece of meat but didn't like it. The other boys watched me. "Are you not going to eat that meat?" One of them finally asked.

"I didn't like it." I replied with a shake of my head.

They glanced at each other, "Well… can we have it then?"

I handed it over wordlessly. They scoffed it up within minutes.

I was amazed at how much more than me they ate. I supposed that was why they were big and strong.

After they left, I noticed that they left their desserts behind. The next day I traded one of their desserts for my meat dish. I thus had two desserts and a little portion of vegetables for lunch. My favorite dessert was Australian crunch. It was chocolate-covered Rice

Krispies with a thin layer of chocolate on top and thick, hot mint custard poured over it.

Not eating a well-balanced diet, however, affected my height. I was shorter than the other boys. Even when I could feel my shoes getting tighter, I didn't want to ask for a new pair, as I knew how expensive they were. I wore them until the soles developed holes, which caused my socks to fray. I cut a piece of leftover vinyl and put that inside my shoe to make it last a little longer. When it rained, the water came through and then my socks got wet. I felt that I was not allowing my feet to grow.

My parents were concerned.

"You are short—how do you expect your child to be tall?" The doctor told them bluntly.

With that in the back of their minds, they were convinced that I would not be tall. Kids often made fun of me because I was short. On a particularly bad day, I said to God, "There are so many hurdles that you have put in front of us, and they seem to be getting bigger and bigger. When will this end?"

Though our food was not a balanced diet, we weren't sick often. Dad did have asthma, which was weather and stress related. Sometimes it was severe. Unfortunately, we couldn't avoid the weather, but we could reduce his stress by doing what he told us to do without arguing or asking for things. If we saw him having an asthma attack, we had to be on standby. If he asked for anything, we ran and got him what he wanted. He was on Ventolin, which was his lifesaver. He always had it in his pocket. He described the suffocation. He wanted to throw a chair through the window to get air. We knew this was serious. He did what he wanted to do—even when we thought he was wrong in his decisions, we didn't say a word. It might have aggravated his asthma, and that was the last thing we wanted.

Dad was a calm person. He never shouted or raised his voice, but his authority was noticed. If we asked for something, however small, all he did was close his eyes for few seconds and at the same time very slightly turn his head left to right. That was it; the answer was a firm no.

Mom Needs a Break

One day my teeth started to ache. Dad took me to the dentist. The dentist examined all my teeth and said that they were overlapping. Since my face was small, he advised removing four of them, two from the top and two from the bottom.

I was scared. I didn't want them removed, and I was petrified at the idea of pain. The dentist assured us that in years to come, it would be for the better. Dad took the dentist's advice and had them removed. I sulked for the rest of the day and swore to never go to the dentist again.

I couldn't eat much for a whole week, only soft food and liquids. I had to take an absence from school while recovering. Once I came back, the other kids crowded around me.

"How come you weren't in school?" One of them asked.

"Yeah." Another nodded, "You were gone for a long time."

A million lies ran through my head, but I couldn't pinpoint a cool enough excuse. "I had to get teeth removed because my face is too small." I admitted quietly.

A roar of laughter swelled up.

"That's so lame!" Came a croon.

"I know! Imagine that!" Came a reply.

My stomach sank further and further with each word until I couldn't bear it anymore and ran away.

Every day, I couldn't wait to go home to be with my family and play with my toys. In the evenings we watched TV together. Our favorite shows at the time were comedies: *Are You Being Served?*, *Dad's Army*, *Some Mothers Do 'Ave 'Em*, and *The Two Ronnies*. We loved British humor and learned a lot of English from watching shows.

We listened to music the British liked, especially Elvis Presley. My sister liked the Bay City Rollers, who wore tartan clothes. Sadhana had a skirt with a tartan design, and we thought she looked like a British girl. But it didn't suit her, and the skirt was quite short. She wore it once and Dad didn't allow it, so she never wore it again.

It was taking a long time for us to adjust. Three years after coming to Britain and we still haven't fully acclimated to Britain. Mom got really frustrated.

One day, she said to Dad, "My sister is getting married in India. I want to go and see my family." Her face softened, "I miss them."

Mom's pain was evident. She was stressed by our situation and constantly looked exhausted. After an in-depth discussion, Dad agreed for her to go.

She wanted to go for two months. However, we couldn't afford for everyone to go. The only option was for her to go and take my little brother, since Dad had to work and would be unable to care for him. It would be hard for us; how would we survive without Mom? Dad would not do any cooking, so my sister and I would have to do that work.

Mom changed her mind sometime before she was to leave because she was worried about us. She talked to my sister and I and said she could only go if we helped Dad with some responsibilities. We both felt grown up and we knew how much Mom needed this, so we happily agreed to help. Mom showed my sister how to make some basic Indian food.

However once Mom left, most of the time we ate frozen Vesta chicken curry, which came with rice. We lived on it for almost a month—Sadhana even added chicken to her diet after this. Mom left during the winter, so we had tomato soup and bread some days. After school, my sister cooked while I set the dinner table. Dad supervised us and at times rested and caught up with news. After dinner I took all the dishes and pots to the sink. Then I wiped down the table while my sister did the dishes. On the weekends, one of us vacuumed while the other dusted.

We missed Mom and thought often about our little brother. We knew she would be fine since she was in her motherland and would be with her family. She needed this break. Still, it was very lonely without her and my brother around, but we took it a day at a time. Sadhana and I didn't argue; we did what Mom had instructed us to do. We took on our responsibilities like adults.

The Blanket

Winters were bitterly cold. Though each of us had our own hot water bottle, it grew cold halfway through the night. We wore socks if our feet got cold. Eventually, Dad invested in electric heated blankets, which were placed under the bedsheet. We each had one, and it was the best investment ever!

The blankets had a few heat settings, so we put them on "high" about half an hour before we went to bed, then turned them down to "low" when we got into bed. Some people warned us that there was a risk of fire, as an electric wire was sandwiched between cloth. However, we took the risk. There were hardly any cases of fire anyway, so it didn't worry us.

My job every evening at eight thirty was to turn on the blankets since we went to bed at nine. I was scared to go up the stairs because I believed someone could be hiding behind the door or under the bed and would grab my leg, so I timed myself. I had to do it in under forty-five seconds.

I flicked the light switch at the bottom of the stairs and then ran up. To enter the first bedroom, I pushed the door wide open in case someone was behind it. I switched on the light. Hardly touching the floor, I leaped onto the bed in case someone was under it. I reached out for the controller and switched it on. I jumped from the bed to the door and switched the light off. I repeated the same process for the second bedroom. Finally, I went up to the loft room which was the scariest. I ran super-fast, making a lot of noise on the stairs. When

I got back downstairs, I was out of breath. Having a warm bed was worth all that effort.

Coming home from school one day, I opened our front door and the wind slammed it shut. Two of my fingers were caught between the door and the frame. The pain was unbearable, and I screamed out loud. I thought my fingers were severed. Dad quickly ran and assisted me. I was crying and he panicked. My fingers were almost black.

Dad took me to the kitchen and ran warm water over them. My legs were shaking. I tried to stay strong and calm. I didn't want Dad to worry, as I thought it might trigger an asthma attack. Luckily the fingers weren't bleeding. We left them under a warm running tap for fifteen minutes. Afterward they felt better, but the fingers were still swollen and black. I couldn't move them, despite it seeming like there were no bones broken. Dad bandaged the hand up so I wouldn't accidentally bang it against anything. At least I was excused from PE at school. The other kids had to play outside in the cold weather.

FOUND A FRIEND

One day on my way home, a boy started to talk to me and asked me about my background. I'd seen him in my classroom, but he had never talked to me before. I figured he didn't want the others to know that he wanted to be my friend.

"What does your dad do for work?" He asked in an accented voice.

"He's an accountant." I replied, "How about yours?"

"He fixes cars." He gestured off in a direction, "Do you want to come to my house? It's not far from here" I agreed. They lived in a big house. He took me to his room. Once we settled down, he started drawing, and I thought he was incredibly talented.

"Where are you from?" I asked as he was showing off his drawing of some landscape scene.

"France."

It clicked. He was also a foreigner. That was why he understood me.

His mom called for him from the bottom of the stairs. "I made some juice!"

"I'll be right back." He smiled before he ran downstairs.

While he was gone, I looked around his room and saw a book about cars on his desk. I flicked through it, marveling at the photos of sports cars. When he came in with the juice, he saw me looking at his book. I quickly shut it and put it away.

"It's okay." He assured me, putting down the juice, "You can look through it." He sat down next to me, "What's your favorite car?"

I considered it," I don't know."

"Ah. Mine's a Lamborghini."

"Lawm-bo-genie?"

"No, no. Lamb-boar-ghee-knee." After several rounds of this, I gave up.

"Are you interested in cars?" He asked after the impromptu (failed) lesson.

"Yes." I perked up, "Very much."

He went to his desk and picked up a card set that explained everything about different cars, such as their speed. "It's yours, a gift from me." He declared

He also gave me a book about how cars worked. It was his dad's old book.

"I can't take this." I fret.

"I insist!"

I couldn't believe I had made a genuine friend, and I thanked him many times before going home. It was one of the happiest days I'd had ever since we landed in Britain.

I went home and told Mom all about him. I couldn't stop talking. I showed my parents what he had given me, and they were excited for me. Learning about cars was my hobby. I was crazy about cars, especially sports cars. I learned the specifications of all the cars and started to learn about how they worked.

The book showed how each part of the car worked: pistons, steering, brakes, clutch, and many more things. I didn't read other books; this book about cars was the only book that interested me. Uncle Pravin knew about cars too. When he fixed things, I was impressed. I wanted to be like him. I was not afraid of using tools, experimenting, and working out how things worked.

Prayers Answered

Life seemed to be at a standstill. Mom prayed every day in the morning after having a wash. She sat on the floor, legs crossed. Her hands were clasped together, and her eyes peacefully closed. She prayed silently for about twenty minutes. Only her lips moved. Hardly any noise came out, just a slight whisper. I wondered what she prayed about.

She cared for everyone and avoided confrontation. She never shouted or talked ill of anyone. I'm sure she prayed about our health and happiness first. We were stuck, so I'm sure she prayed for God to show us a path to a better future.

After six years of living in a small town, wishing we could be in a place where there were more opportunities, finally, we got a break.

Dad came home one day and announced that his company had offered him a relocation to Orpington, Kent, which was about sixteen miles from central London. People often called Kent the "Garden of England." It rests in the southeast corner of Britain. Also included with the relocation was a company car and a raise.

We couldn't believe it. The whole family was jumping in excitement. We would be close to our cousins who lived in the East End of London. Mom teared up. Her prayers had been answered. Now at least we would have more options for work, school, and possibly even business.

That night no one could sleep. It was a Friday night, so we stayed up late and talked about Dad's exciting opportunity and how it would affect us. We wondered what our house would be like. Would there be Indians living near us? Would we meet any Indians in our new school? We yearned to be near other Indians because we knew they would not judge us.

Over the weekend, we started to organize our goods and declutter. Many items had been given to us and we had used them for six years, so they were ready to be thrown away. Dad had enough money saved so that we could buy new items. We wanted to start fresh.

Dad and Uncle Pravin went to Orpington to look for houses. However, housing was significantly more expensive there than it was in Wellington—more than double. After several visits, Dad realized that we would not be able to afford living in Orpington. He started to get demotivated. He had to think of something.

He and my uncle realized the only way for us to make the move was to live further out in the suburbs. They eventually found a suitable house; it was smaller than our current house, but that was what we could afford. Dad fell in love with it. The most attractive thing about it was a big fish tank built into the wall. When we heard that Dad was buying a house with a fish tank, Sadhana and I jumped for joy.

"Please buy it." We begged. "We will look after the fish and learn about them."

Dad put in an offer, and after some negotiations, it got accepted. The mortgage would be a stretch, but with Dad's raise and Mom working to pay the bills, we would just be able to afford it.

We waited patiently while all the paperwork was going through. I was not sad to move as I hadn't made many friends in Wellington. We all wanted to be close to our relatives, who would be thirty miles away instead of two hundred. Dad explained that the new house had a nice garden and a garage, but it was otherwise older and needed some work.

Our current back garden was long and narrow, about one hundred feet by twenty feet, and divided into sections. The first section was a small flower bed. We tried to grow flowers but failed. We didn't want to spend money experimenting, so most of this section was weeds.

There were tulips that grew every year, but they didn't last long. At least they were colorful.

Along the back of our house was a small pathway for the neighbors to walk along to get to the backs of their homes. I often walked along that path to see what others had done in their gardens. Some were really manicured and looked very well maintained. A few were used to grow fruit and vegetables. Sometimes I wished we could have a perfect garden. We hadn't had a garden in Uganda, so we were useless at looking after the garden. Maybe in the new house, I could learn. It wasn't my interest—I thought gardening was for old people—but I could help Dad by mowing the lawn, at least.

We didn't have a garage in Wellington, and we looked forward to putting the car in the garage in our new home. It would be useful in wintertime. Often, we had to scrape ice off the windscreen on cold mornings. Sometimes Dad got a small bucket of warm water, threw it on the windscreen, and turned on the wipers at full speed so the water didn't freeze.

Everyone parked their cars outside their front gardens. All the houses along our road touched each other, and the front gardens had a three-feet iron fences to separate them. Our front garden was concrete, which was great since we didn't need to maintain it. There were hardly any cars on the road. Most people walked to the shops or took the bus. Cars were costly.

Unfortunately, the house purchase fell through as there were defects. It had termite damage and didn't pass inspection. To treat the problem would be too expensive for us. Though it would have been our dream house, we couldn't afford to repair it and the seller would not go any lower. It had been the cheapest house in the area, and now we knew why. We were all very disappointed. Having a fish tank in our house would have been a dream. I thought, *One day I'm going to buy a house and put in a fish tank*. Mom explained that there may be something better for us, and that was why God didn't want us to buy this house.

After several more viewings, Dad found another house. It was about two miles from Orpington in a small town called Green Street

Green. This house was much newer than the other house. It also had a garage, but it only had a small front and back garden. It had a flat roof and looked decent from the outside.

Inside there was a reasonable-size kitchen and a big room that could be used for sitting and dining. It had a wide patio double door, so the room had a lot of natural lighting. I noticed it had a copper-effect wallpaper on one of the walls, which was unique. The rest of the wallpaper in the main room looked like wooden panels. Upstairs there were two bedrooms to one side, a bathroom in the middle, and a small box room on the other side. Halfway up the stairs was a nice big window that had a view to the front. The house was on a dead-end road. There was only one house next to it. Beyond that was a wooded area, so it was quiet.

We all liked it. It was newer so the value had potential to grow. Dad drove us around the area. The schools were far away. There was a Catholic school about a mile away, and I was to be admitted to that school. I scowled. *We aren't Catholic, so why would I go to that school? If it's Catholic, there will be no Indian people.* I told my parents there was no way I was going to that school. Mom and Dad understood.

The only other school was Charterhouse, which was a mile and a half away. It was a mixed school; my sister and I could both attend. However, we would have to walk to and from school on our own every day. We didn't like the idea of that, especially in the winter. But what choice did we have? We accepted.

Dad placed an offer on the house before someone else could place theirs, and we waited for the seller's response. After hard negotiation, they finally accepted £21,000. We had a buyer for our current house at £11,000.

We hoped nothing would go wrong with the purchase. Mom prayed every day. Finally, all the paperwork was ready to complete. Things could still go wrong even minutes before the contract was signed, so we prayed until we heard from Dad. We waited patiently for the phone call. When it came, he declared, "We are moving to Orpington!" We were all excited to start a new life near our family.

The final days in Wellington were sad—not because we would miss people, but because we would miss our home. It had been a cold house that we turned into a warm home. The hard work we had done made it look like new. We learned many skills, like wallpapering, painting, tile installation, drilling holes, and even a bit of gardening. We were sad to leave our first home in Britain, but at the same time we were ready for a change.

I walked from the top floor to the bottom floor, looking at every corner of all the rooms and storing all my memories. This would be the last time we would ever be able to see our home. I thought of the last day in Uganda, when we also had to leave our home. Though we would stay in Britain, moving near London would be totally different to living in Wellington.

NEW START

We all took a last look at our home as we left for Orpington. Mom teared up, and I could see she had many fond memories of our first home. Sadhana was on a school trip and returned on the same day as our move; therefore, she didn't have a chance to see our home for the last time.

We drove to our new home. The journey was long and bittersweet, but I focused on staying positive—this time, things would be different. At least I could speak English now, so I should be able to communicate better. I hoped I'd be able to make friends.

We finally got to our new home. We rested after the long journey and tried to take it all in. As we started to unpack, I began feeling cramped. The house didn't have a loft. It had a flat roof, so there was no space for a room or storage. At least it had double-glazed windows to help keep the cold out, though. There were radiators throughout as well, so the house stayed warm. We used the garage to store the boxes until we organized ourselves. We didn't have many things, so it didn't take long before we sorted them out.

The first thing we did was buy wardrobes for the three bedrooms so that we could hang clothes and place shoes on the bottom. The cupboards came as a flatpack. We had to follow step-by-step instructions from a booklet to assemble them. I did most of the work while Dad supervised me.

We bought blinds for all the bedrooms and curtains for the patio door in the living room. The curtains were blue and made of velvet material. Blue was Dad's favorite color, so he insisted on having blue curtains. They did not match the furniture, but that was his choice.

We went to buy a carpet for the living room. Our walls had wood-effect wallpaper and our curtains were blue. Dad chose a carpet that had a busy blue-and-brown design. After some time, Dad bought green sofas, again in a fabric that felt like velvet. They were on sale, so we couldn't be fussy about the color. At least they were comfortable.

Mom found work at a gas station about three-quarters of a mile away. She started work at seven each morning and finished at three in the afternoon. Dad dropped her off in the morning, but she had to walk home. The steep hill we lived on was challenging for her, but there were no other choices.

She worked as a cashier. She picked up very little English, but for this job she didn't need to communicate much with the customers. She was great with arithmetic, which she learned from Dad. She was very accurate and hardly made any mistakes. Her sweet voice encouraged customers to ask her questions, and with her broken English she managed to communicate.

Her job also involved selling oil. She asked every customer if they needed to buy oil. She got extra money for reaching a certain quota, which served as her motivation. Every chance to earn a little extra would help to pay the bills. Within a short time, she was recognized by her district manager as the highest seller in the area. She got extra money and was liked by her manager and the upper managers.

One night as I lay in bed, I couldn't get to sleep. I was piecing together important things and storing my experiences in a separate part of my brain.

I looked up at the ceiling, deep in thought. I couldn't figure out what life was about or how the world worked. There were so many questions that I couldn't figure out. My questions kept me up all night. How could my dad afford this house? Why didn't God make everyone the same? Why was there so much hatred in the world? Why was the sky blue?

I was fourteen years old. I was too young to understand many things. Still, I genuinely wondered how Dad had enough money saved to buy a house. I asked him the next day. He taught me what a mortgage was, about the interest paid to the bank, and how long his commitment was—typically a twenty-five-year term.

That evening, I worked out my entire life. My dream was to retire at age fifty. Therefore, I would need to buy a house at age twenty-five with a twenty-five-year mortgage. It would take me one or two years to find a house, so I would have to start looking at age twenty-three. I thought if I got married between twenty-three and twenty-five, and we both worked, then a house would be affordable. Dad said that the bank would require a down payment, usually 20 percent of the value of the house. It seemed like an impossible task—just a dream.

Sometimes I felt that I was different to others in the way I thought. I tried to explain my logic to people, but they never understood me. They looked at me as if I were crazy. I didn't speak much in general, especially to people who were not family. Outsiders saw me as a shy, thin Indian boy who hardly spoke. It was hard for me to mix. I lacked education and general knowledge. Inside me, I felt I had more to offer. I was looking for my moment and to be around people who encouraged me instead of demotivating me.

School Life

We moved during the middle of a school year. I would be in the nineth grade and Sadhana in the eleventh. Dad completed all the forms for admission into Charterhouse. Dad's company paid for our school uniforms as part of Dad's moving package.

On the first day, we got dressed in our new school uniforms and Dad drove my sister and I to our first day of school. For other children, the school year had already started. They had all settled and made new friends. We joined in October 1978. We were asked to meet the headmistress at ten in the morning.

The headmistress was nice. When she saw us for the first time, she welcomed us. The boys had to wear a tie as part of the school uniform. I didn't mind wearing the tie as it made me look smart. The headmistress kept looking at my tie. Eventually she said, "Come here." I went toward her.

She knelt down, "I need to show you how to wear your tie correctly." She took off my tie and showed me how to tie it step by step. "This is how it should be worn. Keep practicing and you'll get the hang of it."

Dad finalized all the forms and left us with the headmistress, wishing us well. We waved to him and took a deep breath to face our first day.

The headmistress asked a teacher to take Sadhana to her first lesson. Then she looked at me and I looked at her, and we just smiled at each other. The headmistress led me along a long corridor. We passed some classrooms, and all I could see were white children. No Indians. My heart sank.

After passing about ten classrooms, we reached my class. The headmistress entered the class and I followed. I glanced at the children, and all I could see was a sea of white faces. There was pin-drop silence. I quickly dropped my head down. I didn't want them to see me, I knew at the instance that I was different from them.

The teacher clapped, "Alright, children. This is Sanjay Patel. He'll be joining our class from now on." She turned to me, "Go ahead and find a seat and settle down."

I looked up and scanned across the room to find a seat, I saw a couple in the middle. As I approached a seat, the boys on either side spread out their arms and legs, trying to stop me from taking that seat. There were no other seats except the ones along the window where no one else sat, so I sat on my own.

About ten minutes into the class, I felt a small piece of rolled-up paper hit my right ear. I looked in the direction where it could have come from and saw a bunch of kids snickering. One boy looked straight at me with a stare that could kill. I looked away. Again, a pellet of paper was flicked at me. It wasn't a good start. *This is no better than my old school.* I hoped Sadhana was having a better day than me. I couldn't wait to go home.

We had arranged to meet outside the front gate and walk home together. My sister and I seemed to be the only two who were not white. Our walk was not pleasant. The other kids stood in groups and made snide comments about us as we passed. We tried to ignore what they said and walked on the other side of the road to avoid them.

We just wanted to get home quickly. Unfortunately, the walk home was a mile and a half. Most kids didn't live that far, so the first half mile was the hardest. Near our house was a steep hill that was almost a quarter of a mile long. It was tiring to climb. After walking for about forty minutes, we finally arrived home.

"How was school?" Mom asked with a smile.

Sadhana and I shared a look. We didn't want her to upset her. "It was fine." We hated that school.

Lunchtime also presented a problem. My sister and I didn't want to eat lunch at school. The other kids sat and ate lunch together. We felt left out. Our food was not like the other kids' food, so it was embarrassing to eat in front of them.

Dad arranged his lunchtime around ours. If we timed it just right, Dad could pick us up from school and drive us home, where we ate lunch together, and then drop us back within the hour allotted to us for lunch. As soon as the bell rang, we ran to find Dad waiting for us. It took about seven minutes to drive home. We had the same food every day: egg on toast and tea.

My sister and I had duties to perform while Dad took an afternoon power nap. He would change into comfy pajamas and lie down while my sister made the eggs and toast and I set the table. It took about twenty minutes to get the food ready. We then woke Dad up and sat together to have our lunch.

After lunch, I took the dishes to the sink. My sister washed the dishes while I wiped the countertop and put the table away. Dad freshened up and watched the news. Overall, our time at home was forty minutes. It took another seven minutes to get back to the school, leaving us just enough time to get to class. There was no room for error.

My sister attended Charterhouse School for less than a year. She got a job at the supermarket at the bottom of the steep hill where we lived. I continued at Charterhouse for another three years. School was tough because of the racism. At that time, there were many bullies too. I really did try to excel in all subjects, but I couldn't concentrate on my education and did poorly. Learning the basics of all the subjects was not enough. I just passed basic English, math, physics, chemistry, and biology.

Many English words stuck in my mind. These were interesting words that Ajay, Bobby and I made fun of. One was "vice versa." In math it was "hypotenuse." In physics it was "siphoning." In chemistry it was "the periodic table," and in biology, "esophagus."

In class we had reading time. I would skip class whenever it was my turn to read aloud. I couldn't read as fast as the other kids.

The first time I was asked to read, I froze. I could see all thirty kids waiting for me to read. I was shaking. No words would come out of my mouth.

The teacher sighed, "Come on, we haven't got all day." So, I tried.

My reading didn't flow in the way the writer intended. The words seem to be muddled coming from my mouth. I tried to read fast but missed words in between. The kids laughed, and the little confidence I found went to zero. It was only a passage I had to read, but it seemed to be an epic instead. I went red as sweat beaded my forehead. When my turn was over, I sat down and took a deep breath.

The kids looked at me. "That Paki can't read." One said.

All the children laughed.

I sunk into my seat. *If I were in Uganda, I would have tried hard to be the best student and earn respect from my friends and teachers. Here I'm an untouchable. Is this how the Ugandan Africans felt?*

RACISM CONTINUES

After a few months of living in Orpington, we experienced another form of racism. I was ready to go to school when, in my peripheries, I spotted large writing spray painted on our garage door. **PAKIS GO HOME.**

I quickly ran inside and told Dad. He came out and looked at it for a while. The lines in his face deepened. I stood beside him, clutching my shirt. We had been good people, so why was this happening to us? We had thought we moved to a civilized area and people would be nicer here than in Wellington. Instead, it seemed to be getting worse.

We tried to wash off the paint, but it wouldn't come off. We used different cleaning materials and chemicals, but nothing would shift it. Passersby looked at us as we attempted to take off the sickening words. It was embarrassing. Scraping the paint off was a last resort. We would have to repaint the whole garage, no doubt only for them to do it again. We eventually found some sandpaper, so we tried to sand off the words. They did come off, but the garage paint came off too. We left it like that for few months before deciding to repaint the whole garage door. Luckily, that was the only time such a thing happened. Regardless, the memory scared us every time we stepped out of our door, as the racists knew where we lived.

We were all worried walking on the road—Sadhana and I walking to and from school, and Mom walking from her work. Dad reminded us that, whatever confrontations we may have, we should try not to get angry as this would aggravate them. We were to stay calm and ignore bullies. We were outnumbered by far, so there was no point in trying to attack them. They would beat us into a pulp.

Every day we watched the nine o'clock news. After more than six years, the racism went on. National Front groups were all over Britain, shouting "Wogs out" or "Pakis go home." We saw that the South Asians were attacked by groups of whites. Many South Asians owned small shops; some had windows smashed. Graffiti was scrawled on their cars. Some even had Molotov cocktails thrown inside their homes through their letter boxes.

The skinheads with their shaven heads troubled us the most. You didn't want to mess with them. The boots were their lethal weapons. Skinheads were anti-immigrant. They usually roamed in gangs. There were several incidents when they had stopped me as I walked home and come close to my face, shouting filthy language. Remembering what Dad told me, I did nothing.

One of the girls in my class saw that I was being treated badly. She offered to walk home with me. She lived about halfway to my house, so she gave me company for the worst part of my walk. I noticed that when I walked with her, no one insulted me.

During classes, another girl saw that the boys were picking on me. She talked to me, and I told her my story of how I got to Britain and that it wasn't through choice. Other boys saw me talking to her, "You better stay away from that girl. Her boyfriend is the toughest in our year, so don't flirt with her."

I got scared and tried to avoid her. I didn't know her boyfriend until I saw her with him one day. She asked around if anyone had seen me. No one knew where I was. Her boyfriend was looking for me, probably to beat me up. I hid in the carpark behind a large car.

Then in class, she caught up with me. "I want you to meet my boyfriend."

"No, thank you." I shook my head, looking for an escape.

"You should!" She smiled, "I told him your story. He wants to look after you."

My eyes woke up. Suddenly I felt energy inside, and some hope that things would get better. "Yes, let's meet him."

During the next break, I did. He was very tall and handsome. He seemed tough, but people respected him. He had a great physique and was very smart. He extended his arm to shake my hand. I had never shaken someone's hand. I extended mine. He had a firm grip and introduced himself in a deep voice and with a smile on his face. People saw me with him and left me alone.

Later, I found another friend who lived near me. To go home, he went in a different direction than the others. It was quieter. He was also known to be one of the tough guys, so I felt safe going home with him. I talked about my background as we walked. I learned a lot from him in general conversation. In the morning we met at a certain point at a precise time. We did the same coming home. It was still thirty minutes' walk for me.

This friend was into music. At that time, many different types were popular. I couldn't understand any of it—rock, heavy metal, reggae, soul, jazz, and pop. There were so many artists, I couldn't keep up with the popular trends. One that I liked was Debbie Harry and her band, Blondie. I later enjoyed soul.

I made another friend who also took me as I was. He said a group was meeting up and invited me to join them after dinner, around eight o'clock. I hesitated, but at the same time I didn't want to get left out. This was my opportunity to make friends. I accepted the invitation, and they were thrilled that I would join. I told my parents that I'd be going out to meet friends. They were very nervous, thinking that I would get into a fight. Mom said, "With all this racism, it's dangerous to go out." I was torn. Mom continued, "We are not like them, hanging around in the streets. You will be open to getting into trouble." In the end, I still went.

It was dark and cold. There was no one on the roads. I felt scared and thought I should go back. If skinheads saw me, that would be the end of me. I started to walk fast. Eventually I ran until I got to my friend's house, which was about a quarter of a mile away. I saw my friend with three others. They were smoking cigarettes. I'd seen all of them at school. They introduced themselves and talked to me. They seemed to be friendly. After ten minutes, they asked if I had ever smoked before. I said no.

One boy lit up another cigarette, "Here you go. Try it." Again, I was at a crossroad. If I wanted to be one of them, then I'd have to try it. However, if my parents found out, they would kill me.

I refused many times, but they insisted, "Just one puff."

What the heck. I took a puff as if I'd smoked for years. Then I coughed and couldn't inhale. I quickly put it out, "That's not for me."

They laughed, "Well done, mate. At least you tried." I did it to please them.

They got a big stereo and said, "Let's go down the road and play music at high volume." One boy turned on the stereo and put it on his shoulder. They were playing "Ace of Spades" by Motörhead. They joked with me, "We'll have to get you a black leather jacket, and you'll be the first Indian heavy metal guy." I could see that they wanted to help me fit me into their group, but I was totally different to them. That was the first and last time I went out with them.

I realized that to truly make friends, I had to be similar to those friends, as they were not going to change for me. It was very hard to make friends. Our backgrounds often clashed; I would never be like them, and they would certainly not be like me. Yet I had to live in a white community, so what could I do? Now I understood why Ugandan Indians wanted to go to Leicester.

I'm Not a Boxer

One of the boys in my class was a boxer; no one messed with him. One day, he asked me to hit him. I laughed, "There's no way."

He glared at me, "*Hit me.* Punch me in my face."

I didn't know what he was trying to do. He said that he would not punch back, nor would he try to block my punch. Other kids started to watch us.

He told me to tighten my fist and put them up as though I was protecting my face. I wouldn't do it, *couldn't do it*— I had frozen. He then grabbed both my hands and showed me how it should be done. "Now aim for my face and take a punch." He said.

I punched, but he moved away, dodging the blow. "I don't want you to hit me in slow motion, hit me with a fast punch." He demonstrated with a swift swing.

I focused on his face—if I hit him, I'd be like a hero. So, I tried hard. I took couple of swings and missed every time as he dodged with ease.

"Faster." He demanded. I still never landed a hit.

Later, he told me that he had been watching how kids picked on me and wanted to teach me how to protect myself. I was so happy at his thoughtfulness. He told me that he went to a boxing club and asked me to join. I refused; however, he kept insisting.

After several weeks of him asking, I accepted. We arranged where to meet and he took me there. We got to the boxing club and everyone stared at me as they were practicing. I felt very uncomfortable. I thought they were all racist. They were all white, well built, and tall. My friend introduced me to few people and I started to learn a few training drills.

I had never put on boxing gloves before—they were huge, and I had that feeling people were watching me. I could *hear* them laughing at me. My friend told me to just ignore them.

I had gone there maybe four times when the coach said, "Sanjay, get ready for a spar."

I didn't know what that meant, so I asked my friend who told me that I was going in the ring to fight. I knew I was not ready and refused to go. My friend gave me few last-minute tips and tried to encourage me. Finally, I reluctantly stepped into the ring.

My opponent was about 4 inches taller than me and well built. It looked like he had been fighting for a long time. I wondered then if he was racist. If he was, then this would be perfect for him to take out his grievances on me. I tried to remember what my friend said. I'm going to release the temper that these bullies gave me and I'm going to go for him.

When the bell rang, I didn't know what I was doing, I just kept on trying to punch nonstop and missed every time. He was quick and I was slow to dodge. He never missed a punch. When the referee stopped the fight within the first round, I was bleeding from my mouth.

I was glad he stopped it—it could have gotten much worse. My friend said that I did well and there's lots to learn. I got cleaned up and was ready to go home, still shaken from the punches.

We left the club and went our separate ways. It was about 9 p.m. and pitch black. I was scared since I had to catch a bus home. I was hoping I wouldn't bump into gang of troublemakers. However, a gang saw and approached me. There were three skinheads.

One said, "Hey, Paki."

I ignored him and put my head down, looking at the ground.

"He's not talking." Another said, "Let's just beat him up."

My head shot up, "No! Please! Let me go!"

The third saw I was bleeding from my lip. "Nah, someone has already beat him up, but we'll get him next time."

They left as my bus arrived.

I got home safely, but my parents had waited up for me. They saw my bleeding lip and asked me to explain. I told them the truth; however, they didn't believe me and forbade me from going out—meaning, no more boxing.

They explained that we are not like them, we *can't* be like them. We are different to them.

That was the last time I went boxing.

I didn't know how to fit in. If I wasn't like them, they wouldn't accept me. Some had tried to make friends with me, but they talked about soccer, music, and video games. They spent a lot of money on buying records and they talked about their record collections.

I thought I could at least get interested in music, but we didn't have money for records. Dad *did* have an old radio and a tape recorder though. When a song came on the radio that I liked, I placed a microphone to the radio and recorded the songs on the tape recorder. I made cassettes and played it repeatedly to try to learn the words. I listened to the top 40 songs in the charts and recorded the most popular ones. I was so happy that now I can talk about music and relate with the other boys. However, they listened to different type of music— mainly rock. No one was really interested in Soul music, so I was back at square one.

One day, one of the boys asked me to go to the gym with him to build some muscles. He was in great shape. I declined a couple of times, claiming that it wasn't for me. He insisted though and told me I'd feel good—that I could pick up a brick and throw it through a window without even feeling the weight of the brick.

I laughed at the image. "Okay." I finally conceded.

I went several times and I felt good. Eventually, I entered a competition of who can lift more in comparison to their body weight. I came second.

Everyone thought it was unfair as I was much lighter than everyone else, but I was unbothered. For the first time, I felt that I have achieved something. At last, people started to recognize me for something good. I was being seen. I started to get some respect. I wanted to keep it up with fitness and do it at home.

Dad knew that we looked weak and he encouraged my new hobby, so he bought some equipment that functioned like a rowing machine. It's placed on the floor and has a seat that goes back and forth. As you push with your legs, the springs will pull it back. There were also additional handles that's attached to springs that you pull simultaneously like one would when rowing a boat. You could also detach the springs and attach it just to the handles to tone the arms.

We also had a chinning bar which attached horizontally to a door frame. I installed it onto my bedroom door frame and set a goal of doing five pullups every time I went in or out of my bedroom, increasing by one every week until I reached thirty

It was hard at the beginning. However, after about three months, I could see a change in my shoulders and forearms. I kept on going until I reached my target of thirty a day. With the in-house exercises, I felt much stronger. I hadn't realized that just by focusing I would be able to achieve something.

Dad also bought Arnold Schwarzenegger gym equipment for me. I got even stronger. However, while I had the strength, our diet prevented me from having the shape.

Can't Afford It

One day when I was walking home from school, my friend said that he bought a video game console that was four hundred pounds and each game forty to fifty pounds. I thought he must be rich. There was no way I could buy that expensive machine. This was yet another difference between us.

We saved in my family, which may have caused us to miss out on the fun stuff. In contrast, the British lived from paycheck to paycheck. They enjoyed their lives. There's reason for both sides; neither were right nor wrong—it's just a different way of life. Their parents will give them these consoles for Christmas presents. We would be lucky to get a gift. My parents *did* give us some money during our festivities however, like Diwali and birthdays.

I missed riding a bike, but I knew it was expensive. One day as I was walking back from school, I saw a bike in a skip—someone didn't need it and threw it away.

I went passed the skip for two days and it was still there. One late evening I went to get it. I didn't want anyone to see me and think that I was a tramp going through the skip. The bike was in a very bad state, and I couldn't ride it, so I carried it about half a mile home.

Sadhana took one look at it and asked, "What junk have you bought home?"

"It's not junk." I told her, "I'm going to try and fix it."

All the color of the frame had come off, the brakes weren't working, and there was no chain or seat. The handle was crooked, and the pedals were missing, but it was the perfect size for me.

I've fixed bikes before and was ready to take on this project. The next day, I went to the bike store at the bottom of the steep hill we lived on. I had made a list of all the items I needed. It was very expensive.

The store had a section exclusively for secondhand items like handlebars, pedals, etc. I couldn't get everything at once, so I kept going back until I got most of them. However, I had to buy a few items brand new, so I ended up using all my present money to fix my bike.

Finally, I sprayed it black. I cut a piece of red tape in a shape of a long arrow and stuck it along the frame. I named it -red arrow. I had brought it back to life.

There was a field near my house where I tested the brakes. It was working great. I took the bike to the top of the hill and started to pedal faster and faster and as I approached the end, I braked hard, expecting to slide on the grass. However, the brake cable snapped, and I went straight into the hedge. Luckily, I only had lots of scratches. Without the hedge, I would have ended up on the road and the injury would have been more severe.

Water on the Roof

The house we lived in was comfortable. However, while trying to get to sleep, I could hear the rain, and it kept me awake. I lay in my bed with my eyes open and looked at the ceiling. I noticed water slowly running down the walls. I shot up and ran to wake Dad. We got towels and stayed up all night until the rain stopped. The next day, Dad talked to a roof repair guy to resurface the area where the leak was coming from. It was a temporary fix.

A few months later, after getting quotes, Dad had no choice but to have the whole roof redone with a self-reflective surface. It was more expensive, but Dad wanted the best material, so it wouldn't happen again. The guys went up and down the ladder many times. We couldn't go and see it until it was finished. Once they had gone, it looked amazing and gave us peace of mind.

About six months later, we had very heavy rain during the night. Again, the rain kept me awake. I suddenly heard a roar like a waterfall. I couldn't see any water running down the walls, so I thought we were fine. I tried to get back to sleep, but that noise annoyed me. I got up to investigate. To my shock it looked like water was overflowing from the roof.

I woke Dad, "We really have a big problem."

We went outside in the heavy rain and saw water overflowing from the ledge of our flat roof. It was coming down the sides of the house, front and back.

"Take this," he handed me a bucket, "and take as much water off the roof that you can." He instructed. "If you don't, the weight might cause the roof to cave in."

I hurried to do what he said, but the heavy rain just filled the roof again. I tried for half an hour, but it was no good and went to see why the drainpipes weren't working. When I peaked in, I saw that it was clogged with gravel. The roofers had brushed all the gravel from the roof down the drainpipe. The water had nowhere to go. I had to think fast to save the roof. I thought hard. I thought about creating a dummy drainpipe.

I thought of a physics lesson—how to siphon from a high level to a low level. I closed my eyes and pictured the diagram. I had to get a long pipe. I came down and looked around in the garage and found a hose pipe. Perfect! I attached one side of the hose to the tap in the kitchen sink and filled the hose with water. I asked Dad to block the other end and not let any water escape.

I went up the ladder with the other end. I placed the hose in the drainpipe, about three or four feet. I asked Dad to remove his hand from the bottom of the hose. To our relief, the water started to flow through the hose. We watched it for about ten minutes with smiles on our faces. It was an idea that not many people would have thought of. Now we could go to sleep. The water would continue draining until the rain stopped and all the water was siphoned out. In the morning, the water had all drained away.

We called the roofer in the morning, who never responded. We felt they had done this on purpose because we were Indian. Or perhaps they were too lazy to do the work? We tried to brush it off as a one-time heavy rainfall that wouldn't happen again. However, in the backs of our minds, we knew that we couldn't leave it like that. The thought of how much it would cost to fix was unimaginable. It would be a huge job to take the gravel out of the drainpipe because the drainpipe was buried between the bricks. We left it like that for a few months.

In the winter, it didn't snow as much in Orpington as it had in Wellington. We often saw a lot more rain instead. On one cold evening, it started to rain heavily. Overnight the temperature dropped below zero, so the water turned into ice. We woke up in the morning and saw water dripping from the upstairs ceiling along the inside of the perimeter walls. We couldn't understand what had happened. Dad told me to check the roof.

I got a ladder and climbed on the garage roof. I pulled the ladder up and climbed onto the upper roof. I could see ice along the edge of the roof. The blocked drainage must have iced up. As the ice melted, the water had found cracks along the edges, causing it to enter the house. I had to think quickly as Dad could not climb up to help.

I came down the ladder and got a hammer and a chisel. I got back up onto the roof and started to chip away the ice from the edges so that the water formation was reduced. The ice was solid, and it was hard work. I had to be careful not to cut into the surface of the roof. It took almost three hours of bending down and chipping. I was exhausted and very cold. I came down—and as I was coming down, I heard a crack in my back.

I couldn't move.

My back was bent and I couldn't straighten it up. I slowly came down the ladder in that position. The pain was brutal. I slowly walked into the house, trying to hold myself up. I lay on the floor for about an hour before I could straighten out. The cold had seeped into my back and stiffened it.

It was a weekend, so I rested. I was in pain if I moved. I slept directly on the floor for two days. Mom nursed me and rubbed balm on my back. She placed a hot water bottle on it to warm it up.

The pain ran down my right leg. I could hardly walk. I took few days off from school and visited the doctor. He did some movement tests and said that I had sciatica, a pinched nerve. I had to rest for a week. I got released from school due to illness. The doctor said I could not play sports for six weeks. I was happy because I didn't want to play in the cold weather. I assisted my PE teacher instead.

The doctor gave me a strap to put around my waist as a support. I felt like an old man with back problems. *Now I can't do any fitness at home.* I started to look like myself again, weak and thin.

The Dream

I was not happy in Britain. It felt like I couldn't live a free life. There were always obstacles. I often thought about life back in Uganda. Several times I dreamed that we were back in Uganda. One recurred more often than the others.

In this dream, we ran toward a tall wall. We had to get over to the other side, which was Uganda. There were hundreds of people running toward the wall. Dust flew everywhere. Dad held my hand and carried Sandip. Mom held Sadhana's hand. We were all running as fast as we could. Ropes dangled from the top of the wall. We had to climb up using the ropes. People were climbing halfway, then losing their grip and falling. Dad hurried me, "Sanjay, go up quickly. I'll be behind you."

I thought all the pull-ups I'd done would help me climb this wall. I didn't look behind to see where my family was. I had to focus on getting over that wall because that would be freedom. I hoped Uganda would be like it had been before. As I started to climb, I was doing well. However, I almost lost my grip a couple of times. I had to regain my focus.

I finally made it to the top, and as I did, I stretched out my arms. "Freedom!"

Then someone pushed me. I fell to the ground and woke up.

It seemed so real. I was sweating as though I had run to the wall and climbed the rope.

The second time, when I got to the other side, I took a deep breath, "Last time it was a dream. This time it's real; I've made it back to Uganda." To be sure it was not a dream, I started to pinch myself. I pinched harder and harder, then woke up from my pinch. I looked around the room as I woke up and cried.

I was still in Britain.

The heat I had felt on my face in the dream ebbed away. I was disappointed. I was sure I had made it to Uganda. That really would have been a dream come true.

Punched and Kicked

On the weekends, we spent a lot of time at Uncle Pravin's house, which was about twenty miles away in East London. Uncle Pravin was five years younger than Dad, and they were very close. Ajay and Bobby were younger than me by four and five years respectively. We were all very close and enjoyed each other's company. In fact, we couldn't live without each other. Our wavelength was on par. We understood each other—we could almost read each other's minds. We rarely had arguments. Seeing them was a breath of fresh air. Dad knew that we all needed that, to be with people we loved and who genuinely loved us back.

We made every excuse to see each other and took every opportunity to stay with them longer. My parents, uncle, and auntie usually watched movies at home, which was their relaxation time. These movies were Indian movies, which lasted around three hours. In Wellington we didn't have Indian movies on video cassette. In East London, there were many Indian stores that sold such movies.

We were only twenty miles away from this Indian community. There we could get Indian groceries, Indian restaurants, Indian clothes, and Indian jewelry. There were many Indians. It was good to see our people. However, it was dangerous to walk on the streets because of the National Front groups.

One Diwali, we wanted to get fireworks. We were at my uncle's house, and Ajay and I decided to take a bus to the Indian store that sold fireworks. It was about ten miles away. We were fearless at the time, declaring that if anyone troubled us, we'd whip them with our belts. Unfortunately, all the shops had run out of fireworks, so we headed back.

It was wintertime and about eight p.m., so it had long grown dark. Ajay and I were the only ones waiting for a bus. We saw four boys on their bicycles. They rode past us. Then, they stopped and came back and approached us.

"Oi! You threw a stone at us, didn't you?" One accused.

"No, I didn't," I replied. Before I could say anything else, he punched me in my mouth. I heard ringing in my ears. Another punch to the side of my face.

Ajay started crying, they only beat me up. All four boys punched and kicked me as I fell to the ground. They finally left us alone after a good several minutes and rode off, laughing following in their wake.

Ajay and I were shaken and didn't know what to do. Another auntie lived fifteen minutes' walk away, so we decided to go to her house and call Uncle Pravin to pick us up.

Uncle Pravin was fuming. Once he picked us up, he huffed, "Let's drive around, and let me know if you spot those boys. If I see them, I'll break their arms."

My uncle was a tough guy. He had beaten up many boys in his youth. He had fire in him. I'd heard many stories about my uncle and how tough he was. I couldn't wait to see him in action. Fortunately for those boys, we didn't find them.

The incident had spoiled our mood, however. I got a black eye and a split lip, bleeding from the right corner. Aunt Rangan nursed my wounds. We couldn't even go out with all this racism.

My brother, my cousins, and I mainly spent our time at home or just outside their garden, talking, telling jokes, and playing. We played cricket in the alleyway, and many times we hit the ball into the neighbor's garden. "Why don't you go and play in the recreation center?" They'd shout at us. However, many skinheads hung around in the recreation center, so there was no way we'd dare to go there.

We never talked about education or school. However, we did talk a lot about being rich and owning sports cars, big houses, a boat and becoming millionaires. We all had big dreams but never thought about how to make those dreams come true.

Sandip and I stayed over at my cousins' during long holidays. Before Aunt Rangan went to work, she gave us instructions about where to find everything in the kitchen to make our own breakfast. She warned us not to forget to wash up. I was the oldest, so all the responsibility lay on me. We had good working relationships; each person did their own duties. Two of us made the breakfast and set the table, while the other two cleaned and washed up. We didn't want to put any burden on my auntie, so we did other house chores like dusting, vacuuming, placing the clothes in the washer, and drying them on the clothesline.

Uncle Pravin had bought a folding snooker table. It was small, six feet by three feet. We had to bring it downstairs into the living room to play, as there wasn't any other space. We played for hours just to pass time. At night, we put two single beds together, and all four of us squeezed into them. There was no space for movement, so we all slept straight, facing the ceiling. It was uncomfortable but that was our only option. We didn't mind as we were together. We hated going to school after holidays because we had so much fun together. To be apart even for one day was hard. We couldn't wait for the weekends. They were our lives, and we could not live without them.

Renovation

One summer, Ajay and Bobby came to stay with us. One evening while my parents were downstairs, we huddled around a paper in Sandip and I's room.

"Okay, what if we tried sunken beds?"

"Oh! Yes, that'd look great if we put a platform in the middle."

"If you do that, you should also put a light at the front of it."

"I agree, it'd help add a calming ambiance."

"Oh, I just suggested it because it be easier than getting up to turn off the light at night."

"Sanjay, do you think we can add anything for storage?"

"We probably can... what if we make two small shelving units?"

"That'd work! We can put them at the foot of the bed."

"You should add spotlights too! That'd look really awesome."

"Don't forget the walls! If you want this room to look *really* different, you should do something with the walls too."

"Yeah! Yeah! We should make them all white with red diagonal strips! Like a race car!"

"Or a candy cane... but yeah that'd look really cool."

"We could get some blinds to complement it too."

"Horizontal venetian blinds would probably suit that style. What colors?"

"Red, white, and black?"

"Ah! That sounds cool!"

"And to tie the whole look together... what if we put up two posters of some sports cars?"

"Great idea! Do you want to do your would-be Lamborghini and my equally imaginary Ferrari."

"Sounds perfect."

We laughed, writing out the price for that final detail.

"If only, huh?" Sandip quipped.

As the three of them continued to joke around, I scanned the figures we had come up with. "Let's do it."

They stopped, looking at me.

"I think it's doable." I thought for a little bit, mapping out a way to make this work. "Let's plan it out step by step with timing and costs. We'll decide where to source the materials and what each of our roles will be."

They looked to each other, big grins spreading on their faces, "Let's do it!'

As we delved deeper into planning, it started to seem more achievable. We would need funding, however. I'd have to ask Dad. I hoped he was in a good mood. We all went downstairs.

"Dad?" He stopped his conversation with Uncle Pravin, looking at me with a raised brow, "We want to decorate our bedroom." I gave him the paper, "We want to make all these changes."

He scanned the paper, "No. This is going to cost a lot of money."

I shook my head, "No, look on the side. We calculated it and it's only going to be £140."

"It's going to cost much more than that." He huffed.

"No, trust us."

We continued in that vein for a bit before Dad sighed, "Okay. I will give you £140 but not a penny more—and I want the job completed, not half finished."

We all whooped, but when I caught their eyes, I could see they were slightly tense. Could we pull it off? I started to have doubts. I looked at my plan and the budget. I could see ways going wrong. I had saved thirty pounds, so if we went over, I would put my money in.

The next day, we emptied the room. We went to the store to get all the supplies. We made the platform from pallets that we found by a skip. We followed my step-by-step guide. We scraped the wallpaper off the walls. The walls needed two coats of paint. We applied a glossy red stripe, so it stood out against the matte white. We changed the light to a modern, inexpensive light. We ordered the blinds, which would take about two weeks to be made. It took a week to get it done, and it looked fantastic. We could not believe we had made it happen.

I took pictures to show to some friends at school.

"That's amazing!" They gasped, "Can you do my room next?"

"Let me ask!" I smiled back.

When I got home, I asked Dad for permission.

"No." He shook his head, "If you mess it up, then they'll argue with you about the quality of your work and then you'll be in trouble." His face softened, "I know you're good with your hands, but you're not a perfectionist."

People again asked us to do their rooms, but we declined each time. We had saved a lot by doing the work ourselves rather than getting someone to do it for us. I realized that if you had a thousand pounds in labor costs, you would have to earn £1,200 to have a thousand after tax to pay for the labor. I made a saying based on this: "Saving is like earning tax free."

Later that year, I had three months' break from school before I would go to college. I was looking for something to do. I saw that my neighbor had bought an old Mini Cooper. He had stripped it down and repainted it. I watched him while he worked on the car. He explained each stage in the process and the obstacles he ran into. I was fascinated with what he did and accomplished.

I looked at Dad's car. It was an old white Peugeot 504 with and blue seats. In Britain, cars rusted easily, and his car had rust everywhere. I asked Dad if I could respray his car. The neighbor would guide me. Dad asked me to cost it out. I had to get paint, paint thinner, a spray gun, sandpaper, rubbing-down compound, fillers, and a grinder. The cost came out to £220. Dad thought for a while, considering whether I would mess it up. He decided I would learn from it. The car looked very bad, and it would save him money to have me respray it rather than a professional. He agreed.

It was a big project for me. I was excited to start and nervous at the same time. I found a local car parts store and asked, "If I buy everything from you, will you guide me in how to respray a car?"

He said, "Certainly."

Ajay and Bobby helped. We made a step-by-step list and got to work. We sanded down the areas where rust was showing (mainly under the doors and the trunk). We used sandpaper and wire wool; it was hard work. Once we saw the metal, we applied rust-preventing solution and left it for a few days. Then we applied fillers. When the filler was dry, we sanded it, starting with coarse sandpaper and gradually moving to the finest sandpaper to get the perfect shape and line. We were pleased with the result. We then prepared the surface of the rest of the car and masked off everything that didn't need to be sprayed. The car was ready for spraying.

My neighbor gave me some tips to follow so the spray was even and there were no drips. I was scared, so I practiced on a piece of cardboard leaning against the garage wall. It took some practice, but I finally got the rhythm. I slowly did one panel at a time. It came out great. We waited for few days, then sanded the paint down with very fine sandpaper. I applied a second coat and sanded that. I then applied a final coat. I hoped more layers of paint would prevent the rust from forming again.

We used a rubbing-down compound and carefully smoothed down the paint. It took a long time and a lot of elbow grease. However, we were pleased to see it gleaming. We had to wear sunglasses as the white reflection of the paint hurt our eyes. We gave the car a final polish until every panel was like a mirror.

The days were long and hot, so we started early and finished late. Initially, many passersby thought we were going to do a bad job. They thought we were too young to tackle this big project. I was seventeen, Ajay and Bobby were fourteen and thirteen, and Sandip only ten. As the work progressed, the neighbors saw that we did a great job. The car looked as though it had just come out of a showroom. Dad was very pleased. I felt that if I focused on something, I could do anything.

LOWEST POINT

My final year in high school was a waste. My school slated to be demolished for housing the next year. No one cared about classes, and the teachers were not motivated to teach. I received my Certification of Secondary Education (CSE), however I barely passed on all subjects.

Where was I in life? Most kids didn't go to college. I felt that I was better than this and decided that I needed to go to college. I was searching newspapers to learn how to get admitted to a college. It was all too overwhelming. With no direction, I was totally lost. I didn't know who to turn to for help.

The same neighbor that guided me to repaint Dad's car had bought a Spectrum computer and showed me how he did programming.

"If you're interested in it," he commented, typing away, "you should learn about it. It's poised to become an in-demand career."

I didn't think much of it at the time. One had to be clever to be a computer programmer, and I was not.

Then I saw an article in the paper for a course in computer programming. It was in London. I braved up and called them. They asked me to come meet them. I got there, expecting a big building, but this place was small. I walked inside and met one of the teachers.

I was asked some questions, and she showed me to a small room. She asked me to take an aptitude test. She asked if I'd ever taken one. I replied no. She told me to take a practice test, and then she would time me doing one hundred questions. I would have two hours.

I was good at applying logic, and the practice questions seemed easy. Once I completed the real test, the teacher marked it. She looked at the paper and then at me a few times.

"You got a 98." She gasped, "That is one of the highest scores we've ever seen." She put the paper down, "If you want a place in our institution, it's yours. No further questions asked." She smiled, "If you accept, we'll teach you to be a very good programmer."

I was delighted, "Yes, I'd like to join."

I couldn't believe it. This could be the turning point for my future. I'd be able to earn lots of money. I could buy my own house and a nice car and help my parents financially.

The administrator handed me a sealed envelope, "Be sure to give this to your parents." She said. "And don't open it, okay?"

I had a huge smile all the way home. I was excited to tell Dad. I wanted him to be proud, since I hadn't made good grades at school. I felt my life finally had begun; this was my ticket to the future. I reached home and ran to Dad, who was concentrating on the news. I disturbed him and said, "Dad, I have some great news!" I handed him the letter.

"What's this?"

"Open it."

I had a smile on my face, waiting for him to be happy for me. Instead, after reading the letter, he tore it up and said, "This is not possible." He handed me the torn pieces to throw in the trash can. I didn't understand what could be in the letter that he objected to. I ran upstairs with tears flowing down my face. I got to my bedroom and put the pieces of paper together to figure out what the letter said.

The college wanted £1,500 toward fees and other costs. That was too much for us. My dream was shattered. I was shaken. I didn't know what to do with my life all over again.

Every time I tried to get up, I got knocked down again. I was getting tired and losing hope in life. I didn't blame Dad. It was the situation we were in. However, he could have got me a student loan or found another solution. He just didn't have hope in me.

THE BLACK CAT

I wanted to learn to drive as soon as I was legally allowed. I had a passion for cars and speed. I missed watching East African safari rallies. My dream job would have been to be a rally driver. Dad started to teach me how to drive a car. After an introduction, I took lessons.

The car I learned in was a Mitsubishi Lancer. The lessons were expensive, so I didn't take many. I made sure I passed the test the first time. I took Dad's car to help with getting groceries and taking Mom around to shops. My brother and I went to see our cousins many times on our own.

One day I met up with a friend who lived in Taunton and we got to talking. "You should sign up for this computer course I'm taking at Eastham." He recommended, "It's free since Eastham is a community college."

When he said *computers*, my ears were ready to listen. "Tell me more."

I applied the next day.

The college was far from where we lived, an hour and a half each way by train. I had to change lines twice and then walk for twenty minutes to get there. At this point, I didn't have a choice, so I applied and got admitted.

I made friends very quickly. The students were from all parts of the world. I had friends who were Black, White, Muslim, Chinese, and Indian. There was no discrimination between us. For the first time, I found myself enjoying my fellow students' company. I was, however, struggling with the course. I had expected to learn about computer programming. The course was nothing like what I had expected, and I lost interest.

The college gave me lunch tokens up to certain amount. I had to pay for anything over the value of the token. The cheapest lunch was chips and beans, which was one token plus two pence, so nearly every day I had chips and beans for lunch. However, the cost of travel was expensive. I decided I'd get a weekend job sometime.

Sometime later, a brand-new upscale men's clothing shop was built in Eastham and began hiring staff. I applied and got the job. It was my first real job. I went all the way to Eastham just for an eight-hour job. I was shy and lacked the confidence to talk to customers. The people coming in were trendy, and I looked like I'd just come from a village. Racist comments followed me wherever I went. After about six weeks, I couldn't handle the comments, so I left.

Mom said that there was a Sunday morning job at the gas station she was working at, so I applied without hesitation. The work hours were from seven o'clock in the morning to three in the afternoon. Sometimes it was hard to wake up, as I went out with my cousins on Saturday nights and came back in the early hours of Sunday, but I needed the money, so I had to do it.

I need to save, I thought, so I got a shoe box and made a divider. I placed half of my earnings on one side to go towards gas, entertainment, and other miscellaneous expenses. The other half went toward saving.

I was going to Ajay and Bobby's house when I saw a beautiful Mark 2 Ford Escort, black with rally wheels made with steel spokes and Cibie brand lights. It was for sale for five hundred pounds. I went to my cousins' house and told them. We immediately went to see it. I contacted the seller, and I had enough money to buy it. I bought it for £475 cash, there and then. I loved it! It was old but totally repainted and looked like a rally car. I hadn't even told Dad. He trusted what I did, so I knew he wouldn't be mad.

My uncle checked out the car. He turned on the car, opened the hood, and revved the engine by tugging on a lever. The engine roared. "The engine is good." He smiled.

All my friends loved it. One person said the sparkling wheels hypnotize him when he watched them spin.

I had that car for just over a year. One evening after a party, a couple of girlfriends didn't have anyone to take them home, so Bobby and I offered to drop them off. It was dark and raining. We were having fun in the car, and the bass reverberated across the seats. While driving, I saw a nice wide road that turned left at the bottom. *Let's have fun and try drifting the car like rally drivers do.* I accelerated and turned the corner sharper than normal to get the drift. However, because the ground was wet, the car slid over the central reservation and onto the other side of the road. I saw an oncoming car and quickly regained control, going back to the right side of the road.

Bobby was sitting in the front seat and the two girls in the backseat. He knew what had happened, but the girls didn't. They jumped, "What was that loud noise? What happened?"

Bobby and I didn't know what to say. "I think we ran over a black cat." I spoke slowly. Bobby looked at me, still in shock. "It just came out of nowhere. I tried to avoid it, but I couldn't, and I drove over it."

They let out a soft "ah." "If you run over a black cat, it is bad luck." One of them commented.

The car was barely drivable, but we managed to get home after dropping the girls off.

I stayed the night with my cousin. In the morning, I asked my Uncle Pravin to check my car out. I told him the story of the black cat and how we ran over it. He inspected the car and said my axle had almost snapped off. The car was too dangerous to drive. I lost the car because of my stupidity.

That afternoon, Uncle Pravin went to the scene of the crime to investigate. He came back, face pinched, "You lied to me. There is no way a cat could have gone there. There's a big wall on both sides of the road." We gave up and told him the truth.

I learned a big lesson about not showing off and being more responsible. What if the car had flipped or we had been in a head-on collision? It could have been much worse. I had put our lives at risk. To make matters worse, when Dad heard about it, he was furious. I lost his trust in me.

SHOPKEEPER

One day when I was nineteen, Mom came home crying and said she had been laid off. The gas station had to cut staffing. It would be hard for her to get another job because of her limited English and skills.

Dad thought on the matter before declaring, "I will buy a convenience shop." He intended for me to run it with Mom, figuring that I was not doing well in college. Dad would do the accounts.

When Dad told me so, I laughed, "So when will you help out? You know I have no clue how to run a shop."

"I will only come to supervise now and again. You and your Mom will have to work it out." Dad replied.

I was afraid of the challenge. Mom and I had gained some experience working at the gas station. We were both good with customers, but I had to prove that I was a responsible person. Dad was putting all his savings into this shop. I was afraid we may go bankrupt if we failed. I could not fail.

I left college after attending for a year and a half and didn't finish the course.

We bought the shop from a British man in a predominantly white community. He had owned the store for many years and was retiring. The previous owner gave Mom and I two weeks' training and then we were on our own.

We tried to run the shop like he did and didn't move anything until we got settled in. The British customers saw us as the new owners and started going to other places. We were different from the former owner. Customers had bonded with him, but they didn't like us. We soon began believing we had made the wrong move by buying this shop.

Mom was the cashier. I did everything else. We were a good team and didn't argue at all. I cleaned the shop from top to bottom and rearranged items in an order that made sense. I was a logical person and applied logic in everything I did. I brightened the store and placed attractive offers in the window, cheaper than any of our competitors. *We must get people in the door even if we lose money in the beginning.* I thought. *We must offer them the best customer service, so they start to build a bond with us.*

We introduced additional lines and did raffles at Christmas. We even sold the clocks that Dad had bought in Wellington from that con man. We made it a fun shop. I started understanding what customers' requirements were and made sure those items were always in stock. We had a small stockroom at the back of the store. I bought offer items in bulk to maintain higher margins. Mom worked on excellent customer service. The business started to build, and customers began to come back. I did cash and carry once a week. I priced the items, stacked the shelves, placed orders with suppliers, and managed the day-to-day running of the store. Sadhana and Sandip hardly came to the store. Dad visited once a month.

We had competition up the road. The owner would come talk to us, check our prices, and undercut us for drinks. Schoolkids came during lunchtime to buy those drinks. I placed all the drinks in the freezer hours before the kids came, and then put them out in the fridge. The kids paid extra for cold drinks. The other shopkeeper kept his drinks outside. He couldn't work out why the kids came to our store and not his.

I picked up business skills very early on. It was a matter of do or die. My mind worked at a hundred miles per hour to find ways to increase business. I noticed that by placing day-to-day items at eye level, they would sell. It was convenient for customers to quickly run in and out. I learned that they were not buying other items, so I had to think hard about what to do. I decided to place the day-to-day items at various heights and placed the low selling items at eye level. When customers came in, they saw the other items and started to buy them. They had not been aware we stocked such items. This increased our sales dramatically.

I also priced three day-to-day items at cost as loss leaders. This made us appear cheaper than any competitors. Customers would come in for those items and pick up other items for which my prices were slightly higher, making up the margins. Mom and I gave the best customer service and made sure we built rapport with our customers, so they wouldn't go anywhere else. We cleaned the store every day, so customers enjoyed coming in.

One day our dairy supplier increased the price of milk by a penny. Therefore, I had to increase my price. A regular customer came in the shop and saw we had increased the price of milk. "You bloody Indians are all rich." He spit, "You're charging us poor people higher to pay for your rich lifestyle."

I was bewildered. *Does he have any idea how we came to this stage? If only he knew.* Not for the first time, I had the desire to tell all the British people what we had gone through. I thought then that I should write a book, but I wouldn't know where to start. It was a silly idea. Whenever I got racist comments, I always came back to thinking, *I must write a book about our journey.*

Due to racism, we had a break-in at our warehouse and our store window smashed. Kids often stole from our store as well. At lunchtime we got between five and fifteen kids coming at the same time. Mom caught several of them stealing. What could we do though? They would just abuse us or ransack the place. We decided to put up a sign: *Only three kids at a time.* This controlled the kids coming in, and theft went down considerably.

We had a living area above the store, which had not been lived in for many years. It was a mess. I cleaned it up and gave it a fresh coat of paint. I installed nice blinds and new carpet. I repaired the toilet and got the kitchen cleaned up. It was like someone had breathed life into the old apartment. It was ready to rent out. This provided an extra income that the previous owner hadn't considered. I had increased store revenue, and we added more value with the accommodation above the store.

Three years later, a friend at my regular cash and carry informed me that they had received information that a huge supermarket, Tesco's, was to be built very close to my shop. I told Dad, and we decided to sell the shop before they started to build the supermarket, as it would crush us. We quickly got the shop ready for sale and managed to sell it in good time. Dad later told me that the shop didn't make much profit after we sold it.

The shop had paid for our day-to-day living. I didn't take a salary; however, Dad gave me money as I needed it. After we sold the shop, Dad gave me a car, the Datsun Estate I had used for my cash and carry, as a reward for my hard work.

During this new downtime, I noticed that racism seemed to be decreasing. Most Indians owned convenience stores, which they opened for long hours. When the large grocery stores closed at six or seven o'clock, the Indian stores were open until ten or even eleven. If the other shops were closed, the locals had nowhere else to go than the Indian stores. Slowly the customers began to communicate and become regulars.

Additionally, the new generation of Indians, the ones born in Britain, grew up British while learning their Indian culture from their parents. I know of friends and family whose children married whites and have been together for many years. Things had changed for the better. Yes, there was still racism in some areas, but nowhere near what it was in the 1970s and the early 1980s.

The more the British understood our culture, food, loyalty, and attitude, the more we mixed. For many years now, for instance, chicken tikka masala has been the number one food in Britain. The British had come to understand the way we lived and finally accepted us as we are.

World of Computers

I managed to find a job at a computer store as a sales assistant. Even though I had taken a course in computer technology, I had never actually used a computer. I didn't know what a mouse was or even how to navigate around a screen. The other sales staff thought I would be useless at selling.

For the first few days, I didn't want to serve any customers as I wasn't equipped to answer their questions. It was Christmas time, and most customers asked the same question: "What is the difference between the Atari and the Commodore, and what packages are included?" I thought If I learned that much, then I could at least assist the majority of the customers.

I took all the leaflets and brochures in the store and studied them at night and on weekends. I reviewed the information fully and got my sister to quiz me.

The next day at the store, I walked in confidently and approached all customers willingly. I got noticed by the higher management. I was great at customer service, and my sales figures started to go up. I saved money and kept my expenses low.

My dream was to work at a reputable store in London, Selfridges, where we had a concession. Three weeks after joining, my managing director asked if I would like to work there. I accepted without hesitation.

I went there the following day and noticed the store was huge. Our concession stand was in the center, near the escalators. When I got there, the manager introduced himself and went for a break. It was a small stand that only required two salespeople on weekdays and a Saturday staff. I scrutinized the stand and noticed it was coated in layers of dust, so I started cleaning up. It took three days to clean everything.

The Selfridges floor manager saw an improvement in our stand and reported to my managing director what a great job I had done. After a few months, the managing director offered me a position as the manager of their Selfridges stand. I was delighted, I had gotten my dream position. I could save more with the better pay package.

I increased sales and asked to hire more staff as it was getting busy. My managing director allowed me to interview for my own staff. They had full confidence in me. I was starting to feel proud, like I had achieved something in life. Was this my turning point?

One of my Indian friends from East London had been working for a low-end men's clothes shop for many years. I asked him if he was interested in working with me because I knew he was a great salesman. He accepted.

Then I asked Sandip if he'd like to work every Saturday, as he was studying at that time. He too accepted. Bobby was looking for a job, so I recruited him as well. It was the best time. We worked together and increased sales to their highest level. It didn't even feel like work. We had each other, and who better to work with than your friends and family? We had great teamwork. We made good bonuses, and I built my savings with the goal of buying a house.

Selfridges in itself was also great. It was in central London. Customers from all over the world would come and visit. It was a high-end department store, so the majority of the customers were well dressed and well mannered. There was no racism within the store, so it felt free, and I built confidence in myself. Anything I did, people listened to me. I had shown them that I could do it. I gained respect from my managing director and the Selfridges floor manager. I made friends with other Selfridges staff. They recognized me as the manager of the computer store.

Who Is She?

While walking through Selfridges' departments, I went past the perfumery department. Something smelled great—a very powerful, rich smell. I looked around to see where it came from and saw a beautiful girl behind the counter. She looked Indian. I had to rush back to my department, so the incident quickly left my head.

A few days later, when I was having lunch in the staff restaurant, I saw that girl again in the distance. She looked stunning. I had to get to know her. I was very confident in talking to anyone, so I thought I'll just approach her one day and talk to her. I felt that she could be the one.

For several days I watched her from a distance. I told my friends about her. One at a time, they went to see her, being discreet. They all got excited and said I must pluck up some courage and talk to her. I tried several times, but each time I approached her department, I chickened out. By then many people knew that I had my eye on her.

One of my friends grabbed my hand and said, "Let's go. It's been two months and you haven't even said 'hi' to her."

I took a deep breath, "Okay."

He tugged on my hand and led the way. We took the escalator down to the ground floor. She was right there by the escalator, which sent me into a panic.

My friend started to talk to her. He was a natural. I just stood there like a dummy. I couldn't join in the conversation. He then introduced me to her. In the excitement I accidentally knocked over part of her display. Luckily, nothing broke, and we all laughed. She seemed very friendly and had a beautiful smile and a melodic laugh.

I melted.

I said a couple of introductory sentences, but then we had to leave her as she was serving customers. I felt something strong. I had never fallen in love before, so I didn't know what it should feel like. I couldn't stop thinking about her. I had spoken to many girls but never had this feeling.

"Now it's all up to you." My friend laughed, clapping my back.

I went to her counter several times, each time making an excuse for why I walked past her counter. Her friend noticed that I kept coming and realized that I liked her. One day I again went to the counter, and she wasn't there. Her friend saw me searching for her.

"She has a day off today." She explained. "And listen, she's not what you think she is. She is a bad girl." I was pissed and just walked away. I didn't want to hear any more.

A few days later, I saw the girl I liked having lunch on her own. She was sitting in the smoking area. I hated the smell of smoke, but I wanted to join her. I didn't know what she would say if I asked her if I could sit at her table. I knew she was friendly, so I was hoping she would be fine with that. I approached her and, as kindly as I could manage, asked if I could join her for lunch.

"Sure."

But how could I eat? The most beautiful girl I'd ever met was sitting in front of me. I played with my food and tried to talk at the same time. A thousand thoughts were running through my mind. I didn't know what I was saying. She was very chill and talked as though she had known me for a long time.

I called her once a week to try and sync our lunch breaks. I wished I could have lunch with her every day; however, I didn't want to move too fast. Each time we had great conversations. She was a fun person and easy to talk with.

One day while we were having lunch together, one of her work friends asked if she could join us. We said sure. We continued talking. It must have seemed like we were flirting with each other, because the other girl said, "I think I'll leave you two lovebirds alone." She picked up her tray and moved to another table.

One day, I called her and asked if she'd like to go for dinner. She said, "Do you mean lunch or dinner?"

I always got lunch and dinner mixed up. I said, "Dinner."

She said, "Hmmm, let me think about it and get back with you."

I realized that I had just asked her out to an evening meal by mistake. Oh my God! What had I done? She called back and said, "Thanks for asking, but I'd better not."

I couldn't get to sleep. I was confused about what to do. I was totally head over heels over her and I knew she was the one.

At one lunch, out of the blue, she said she was married. I didn't understand. Why had she acted like she was single? She looked too young to be already married. She had never mentioned this before, and I didn't see a ring on her finger. There were hundreds of questions going through my mind. I was heartbroken but didn't want her to notice. As far as she was concerned, I was just a friend. I decided that I was not going to see her again. I wanted to forget her and move on.

Unfortunately, that only lasted a few days. She was on my mind all the time, day and night. I had two options: I could either leave her and never see her again, or we could just be friends for a long time. I tried not contacting her, but after experiencing that agony, I decided to try being friends.

She eventually moved to another department store. True to my decision, I kept in touch with her a couple times a year.

Visit to India

It was time for me to visit my grandparents in India. I was now twenty-three. I went with my brother, two cousins, and one of my best friends from East London. We were going on a ten-day tour of North India, but we wanted to do it on a budget. My friend had two uncles who arranged the tour. We were prepared to live rough and go on an adventure.

We visited many famous cities and landmarks, including the Taj Mahal. Our trip also took us to Srinagar, where we experienced snowy mountains. We were not prepared for the snow and only had shirts on. They provided us with long coats to go farther up the mountain on a bus. Our hearts lurched in our throats whenever the bus drifted too far to the edge, but the view was definitely worth the palpitations.

The trip was just over a thousand miles. The two uncles drove the minibus: one drove at night while the other drove during the day. We slept in the minibus and only booked one bed at hotels to take a quick wash. We planned so we stopped at a city during the day and toured. At night we drove to the next city.

When we got back home, we had a good wash, ate, and rested. It was a journey we would never forget. We ended up spending £44 each for everything. We learned many things and had unbelievable experiences.

However, once we were back at my grandparents' house, I fell victim to sciatica again. This time it was very bad. It happened two days before we were due to leave for Britain. The pain was so intense, I didn't know how I would sit on a plane for more than ten hours. I could hardly bend or walk. I could not stay in India because I would be stuck there if my pain worsened. I had to get back to Britain no matter how much pain I was in.

The whole trip, including going to and from the airports and two flights, took almost twenty hours. I was in extreme pain the entire time. I was counting every second until I could find relief. Once we got to our house in Britain, I had Ajay and Bobby provide support on each side as I limped in the house.

I gasped to Dad. "I need to go to the hospital right now."

"Get some rest and have something to eat before you go." Mom fretted.

I shook my head, "No. I need to go *now*."

Dad drove me straight to the emergency hospital. They conducted a quick examination and admitted me. I didn't even have the opportunity to grab a change of clothes. I hadn't been expecting to stay at a hospital; I thought they would just give me an injection. The doctor said the situation was severe and I must not move at all or it would get worse. I was taken to the ward, which had six patients. All of them looked over seventy. I was only twenty-three.

That night I cried. I had not cried for many years. I thought of my life in Uganda and how it had changed here. I had endured all that hardship, and now I had this extra issue. At my age I should have been playing sports and in my best health. But instead, I was stuck in this ward with seventy-year-olds.

The doctor hung traction around my waist. The weights hung off the foot of the bed. With that contraption, I was not allowed to move. I had visitors every day, which kept me going. Even my managing director sent his personal assistant to see me with a small gift and "get well soon" card.

After I had spent about a week in the hospital, one of the older men got released and was replaced by a young boy. He was in a bad state. His parents told me that he had been on a motorbike when a car crashed into him, leaving him paralyzed from the neck down. *I'm in better condition than him.* I realized.

I started to think positively. I thought of the people in India living rough. *Okay,* I thought, *I have all this free time. What shall I do to keep my mind active?* I considered lots of things and then thought about a project to build low-cost houses. I would design the layout that was economical to build and efficient. I brainstormed, made lots of calculations, and did some drawings. I designed a whole community. I knew this was just to pass time, but I got interested in the idea of properties as an investment.

I decided to figure out my finances and how I could buy a house. What expenses would I have to pay? How could I save on the income I was on? Some visitors brought me books to read, but I hated reading, so I left them aside. However, I picked up some home and car magazines that interested me more. During the month I was in hospital, I promised myself that I would stay positive and focus on my goals.

My priority for the next two years was to buy a house and get married. I thought girls wanted to marry someone who had a house and didn't live with his parents. I realized I had to be marketable, so the house came first.

After I was released, my managing director wanted to meet with me to discuss an opportunity. He told me that he wanted to transfer me to their flagship store on a busy road, where I would be the general manager. It would mean an increase in salary. I jumped at the opportunity, thinking this would help me buy my house. I would miss my family and friends at Selfridges, but this was an opportunity that I could not pass up.

In addition to base salary, I'd have a performance bonus. The store was in a location with a lot of competition. I felt ready for the challenge. This store had three sales floors, offices on the fourth floor, and a staff rest area and kitchen on the fifth floor. The main floor had computers, peripherals, and accessories. There was a business center on the second floor and music demo room on the third floor. My office was on the fourth floor.

I initially was overwhelmed with the responsibilities. It was a huge operation with six full-time staff, three part-time staff, a senior sales assistant, a business manager, and an assistant manager. I had an office manager for office duties, cashiering, and administration. This was much different to anything I had managed before. However, I felt that if my managing director believed I could do the job, then he had faith in me. I couldn't let him down. I was going to run the business and put processes into place to make it run smoothly.

I started as I did at Selfridges—I cleaned. I rearranged the inventory so it was logical and customers could see all items. Sales slowly increased, and I got good bonuses. I was myself again.

Home Sweet Home

I needed to think about buying a house. Interest rates had increased to around 13 percent and were going higher. No one was buying. The housing market was collapsing fast. I found two houses, but they had issues and did not pass inspection. People said that I shouldn't buy now as the interest rate was high.

I was keeping an eye on property prices and interest rates. I knew that once the rate went down, prices would increase. Therefore, this was a great opportunity to buy a house at a low price. I did my calculation and worked out that by paying a high interest rate, I could save almost 40 percent off the price of a house.

I found a house that had gone down forty thousand pounds in price; however, it was still ten thousand pounds more than I could afford. I went to eight lenders, but no one wanted to lend. They considered me a high risk since I wanted to borrow five times my income. The ninth lender said that if I could show her how I could repay, then they would consider me. I told Dad of the situation. He did his number crunching, handing me a sheet a paper, "Here you go. Present this to her." It was a spreadsheet of my financial situation. I made a deal with Dad to make it work. It was a tight budget, but I needed to buy a house.

I showed the lender the spreadsheet and explained the figures. She analyzed it and asked lots of questions. She said she would speak with the underwriter to see if they would approve. The next day I got a call from the lender, and they told me that the loan had been approved. I was very happy that I could move forward.

Dad and I made a deal that he would rent his house. My family would move in with me for three years. Once I got married, he would move out. He would earn income from the rent and help me pay for some of my expenses. Financially it made sense. It would be a win-win situation.

I finally got the keys to my house. The house was a single story with a large open-plan living area, a dining room, a breakfast room, and a conservatory overlooking a beautiful long garden.

The house was old and needed a lot of work. We were not afraid of challenging work. Sandip and I had done many projects together and felt we could make it livable. Before we moved in, Sandip and I ripped out the whole kitchen and redesigned the layout, so it was functional. We purchased flat-pack cabinets and installed them, as well as the sink and appliances. We did the backsplash and hung wallpaper in the remaining area. All the carpets smelled, so we had them changed.

Then we could finally move in. It felt good. I had achieved another goal: to buy a house by twenty-five.

I was the manager of a computer store and owned a house. I had a separate savings fund to buy a car. I promised myself that I would drive any car, but once I was twenty-five, I would buy a sports car. All my friends in East London had sports cars and I had a Datsun Estate, which people made fun of.

Sandip and I found a beautiful Alfa Romeo Sprint with a body kit, painted all black. I had never seen one of these on the road. I fell in love and negotiated with the seller to buy it for six thousand pounds. I paid cash for it. It was gleaming and very sporty looking. It was a beast.

I drove it home to show Dad. Dad didn't say much except "Do you want to die?" Because it looked fierce and fast, he thought I would cause an accident. I couldn't stop looking at it. It was a dream come true for me. I felt I was starting to build my life and live a little.

I FOUND MY PARTNER

My target age to get married was twenty-five, and I was getting nowhere trying to find the right girl for me. I met with several girls as candidates for marriage. No one seemed suitable for me, and I was not suitable for them. "Don't worry." One of the girls told me, "You will find the one, and you will feel the connection straight away." I smiled back politely but didn't reply. *People always say that.*

My parents were going to India for a month and asked if I wanted to join them. I had three weeks of vacation saved and thought I could look for a wife in India. I accepted and went with them. It felt awkward, but I was willing to take a chance. Once we landed in India and got to our village, we were greeted by my grandmother (My granddad had passed away a few years back).

Within few hours of me entering my grandmother's house, people from the village started to ask if I had come to find a wife. I couldn't believe how word spread in the village. Within a week I had seen about a dozen girls. Unfortunately, they weren't suitable. Nearly all wanted to marry me because they would have the opportunity to go to Britain for a better future. I didn't understand that. Initially Britain hadn't been good for me because of racism. I didn't want to take an Indian girl to Britain as I wouldn't want her to experience what I had experienced. All the girls seemed nice and cultured, but they would not fit in in Britain as most couldn't speak English.

I'd had enough and was ready to go home. It was a tiring process to meet girls at third parties' houses. The girl and I would have a chat in a room, and then come out and give our opinion. It felt weird and didn't seem natural.

"This is not going to work." I sighed to Dad, "I don't want to see any more girls."

Uncle Pravin called Dad from Britain a few days after. "While you are in India, I've seen a girl who may be suitable for Sanjay."

I was hesitant when Dad relayed Uncle Pravin's information to me. However, since my uncle had recommended her, I didn't want to be disrespectful. I agreed. "After her, though," I declared, "I will not be seeing any more."

Dad nodded. "She will be the last."

We decided to go to a mutual acquaintance's house to meet her. When we got there, I saw five men in a room. They introduced themselves. They were from the girl's family—father, brother, and uncles. I looked around the room but couldn't see the girl. I hadn't really dressed up. All the girls I saw prior were from the village, and I didn't want to make them feel inferior, so I dressed down. This family was from a big city, however, and I fidgeted with the hem of my plain T-shirt and the creases of my jeans. I was severely underdressed.

The men fired questions at me and cross-examined me. Once I was approved by them, they telephoned the girl and her mom and aunties and cousins to come.

After an hour or so, a line of women walked through the door. I saw one girl who I thought was her. I thought she was OK. Then I looked away trying not to get caught looking. After about ten minutes the girl's dad said, "You can go into the back room. She is waiting to meet you, and you can have a talk." I was nervous and didn't want to go through this again, but I walked to the door and slowly opened it.

She was sitting on a chair with her head down, so I couldn't see her face. I sat on the opposite chair, "Hi, I'm Sanjay."

"Hi." Came the soft reply. "I'm Jayshree, but some call me Chaka and some call me Jay."

"What is your preference" I replied.

She hesitated for couple of second "Jay" she answered as she lifted her head up slightly.

I was expecting to see the same girl who had walked into the house. However, this girl was wearing different clothes. She slowly looked up at me. She had a pretty face with soft, clean skin and a beautiful smile. She had petite figure and looked elegant. I spoke with her in Gujarati and, at times, some English. I was pleased that she understood English. She smiled constantly during our conversation with a giggle now and again. We exchanged questions and seemed to feel comfortable with each other.

I told her that I was a manager in a reputable computer store. I had a house and a sports car. She worked for an insurance company and had a master's degree in accounting. Most of her family lived in America, so she was aware of Western lifestyles and often wore Western clothes. In my mind, she was everything I was looking for. I had found the one.

We both walked out of the room. She went to her family, and I walked to where my parents were standing. I could hear giggles and laughter from her side of the family. Perhaps she was making fun of me—or maybe she was saying yes.

"So?" Dad asked with raised brows, "What do you think?"

Without hesitation I replied, "She ticked all my boxes, so I have no reason to say no."

"So, it's a yes from you?" Mom asked.

"It's a firm yes."

Her dad walked over to us with a smile on his face. "And what is the decision over here?" From his face, I could tell it was a yes on her side.

"Yes."

Both the families announced the news. I couldn't believe what I had done. It happened so fast, but I was happy. I was hoping she hadn't been forced by her family. I had heard many stories of Indian families forcing their daughters into marriages of their choice and not hers.

Her parents said that they had to go to America for two years due to their visa application. They gave us a choice of when to arrange the wedding date. The options were to get married before we went back to Britain, or to get engaged now and get married in two years when they came back from America.

Dad asked me to make the decision. *If I wait for two years, there will be extra cost and hassle, and I will be two years older.* I was ready to get married and couldn't wait two years. I decided to get married before we went back to Britain.

"Is it even possible?" I asked Dad.

Her dad came over to us and asked if we had decided. Dad said, "Yes, let's arrange the date." Her dad called the priest to match the stars and see if we were compatible. If so, what would be the best date for marriage? We met on March 31, and the priest said the best date would be April 9.

Wow! That's too fast. I wanted at least my brother and sister to be at the wedding and was hoping Ajay and Bobby would also be able to come. Dad called Sadhana who then lived in in Africa and Sandip in Britain and announced the news. They were excited but in shock. We called all our relatives and invited them over the phone, as written invitations would not reach them in time. Mom's and Dad's families, who lived outside India, were upset that it was impossible for them to attend the wedding. Sadhana, Sandip, Ajay, and Bobby arranged flights and said they would attend.

We got the arrangements underway. I had no time to have clothes made, so I wore a suit that I had packed just in case I had to attend a wedding while in India. We had a standard wedding, nothing over the top, as we had less than a week to organize it. We still had three hundred people attend.

In our village, we invited virtually everyone as we considered them family. Everyone knew each other. I was twenty-six years old by then and Jay was twenty-four. We were at the right age. It wasn't ideal, but we took the chance. We met several times before the wedding. We each felt that we had made the right choice and were happy.

After the wedding, we went to Goa for our honeymoon. We got to know each other better and started to build strong feelings for each other. It was weird but felt right.

After six months, Jay got her visas and came to Britain. Our lives began a new chapter. I took a week off from work to tour her around London. I bought her Western clothes. I wanted her to feel comfortable as she didn't have any relatives in Britain and trusted me with her life. She was very brave to come to a foreign country, not knowing anyone and relying on me.

Since she had done accounting, she loved figures and asked to help with my accounts. I gave her all my house expenses and my statements so she could do some number crunching. She noticed I had only £147 in my bank account. She was shocked. She went through my bank statement, saw a £960 payment, and asked what that was for. I replied, "That's the mortgage."

"I thought you said you had a house?"

"Yes, this is my house." I replied.

She was fuming. "This is not your house. It belongs to the bank. You have an £80,000 mortgage. How much interest are you paying?"

"Fourteen and a half percent." I answered hesitantly.

The debts shocked her. She wondered how we were going to survive. My parents and brother had helped pay some part of the bills. "I cannot just sit at home." Jay declared. "I have to find work." A friend recommended an accounting job, which she took.

When we got married, Jay said that her intention was never to marry a boy from Britain, since she had no relatives in Britain. Her only interest was in marrying someone from America. She had seen many boys in India—some from rich backgrounds and some very educated—she had turned them all down. It was destiny that she met and said yes to me.

I totally understood her situation. As part of my commitment to her, I suggested that she ask her sister in America to sponsor us for a green card. Once we got green cards, we could move to America.

Once Jay came to Britain, she asked her sister to start the process of sponsorship. It was a long process that could last years. We let her do what she needed to and didn't push her.

It's a Boy

A couple years after our marriage, we were blessed with a baby boy, who we named Jaime. I had been getting promotions at work, and my income was slowly increasing. With my wife's income, we were staying above water. My parents helped with babysitting so we could work.

Sandip had received his bachelor's degree. I wished I could have studied like him, but even though we got along well together, our mentalities were totally opposite. I was more daring, a risk taker. I would not think too much before doing something. I wanted to try everything and live freely. I was always wheeling and dealing, trying to make quick money when opportunities arise. He was more educated and didn't take risks. He was organized and practical and didn't make hasty decisions. Dad often took my brother's advice on many things.

My thought process was abnormal. Few people understood my logic; some may have thought I was mad. I thought of many ideas, but I was not good at presenting or implementing them, so they remained. All my close friends knew I was different. Some joked about my silly ideas. However, they still respected me as one of them and we treated each other like brothers.

Every weekend before I was married, Sandip and I met up with them. We had a group of ten or twelve people, a mix of boys and girls, all Indians from East London. We went to many eateries—from hole in the wall to five-stars restaurants. Eventually we realized that we were spending too much. We decided to cook at home, so we all helped. We bought the ingredients, cooked, and drank in the comfort of our own homes.

We were all about the same age and fooled around. No one in our group was educated, so there was no inferiority. We all had big dreams and often used a line from a TV show: "This time next year, we'll be millionaires!"

We joked and often talked about how we would make money, since no one really had professional jobs or education. We had made it this far through contacts and helping each other. We often talked about opening restaurants, as making food was becoming something that we experimented with and enjoyed. We specialties were Indian curries since we all liked hot and spicy flavors.

After I got married, I drifted away from the group. I wanted to concentrate on my family. I had a son to care for, and I could not waste money.

My parents helped to look after Jaime from the time he was born until he was five or six years old. They traveled to India during the winter months and took him with them—otherwise we would have had to take time off work to take care of him. We tried putting him with babysitters, but he cried a lot. The babysitters said he was upsetting other children, so they refused to take him. He also cried at nursery and asked for his grandmother. Mom asked the teachers if she could help them and be with him so he wouldn't cry.

Later we realized that since he was with my parents most of the time, he only knew Gujarati and did not understand English. From then on, we spoke to him in English at home. Then he started to enjoy playing with his friends as he could communicate with them.

One winter, my parents wanted to go to India. By then they were getting old and couldn't take Jaime. Jay and I were stuck about what to do. We had holiday time, so we decided I would take mornings off and she would take afternoons off.

I took my son to nursery in the morning and picked him up at midday. We took the train to London. I met my wife at the train station, and she brought our son home to look after him in the afternoon. It was a struggle, but we had no other options. We used all our holiday time to look after him.

As he got a few years older, we met a couple of Indian families whose children went to the same school. They offered to pick my son up from school with their children and look after him until we got home. We were very grateful to have them in our lives, and they quickly became like family.

THE BREAK

I realized that interest rates were going down, and house prices were increasing. Interest rates tumbled down to around 6 percent in four years. This is what I had been relying on.

I realized there was a chance to invest in properties. However, I had no savings. I was missing this opportunity. For a couple of years, I was telling everyone how the property market was shooting up and people were buying investment properties. I was hungry to find out how to buy an investment property without money.

I desperately searched for ideas. I saw an advert from a developer who was building apartments that would have shops and fitness centers and a brand-new community. It looked modern and it was near a train station. It got me interested.

I went to the developer, who had a show home. He said the build time was two years, so they were selling apartments off plans. Since it was a new scheme, they wanted a 10 percent down payment. They would pay 5 percent and I would need to pay 5 percent. When the build was thirty days from completion, their lender would require a total of 20 percent. The builder was also offering guaranteed rental for two years after completion at 6 percent.

I was excited. I only needed £7,500 pounds now, and £15,000 in two years. I would be betting on appreciation. For two years while the building was being developed, I would have no monthly payments. For two years after completion, I would have guaranteed rental. My bills would be paid from the rental income. What would the value of the house be in four years? If the property went up £30,000, taking closing costs into account, I would have doubled my investment, risk-free, in four years.

I looked at my bank account. I only had four thousand pounds. I didn't want to ask anyone for the remainder, and I couldn't use all my savings. I thought that my house's value must have gone up. Perhaps I could free some equity from my house and use that for the deposit on the investment house. When I checked, the price of my home had indeed gone up substantially, and I managed to get out £30,000.

Jay found out that I had increased our mortgage to buy an investment property. She hit the roof. "We are supposed to reduce our mortgage, not increase it!"

Again, I had the issue of explaining my thought process. It was true that, without her consent, I bought my first investment property. She slowly saw the upside and started to think like me, but she didn't want to get involved with my investment ideas. She gave up arguing against me and just trusted what I did. I looked for other deals and bought several more properties.

The company that I worked for was not doing well and was spiraling into liquidation. Another company bought it; however, they were investors and had no idea in running a computer-based business. Due to the liquidation, all the company's buyers left. There were no buyers or product managers.

The new owners held a meeting of all the store managers and asked, who had been a retail manager for longest. I put my hand up. They called me to their offices and offered me a role as a buyer. I was not expecting that as I had no experience as a buyer. They offered me a good wage and said they felt confident I would do well. I accepted as I was always looking for an opportunity, yet I knew it would cost me my job if I failed.

The previous buyer had worked for me as my business manager, so I asked him to train me before he left. He said he could only spare a couple of hours as he was leaving the company. I made notes of what he said. It was overwhelming. *I have taken on a challenge way above my head*. I quickly realized.

The company had thirty-four retail stores and a trade arm. I was the buyer for all of them. I thought of the days when I had placed orders at my grocery store. All I needed to do was multiply everything by thirty-four, plus additional for trade. I was trying to keep a sinking ship afloat for as long as I could.

Business was fine for a short period. However, we needed financial backing to fulfill orders. The investors were not willing to pump in more money. I eventually thought of ordering components and build our own branded computers as we received orders. We had competitive pricing but were not selling them fast enough. Customers did not want to wait for their computers. They wanted to take their purchases with them. If we didn't have stock, they would go somewhere else. The company folded, and I was without a job.

Next Opportunity

I thought that after ten years working in retail, this was an opportunity to do something different. I had no idea what though. I had lots of retail experience, but I wanted to keep my options open. I felt at my age, I needed a more reputable job. I had an interest in properties, and this was a great time to think about properties and investments.

In those days, the internet had hardly been heard of. People depended on paper-based advertisements. I thought of opening my own publication focused on properties. People would pay for advertising, and I would give the issues free to people commuting on the train. But this took too much organizing, and I didn't have the skill set to follow through.

The other idea I had was to advertise homes priced at £150,000 and below. I would go to all the estate agents and ask them to advertise any properties for that price. I would target first-time buyers. This was a great idea, and I started to get some interest. However, it would take time to set up and would not bring in income straight away, so I decided to drop it. Jay wanted me to have a steady income. We needed savings and could not take risks.

After a couple of months, I read an advertisement seeking a financial advisor for a reputable bank. It stated that they would provide training at their expense. The pay would be base income plus commission. It was perfect and provided me with learning experiences. This could be an opportunity to show everyone that I was not stupid and uneducated. I wanted to make Dad proud. It was a long shot, but what did I have to lose?

I applied for the position and got an interview. I was confident in speaking and could talk my way through an interview. The next stage was a full-day interview competing against other candidates. This involved decisions, presentations, debates, mathematics, and comprehension. It was a grueling day and took every ounce of energy out of me.

I was competing against fifteen others. Most had master's degrees; some had held high positions. I was the oldest candidate. I was happy to make it through to the next process, which was to meet the regional manager for a final thirty-minute interview.

We started off very formally. Later he got interested in my background and asked me more personal questions.

"Where do you see yourself in five years?"

I laughed, "I want to be a property tycoon."

He smiled, eyes crinkling, "Well I wish you well in that endeavor."

The interview ran for an hour and twenty minutes. He said he would love to have me in the team. However, I would have to pass all the certificates. He arranged for me to take the residential training.

It was a six-week training in a hotel, from Monday to Friday. We could go home for the weekend. There were fifteen candidates in my group, all white except me. I was hoping there would be at least one other Indian person. The others didn't know each other, but they mingled and started to connect. No one came to me. I immediately felt like an outsider. At the orientation we were taught how to study and were given a big box to take home. For the first week, we were asked to read through some exercises.

We took our boxes home. It was a heavy box full of exercise books. I couldn't believe how much reading was involved. I had not studied before, so this was overwhelming. *There is no way I can do this.* I was not a fast reader and struggled with comprehension. How was I going to pass? I read a few chapters and fell asleep. I could not stay awake. I couldn't focus and started to give up. My mind wandered off. I had to read one sentence several times before I understood it. I lost interest. I was just reading for the sake of reading; nothing was registering.

My family knew this was too much for me and that it wasn't for me. This was too much of a challenge. As I closed my eyes, many thoughts passed through my mind. I had been bullied and called a loser. I started to feel down. I took a deep breath. *No, I will not accept that. I am better than that. If I focus, I can do it. God has given me this opportunity, so I'm going to take it. I always want to have a positive attitude, and this is a challenge I will take on.* I immediately got a rush of energy. *When others take six hours to read it, I will take twelve hours, but I will get through it.*

The next day, I planned my day and set my study times from eight in the morning to ten at night, with four fifteen-minute breaks and thirty minutes each for lunch and dinner. I started to understand the material clearly and got interested in the subjects. This was exactly what I had been looking for. The subjects were all about what everyone would experience once in their lives. The areas included investments, taxation, pensions, mortgages, inheritance tax planning, and health and life protection. Every subject was applicable to everyone, and I would be able to advise them. I focused hard and tried to understand every sentence before moving on to the next one.

After the first week of home study came the residential classes. I was doing well. I studied until late at night while the other students went to the bar after class and after dinner. They hung around the bar or just socialized. I only joined them for dinner, since it was provided by the hotel and the table was set for our group. Afterwards, I went back to my room and studied.

For six weeks I hardly slept. My only aim was to pass the test. It was tough, but I had to do it. I prayed to God before our final exam, "I have put every ounce of my energy into passing the test. You gave me this opportunity, and I have shown you that I would work my hardest. Please don't let me fail."

I went to take the exam the next day with the other students. I was laser focused. I didn't let any of the other students talk to me. I had only one mission: to pass the exam. I saw the students leave one by one. I wanted to use all the time allotted. I was the last student out of the examination room. *I studied for six weeks, and I must pass.* I checked my work repeatedly for any mistakes until I was happy that I had done the best I could. I left the room with a minute to spare.

The next day I got my result. I had passed. I teared up. I had just done the impossible. I found out that only five students passed out of the fifteen, and I was one of them. I couldn't believe what I had just achieved. I felt if I could do this, I could do anything.

I told Dad with excitement that I had passed. He was incredibly pleased. I would be in a position in which doctors, lawyers, dentists, accountants, and everyone else in the professional sphere would come to me for advice.

As a financial advisor, I understood how life works and all the stages in life. I had my own office in the bank and gained the highest respect from the bank staff. I was the financial advisor for three branches in the heart of central London. These branches were in prime areas.

I was with the bank for four years. The bank had their own products to sell and advise upon. Many times, the products were limited and did not fit the customers' needs. I didn't want to sell something that was not right for the customers. I decided to become an independent financial advisor so I would not be restricted to the bank's products. It was a risky step for me to take as I would be purely on commission, without any benefits or a base salary.

Jay became a mortgage broker. She was doing very well. In fact, she was the number-one salesperson in her region. With her income, I could take the risk of going independent. She was now the backbone of our family.

While I looked for an independent company, I wanted to renovate our bathroom, which hadn't been updated for over twenty years. It still had an avocado-colored bathtub, sink, and toilet. I thought I would use this time to get a renovation company to change all the hardware and tiling.

I purchased all the items but couldn't find anyone who could do the job soon. They gave me dates that were two to three months out.

I had the bathtub, sink, and toilet in our conservatory. I couldn't leave them there for that long. I looked at the work and thought, *Maybe I'll do it myself.* It would be a massive task as I had no experience with plumbing. I had done some tiling before, so I was confident at that. I felt up for this challenge. I would focus, learn, and save money at the same time.

I went to a local plumbing store.

"Excuse me." I called over the manager. "Would you guide me in how to change out a toilet, bathtub, and sink? If you do, I'll buy all the materials from you."

"Sure." He replied without hesitation.

I drew diagrams, calculated measurements, and took photos of my task. It would be a challenge as we only had one bathroom and five people lived in the house. I worked out step by step what I needed to do at what time, as the bathroom was constantly used.

I started by replacing the sink, which fit perfectly. The next task was the toilet. The toilet was hard to take out, but with the help of some suggestions from the plumbing shop, I managed to replace that too. I laid the floor tiles, then mounted the toilet on them to make a professional finish. The final item was the bathtub. Further complicating matters, I had the one with jets. It was an offset tub.

I first tiled the wall and then installed the tub. Jay helped with all the grouting. It took me two weeks, but I was pleased with the finish. I had also saved a lot of money doing it myself. Most importantly, I could say I did it myself. I always said that saving was earning tax free.

I joined a private company as an independent financial advisor based in heart of London. Since I was self-employed, I had to create my own leads by prospecting and referrals. I started slowly as I was not used to prospecting. Working in the bank was easier. Cashiers and personal bankers would pass me warm leads by talking to the bank's customers.

I was constantly thinking of how to make money as my income wasn't enough. I thought of buying another investment property, but how would I get the money for a down payment? I went through advertisements, brochures, and magazines—anything that would indicate how I could make money.

I received an invitation to open a credit card. They would give an eighteen months' balance transfer from another credit card at 0 percent interest.

I thought, *Wow! Zero percent interest! How can I make that work to my advantage?*

I had a credit card with a £10,000 limit, so I could spend £10,000 and transfer the balance to the other card so I wouldn't have to pay interest for eighteen months. I read all the small print and started to think. My brain was working overtime. I looked for another off-plan property with similar deal to my previous investment. After several weeks, I found another scheme. It was again in a new up-and-coming area with growth potential in the next five years. I took a chance and paid the 5 percent down payment to lock in the purchase price.

I got to talking to the developers, who agreed pay me a referral fee if I found other investors. I discussed this with several people and decided to hold a small workshop demonstrating how to invest in off-plan developments. The potential tenants would need to be professionals. Where would professionals typically be? I realized that researching would take time, and there were many variables. How would I find up and coming areas?

I thought long and hard. Then I noticed that Starbucks cafes were popping up in certain places. Professionals went to Starbucks. I thought that Starbucks must have done all their market research and analysis before they built. So, off the back of Starbucks' in-depth research, I looked for new off-plan developments near newly opened Starbucks.

Jay didn't like that I wasn't making a consistent income. My concentration was in properties. I was passionate about learning property investments and searching for new schemes. I told her that I would work on growth, and she could work on income. My aim was property appreciation. I was looking only for off-plan developments with long completion dates in areas where the values were low but would increase in five to ten years. London was small, so eventually the outer circle of suburbs would grow.

I saw that a developer was building a five-star hotel next to the River Thames. They were selling individual rooms and offering five years of guaranteed rental at 6 percent. They were asking for a 35 percent down payment. The build time was three years. I was excited with this new opportunity.

I tried to convince Jay. "Are you crazy?" She huffed, "It seems like a scam to me." She didn't like to take big risks. She was totally against this investment.

I wanted it badly. "It's a brilliant way to invest." I argued.

I contacted the developers and attended their presentation. I was sold on it. "I'm going to go for it." I declared to Jay. We got into an argument because she thought that if this failed, we would lose a lot of money. It could drain us.

I did my calculations and ran through the numbers. I took a calculated risk and went for it. I freed more capital from my house and paid the deposit. I had just got my fourth investment property. I could see house prices were increasing steadily.

I remembered my interview with the regional manager who had asked me, "Where do you see yourself in five years?" I had told him that I wanted to be a property tycoon. It had taken me longer than five years, but I had taken calculated risks. I was starting to think that I was somebody. People came to me for advice. I proved to myself that by focusing and wanting to be noticed, I could finally get to where I felt comfortable.

THE CONSERVATORY

Jay's cousin was getting married in India, so she wanted to attend. She deserved a break, and all her family would be there too, so I agreed. I thought that while she was gone for almost three weeks, I wanted to surprise her with something. Jaime and I thought hard. There was a project that I had always wanted to do, and that was to replace our conservatory with a new one. We had investigated it before, but the cost came out to around £10,000.

Our current conservatory was old and falling apart. We weren't using it except as storage. Jay had always wanted it changed, but we couldn't justify the cost. I looked at the options and found a suitable one. A company would deliver the parts, and we would have to build it. The parts came with instruction manuals. I couldn't believe the cost; it was only £2,500, and at that time they had a deal giving away free wicker furniture.

I kept it as a surprise from my wife. I ordered it so the parts would be delivered the day after Jay flew to India. I had to work fast as I wanted it fully installed before she came back. Jaime and I dropped her off at the airport and returned home.

I dismantled the old conservatory and set it aside. I advertised it in the newspaper for £150. The next day I got a buyer who paid £125 and took it away.

The new conservatory was six inches larger than the old one. Therefore, I had to extend the cement foundation by eight inches. I let the cement dry while taking couple of days to work out the installation instructions. Each day after work, I did a bit at a time and slowly got the main structure up.

A week before my wife was due to come back, she called me in hysterics. I was shaken from her cries and stayed silent. She breathed deeply a few times and told me that just a day after her cousin's wedding, her dad had been involved in a motorbike accident. He fell over, banged his head on a hard surface, and was in coma. Two days later, she called back to say he never recovered consciousness and had passed away.

I was in shock. He had been healthy. He was a great man. For a couple days I felt numb and thought of her and her family back in India. I wanted to do something for her but felt helpless. I asked Jaime, "What should we do for Mom?"

We thought of many different ideas. I had no motivation to finish the conservatory. It sat there, half complete. The weather was pouring down rain.

"Mom will be back in a couple of days now." Jaime noted. "When will we complete the conservatory?"

I looked at it for few minutes and thought that it would be good to get it completed by the time she came back. I hoped it would take her mind off the sadness. However, I had no desire to complete it, I lost motivation and the strength. I was weakened by the news. Thinking again what this would mean for Jay when she comes gave me a burst of energy within. I shook of all the negativity and said to Jaime, "Let's do it now."

This was for her. I had to complete it, even in the heavy rain. I put on my raincoat and got my tools. The roof was the final piece of the puzzle and the most technical. All the slots had to fit in perfectly and be aligned. I could hardly see in the pouring rain, and the screws were tiny. My hands were cold and soaked. My only thought was that I had to get it done before she came. Since it was wintertime, it got dark early. On top of that, I was working on the roof, so I was on the top rung of a ladder. I finally finished late at 11pm that night. She would be back in three days.

The next day it continued to rain. That was a good test to see if there was any leakage. Luckily it was well sealed. I just had the floors to lay; then it would be fully complete. I let the floor dry for a day. On the day before she came back, I laid the floor. It looked beautiful. I positioned the wicker chairs and put some plants in the corners.

Jaime and I picked her up from the airport and comforted her. We drove home and she entered the house.

We had drawn the curtains before we left, so she wouldn't see the conservatory. As she entered the front room, she felt it was dark and opened the curtains. To her surprise, she saw the conservatory.

"How could we afford this? It's beautiful!" She didn't believe that we built it for only £2,500. Once she settled down, I explained how we had planned to surprise her.

She was silent for a bit before she smiled. "Thank you."

THE GREEN CARD

In 2005 we received news that our application for American visas was in its final stages. Some documents were needed from us. We also had to get medical exams done and obtain police clearance.

We hadn't been thinking about our intention to go to America as Jay had settled in Britain. She was very happy with my family; she had a stable job that she enjoyed; we lived a comfortable life. "We are set in Britain. There is no need to go to America." She said when I shared the news with her.

Jaime was doing well at school and had made lots of friends. We lived in an area that was predominantly white. Racism was not as prevalent as in years past, and my son's friends were all white. They didn't see any difference in him except the color of his skin. He was a noticeably a confident child, and other children followed his lead. I was happy that he didn't have to experience the racism that I had growing up.

We weren't sure if Jaime would make friends like the ones he had in Britain. He was great at soccer and was a B team captain in rugby. His favorite sport, like most Indians, was cricket. He had joined a private cricket club. He was more of an all-rounder, but he was a great baller. He would miss all this if we moved to America.

At this stage we had decided that we would go through the application process but had no intention of leaving Britain. It was too high a risk. Many friends told me that they knew people who moved from Britain to settle in America but didn't like it, so they came back. I heard no one saying that they knew someone who settled in America and liked it. People who moved from India to settle in America did well. There were more prospects in America than in India. People in Britain had established themselves in Britain, so there was no need to move to America. I couldn't think of a single reason to move to America.

As part of the process, we had to make an entry into America. In November 2005, Jay and I flew to America for three weeks. We stayed at my sister-in-law's house in Texas. We rented a car but stayed at their house most of the time, since we didn't have any intentions to live in America, therefore we had no reason to tour around.

My wife's cousin was twenty years younger. She knew that we came from Britain. We used to party a lot and go to nightclubs. She planned to show us the nightlife in Dallas. She arranged for about five of her cousins and their partners to go. She introduced them to us. They seemed nice and much more modern than I expected, since most came from India.

We went to couple of nightclubs, and they seemed like clubs in Britain. We hadn't gone to a club in a while since we felt too old. The cousin and her crowd liked us and tried to convince us to move to America.

A week before we went back to Britain, we decided that since we were there and had paid for the car rental, we may as well look around at schools and housing, just to pass time.

We looked at some school districts. Since I liked new, developing areas, we looked at up-and-coming residential neighborhoods. We found the perfect area, which was Keller, Texas. It was about thirty miles from Dallas and twelve miles from Fort Worth.

There was new housing being built. We saw several model houses and were blown away by the sizes and cost. Houses in London were very small; these were more than twice as big. The cost was also less than half the price of my home in London. We drove up to a school that my son could go to. School was letting out, and all the children were coming out. We waited until all the children were out of the school, and then went in to see if we could book an appointment to look at the school. We didn't know the process, so we just took a chance.

As we were about to enter the school, we were stopped by an official-looking man. "Can I help you?" He asked in a deep voice.

"Pardon us." I responded, "But we're from Britain and wanted to look at some schools for my son."

"I see." He smiled, "Welcome to the States." He gestured to the school, "I'm the principal here and I have some time, so I'd love to give you a tour."

I was impressed and felt privileged that we didn't have to book an appointment. He made it so easy for us. I was grateful for his kindness. Such a thing would never have happened in Britain.

The school was massive compared to the schools in Britain. Everything seemed two or three times the size. The school had all the facilities. However, in America they didn't play rugby or cricket, so even though the school was great, I could not see my son fitting in and being happy.

There were other factors as well. Jay and I would both need jobs. We would have to make new friends. We'd need to learn the American way of life and how to drive on the other side of the road. We'd have to sell our house in Britain and go through all the hassle of moving. It just was not meant to be. I was drifting away from the idea. We were fine in Britain. Why move? I couldn't think of one positive thing to change my mind.

Jaime was against the move. Jay was largely impartial and told me to make the decision. She did say she felt there would be too much to lose and it was very risky. On our last day at my sister-in-law's house, we stayed up discussing the options. I came to the decision that it was not for us.

In the back of my mind, though, I believed I would have taken the risk. When I woke up on the final day, I kept asking myself, *Is there not even one good reason to move? Give me that reason.*

I drew back the curtains to let the light in the room and saw a beautiful blue sky. The sun was rising. I had found my one reason. It was November, and for all the three weeks we were in America, the sun was shining, and azure colored sky. It wasn't as cold as Britain. To see such weather in Britain, we would have to wait until summer. The weather was one good reason to live in Texas. It was better than the gray clouds in Britain, which made me feel dull and sad.

While Jay packed to go back to Britain, I grabbed a local newspaper for something to read on our journey. We got to the airport and said our goodbyes to my brother-in-law, sister-in-law, and two nieces. It was an awkward moment. We had mixed feelings about what we wanted to do, to stay in Britain or immigrate to America. They had spent much time and money to get us our green cards. I felt obligated. It would be hard for us to say that America was not right for us.

Once we said our final farewell, I felt numb. I couldn't think what the right thing to do would be. Jay and I had made our minds up that it was too much risk and hassle to move to America, and we didn't want to think anymore. We decided to tell our family that we would stay in Britain.

Even so, we had to return to America as Jaime also had to make an entry. We wondered if it was even worth it, since we didn't want to live in America.

We hadn't told anyone of our America opportunity except for our family. One day during work, I went for lunch with a colleague. *Let me tell her so she can give me advice*, I thought.

"I have an opportunity to immigrate to America on a green card."

She gasped and smiled widely at me. "That's great! When are you going?"

"That's the thing—I'm not going."

She drew back "Are you out of your mind? People hang off airplane wheels to go to America, and you have a lottery ticket that you are just going to throw away?"

I thought for few minutes, "We are settled here, and we would have to start over from the beginning."

"Think hard." She urged. "Don't just let this opportunity go."

I knew she wanted the best for us. However, perhaps she did not know our whole situation. To be nice, I said, "Thank you for your optimism. I will discuss it with my family again."

I went home and we didn't discuss it again. I knew that the topic had ended.

I had stopped going to the office and started working from home to save money on travel and other work-related costs. One day while working from my home office, I saw an old newspaper on the side of my desk. It was the local newspaper I had picked up when we left America. I went to move it off my table, and from the corner of my eye I saw a small article about a house for sale for $150,000. It was a five-bedroom, three-bath house in Keller. That was the area I would have moved to had we gone to America. I couldn't believe the price. I read the article word for word. Surely it was a misprint.

I went onto some websites and looked at houses in Keller. They were all around that price, some more and some less. I looked at new developments and again was surprised at the price and the size of the houses. They were two to three times bigger than my current home. I thought that price must be just for the land.

I called Dad to verify. "Yes, it looks like that is the price of the house and land." He confirmed.

I wondered how much that was in pounds. I looked at the conversion rate for the first time and saw it was 1.99 dollars to a pound. I didn't know if that was good or bad, so I looked at the conversion history. It showed that the dollar was at the weakest it had ever been. I would get great value for the money. One hundred and fifty thousand dollars equated to around seventy-five thousand pounds.

Adrenaline rushed through me as I realized this would be the best time to move. I told my wife and son. They weren't interested in my findings, so I thought it was too good to be true. We didn't discuss the subject again for another few months.

Then a family member who was a big businessman asked me when we were leaving for America. I told him that we had decided not to go.

He was completely shocked at my response. "Look, I've known you for many years, and you are always talking about ideas that you have. You are an entrepreneur, and America will give you opportunities."

I was surprised. *Now two people have told me to go. But is that enough, or do I need more justification?* Obviously, I wouldn't decide to go solely based on their words, but still... Am I missing a chance that I've always looked for? *Is God trying to tell me something?* I always was asking God to give me that one opportunity. I'd knocked on so many doors only to find dead ends. *Is this door the one I've been looking for, or is it a dead end? If I don't open it, how will I ever find out?*

What should I do?

We booked our trip to America with Jaime for his entry. It was April. This time we only went for ten days. We stayed at my sister-in-law's house for seven or eight days and started to get bored. They lived in a suburban town, and there was not much to do there.

"Dad, can we just go for a ride?" Jaime sighed.

I replied, "Do you want to see the area where we would have stayed if we lived here?"

That didn't excite him, but he shrugged, "If there's nowhere else to go, then let's go."

After a one-hour drive, we got to Keller.

"Can we see the school I'd be going to?" He asked.

"Sure."

I showed him two schools. One was almost five times bigger than his current school, and the other was three to four times bigger. He was impressed from the outside. "Can we go in to see?"

We again went in as classes were letting out and went to a window. It seemed like a reception window. We tried to explain to the reception person that we were from Britain and would like a tour of the school.

A student overheard us. "I'm a senior at this school and I have some free time. I would love to show you the school." We were impressed. She didn't know us, but she was willing to use her free time to show us the school.

All the classrooms were tidy and well organized. She took us to the sports hall and the gym. Jaime was blown away by the size and all the gym equipment. After the tour, I saw a glimpse that he really liked the school.

"Okay." He said, "So if this is the school that I'd be going to, where would we live?"

"Let's go to some model houses." I replied.

While driving around all the neighborhoods, we were amazed by the size of the houses compared to London. We took videos while we were driving. We couldn't believe that we could own one of these houses. They were all detached, which would have cost a fortune in London.

We entered three model homes. While we were looking, I could see my son's eyes just staring at the huge space and architecture. He shouted while I was talking to the salesperson, "Dad, will our house look like this one?"

"If we move, then yes." I responded. I thought, *Wow, I have his interest*, which was very important to me. If he wasn't comfortable, then I would think that we had made the wrong decision. So far, he was impressed. Just to give him a picture of what it would be like, I said, "If we come here, you will have your own bedroom with a bathroom. We will have a game room with a full-size pool table, a foosball table, a dart board, a table tennis table, and a media room for movies."

His eyes lit up and a great big smile spread on his face. "No way."

He didn't believe me and kept on questioning me to confirm that I would keep my promise. He frowned, "But they don't play cricket or rugby." I assured him that they played football—or soccer as they said in America. I told him baseball was like cricket and American football was like rugby. I also told him that he could drive at the age of sixteen in America, so if things worked out, I could buy him a car at sixteen. He was excited by all the promises I was making, and for once I thought, *This could work*.

I asked Jay for her thoughts. She was on the fence, "You two decide. It's always been your dream to come to America, so I'll leave it to you. I am happy in Britain, but your decision will be final."

I had a hard decision to make. All my friends and family were telling me not to go, but I could see that America could give me opportunities. If nothing else, then at least there would be beautiful weather. I had to put my logical hat on, do some number crunching, and think of every minor detail.

I first analyzed what people had said of the reasons why people from Britain could not settle in America. These were typically Indians. I found the reasons to be very similar among them all.

Generally, Indians in Britain came from Africa. They had been settled in Britain for many years and wanted to go to America for opportunities. Most went to New Jersey, Chicago, or California. Once they arrived, they typically stayed with relatives until they resettled. Though staying with friends and relatives for a few days was fine, over the long term, it could cause issues. Everyone wants their space, and sometimes it's hard to live with others whose habits can be annoying or do not fit in with yours. Therefore, living with other people for long periods does not work.

Some lived in apartments to begin with until they could buy a house. This caused them to think, *In Britain we lived in a house, and here we must live in an apartment. It seems like we are going backward.*

In the East, the weather was cold with some parts colder than Britain. People who moved because they didn't like the British weather were in for a surprise. In California, the weather was much nicer than Britain. However, house prices were much higher, so one's income had to be substantial to afford one.

The other reason people went back to Britain was that they missed their friends and family. They often said there was no culture in America. Most people didn't sell their homes in Britain when they went. It was a safety net they could go back to if they didn't like it in America.

Jay and I kept discussing it. Were we going to move forward? Everyone else seemed to be doing well—owning businesses, buying bigger houses, getting job promotions—and we seemed to be at a standstill. How were we going to move forward?

I was desperate to make bigger moves and was constantly thinking of ways to make money. My wife pressured me to get a job that had a base income and not just commissions. I was getting frustrated at not being able to find a solution. In the end I said to Jay, "If you want a bigger house with no mortgage, several servants, and nice cars, and you don't want to work, then we just need to move five thousand miles east. Let's immigrate to India."

"Are you out of your mind? Don't come up with your silly ideas." She admonished.

I wanted to do something with my life and be adventurous and think outside the box. I didn't want to think like everyone else. *If you follow 80 percent of people who have average, steady lifestyles, then you will become like them. The 20 percent who don't follow such lifestyles will either become well off or wish they had followed the other 80 percent.*

Once I asked a wise old man what he would have done differently if he could go back in life. He said he would have taken more risk. *I don't want to say this when I am old. I'll have to take more risks—but they will be calculated and not gambles.* In terms of moving to America, I didn't have the courage to make it work. It was a risk. Could I make it a calculated risk?

With all this negativity, why were we even thinking of going to America? Where would we go if we decided to stay? My sister-in-law lived in Texas. Should we go to the East Coast, go to the West Coast, or keep to the area I had already seen—Keller, Texas? Keller didn't sound exciting. However, I'm all about logic, and to me Keller was the most logical place to start. My sister-in-law lived about seventy miles from there, and one of my wife's aunties lived twenty miles away. I thought if we didn't like it in Texas, then there were another forty-nine states we could go to.

Keller would be the place. We were not going to stay with relatives or in an apartment like most people did; we were going to buy a house. We were relocating for a better life; I wasn't going to settle for anything less than what we had or did in Britain.

Even though relatives offered to have us stay at their houses, I knew this would not work. I made up my mind that we would buy a house. This house had to be bigger than our current home, which was about eleven hundred square feet. Almost every house in Keller was bigger. I had told Jaime that the house would have a game room and a media room. I needed to keep my word.

I decided to sell our current home and use the funds to buy a home in America. My aim was to be mortgage-free at the age of fifty. If we move to America, with the equity in my house and the dollar to pound rate conversion of almost two to one, I could buy a House much bigger than ours in cash! I would have exceeded my goal and would be mortgage-free at the age of forty-one. I decided that once the decision was made to move, we would not leave an option to go back. I had to make it work. Coming back would cripple me financially. I had to get it right and synchronize our move.

The Big Decision Is Made

Jaime would be a freshman at his new school in August 2006. A house and a residential address are needed by July 2006 to register him for admission. I'd have to move fast. Where do I start?

I picked up the newspaper that carried house advertisements for Keller. A house was advertised for $152,000 that had five bedrooms and three thousand square feet of living space. Underneath the description was a phone number for an agent. *It's worth a shot*, I reasoned, dialing the number.

"Hello?"

"Hello." I looked at the newspaper in my hand, "My name is Sanjay. My family and I are moving to America from Britain soon. We were looking for some houses in the Keller area. I'm planning to fly there in a few days and stay for a week. Would you be willing to help me look?"

"Yes, of course! Have a list ready of what features you're looking for and we can start from there. I look forward to working with you."

"I look forward to working with you as well."

As soon as the call disconnected, I booked my plane ticket.

I made a detailed spreadsheet of my finances. I was on a tight budget and my calculations had to be accurate. I accounted for unforeseen expenses; however, I could not predict certain things— mainly when my Britain house would sell or when Jay and I would find jobs.

I got to the airport, ready to board the flight for America, and I wished my wife and son were with me. It was all on me. I felt that I needed them to help me make decisions but they both trusted my judgment.

I was restless on the flight. I didn't want to question myself. I only thought of moving forward. I kept on reviewing my plan to make sure there was nothing I had missed. This was it. I landed in America, rented a car, and drove to my sister-in-law's house.

The next day I met the realtor outside the location where we had planned to meet.

"Sanjay?" A professionally dressed woman greeted me.

"That's me."

She smiled, "Alright, jump in." She handed me a pad and a cold bottle of water, "Us the pad to note down all your likes and dislikes for each of the houses we view. At the end of the day, we will go through your notes. Based on your likes, I will find more houses the following day and arrange future viewings." She handed me some flyers, "These are the houses I'm planning to show you today. Please feel free to look through them as we drive around."

We started looking at houses priced at around $150,000. Most of them needed renovations as they were pre-owned homes in older communities. All my life I had looked for deals to save money. I believed these houses would be fine for me until I realized that housing prices in Dallas didn't increase as much as they did in Britain, so a home wouldn't be an appreciating asset. We looked at several the first day, and the realtor read through my likes and dislikes.

Three days passed, and I didn't like any of the houses. Since the houses were bigger, they required a lot of work. Having three or four bathrooms was great; however, all the bathrooms needed to be renovated. It just seemed like too much work. The realtor saw my frustration and asked if I wanted to see some new builds. I wasn't prepared to spend too much. However, I was running out of time, so I agreed to see new properties.

Several times we passed a beautiful neighborhood that was halfway developed. I thought, *I would love to live here, but it is too expensive.* We went to another new community where they were almost finished with construction. We saw several new houses priced around $180,000. These were nicer than the older homes, and I got excited.

"Does this house have air conditioning?" I asked as we toured a new house.

The salesperson laughed. I thought I had asked a stupid question, but she answered honestly, "You would die in Texas if you didn't have an AC unit." She gestured to the flyers in my hand, "All new houses will have air conditioning in Texas."

In Britain, air conditioning was a luxury. Even sprinklers were included with new houses. I couldn't believe what I would get for the price.

There was one that I really liked. It wasn't perfect, but it was almost what we wanted. I took photos. "This could be it." I declared to the realtor.

I thought of placing an offer the next day after speaking with Jay. I called her and explained in detail all the features of the house. She asked me if the kitchen was big and if it had an island. That was her only request. This kitchen didn't have an island, and I would have to look again to see if it was functional.

On the fifth day, I walked into the house again—this time with a critical eye. The downstairs seemed small, the living room was an odd shape, and the kitchen layout was not functional. I looked at the flow, and something just didn't seem right. I would be forcing myself to buy this house, and I knew Jay would not be happy with the kitchen. My realtor was understanding, "Let's keep looking until we find the right house."

We had looked at five or six houses everyday over the last five days. We were both exhausted. She knew I kept talking about that new, nicer community—the Heritage. It was out of my price range. She asked if I wanted to see couple of homes there. I decided that I had come here to better my life and would not go for second best, which I'd done all my life. I agreed.

We concentrated on the Heritage community. We saw one house that was about $210,000. It was a short sale. I thought I could offer them $190,000. My realtor pointed out the negative things about the house: it was dark inside, three sides were overlooked by neighbors, and the build quality was poor. I thought she was probably thinking of her commission and not my needs. She was saying too many negative things about the house. I was put off. However, she was right. It was not my perfect house. Again, I was trying to cut corners and find a deal.

We saw another pre-owned house priced at $250,000. It had about 3,500 square feet but needed some renovation. Another brand-new house was $239,000 but smaller at 3,100 square feet. My realtor was confident I would love the new house and was waiting for me to place an offer. She was surprised that I wasn't as excited as she was. "This has everything you've been looking for   a big kitchen with an island, a game room, a media room, and two living rooms, one of them large."

It was my final day, and I had to decide. "Place an offer on the pre-owned house for $230,000. If they accept it, then I will go for that one. If they don't, then I'll place an offer on the new house."

I could see her face drop. "Reconsider your decision." She urged.

I frowned. *Why is she leaning toward the new home? Does she get more commission on the new home?* I kept to my decision. She placed the offer on the pre-owned house. A few hours later, she called me and said they had countered at $245,000.

I wasn't prepared to go up. Without hesitation, I asked her to place an offer for the new house at $230,000. They accepted that offer with the condition that we close by the end of the month. I didn't even tell my wife this time; I just signed the contract.

The realtor said she had a mortgage broker who could help with the mortgage and immediately gave me his contact details. I was excited. I took photos of the house to show my wife and son. The Heritage offered six resort-style swimming pools, four tennis courts, a beautiful club house, basketball courts, and trails for walking and cycling. It cost $400 per year in homeowners' association fees. It was too good to be true.

"I may have gone over our budget." I started on a call with Jay, "But I bought us the house of our dreams." I could not have been happier.

I had enough equity in my house in Britain that I could buy this house for cash and still have money left over. Even if we didn't have jobs for a year, we would manage. I had accomplished stage one of my plan.

We were super excited, though the move was bittersweet. We would miss our friends and family in Britain. I promised my wife and son that if ever they wanted to visit Britain, I would buy the tickets without hesitation.

Once I returned to Britain, we placed our house on the market and hoped it would sell by the end of June. I would be free of the mortgage for the new house and all three of us could move to America at the same time. I had to have plan B in case the house didn't sell by then. I started the mortgage process with the mortgage broker in America.

In Britain, our credit score was 999. However, in America, it was zero. We got an investment loan at 7 percent. I knew this was expensive, but it was only until our house sold in Britain. I had to bite the bullet and pay the higher rate to be able to move forward. I started to arrange for international movers and to sell household items.

Unfortunately, we were not getting any viewings for our house as the market was down. It wasn't a good time to sell. I quickly realized we needed to switch to plan B. Since my son was starting school in August, he had to be in America at least two weeks before, so he could get familiar with American life. My wife continued working. I wound down.

I announced our move once I had got back from America. My coworker was happy that I made the right move. I thanked her for encouraging me to chase my dream. God has given us each one life, so we were going to live the best we could.

It would not be a smooth ride. There would be hurdles. However, we would cross those bridges as they came. We faced many obstacles in life, and we would tackle them just as we had all those that came before.

We had to make a decision: should we sell all the large furniture and just ship our clothes, or take some furniture? I thought hard and imagined both scenarios. We would be in an unknown environment, in a large house with new furniture. We would be sleeping in new beds and sitting on new sofas. It wouldn't feel like home initially. It would feel like a hotel or vacation home, and we may not feel comfortable. I thought if we at least took our own beds, sofas, dining table, and so on, it would feel like our home. We could change them later. I made the decision to ship the good furniture and sell or give away older items. Since our house was still not selling, we changed agents.

We managed to get our mortgage approved after several emails and document requirements. We closed on our new house on June 30, 2006. We had no choice then but to implement plan B, which was for my son and I to move to America and for my wife to come as soon as our home was sold. It was a sad moment to leave Jay behind for an indefinite period. I was hoping it would not be for long.

It was a very emotional trip as we drove to the airport. I was leaving behind the country that I had lived in for more than thirty-three years. Most of those years had been a struggle. However, I had met many great people, and my friends in East London were like family. I would miss them. In the back of my mind, I thought, *I'm only a ten-hour flight away. I can fly back anytime I want to and keep contact with them or they can visit us in America.* I was looking forward to our new life. I would change my thinking about cutting corners and reach for the best in life.

WELCOME TO AMERICA

We landed in America and were welcomed by my wife's auntie, uncle, and cousin. They were excited to see us but sad that my wife wasn't with us. I couldn't wait to show my son our new home. We picked up a rental car and drove straight to the show home where the keys of our home were waiting.

Jaime's eyes lit up when we drove around the area. He was wowed by the size of the house. We entered the house, and it felt good, but I wished my wife were with me. Jaime ran around the house, opening all the doors. "Where's my bedroom?" He hollered from further in the house.

"The whole of the upstairs is yours." I shouted back.

In Britain, he didn't have a true bedroom. I had made a one-bedroom into a two-bedroom by building a partition, and his bedroom was about six feet by six feet. Later we built a loft conversion, and he moved into our bedroom, which was about ten feet by ten feet. Here in our new house he had the entire top floor. His bedroom had an ensuite bathroom with a large game room and a media room right next door. He was in heaven, which made me feel that I had done the right thing.

We didn't have any furniture. It was supposed to come two days after we landed, but it got delayed for two weeks. We slept on the floor and used a cool box to store milk, bread, cheese, and eggs. We ate out during the day as we had no kitchen utensils.

My uncle lent us a TV, which we placed on the floor but didn't otherwise use. Jaime's school would start in two weeks, so we spent time driving around and getting familiar with the area and the American way of life.

I went to open a bank account and was told I need two proofs of identity. He asked if I had a driver's license. I had a British license and an international license, but neither of those would work. I realized that I would have to take a driving test to get a driver's license. In Britain it took three to six months to get a license if you passed the test the first time. I panicked when the banker said that to buy a car and get insurance, I would need a Texas driver's license.

I can't afford to rent until I pass the test. It could take several months. "Are there any other options?" I asked the banker.

He smiled, "Don't worry. All you have to do is go to a testing center and take the written test. If you pass, you will be allowed to take the driving test. If you go early in the morning, you'll be able to get your license straight away."

There's no way it's that easy. I believed I had to drive as much as possible because in America, cars were driven on the opposite side of the road. It was a long shot, but since I'd been driving for twenty-five years, I was just going to take the written test. I got to the test center and took the test without any revision. I failed by two marks.

I went home and flicked through a driving book my sister-in-law gave me. Then I retook the written test. This time I passed. I was very relieved. The next day I took my driving test and passed. I couldn't believe I passed in three days. In Britain, this would have been much bigger a hassle.

Now that I had passed my driving test, I could look for a car. In Britain both my cars had been on their last legs. I would have had to buy cars there too, so this expense would have been the same whether we moved or stayed.

In Britain, I had bought cars that cost around five thousand pounds as I couldn't afford much more. They were older, and I was always spending money on repairs. I was not going to go through that again. I would buy a more reliable car.

I looked at many options. I asked an American acquaintance for his recommendation. "Lexus or Mercedes." He replied without hesitation. He had a Lexus himself, and my realtor had a Lexus as well. I asked my realtor if she had any issues with her Lexus.

"No." She replied with a hum. "It's always been reliable for me. Would you like me to recommend the salesperson I always buy from?"

I went with her suggestion and met the salesperson. He showed me a couple of options. I decided to get an SUV, since I'd need the space to transport large items. I selected a three-year-old Lexus RX300. It was beautiful and fully loaded. It did have 88,000 miles, but I took a chance as these cars were robust and rarely went wrong. We had never had satellite navigation in a car nor air conditioning nor a luxurious interior.

Before my son's school started, we made many purchases for the house. We wanted to get it set by the time my wife came. I had sold one of my investment properties, and from the equity we made some purchases. As promised, we bought a full-size pool table, a table tennis table, a dart board, a foosball table, and extra furniture. We set up the media room with cinema seating, a projector, a huge screen, and surround-sound speakers. It felt exactly like a theater. We bought bicycles so that we could ride on the bike tracks and tennis rackets so that we could play on our community tennis courts. We were living life to the fullest and couldn't wait for my wife to join us.

Our furniture had got delayed for another week. We ate out a lot and tried different things. In Britain, eating out was expensive, so we only went out on special occasions. In America, it sometimes felt cheaper to eat out than make food at home. Obviously, it was less healthy, but we didn't have much choice.

Jaime wanted to try Asian food, so we went to an Asian restaurant near us. It looked decent and it was crowded, so we reasoned that it must be good. We ordered several plates to try everything. We started with sushi, which we had never tried before. We attempted to use the chopsticks provided and carefully pick up a piece of sushi. We saw green paste on the side. We didn't know what it was. It looked like avocado. We each spread a thick layer of it on the sushi and looked at each other.

"Let's do this."

We simultaneously shoved a whole piece of sushi in our mouths. The fire started instantly. That green paste went straight to our noses and tears came out of our eyes. Sharp pain rushed to our heads. It was like brain freeze. We finally recovered and learned that it was wasabi. It gave same effect as eating a spoonful of Coleman's English mustard. That was a day we would never forget.

First Day Troubles

The time came to prepare Jaime to go to school. I had contacted the school to find out where and when my son needed to catch the school bus. Because of my British accent, she asked me to repeat what I was saying several times. I repeated myself until she finally gave me the time and place for the school bus.

Jay told me that I should drop him off at school. I was adamant that he needed to learn and start making friends on the bus. He was thirteen years old and I didn't want to hold his hand. Since it would be everyone's first day of school, it would be a good start. Otherwise, the rest of the kids would start to make friends and he may get left behind.

On his first day of school in America, many thoughts were running through my mind. I hoped he would do well, make friends, and just be happy. It was a big day and a new life for him. I hoped I made the right decision and America would be better for him. I watched him catch the bus and waved at him. He glanced at me for a split second and climbed on the bus. Within seconds the bus drove off. I waited until it disappeared into the distance.

I went home. *I am in America. Is this real or a dream?* I pulled myself together and looked at my list of things to do before my son came home. I went shopping and continued ticking off my list.

Soon it was time for Jaime to come home. I waited at the bus stop where I had dropped him off. I saw a bus coming. I was excited to see him and talk about his day. It was almost 100 degrees outside, so I had a cold bottle of water for him. The bus stopped and a few children came out, but he wasn't one of them. I waited for another bus. I saw one at a distance. To my horror, he wasn't on that bus either. I was questioning myself about where he could be. Should I wait for another bus, or was this the last bus? If I waited, how long should I wait? I started to panic.

I decided to drive to his school. If I saw a bus pass me, then I would follow it and see if he came off. I saw a bus in the distance and prepared to follow it. *He must be on this one.* But no, he was not there. I was really scared. It was his first day at school, and he had vanished. I quickly drove to the school. No other bus passed me.

It was now thirty minutes after school had finished. There was not a single person at the school. It was empty. Where could he have gone? I tried to find a teacher but couldn't see anyone. I was in total panic. I couldn't remember if we had discussed how he should get home. I ran back to my car. I was sweating and thinking what wrong I had done.

Coming out of the school, there was a crossroad. I stopped to think. If he missed the bus, he would have no idea how to get home. How could he even think of what road he should take? Now I had a bigger problem: which direction would he have gone?

I had lost my son. I was tearing up and thinking he must be in utter panic. He didn't even know our address. *Jay's going to kill me.*

I decided to start driving my normal route home and keep driving until I found him. I feared someone may have kidnapped him. Should I call the police? There were so many roads to cover. We lived about two miles away from the school, and there were four ways to get to my house—provided he took the right road at the intersection.

I didn't care about the speed limit. I had to cover as much ground as possible while I had the chance. As I raced around the roads, I saw him at a distance. He was running in the rough up an incline. It was over 100 degrees. I was very happy to see him; he was pleased to see me.

As he stepped into the car, he was obviously upset. Sweat ran down his face in rivers.

I was prepared for him to lash out at me, and I would take all the blame. "Why were you running off the road?" I started, handing him the cold water.

"The cars honked at me when I was running in the road, so I moved to run in the grass instead." He crossed his arms, "Let's go home and I'll explain everything else."

A day before, he had asked me if he could have a phone. "Jaime, I have bought you everything that I agreed, so don't push it." I had replied. I knew most kids played on their phones all day, and I didn't want him to do the same. I put my foot down and refused to buy him a phone. I had spoiled him enough.

Back in the present, he said, "Dad, I need a phone."

"Yes." I agreed immediately. "We will go today and get you a phone."

When we got home after buying him a phone and some food and he had cooled down, he explained. "I remember us driving up the steep hill to get home. After that, I just hoped I was going in the right direction." He frowned, "The bus I got on this morning took me to the wrong school."

I frowned in turn. "How? I know the pickup location and time were correct."

He shrugged, "The school looked different so I didn't know where to go. A teacher saw me and asked what class I had, only to tell me 'We don't have that class. Are you sure you're at the right school?' When I told her what school I attend, she told me that I was at the wrong school and arranged for a bus to take me to the right school."

It dawned on me then. I had made arrangements for the return bus. He could not get on that bus because the arrangement was for the wrong school.

I dropped him off the next day and contacted the school district about what happened. The lady said there must have been miscommunication as there was no bus service for us to get to that school. We lived too far away. Both the school names were almost the same, and because of my British accent, the woman I had spoken to before had misunderstood what I said.

I told Jay what happened. She couldn't believe what I had done. She was extremely annoyed with me and my way of thinking about letting my son learn the hard way. I felt it was not wholly my fault as there had been miscommunication but took the full blame regardless. Due to my stubbornness, I had caused this unimaginable incident.

Our furniture came not long after Jaime started school. We spent time arranging it, opening boxes, and organizing everything in the right places. Finally, we got to sleep in our own beds and sit on comfy sofas. While Jaime was at school, I got a lot of work done setting up the house. Jay was going to visit us in October, so I wanted to make it perfect for her.

Together Again

Jaime and I were very excited for Jay to come and see the house for the first time. We picked her up from the airport. As we approached the house, she gasped, "I love it. It's huge." We walked in and she immediately went to see the kitchen. "I love it." She declared with a smile.

I gave her a tour around the house and showed her some of the purchases we had made. She adored them all. "It's perfect. You did a great job picking this house."

In fact, I felt it was my realtor who had pushed me toward this house. She knew me better than I knew myself. I was glad that I had bought this house instead of the pre-owned house. All along, she had had my interests at heart.

I showed my wife my new car. We went for a ride around the area, and I introduced her to some of the Indian friends I had met who lived near us. Jay was happy about us settling down. Jaime had started to make friends at school.

I was still looking for a job, and our house in Britain had still not sold. Jay spent a week with us before she had to go back.

I had to find a job. I made it my main priority after dropping Jaime off at school. From nine in the morning to five in the evening, I applied for jobs. I sent out application upon application for all types of work with no response. I even took on a job as a mystery shopper, which only lasted four days.

Eventually I obtained an interview to work as the manager at a gas station. They offered me the job. However, it was a night shift. They wanted me to start straight away. I declined as Jaime would be at home with no one to look after him.

I went to job fairs and approached the counter for a mortgage service company. They offered me an interview and offered me a position higher than I applied for. The job was in Dallas. It was from 8:00 a.m. to 5:00 p.m. I'd have to leave home at 6:30 a.m., and I'd arrive home at 6:30 p.m. I wanted to accept it, but how would Jaime get to school and come home?

That day Jaime said that he had made a friend, and his parents wanted to meet us. That evening we went to their house and talked about our journey to Texas. They asked what I did.

"I'm currently unemployed." I told them. "I do have a job offer, but because of issues regarding Jaime's transportation, I can't take it."

Without hesitation they said, "If that is only your worry, then we will pick up Jaime with our son and bring him home." I was amazed as I had only met them once. This was a blessing. Who would do that for a stranger?

I didn't have any other job offer, and the country was heading into a recession. The country was showing some issues in the mortgage market, but I didn't understand how it worked despite being an expert in Britain. I didn't know what job I had applied for, but I accepted the offer anyway.

In Britain, I commuted by train every day, so I was hoping there were trains to get from Keller to Dallas. To my surprise I saw that a train station was located under the building I would work at. I looked at the train maps. I would need to catch a train at a station that was twenty minutes' drive from my house. The whole journey was an hour and twenty minutes each way, but I would save immensely on gas money.

My first day at work, I was joined by other new employees. One of the directors did an introduction and an overview of the company. He said that in this role, there was potential to make commission.

My ears opened as I had thought this job only had base pay. *This is great. The harder I work, the more in commission I can make.*

I struggled a bit in training. There were terms used here that were not used in Britain's mortgage market. Regardless, I worked hard and tackled all compliance courses unafraid. After a few months in the job, I was among the company's top performers. I enjoyed my work—helping struggling homeowners to pay their mortgages gave me a sense of happiness. That I made more money in a few months than I had ever made in Britain was a bonus.

I made many more work friends here as well. Most of them knew me as the British man. I found that Americans loved my British accent. It was the first time I felt people were noticing me and wanted to talk to me. I had never felt like that in Britain.

Jaime too become very popular at school because of his accent and made many friends. He immediately got recognition from his teachers. Most of the children in the school knew him or had heard of him.

My son and I were taking it a day at a time and missing Jay, and she was missing us. Finally, in April 2007, we sold our house in Britain and she joined us in America.

I looked for a car for my wife. I was looking for a nice one as she had worked so hard. She deserved a nice car for her troubles. I thought back to what my acquaintance said when I was looking for a car for myself. *I have a Lexus, so I'm going to buy her a Mercedes.*

I bought her a beautiful silver Mercedes before she came to America as a surprise and a welcome gift. One of my dreams was to have private-number plates on a car. My number plate was LEXUS 1 and hers was MERC 1. It would have taken me another ten to fifteen years—if not a lifetime—to reach this stage had I stayed in Britain.

Jay said that she wanted to take a break from work. I was happy with that; I made enough to support our expenses. On the weekends, Jaime and I spent time together playing tennis, darts, pool, and table tennis. We went for bike rides. We watched films in our theater room. Life couldn't have been better. I often thought back to how I had started off in Uganda and all the struggles in Britain growing up.

After six months' break, Jay got bored at home and wanted to look for work. She applied to many places; however, the country was in recession.

A lot of homeowners were struggling to pay their mortgages. Adjustable rates kicked in, and they could not pay the high rates. The economy spiraled. Properties in Dallas didn't increase much, so it didn't affect Texas too badly. The hardest hit states were California, Florida, Michigan, and New York. Many other states were also affected to a smaller degree.

The company I worked for was hiring because homeowners were in desperate need of advice on what to do. The phones were blowing up. I asked Jay to join me. She did and got the job. I stopped riding the train and we commuted together by car.

She made the same if not more commission than me as she was in a different department. We were both making good incomes and building our savings. We put away the maximum amount in our 401(k)s and took advantage of tax-free saving as we were high-rate taxpayers. I thought that in the next three to five years, the market would pick up.

In Britain we hadn't had much surplus income. I had only contributed the minimum to my retirement account, which didn't build up too much. *Why save for retirement when we are struggling now?* It made sense to save more when we were high-rate taxpayers because it was value for money, and we were closer to retirement.

Property prices in Britain went up slightly, then stabilized. The American market sent a ripple effect throughout the world. I didn't want to buy any properties in Dallas as it was an unfamiliar territory and a market that generally didn't go up. My plan was to save for any opportunity that arose and spend on travel, as that was our passion.

My work colleagues and I were always thinking big. We talked about investing, opening businesses, inventing something, and collecting royalties. The job we did paid well, but it was getting repetitive. How long could we do it for? I was itching to do something different, to be more flexible in my work.

My colleagues and I discussed how much money we wanted to make. We agreed that we didn't want to win the lottery. That was an insane amount of money, and there would be other issues if we became filthy rich. No, the big question was how much would we need at retirement?

One colleague and I calculated in our minds and came up with a figure in the millions. We both laughed, "Okay, let's stop dreaming and get back to work. This is not achievable in this lifetime."

Privately, however, I challenged myself to hit our target. It wasn't impossible, but it would require risks.

LIVING LIFE

Until Jaime graduated high school, we kept control of our finances and worked on savings. We bought a car for him as promised. One thing that my wife and I had always wanted to do was travel.

In Britain, I was known for finding great deals, and I had come to the same fame here. Some called me "dealfinder.com." I was always finding deals or schemes that got me what I wanted and without having to pay much for it.

In Britain, I had had many credit cards. I had decided that after moving to America, I would not use credit cards. I would pay cash for everything. I just wanted a simple life. I did not want to think about checking my statements or get worried about stolen credit cards.

In America, however, it was a whole new game with credit card points. I found out that in America, people used points to travel. I didn't have many points in Britain, and I didn't travel much, so they would have been useless to me then. Since we wanted to travel now, Jay and I both collected points. Once we had enough, we booked ourselves a vacation. I had one card for flights and one for hotels. I constantly kept an eye on deals. Within four years, we had traveled to several countries.

My work colleagues wondered how I did it. It was matter of thinking outside the box. Most of the vacations cost less than half the price of normal tickets by using airline points.

I opened a credit card that gave two free stays in any hotel under their brand worldwide after spending $3,000 within three months.

I had some big expenses; I timed the spending so as soon as I got the card, I spent the $3,000. We used the two nights free at a newly opened Park Hyatt in New York. Normally it would have cost $2,200.

For the first time in my life, I was looking for the most expensive hotel in America. Normally I would look for the cheapest. The Park Hyatt was a hotel that very wealthy people stayed at, and we had squeezed in two nights for free. I've always wanted the best and found ways to get what I wanted by thinking of ways to get the best deals.

Many times, I used websites that offered "mystery" hotels. I always got four- and five-star hotels at ridiculously cheap prices. It was a risk to book a mystery hotel—these were hotels for which you only found out the name after you'd made a payment. *As long as it's four or five stars, we will be guaranteed of a nice hotel*, I reasoned. We went to several of these, and each time we got an outstanding hotel.

We traveled a lot, and we didn't go anywhere unless it was a great deal. In Britain, we had gone to travel agents and brought home holiday brochures. We flicked through the pages, looking at all the beautiful beaches. We hardly traveled when we were in Britain. In America, we traveled at least two or three times a year. Most were all-inclusive vacations by the beach. I felt that in America, there were more options and more ways to save money than in Britain. Everything seemed to be easy.

After a few years in America, we felt that we had made the right decision to move from Britain. The weather in Texas was gorgeous. We got great value for our money and opportunities. Our biggest expenses were the property tax and medical insurance, but this was a small price for the overall quality of life.

One of my dreams was to own a boat. In Britain, that would not have happened in this lifetime, but it was possible in America. My friends and I often went to a lake near us and watched the boats go up and down the lake. The people looked like they were having so much fun. I said to my friend, "One day I'd like to own a boat."

A couple years went by. My friend's neighbor said he was selling his boat. It had been in storage for five years. He had used it when his kids were younger, but they didn't use it anymore and it was costing him storage fees. He said he was selling it for $1,500 but it was in bad condition. My friend called me and asked if I wanted to go into a fifty-fifty partnership.

"If it floats, let's buy it." I agreed.

My friend's neighbor took the boat out of storage, and we cleaned it up. My friend was an engineer, so he worked on getting it started. After several attempts and replacing old parts, we managed to get it started. His neighbor taught us how things worked and helped us with getting it in the lake.

The boat had a small hole, and water was coming in. We quickly got it to shore and took it back home. We repaired the hole and tested it before we tried it out again. Now it was watertight.

The seats were all torn up, so my job was to install new seats and seat covers. We cleaned the boat from top to bottom, and it looked beautiful. It was a small speedboat that carried six people comfortably. However, we could get away with eight people. I couldn't believe it; I owned a boat. It was one of my dreams.

I was so happy that we had moved to America. There were so many things that I accomplished in a short time just by moving. We took the boat out several times a year. The kids enjoyed the doughnut rings. I loved the speed and watching the sunset from the boat. We even took it out on the Fourth of July and watched fireworks from the middle of the lake, along with hundreds of other boats.

After a few years, we decided that the kids were growing up and we went to the lake less. We decided to sell the boat. We got back what we had paid and so we hardly lost any money on it. My dream of having a boat was complete.

Third Income

Jaime was at the University of Texas in Austin (UT), and I was forty-seven years old. My wife and I were empty nesters. My son grew up quickly and made lots of great friends at UT, so he became independent very quickly. He studied hard and played harder.

His friends were from all parts of the world. However, he had no Indian friends. He never seemed to get along with Indians. I had been the opposite when I was growing up. I only got on with Indian friends. The generations had changed. He had heard no racist remarks nor been threatened by anyone. It was different from when I was a child.

Jay and I had decided to have one child as we wanted to give the best to one person. We didn't want that child to struggle in life like we had done. It was not an easy decision, but I've always followed my instincts. I hoped this was the best thing for us, given our circumstances in earlier days.

I noticed that Dallas was buzzing. The whole of the metroplex infrastructure was undergoing a huge redevelopment program. Every day, driving to Dallas to go to work, I saw new overpasses and lane expansions. Something was happening. I put my investment cap on and wondered why Dallas would spend so much money on infrastructure.

A lot of other states were still coming out of recession and didn't have much to offer by way of jobs. Dallas was still affordable, so people were flocking to Dallas. In 2012, I decided it was time to invest again in properties, as I could see a wave coming. When you are young, you work for money. You save and then let the money work for you. I had saved enough. I had to find a third income. I had to plant seeds and start planning for my retirement.

I have a passion for property investments, so I bought a condo on a main street in downtown Dallas. There was a tenant in the condo already. I made a deal with him that I would not increase the rent if his payments were made on time and he didn't call me for minor issues. He agreed.

I was only looking at appreciation. I estimated that the condo's value would go up in the next five years. If there was no trouble from the tenant and his rent covered my costs, then I would be happy. People thought I was crazy to buy during a slump. I could see a vision that they could not see.

OVER THE HILL

I was a year away from my fiftieth birthday. I'd always wanted a sports car, and I had my eye on a Maserati for my fiftieth. *Before I die, I want to fulfill my wish.* However, I needed to have a target and justification.

A Maserati was an expensive car. There was no way I could afford it; I would just have to have it in my next life. I kept on looking at a certain Maserati on the internet. It was an older version, more classic. The newer models were too expensive. This was the Maserati coupe cambiocorsa.

I told Jay about my fiftieth birthday present. She thought I was insane. I felt the same way. It was not realistic. However, I had always got what I wanted. Was this just a dream, or could I make it real? I kept on looking for this particular model. Such cars were rare, and most of them were in California, Florida, or New York. I never saw this model in Dallas but searched regardless.

I saw one at a dealership in Dallas; it was the exact color I wanted. I called the dealer and confirmed they still had it. I asked Jay if she'd like to come to see it. She said, "Yes, but you are not buying it."

"I've only seen this model on the internet. I want to touch it and sit in it." I assured her. She knew this was my dream, so we went.

As we approached the dealership, I saw the car in the distance. It was beautiful. My heart was racing. As I got out of my car, Jay warned, "We are only going to look at it."

"Of course."

I instantly fell in love with it. Jay walked around it once. "I'm going to the car." She announced after finishing her lap, "I'll wait for you there."

I looked around the Maserati in detail. The rims were unique. I had never seen rims like that before.

"Can I test drive it?" My heart was racing as I asked the salesperson.

"Of course!"

I turned on the ignition and immediately the sound of a finely tuned engine went straight through my body. I drove it around few blokes and fell in love, but it was just a dream.

The salesperson and I went back to the office. Jay was still sitting in my car, on the phone with someone.

"Well, what do you think?" He asked.

"I'm not sure. It's too expensive."

He smiled. "How much are you willing to pay for it?"

I wasn't ready to buy it, so I gave him a ridiculously low figure—seven thousand dollars less than their asking price.

We went back and forth, and I would not budge. After about forty minutes of negotiating, he gave his final price and asked if I could increase my price by $200 and pay cash.

Was this really happening? I could own my dream car. Where else would I find this car? It was perfect for what I wanted and at a great price. If it needed repairs, since I had picked it up cheap I would have money for them.

My heart pumped faster.

What should I do? I could walk away without buying it and regret it, or I could buy it and live my dream. It totally didn't make sense to buy it. It was not practical. I was thinking with my heart, not my head.

It didn't take long for me to say to myself, *I've always saved, been cheap, and struggled. What am I living for?*

I took the offer and paid cash. I had just bought a Maserati and Jay didn't know it. She was still sitting in the car, not knowing what I had just done.

I tried to justify it to myself. *I want to live my life. I hit my goal. And I have not overspent on the car.*

I finished up the deal and would be able to pick up the car in two days. I went back to my car and drove for a few miles. My heart was pounding. I didn't say anything to my wife. How could I tell her that I had bought a Maserati?

She suspected something. "Don't tell me that you bought that car."

"I did."

She hit the roof and started telling me off. All I could do was listen and hope that she would run out of steam. She was pissed. I began doubting myself. Had I done the right thing?

She calmed down and came to terms with my action. She thought that it was my lifelong dream, and I had fulfilled it.

I was approaching my fiftieth birthday and reflecting on my life. I'd been through getting kicked out of Uganda with absolutely nothing and ending up in Britain. People in Britain had mixed opinions about Ugandan Asians coming to Britain. Some were extremely nice and others were not. We went through financial problems and lived on the poverty line. Times were tough in those days.

I often thought that I had lived three lives: one in Uganda, one in Britain, and one in America. I wondered what my life would have been if I hadn't moved to Britain or America. If Idi Amin hadn't made the decision to kick the Ugandan Asians out, would we have been safe in Uganda, or would he have still terrorized us? Would we still be alive there if the Africans had turned on us? Their leader would have taken their side, not ours. Amin would definitely have made life hell for us if we stayed. Maybe his decision to expel us was better than us living in terror. When we left Uganda, the Africans celebrated our departure. The Africans didn't want us there, even though we held up the country's economy and kept the country from going underwater. Time took its course. The Ugandan Asians resettled, and Uganda stabilized after many years.

Jay asked if I wanted to have a fiftieth birthday party. I never liked to be the center of attraction, so I point-blank said no. She kept insisting that I should as it was a milestone, and I had achieved so much from the little I had. It was time to celebrate fifty years of my life.

The more I thought about it, the more I justified why I should do it. I still didn't feel old, and I had great friends and family asking me to throw a party. If I didn't do it now, when was I going to do it? Not at sixty or sixty-five or seventy. Never. Who knew what tomorrow held for me? I wasn't getting younger.

I decided to go ahead with the party. We invited 120 people. None of my family from Britain were able to attend, which made me sad. However, Jay's family and our close friends were able to attend.

While I was giving a speech to my guests, Sandip arrived as a surprise. He only came for my birthday, stayed two days, and flew back.

I had gone to hundreds of people's birthday parties and had seen them blow out the candles on a cake. This time it was my turn. I looked at the cake; it had a picture of my Maserati. The guests sang "Happy Birthday," and I realized I had never had a birthday party before. It was time to allow myself to be celebrated.

Getting Down
to Business

We lost a very close friend to cancer. She was forty-eight years old and always kept herself fit. I kept on thinking, *No one knows when God will take you.* I decided that from then on, I would do what I wanted to. Who knows what would happen tomorrow?

Work was getting stressful, and I wanted a change. I had been at the same job for a while, and it was getting more and more stressful. I was thinking of buying a business where I would be in control of my own workload. I had been a manager in retail before, a long time ago. I was prepared to take the plunge.

During this period, I tried different things to cope with stress, including workouts, yoga, relaxing at home, and watching movies. Nothing was working. One day, while I was buying groceries, I saw a child painting set. *Why not try painting?* The set was only five dollars. I also picked out a paper to paint on.

I was excited as I had never painted before. I did my first painting and showed it to Jay. She laughed "That's like a five-year old's painting."

I laughed with her. She wasn't wrong. "Obviously painting is not for me."

"Since you've got the paint, you may as well paint another one." She pointed out.

I considered it, "You're right—what have I got to lose?"

This time I looked at some photos I had taken of landscapes. I used the photos as a guideline of what to paint. The next one came out much better. I showed it to her, and she liked it. I was impressed and put it up on social media. I got many likes. I did another one and got the same reaction. I was on a roll. I could not wait to get home from work so I could paint more. I was getting hang of painting. I took more care and put more detail in the paintings. Who would have guessed that I would paint to relieve stress?

Initially I painted on paper. I later tried a small canvas and moved to a larger canvas. I wanted to add a symbol in each painting to make it unique. I thought about the most important thing in my life—my family. I wanted something that showed being free and seeing the world from above. After thinking for some time, I discovered it was simple. I added three birds flying to represent me, my wife, and my son. The birds were hidden within the paintings, so the viewer needed to look around the painting to find them, at the same time absorbing the details of the painting.

I was still searching for a business. If I bought a gas station, restaurant, liquor store, or other retail establishment, I knew I would be subjecting myself to more stress, not less. It may mean staying open for late nights. I'd have to think about inventory and ordering regularly. There was the possibility of theft. I also didn't like the idea of opening on weekends.

What business would work for me? I thought long and hard. I wanted a business that would suit me, that didn't need inventory, that didn't require late nights or weekends. I wanted a business that I could run alone, without staff. It was impossible to find a business that had all those things. However, after researching for a long time, I found two possibilities.

There was a shipping store in a great location. The business opening times were perfect. I would be free after three o'clock on Saturdays and closed on Sundays. I would hardly need any inventory, and it was a clean business.

The other was more of an investment. Part of my vision was to own an office building, or a retail center comprised of several stores. My goal was to achieve this by the time I was fifty.

I found the perfect one. This investment was an office building consisting of ten units. Each unit were rented out. Both options had risks. I remembered what the old wise man said to me: that he would have taken more risks in life. *I'll take the risk, but I must run my numbers as this could cripple me if it goes wrong.*

I was planning to leave my job to manage my new businesses. This would be perfect for me, and it would give me a challenge to increase the revenue. It was December 2014.

I was getting overwhelmed with buying two businesses at the same time. Both would close in February 2015. In January, reality kicked in, and I questioned myself. *What am I doing, buying an office building which I have no idea how to run it and a shipping business for which I have no experience?* I kept on saying, "Go big or go home." Many times, I felt like throwing up as my worries overwhelmed me—what if it all went wrong? Is it too late to back out?

The shipping business was not a huge investment, so I paid cash. I didn't want the worry of paying loans. The investment property was a monster; I'd have much more to lose.

As soon as I bought the store, the revenue spiraled downward. I was losing customers. I didn't know anything about shipping or printing. The store looked a mess, and I was demotivated. What should I do? We were surviving on my wife's income. She was once again holding me up and supporting me.

I tried to get out of the office building transaction. I looked for reasons why I didn't want to go through with it. But I'd lose the earnest money. What should I do? *God has again given me these opportunities. To move forward, I will have to go through to closing and make it work.* As I've always done, I had to work hard and focus.

I closed on the office building in February 2015. Within four months, three of the tenants defaulted, saying they could not make their payments. I couldn't believe it. I contacted my broker for help, certain that these tenants could not break their leases, "Let's sue them."

My broker calmed me down, "These people don't have the money. If you sue them, then you will have to pay attorneys' fees. Most likely you will not get any outstanding rent back. We will just have to look for replacement tenants."

I was getting worried. I hadn't realized these tenants could do this. This was something I had never had to deal with. The tenants in my residential investments had always paid up. Was it only businesses that did this? I was shaken up. What had I done? Would I have been better off with my original job?

I was so stressed, I thought it would kill me. I was getting disoriented and felt like I was losing control. I prayed every day, but the more I prayed, the more issues came up. For the first time, I felt that I had failed. I had let my wife down. She had repeatedly warned me not to gamble like this, and said we were only suited to be employees. At least then we would have regular income and, if lucky, would be able to retire at sixty-five.

She was right. I had taken on more than I could chew. What was the solution?

I am better than just giving up. I told myself. *I have no choice except to think positive. I have got through many hurdles in life and moved forward. This is a challenge I took on, and now it's time to roll up my sleeves and get to work.*

There was a great program I watched called *The Profit*. Along with many other things, this taught me that any business should have the "three Ps,": people, product, and process. I didn't have any employees, so I was "the people." I knew I had to give the best customer service to every person who came through the door. As for products, I studied each item line and adjusted the pricing. I did promotions and positioned items in more logical places. To address process, I looked at how I could do things more quickly so that I could be more efficient. I cleaned the whole store from top to bottom. I worked until I had no energy left.

My mind was working a hundred miles an hour, thinking about how to make the business the best I could make it. I had competition all around me, so that made it tougher.

The walls of the store were gray. Instead of spending money to brighten them, Jay suggested that I hang my paintings up. Since I had painted them as stress relievers, they might help me. I hung eight pieces. They looked great. They became conversation starters. Customers noticed the hard work I had put into the store and loved my paintings. Business started to pick up.

I set targets for myself. I shook off all negativity and focused on sales. It took about seven months to turn the shipping business around.

One customer asked me how much one of my paintings of a wave was. I laughed, "It's not for sale."

"Are you sure? I would like to buy it for my son. He's in the navy and would love it."

Since I didn't really want to sell it, I said, "Two hundred and fifty dollars," thinking that would put her off.

She handed me her credit card, "I'll take it."

I could not believe it. "I only started painting a couple years ago. This piece was done with a kids' paint set."

"So? It's beautiful and I would be glad to have it."

I told Jay, and she encouraged me to paint more. I bought larger canvases and painted on the kitchen worktop. I got into a rhythm. Straight from work, I would quickly eat and then paint each night for two or three hours, as well as over weekends. I started to sell more paintings and held art shows at my store.

I was fifty-three years old. I could see that if I worked on the office building and made money, I would have all my big goals in sight. These were goals that I'd never thought I would achieve. I needed to work hard and take some calculated risks. However, I constantly worried that if something happened to me, my wife would be unable to manage the office building. With all the issues it had, she would be unable to cope. This was a big fear for me, so I had some renovations done and was able to sell it for a decent profit.

At the end of February 2020, I heard about COVID-19. No one knew what this was or how it would affect people.

A week later, there was a sell-off due to the uncertainty of this so-called COVID-19 virus. There was a huge panic regarding this virus. Most of 2020 was unstable. The market was volatile and crashed in early March.

As the virus slowly worked its way into America, we learned that Europe was going into a lockdown, as this virus was uncontrollable and deadly. The whole world was affected. No one had a clue of how to stop it. Medical professionals were advising people to social distance at least six feet, wash hands, and wear face masks.

During lockdown, the number of people infected gradually slowed down. People worked from home and schools closed, sending a ripple through the economy. Only essential businesses stayed open. I noticed that even though the stock market was trending down, this was a great time to buy. Once everything went back to normal, stocks would go up.

By the end of March 2020, I was all in again. The market started to climb. People's needs had changed. Certain sectors, however, were losing money fast, and the unemployment rate was at the highest it had ever been. I traded cautiously as there was still many uncertainties. I wanted to stay safe.

Though my shipping store was considered an essential business, I reduced my hours and closed at one o'clock instead of six o'clock.

Even though it was a sad time, I wanted to stay positive. I had always wanted to be a realtor. Therefore, straight after I closed my store each day, I went home, took a shower, ate, and studied. It was a tough course. I even woke up at three o'clock in the morning and studied before I went to work. I was not good at studying, but I wanted to prove to myself that I could do this. I hadn't studied in over thirty years. It was a challenge I wanted to take on.

The course required 180 hours of study. It involved passing six classes before I could sit my actual exam. Lockdown was a great time to concentrate. We didn't go out to eat or socialize with friends, as there was a risk that someone could catch the virus. I focused on studying.

I passed all six courses in three months. Then I applied to sit the actual exam, which included a national and state exam. I had studied for more than five hundred hours and reviewed more than seven hundred questions. My aim was to pass it the first time. I thoroughly learned all the course material.

I passed both the national and the state exam on my first try. I felt I had just done the impossible. Many people had to retake these exams several times in order to pass.

I was now a realtor. That meant I would be able to buy and sell my own properties and save myself the realtor costs. I had experience in commercial properties, since I had bought my own office building and leased it. My experience was broad and deep.

It was time for us to move to a more central location. We chose Colleyville, Texas. Jaime moved in with us from Arlington, VA, due to COVID-19. Even though times were hard, we felt that we needed to keep moving forward.

We purchased a home near the Dallas–Fort Worth airport. The house was a new build with modern design. It was our dream home—and it cost almost three times than our existing home. My wife, my son, and I all felt that even though it might not make sense to upgrade, we wanted to achieve our goals and live with no regrets.

As a realtor, I got the realtor commission from the builder, so I again saved money. We went through our calculations repeatedly to make sure we were within our budget.

Parting Message

Looking back at my life, I think of my time in Uganda and how life had been there. Then we moved to Britain, where we struggled for almost thirty years. In America, we had finally settled and were enjoying life.

My story is about staying positive, looking for opportunities, and keeping focused on your goals. It's about not being afraid of hard work and putting passion in everything you do. It's about thinking for yourself and finding your own path instead of following those that other people pave.

Life is an adventure, so think outside the box. God has made this beautiful world for you to explore. Don't have a narrow mind. There is positivity in everything. Spend your time creating solutions, not problems. Think logically and stick to your plan. Take calculated risks. Taking no risks is a risk in itself. We don't know when our time is up, so (within reason) live life to the fullest.

When I was young, I was dark-skinned, shy, small, and weak. I was uneducated. People didn't notice me when I walked through the door. I just wanted to be liked. I had done nothing wrong to anyone. I built my character so that people would like me.

Slowly I made friends by being a good person. That was the only quality I could rely on. I learned to build on that. I gained trust and loyalty. At a young age, I felt I was different to others. My mind worked in an unusual way that no one could understand. I knew I was different, and I had difficulty communicating and explaining my thoughts. People thought I was weird. Most of my life, I did things to show people that I was not mad. People started to like what I was doing and found that I was an "all-rounder." Many people came to me for advice. I had experience in many things. I became a consultant.

This book was written to inspire and motivate. Follow your dreams and set goals. God has made every one of us different. No one knows their talents until they have tried everything. You will find your talent. Luck doesn't come overnight. It takes time, so be patient. I've found that if I want something, I will only get it if I put every ounce of energy and focus into getting it. That approach has worked every time.

GLOSSARY

Asian- In the context of the United States, 'Asian' is assumed to mean someone of Chinese, Japanese, or Korean descent. In the context of Britain, however, it is assumed to mean someone of Indian or Pakistani descent.

Bhajia- A spicy hot vegetable snack or entrée that is battered and deep fried.

Caste- Hereditary social classes in Hindu society.

Chapati- A think pancake of unleavened whole-grain bread cooked on a griddle.

Dal- A dish made with lentils or other split pulses.

Diwali-Festival of lights –5 days of celebration that family gather to pray for prosperity and bloke out darkness and evil with extravagant display of light, candles and firework.

Gam-A village.

Indian- A native or inhabitant of India, or a person of Indian descent.

Khichdi- Indian dish made with rice and dal, it's light and easy to digest.

Lassi-refreshing drink made with yogurt, water and salt or sugar.

Mangalsutra- Symbol of marriage indicating the love and commitment the husband and wife have towards each other.

Ras-Mango pulp mixed with milk.

Sari- A long, thin piece of colorful printed material that wrapped around the body in a particular way.

Shak- A dish made up of several different combinations of vegetables and spices. May or may not be either spicy or sweet.

South Asian- Following the American context, 'South Asian' refers to a native or inhabitant of, or a person descended from, the South Asian countries—India, Pakistan, Bangladesh. Nepal, and Sri Lanka.

Ugandan Asian- The term 'Ugandan Asian' follows the British context. 'Ugandan Asian' is used to describe those of South Asian descent who were brought to Uganda by Britain and settled there.

Ugandan Indian- 'Ugandan Indian' is used to describe those of specifically Indian descent who were brought to Uganda by Britain and settled there. Once the Ugandan Indians immigrate to Britain, they are thereby referred to as simply 'Indians.'

* Note: in this novel, the American context is to be assumed unless otherwise specified.